“A handbook to consciousness as [illegible]

Alliende’s book interweaves scienc[illegible]-ogy, string theory and memoir in a [illegible] of the [illegible] and nature of consciousness. The unive[illegible] planet, nature and everything else in existence consists of fractals, says the author, with each individual component containing the same core characteristics as the whole of existence. Alliende investigates and painstakingly demonstrates how the evolution of life, society, the developmental path of the human psyche, the chakra system and the author’s own life have all developed according to a similar pattern and structure. This ambitious and comprehensive work, which is both scientific and arcane (bordering on overwhelming; this is no quick, light read), reveals intensely personal information. The author harnesses his wide-ranging material with a framework based on Timothy Leary’s eight-circuit model, exploring consciousness and all its components, from the material plane of survival to the causal plane of spirit. The interwoven autobiography illustrates and makes accessible the theoretical sections of the text, while also providing a model for living in connection with the greater consciousness. Alliende is a transpersonal therapist who regularly practices and guides others through many of the consciousness-enhancing techniques he surveys (from meditation to gardening and other community-building concepts) and shares experiences about raves and hallucinogenic drugs. Exercises throughout the book encourage the reader to join him in moving from passive understanding to actively expanding awareness. Of these, the meditation techniques are particularly well-crafted and inviting, while other suggestions are more likely to spark thought than follow-through (“Go to a school and witness the teaching process”). Also thought-provoking is his suggestion that the Internet and social media link us all to a greater consciousness. That link, and increasing reliance on technology, he argues, could help save the Earth—and our continued existence.

An academic and experiential guide that requires rereading for absorption.”

-Kirkus Indie, Kirkus Review

Dimensions of Being
An Explorer's Guide to Consciousness

By
Eugene A. Alliende

Cover art by Amoraea Dreamseed
www.Divine-Blueprint.com

To contact author, please e-mail at
ealliendea@gmail.com or join the discussion at
www.dimensionsofbeing.com

ISBN: 1478151870
ISBN 13: 9781478151876

Dedicated to Christina,
whose endless unconditional love, support, and light
are an inspiration to my life.
And to my two beautiful children, Mateo and Emma, who make this life a most
magical and beautiful journey.

Contents

Preface

Ever since I was a young boy I have been intrigued by the wonders of our mysterious universe. Early love for Nature and animals blossomed into a genuine thirst for knowledge when my uncle Rodrigo gave me a book called *God and the New Physics*, by Paul Davies.[1] This book sparked an intense interest in the deeper questions of humanity, such as who are we, where do we come from, and what is the purpose of life. My approach in those early days was scientific, grounded in understandings based on sensory-dependent empiricism and the mathematical proofs of the scientific elite. I thought the new physics had all the answers, and I was committed to becoming a researcher in that field.

As time went on I entered college, and through some life-changing experiences I encountered the most mysterious aspect of our universe, my Self. I quickly learned that the answers I was seeking were not out there, but within. I began to meditate and explore the inner terrains of my being. I kept detailed notes of my experiences, discovering that the spiritual wisdom traditions were correct in saying that all answers are truly found within.

Meditation became my technology, my brain my lab, and my Being the environment in which I conducted my experiments. As my meditations deepened, I began to wake up to the spiritual nature of our Cosmos. My eyes were opened to the vast suffering of our planet and my mission unfolded as one of healing. The guide that you are about to read is based on some of my inner discoveries, coupled with the synthesis of many schools of thought and the work of other explorers of consciousness. Enjoy the journey, and take advantage of this lifetime to explore the nature of *your* Being. *Namaste!*

Baltimore, Maryland
Spring 2000

Preface to Second Edition

The book you are now holding was first written in the spring of 2000. At the time my fiancé, now wife, and I were living in Baltimore, Maryland, while she completed her Nursing degree at John's Hopkins University. While she went to her classes, I'd spend my days writing, meditating, practicing Yoga, and living a generally contemplative life as I completed my Master's degree in Transpersonal Psychology. Many of the ideas and constructs in this text were developed based on observations derived from intense meditative, yogic, shamanic, and entheogenic explorations on the one hand, and from intensive study of the established research of various fields on the other. As a consequence, the book turned out to be rather idealistic and "far out," as my brother liked to point out. Now, twelve years later, as I attempt to complete this work, I find myself and my ideas much more grounded. This grounding has occurred from the sixteen years of working as a traditional and transpersonal psychotherapist. My work with people struggling at the various stages of consciousness has inevitably informed and elucidated the various dimensions that we are about to explore. Also, the experience of becoming a father to two beautiful children, now fifteen and twelve, within the householder role has given the exploration of consciousness a depth and richness, through relationship and personal inner development, previously barely imagined.

Today, as I write, is May 10, 2012, seven months before the end of the 5,125 -year Long-Count of the Mayan calendar and the alleged galactic alignment of December 21, 2012. Coming of age with this looming meme has inevitably influenced much of my thinking, as this temporal Singularity beckons with shiny promise of a new golden age, or dark apocalyptic demise, or, the most improbable scenario, business as usual. Whatever the case, these times are buzzing with a transformative undercurrent that is hard to miss if we take a moment and tune in. And if we take Terence McKenna's "fractal Novelty Wave" theory of time seriously (this and other similar theories will be explored in Part 2), these last few months represent a compressed resonant recapitulation of the previous 13.7 billion years of cosmic evolution! In other words, according to this theory, these next few months will see more change happen in terms of information processing and exchange than has been seen in the previous twelve to fifteen billion years. Seems like a perfect time to embark on this intellectual and experiential journey through Consciousness. (Note to reader: the last round of revisions occurred after the end of the Mayan calendar, December 21, 2012. The media-hyped apocalyptic end of the world did not occur, we did not disappear into the black hole of the galactic center, aliens did not suddenly land on the White House lawn, planetary magnetic poles have not yet shifted, and the solar flares have yet to engulf our blue planet. Yet the premise of evolution and transformation this book outlines will hopefully be recognized as the basic pattern that governs the process we all find ourselves embedded in; a process that seems to be accelerating with the passing of each day. Unprecedented change *is* happening, and this text is a humble attempt to contextualize this transformation within the whole of Cosmic evolution.)

What new information can be conveyed in these times, when all info and human knowledge is literally in the back pockets of the typical teenager, awaiting the tender stroke of a finger? The overwhelming information overload of the day has created an ocean that at times dissolves into noise, losing any coherence or ability to inform. My attempt here is to bring together diverse fields of understanding, from the depths of Mystical wisdom to leading-edge research from our empirical sciences, in order to paint a story of the journey of Consciousness. The hope is to provide the reader with a visionary, intellectual, and hopefully experiential journey through the various dimensions and contours of Being. The basic premise, then, is that the universe is an organic, interrelated, interdependent evolving Being moving toward ever-greater acts of novel self-creation. We represent the leading tip of this evolving Cosmic organism, with the promise of awakening *as* this totality. But let's not get ahead of ourselves.

Finally, as I complete this book, the words of my mentor twelve years ago while acquiring my Master's degree through the Institute of Transpersonal Psychology (ITP) echo in my mind: "I can't find you in your words." In other words, when writing about consciousness, it seems necessary and appropriate to include the view from within. Thus I have woven personal and transpersonal experiences, my own and my clients', to illustrate and give greater depth to the understanding of the Dimensions of Being. I hope you enjoy this most miraculous and mysterious journey through the Dimensions of *you*r personal and collective Being.

Paloma, California
Spring 2012

Preface to Third Edition

As most authors, artists, poets, or composers would undoubtedly agree, no work is ever finished or complete. A person's expression is rather an evolving reflection of an interior that is dynamic and alive; always shifting and growing as new personal and collective experiences are encountered in this most mysterious of lives. The book you are now holding represents the third incarnation of my ongoing explorations of Consciousness. What first started as a thesis for my Master's degree in Transpersonal Psychology in the year 2000, has now morphed into an ongoing work that probes deeply what it means to be conscious in a world that is in a perpetual state of transformation and becoming.

Today is February 20, 2017, five years past the much anticipated Mayan "end date" of December 2012. As antiquated as that conversation might seem at this point in time, we will explore how what we are currently living is in perfect alignment with those deep visionary premonitions of our indigenous ancestors. We *did* complete a historical cycle, and what we are now witnessing and living is nothing other than the birth pains of a new Consciousness that is actively attempting to birth itself. A new Consciousness that is not guaranteed, however, but that is nonetheless trying relentlessly to push through the crumbling structures of the old Consciousness that have totally become obsolete when viewed in the context of whole system's thinking. The shadow side of the collective psyche is on the loose, manifesting as the "other" and instigating fear, hate, and greed in those living in the old paradigm. Of course, this is how evolution has always done it; the new levels evolve out of and replace the old levels, which in turn become old and obsolete if destructive, or integrated if useful for the furthering of evolution.

If anything, our journey through the various evolving dimensions of Being will hopefully inspire a sense of trust, hope, and optimism in the processes that we are a part of, for we will recognize that there is a deeper Intelligence at work that transcends the silly human games and dramas. Behind all the forms and perceptual appearances we will recognize that there is a Silent Awareness that quietly beckons us toward the higher ideals of unity, harmony, beauty, compassion, and love. With these realizations we can, we must, build the next world, the next stage in an evolutionary saga that has been coalescing and unfolding since the beginning of time. No matter how crazy things get, never forget to take a step back, take a deep breath, and marvel at what a true miracle it is to be conscious and alive, in this very moment!

Paloma, California
Spring, 2017

My Journey Through Consciousness: Brief Autobiography

My Journey begins August 4, 1973, in the midst of revolution and change. As the tyrannical militaristic forces of Augusto Pinochet take hold of a struggling democratically elected Socialist government, I am born into a young emerging family. The tense political atmosphere into which I am born in Chile does not take away from the joy and love that my parents create for this new family. The first fundamental connection-imprint (this concept will be extensively explored in the following pages) to this world, which sets the stage for all subsequent development, occurs through the relationship to the mother figure. In my case, this connection-imprint is ideal, laying the secure and trusting foundation in my being that later blooms into a fearless curiosity for knowledge and the unknown. My mother represents and embodies the ultimate archetype of *Mother* for me. She radiates an unconditional love and a nurturing energy that are my gateway into this world. Her love, friendship, and support have enabled me to confront the tides of our crazy world with self-confidence and a loving attitude that is but a reflection of her up-bringing.

My second fundamental connection-imprint, which establishes itself as I mature into an intrusive, curious little boy, occurs in relation to my father. He represents courage, strength, and wisdom. Expanding my horizons of the world through organized family trips to the mountain peaks of the Andes, exploring the beautiful lakes at the feet of breathtaking volcanoes in the South, and later immersing ourselves in the flowing frontiers of music, my father is fully present in those crucial early years of my life. He introduces me to countless new worlds and experiences that eventually evolve into an appreciation for music and nature that is to set the stage for the ineffable connection that I presently have with the universe. My first two stages of development, physio-survival (mother connection) and emotional-territorial (father connection), are successfully imprinted, as my parents set the emotional and integrative foundation of well-being that has enabled me to live a healthy and happy life. To this very day my father and mother are two central figures of support and love that exist within my being, and that will always be.

Music is the word that most stands out when I think of my late childhood. Through music I find common ground with many peers who teach me much about friendship and relationships, both human and musical. The biggest lesson I acquire from my musical training and subsequent jam sessions, and that carries over to this very day in all areas of life, is that in order to harmonize and be in tune with others, I must first listen. Everyone wants to be heard and express him or herself loudly, but few know how to listen. My jam sessions are never quite the same after that simple but all-embracing insight. Rock climbing is another major influence in my young life, balancing in a physical activity that strengthens my body as well as my mind. The biggest lesson I learn from rock climbing is, "fear inhibits movement." The minute fear creeps into my next move, I fall.

By age seven we migrate to California in response to extreme militaristic oppression and a lack of economic opportunity that our struggling country experiences during those dictator-controlled years. This is a turning point in my young life, for I am now exposed to novel peoples, strange cultures, bizarre customs, and intriguing religions that our homogenous all Chilean-Catholic country fails to offer. My young eyes are opened to fantastic new foods, fads, and toys that expand my sense of possibility exponentially. My thinking-reflective mind begins to expand and evolve. I begin to question, read, and debate ideas with adults who "know" they know more than I do. After reading George Orwell's *1984* [1] and Aldous Huxley's *Brave New World* [2] in an honors history class in eighth grade, my intellectual life is transformed forever. Poverty, social and political injustice, police-state control, and the inequality of resource distribution are now a manifest reality that my innocent childhood mind had previously failed to perceive. I become very introverted and alienate myself from other peers, whom I think to be all too immature, while them seeing me as extremely weird. I immerse myself in an intellectual world of thought and observation, trying to understand and learn everything I can as I basically inherit the scientific mind of our Western-rational culture. I become addicted to knowledge, reading Western philosophers and devouring scientific theories of our universe. My third, symbol-logic brain is overly imprinted with information, creating a know-it-all, hyper-intellectualized kid. My profound love and interest in nature blossoms into a fascinating thirst for understanding about how things work.

With the book *God and the New Physics,* [3] by Paul Davies, my labeling-thinking mind is blown, planting the seed for an intense interest in physics and the ultimate questions of humanity. Intrigued by quantum physics and the concept of an infinite singularity outside of time, I begin to form an intellectual-conceptual model of our universe, where it came from, and its evolutionary fate. During this time my social life is null. Content with the love of my family and intellectual interests, I see no need to partake in trivial worldly social rituals. The cliques and fads of high school seem ridiculous and irrelevant, nothing but silly games, so I believe, as I immerse myself in a rich inner mental world of thought.

One day, browsing through some books in our school library, I spot a fellow jazz band member reading a *Scientific American* magazine. I sit next to him and start up a conversation on the nature of time and existence that is to last several years. It is the beginning of my sophomore year in high school and I finally find someone who "knows." We exchange books and discuss them to all hours of the night, fascinated with concepts and each other. In school we consider ourselves alien anthropologists observing intriguing creatures of all forms, interacting in the most curious fashions. We do not fit in, but we feel that we are somehow above the masses with "more important" things to think and talk about.

Junior year comes around, along with a new and most-fascinating topic, girls. My fourth brain begins to activate hormonal mechanisms in my body that are completely out of my hands. Physics and the nature of reality become secondary priorities next to the new and exciting unknown realm of sensuality and sexuality. With this new interest we, sure enough, manage to make many other friends as we are now "accepted" into the various social groups. Eddie, my intellectual companion and best friend, and I now begin to experience the "social realm," as we explore various identities and personas during these most awkward adolescent years. Some alcohol experimentation opens up a previously unknown state of oblivious consciousness where social boundaries become numbed, allowing deeper entrance into the more "popular" social groups of high school. We continue our philosophic perspective, but now it is all about freedom. We are young, dumb, careless, and free. No concerns but that of partying and having fun.

Then one fateful day during the end of my senior year in high school, a friend of ours pulls out a strange-smelling cigarette. With a sense of caution, fear, curiosity, and adventure, Eddie and I try it. Colors suddenly explode into life, sounds spontaneously become more melodious and sweet than before, and the food reveals a texture and depth never before experienced. Our senses seem to open up to a world of sensory pleasures previously unimagined. Our philosophic discussions reach new heights; a level where instead of talking about physics we are now *experiencing* physics, so it seems. Vibrations of different frequencies interacting, resonating, merging, co-creating one another in inexplicable harmony and beauty. Our thought patterns are elevated to a self-reflective flow of understanding and insight that makes life and its experiences the most amazing and wondrous phenomena. We no longer understand, but boy is it fun to exist! The free-floating, fifth hedonistic neuro-somatic circuit is now in full bloom. Here and now existential joy is all there is.

As the flow of time inevitably continues, I eventually enter the University of California, Davis, as a civil engineering major, since that is a field of applied physics. Dorm life is interesting but lonely. I miss Eddie, my brother, and my family. Classes are hard and somewhat dry. The fun of theoretical physics and abstract speculation is nowhere to be found in the monotonous formulas blared out by uninspiring professors. I am ready for the next message.

Eddie, of course, comes to visit me one day and says, "I've got something that will change you forever. Get ready, we are going to a rave." Intrigued and ready for a change, I get dressed and we drive down to San Francisco. He gives me a small square piece of paper with a pyramid printed on it and says, "No expectations, just feel it." As we drive across the Bay Bridge, I put it in my mouth and take a deep breath. After we park the car, we walk into a bass-pounding, strobing-flashing, color-filled warehouse, and I immediately feel my body begin to pulsate with the never-ending beat. People around me seem beautiful and perfect, all grooving to the thumping beat.

After about an hour of dancing I begin to feel the music in every atom of my shivering body. The lights, sounds, people, and the entire universe begin to somehow melt and merge, as the notions of a within and without, self and other, begin to slowly disappear. To my utter shock, the apparent boundary between "me" and the ocean of energy around me begins to evaporate. I close my eyes as the energy becomes too intense. Suddenly, everything begins to converge and unify within, as a perfect Oneness is revealed at the core of my being. It is beyond anything I had ever dreamed of or even thought of as being possible.

All of a sudden, there It was! The Singularity outside and beyond time, the Source of all creation, God as pure Energy and Love, inside my own Being! Revelations, images, and love flash light-speed before my bewildered consciousness, revealing the answer, the purpose. This moment was the purpose of universal evolution; the universe finally becoming aware of itself. "I" was the creator, and "I" was in everyone and everything throughout space and time. Pure Consciousness *was* the Singularity, beyond the boundaries of space-time, duality, and the cycles of birth and death. My whole life had been a preparation and an unfolding journey leading toward this ecstatic revelatory moment. We are not separate beings, but are rather One Energy Force taking on different manifestations for the dance. Time-space, reality, and existence were just holographic, fractal projections of Consciousness, not my consciousness, but the Pure Consciousness that is the formless Void, the Buddha Nature within all things.

The party ends, but my perception is blown to pieces. The sunrise-streaked city is now raw energy, as the undifferentiated sounds, lights, emotions, buildings, thoughts, people all move in a disorienting unitive flow. Eddie and I spend all day together trying to grasp, with what little minds we have left, an experience that is so beyond conceptual comprehension that I cannot believe it is not culturally talked about.

The next day I am down, depressed, and confused. What just happened? There is nothing in my mental models to which I can reduce this all-out revelatory experience to. At this point in my life, I don't even know what the word mysticism means, let alone knowing that it is an experience available to all human beings. I just plainly do not understand. How can I get back to that complete understanding, Love, Unity, Beauty, without drugs? Or is this merely a drug-induced experience, unavailable unless triggered by a psychedelic substance? Up until this point I had no interest or knowledge of drugs, except for the brief and limited past-year alcohol and cannabis experimentation. But this did not feel like a drug. It felt like a secret key that revealed the deepest mysteries of the universe. What the hell was that?!

The next day back at UC Davis, I go straight to the medical library and look up LSD. I check out every book I can find on the subject and begin to unravel a whole new world, perspective, philosophy, culture, and era. I encounter mysticism, shamanism, Ram Dass, Alan Watts, meditation, Timothy Leary, Charles Tart, Zen, Terence McKenna, Buddhism, Yoga, psychopharmacology, neurology, Stanislav Grof, Maharashi Yogi, D.T. Suzuki, etc. I begin to slowly realize that life is a spiritual journey of unfolding and expanding consciousness. Psychedelics provide an apparent glimpse into the eternal in the right set and setting, but ultimately it is a conscious process of work on oneself that uncovers gradually one's true nature.

My major in college changes soon after to psychology, since it is all in consciousness, even physics. I take a yoga class and begin to meditate regularly. A Tantric Yoga monk happens to cross my path and I dive deep into study and meditation under his guidance. He initiates me into his Tantric lineage and I receive a secret power mantra. My spiritual evolution begins to accelerate and a mindful lifestyle inevitably follows. Everything begins to fall into place and I begin to understand my role in this sick planet. My eyes are opened to the vast suffering of humanity, to the alienated souls that are screaming-out for something authentic, something real that TV, money, sex, power, status, and things just can't offer. I realize that the more I work on myself, the more I quiet the limited labeling and judging thoughts, the more effective a channel I am for healing and change.

Eventually I move into the Domes, a sustainable agricultural cooperative community in Davis, and meet my Davis family; a group of beautiful, inspiring, creative, conscious individuals who are all about evolution and change. We grow up together, and conspire to transform our contaminated Earth into the garden we all dream of. We discover love as the only way, and community and family as its manifestation. We learn to grow organic fruits and vegetables as we attempt to reconnect with our sacred Mother Planet. I meet a woman whose endless teachings and love inspire me complete, and we never leave each other's side from that point on. I learn, and continue to learn, the deeper lessons of Love accessible only through an intimate relationship with another.

After college she and I decide to travel and be together. We explore and travel for years, encountering shamans, witches, wizards, hipsters, healers, scientists, activists, travelers, priestesses, foreigners, and generally cool people who expand and enrich our world-views tenfold. We live deep in the jungles of Hawaii, practicing Yoga and meditation by majestic waterfalls and eating mangoes off the trees. We circumnavigate South America, tasting the cultures and touching sacred lands. I keep detailed journals of my ever-expanding world-views and spiritual perspectives, as insights from within and without guide me toward my unfolding life's purpose.

After years of traveling, my partner and I decide to pursue higher education. Both wanting to be a part of the planetary healing, we explore the best way to "bridge" the two worlds: the enchanted spiritual world available to an awakened being, and the suffering world of the masses. She pursues a nursing degree at Johns Hopkins University in Baltimore, and I dive deep into the study of Consciousness while completing a Master's degree in Transpersonal Psychology through the Institute of Transpersonal Psychology (ITP). The book you are now holding was birthed in those quiet seaside days solely dedicated to contemplating the deeper mysteries of mind and the cosmos.

After my partner and I graduate from our respective programs, we decide to formalize our intimate connection and unite in sacred marriage. We settle down in the beautiful foothills of Northern California and create community with family on beautiful, rolling-hill, oak-filled land. We have two beautiful children and attempt to grow an organic and regenerative permacultural life. We cultivate an organic garden, install solar panels, and cooperate with family and community to raise happy, grass-fed, hormone-free organic cows. My partner works for a Women's Health Clinic in town while practicing the Earth-based *Wise Woman's Way,* and I dive deep into the world of psychotherapy as a licensed Marriage and Family Therapist (MFT). I intern and become licensed while working for the County Mental Health department, and immerse myself in a world of clinical symptoms and disturbed individuals. I acquire experience working with a spectrum of disorders in kids, adolescents, and adults, and learn the traditional evidenced-based psychotherapeutic techniques of the trade.

After four years of County work, I am offered a position in a Native American Health clinic as a mental health professional. I accept and join a multidisciplinary team of health care workers that includes native elders and healers from the Miwok tribe. I explore Native spiritual practices and begin to apprentice with elders, learning the art of the sweat lodge. I begin to learn about local herbal medicines and discover the use of the elements in the sacred medicine wheel. I continue to work with a spectrum of ailments and disorders, but this time within a mostly Native American population.

Four years later I am offered a space in a Holistic Healing Center called Global Healing Arts. Along with two acupuncturists, two massage therapists, a tai chi and yoga teacher, and a nutritionist, we have created a healing center that integrates techniques from East and West, North and South, to heal in body, mind, and spirit. There I open a private practice and provide traditional and transpersonal psychotherapy services to children, adolescents, adults, and couples. I facilitate a weekly meditation group and host deep exploratory sessions in Consciousness. My kids continue to grow, and my priorities, love, life, and joy become inextricably interwoven to their beautiful unfolding lives. I continue to meditate and practice yoga, but only to remain connected to that which is sacred and ever-present. At this point my spiritual practice is my life, and every encounter becomes an opportunity for growth and healing.

And so as my son reaches sixteen and my little girl thirteen, and as my life is stable, healthy, and rooted, I take a moment to complete the book I started seventeen years ago in Baltimore, Maryland. My ideas have surely matured and become more grounded, for the data from the last seventeen years has been derived less from inner shamanic and mystical experiences and more from my experiences with clients in diverse states, stages, and levels of consciousness and pathology. But as you will soon discover, the ideas presented continue to push the envelope of that which is possible. What else are we to do at the edge of the Galactic Alignment, the end of the fifth world age, the year of the dragon, the apocalypse? We are being signaled toward yet another spiral of creative emergence and evolutionary change, and things are about to get interesting. So enjoy the ride, for we are living in a time that has been building momentum ever since the Big Bang. Pause, wake up, and take a moment to notice what's around and within you in this very moment. From this moment we can watch the unfolding drama of our lives and the universe, and marvel at the sublime beauty and mystery that it all is. And through that awakening we can begin to heal ourselves, our families, our communities, the planet, and all sentient beings across all time and space.

On Drugs: Medicine or Poison?

Most interestingly, the most shocking element to the readers of the previous edition to this book was the discussion on drugs. There are perhaps very few subjects that trigger such emotional responses in people, on both sides of the argument, as does the open conversation on drugs. Yet a comprehensive exploration of Consciousness would be totally incomplete without some mature discussion of the various substances that trigger altered and augmented states of Consciousness.

As a psychotherapist working with a plethora of psycho-emotional disorders, more often then not including the dual-diagnosis of substance abuse and addiction, I am acutely aware of the dangers that some of these substances pose to the individual, their families, and society as a whole. However, there is a class of substances that has been misguidedly included in the schedule I, dangerous drugs of abuse without medical utility list. These substances are called psychedelics, hallucinogens, or entheogens (these terms will be defined as we proceed). There is now sufficient medical, scientific, and anecdotal evidence, past and present, that supports the notion that these substances are *true* medicines, in that they facilitate and promote healing in the right set and setting. As medicines, a new ethos should be established as to 'best-practices' approach in order to understand how to optimally use these medicines to catalyze the healing response. Even though the evidence is clear, the legal system has relegated these psychoactive neurotransmitters into a category that inhibits any further study, therefore slowing down any potential progress in this area. There is evidence, however, that things are beginning to shift, as more studies are being funded to research the therapeutic, creative, spiritual, and medicinal value of these substances. We will explore these miraculous neuro-molecules in greater depth as we proceed with our explorations.

What is the difference between a medicine and a poison? A poison is a molecular substance that causes damage to the organism in some way. Certain drugs are *neurotoxic*, poisonous to the nervous system, in that they damage neural tissue and its ability to keep the organism in a state of equilibrium. Some well know neurotoxic substances include methamphetamine, heroin, and cocaine. A true medicine, however, should be *neurotonic* or *neurogenic*, with the capacity to strengthen and stimulate neural growth and connectivity. There are very few substance that can claim to have this potent ability. Psychedelics and entheogen are perhaps the only true holistic (addressing somatic, emotional, psychological, and spiritual dimensions of Being) neurotonic substances, as they are sourced in Nature, and are increasingly demonstrating a capacity to stimulate neural growth and connectivity. We will explore the current research, and how various psychoactive drugs work in the brain as they relate to the various dimensions of Being.

Even though we will be exploring the vast potential of these psychedelic medicines, it is worth noting here that they are not for everyone. Despite the fact that they have been determined to be non-toxic, benign to the physical body and nervous system, and non-addictive, they nonetheless can be emotionally and psychologically dangerous if taken by unprepared and careless individuals. Particularly, the argument will be made that no substance, psychedelic or otherwise, should be taken during adolescence. These tender years are subject to intense and exponential brain development, where all functions from social awareness, to emotional regulation, to ability to focus and self-regulate, to hormonal balancing, to all cognitive abilities are being wired and developed. Teen years should be nurtured and protected by an environment of health and wellbeing so as to cultivate optimal self and brain growth. These molecules are not toys, but serious and powerful tools of consciousness that must be treated with caution and respect.

As we will soon explore, these medicines have ancient historical roots in our indigenous ancestors that span the globe, and have been used ceremonially for healing, vision, and transcendence by people of the Earth in every continent for millennia. In fact, as we will soon reveal, the indigenous and aboriginal peoples of the Earth have much to teach us during these times, as the human species continues to unconsciously accelerate towards catastrophe and its own self-demise.

Introduction:

Considerations for Exploring Consciousness

> *Within the province of the mind, what I believe to be true is true or becomes true, within the limits to be found experientially and experimentally. These limits are further beliefs to be transcended.*[1]
>
> *- John Lilly*

It is with the spirit of John Lilly, a pioneer in the exploration of consciousness, that we undertake this journey. As the title of this work suggests, this is a manual or guide that attempts to provide the explorer of consciousness with a general map of the terrain that is Consciousness. In a sense we are all explorers of consciousness, for we possess that most mysterious ability to be aware, conceive, and perceive. This faculty of consciousness (the term will be defined as we progress through our explorations) is one that evolves and develops through various levels and stages, always striving and moving toward higher and more integrated forms of self-expression. The point of this guide, however, is to encourage the reader to explore the various dimensions of his or her *own* being, for consciousness is the most intimate aspect of who we are. In fact, it will become clear that all we are is Consciousness. All events, internal or external, physical, emotional, intellectual, or spiritual, are only meaningful for the individual who *experiences* subjectively those events. In other words, all that we can experience occurs within the context of consciousness or awareness, the very faculty that makes experience possible.

In this work I have provided three components to each section. One is theoretical and weaves intellectual images in order to create a general conceptual understanding of the dimensions of being; the second is experiential and is designed to encourage personal exploration in the various domains and dimensions; and the third is biographical, so as to provide a view from this explorer's inner experiences. It is my hope that by exploring the various dimensions, this manual will inspire and serve as a humble guide to anyone wishing to explore deeply the different levels of his or her being.

As William James popularized, "the map is not the territory," [2] reiterating the ancient Taoist realization that "the Tao that can be told is not the eternal Tao; the Tao that can be named is not the eternal Name." [3] As these two explorers of consciousness, William James and Lao-tzu, intuitively understood, no map, model, or concept, no matter how complete or integral it is, can ever convey the reality of subjective *experience.* As we will discover, Consciousness is the source of experience and is primary to all phenomena. Labels are creations of the rational faculty of the human intellect, thus being limited to the organism and the structure of its brain. The realm of labels, concepts, symbols, thoughts, ideas, and metaphors is a reality unto itself, as we will soon clarify, and is unique in nature. In their attempt to reflect reality, our mental representations have instead created a whole new order of reality. In this effort, however, we have mistaken our symbols, labels, theories, and maps for the actual territory, forgetting that these are emergent properties of mind that have their own intrinsic laws, principles, qualities, and defining parameters. With this in mind, we can undertake the pursuit of conceptual model-theory building without confusing it for the reality it is trying to express. Shunryu Suzuki advises us, "Forget everything, then your mind is calm, and it is wide and clear enough to see and feel things as they really are without any effort." [4] As this Zen master points out, reality is vast and infinite, always mysterious and with new lessons to convey. It is only when we release our ceaseless compulsion to label and describe that we are able to experience reality directly, "as it really is."

In the following exploration of the various dimensions of being, it is precisely this attitude that will allow us to witness the structures that conspire to create our current experience. We will use various techniques to achieve this task, but ultimately it is a clear and uncluttered mind that enables the "scientific" and "objective" analysis of who we are. In this sense we are scientists who are exploring that which explores, and here we ride the leading edge of research. Our lab is ourselves, and this discipline considers any and all states as data. [5] We are born with our Self, and we die with our Self, making the introspective search one of utmost importance. I encourage the reader to take this opportunity to explore, in a playful manner, the realms that make up his or her individuality, and those higher and subtler frequencies that unite all forms. The approach is a "scientific" one in that it is a systematic observation of the suggested dimensions, gathering the data from one's own experiences. It is also a playful endeavor in that it is your own research, thus not limited by the constricting doctrines, paradigms, and dogmas of our existing religious and scientific institutions. Here we follow psychologist and author Robert Godwin's aspiration to create a work for "the cage-free intellectual or 'free-range' spiritual aspirant rather than the sterile, 'unfertilized egghead' of contemporary academic hyper-specialization." [6] In other words, the following chapters are poetic and artistic descriptive renditions of aspects of reality with approximate scientific articulation—approximate due to the fact that scientific articulations develop, change, and evolve over time as the mental structures of consciousness that create them develop, change, and evolve over time. In this regard, this work has no inferred authority, is not conclusive, exhaustive, definitive, or even "factual." In these words I only offer a humble myth, based on my interpretations of the discoveries of science and my own explorations. I encourage you to create your own myth!

Much of the information within this text in the fields of cosmology, physics, biology, neurology, psychology, anthropology, history, shamanism, and mysticism is more or less consensually agreed upon within the respective field, and can therefore be found in your standard high school and college textbooks. Dates and time periods may vary depending on source. What I've done in this work is to integrate and interweave all these various fields of knowledge into a coherent story, with Consciousness unifying them as their ever-present protagonist. Dates are used to give a general sense of the time-space sequence through evolution, using the discoveries of science to tell the story, but should be taken as general approximations rather than as fact.

Diverse authors and explorers of consciousness have been quoted and referenced throughout this work, for their research, synthesis, and discoveries have enriched and illuminated my mind throughout my journey, thus helping shape many of the ideas herein. I encourage the reader to journey with the various authors mentioned in this book for a more in-depth view of their respective subjects, for here I only scratch the surface of what they have to offer. One such explorer is integral philosopher Ken Wilber. He is referenced extensively throughout these pages, as his work in integrating all fields of human knowledge is unparalleled. Although framed in the same model of ascending consciousness, this work breaks from Wilber's model in some important ways that will become apparent as we progress. Of importance here, however, is to mention and acknowledge what Ken Wilber has identified as an "all level, all quadrant" [7] approach when studying consciousness. His integrative approach, mapped and graphed in a grid of four quadrants and nine to thirteen levels, postulates the various dimensions of being as existing in four different but related manifestations. These four manifestations include:

- Individual interior-subjective, mapped in the upper-left quadrant ("I" dimension—sensations, emotions, thoughts, visions, illumination, etc.);
- Individual exterior-objective in the upper-right quadrant ("it" dimension—brain stem, limbic brain, neocortex, pre-frontal cortex, etc.);
- Collective interior-subjective in the lower-left quadrant ("us" domain—archaic, magic, mythic, rational, integral, etc., cultural structures);
- Collective exterior-objective in the lower-right quadrant ("its" domain—hunter-gatherer, horticultural, agrarian, industrial, informational, global, etc., techno-social organization).

In this book we will discuss the collective, or phylogenic, origins of the particular levels or stages of consciousness, and the individual, or ontogenetic, forms and manifestations of those levels (lower and upper quadrants, respectively) in different sections. *Phylogeny* is defined in *Webster's Dictionary* as the origin and evolution of any plant or animal group, race, or species, and *ontogeny* defined as the development of a single organism, in our case *you*. The distinction between internal-subjective sentient states (sensation, emotion, thoughts, concepts, identity, illuminations, etc.) and external-objective material structures (organismic states, limbic-hormonal system, neuronal activity, brain structures, neurotransmitters, DNA information matrices, microtubules, quantum resonance, etc.) will not be explicitly differentiated. They will be discussed simultaneously, within their collective and individual manifestations, in order to convey their inextricable interrelatedness and interconnectedness. The perceptive reader will be able to differentiate between objective and subjective phenomena, but will ultimately come to the nondual realization that "form is emptiness, and emptiness is form". [8] In other words, subjective and objective events are a simultaneous, a-casual manifestation of Consciousness's urge to express itself. Whether we talk about neuroelectrical signals or habituated thought patterns does not ultimately matter, for they, being two sides of one coin, manifest within the Empty embrace of Awareness or Consciousness.

Awareness, Consciousness, Self, Being, and Spirit will be used interchangeably in this work and will be the protagonist in our story of evolution and development.

Before we embark however, we must first ask ourselves a most fundamental question, "what is the only thing I know for sure, right now, without a shadow of a doubt?" Take a moment and ask your self that question before you read on.... What I discover when I ask myself that question is that, the only thing I really know fore sure, right in this moment, is that I Am. I Am, I exist in this moment, that is it, the rest are abstractions, ideas, notions, or perceptions of an "external" world which is really an inner experience apprehended from within. Other then this immediate sense of being Present, right now, all else appears as arbitrary thoughts that clumsily attempt to capture and reflect 'outer' sensory experiences that are really subjectively and intimately apprehended by a mysterious interior Source. An inner Essence that seems to transcend our ability to conceptualize, for as we look into it we discover that it has no form, therefore formless; it does not change over time, therefore timeless and ever-present; and its boundaries nowhere to be found, therefore infinite. This is Being, this Consciousness, this is Spirit, this is your deepest Self.

In our story, this inner 'I Am' Essence that appears to exist originally in and as a state of pure potential, unmanifest, and formless, will be seen as the mysterious sentient Witnessing capacity within all levels of manifestation, from the mineral world to Omega, from the embryo to enlightenment. Along this journey through space and time, various mechanisms and technologies (Wilber's exterior-objective) will manifest in order to aid Consciousness in its reception, interpretation, projection, experience, and creation of reality. From this viewpoint, what we call "reality" is seen as co-created by the evolution of Consciousness and its filtering mechanisms and technologies. These organic technologies act as "reducing valves" that dictate and determine the particular relevant signals that are to be "experienced" and "perceived." These "valves" collapse pure potential into actualized realities from what Aldous Huxley called "Mind-at-Large." [9] Following Huxley's observations, we will consider our organism and its brain to be a series of reducing valves that filter out an ocean of signals that are redundant for an earthly existence. When the filters are bypassed and the "doors" of the reducing valves are swung wide open, we will explore how the inner being is privileged to the vast transcendental view from and as the One Mind of Mind-at-Large.

This brings us to an important consideration of the relative nature of phenomenal reality. It has become apparent through advances in the study of neuroscience that what we call "reality," in its myriad and diversified forms, is a relative construction of individual nervous systems and the networked information processing capacities of the brain. As psychologist and '60s cultural icon Dr. Timothy Leary points out, "All events in nature, including human behavior, exist for us only as registered, recorded, and mediated by the brain. The dimensions, variables, divisions, groupings, lawful relations defined by science, and all other fields of human endeavor are based on, filtered through, determined by the receptive, integrating, and transmitting characteristics of the brain." [10] In other words, what we perceive and experience is relative to the receiving structure and its filtering tendencies. These filters, in our case the sensory system and the brain, select, define, organize, and focus on energy frequencies that are relevant to that organism's current experience and its level of awareness.

In this manual we will define the various levels of information reception, integration, and transmission. We will see how each of those levels functions as relative "perspectives," selecting the stage-related frequencies that are relevant to the organism at its particular stage of evolution. We will explore how each level is a layer of filtering devices that include genetic templates, developmental imprints, conditioned networks, and learned responses. These so-called layers and levels in turn combine to reveal a particular aspect of reality, a relative angle of knowing, a distinct perceptual vantage point, or a specific interpretation of phenomena. The point being that what we perceive and experience is directly and fundamentally tied to the level of consciousness in which we reside. In fact, we will explore how each level has its own distinct identity, motivation, mode of knowing, behavioral response, and basic reality.

These stage-related reality constructions, projections, and perceptions are all mediated, of course, by the evolution of the transceiver (or what we will call "reality creators"), in our case the multileveled brain. This evolving transceiver (receiver-transmitter) co-creates its environment as it informs the inner silent Witnessing Awareness of the diverse frequencies of the "outside" world, filters and reconstructs them "inside," to then project its particular version "outward" in an evolving, self-referential feedback loop. The transceiver is the genetically templated hardware, the co-evolving "objective" shell of Consciousness used by it to define, determine, and create its reality sequence. This evolving transceiver can be visualized as an antenna, receiving and transmitting specific signals at the various stages of development. This visual insinuates that Consciousness is not created in the structure (i.e., brain), as the images on TV are not generated by the box, but is rather a field that is networked and transceived in a vast web of coordinated information sharing and processing. All of these notions will ultimately lead us to the exploration of the various levels, layers, or circuits of the nervous system and the triune brain, the most evolved known antenna of our planet. We will unravel how each of those layers defines what we call reality in its own information processing terms. Timothy Leary's greatest contribution to the exploration of consciousness, in my view, is his eight-circuit model of consciousness, otherwise known as his Leary Theory. [11] Leary's eight-circuit model will be extensively quoted throughout our journey, as it follows the same basic outline, but will be updated with the most current neurological findings in neuroscience.

My hope is that this text not only serves as an exploratory guide, but also one that strongly inspires the development, strengthening, and health of all levels. Wilber addresses this call toward wholeness in his approach to integral psychology. [12] His main line of reasoning is that all levels develop at relatively different rhythms, and that there are various "streams, lines, or modules," such as cognitive, moral, affective, linguistic, kinesthetic, somatic, interpersonal, musical, etc., that develop independently but progress through the same general developmental and evolutionary sequence. One can be having high mystical experiences of Unity while at the same time be suffering from physical malnutrition and emotional alienation, for example. The point being that all levels must be developed, worked with, and integrated, or else unbalance and stagnation become inevitable. Within the context of each chapter we will have exercises for the exploration as well as the development of those levels addressed. Therefore, this can also be a guide promoting health and wellness for the whole being, in which no level or structure is omitted or overlooked.

Finally, before we begin our tour of Consciousness's epic saga through time and space, I would like to postulate, based partly on the answer to our first fundamental question, that pure Consciousness *is* the foundation and ground of everything, including matter. In alignment with the perennial philosophy, a term coined by Leibniz and popularized by Huxley, [13] we will view all of existence as an expression and manifestation of a single, universal underlying Ultimate Reality that is unified and One at its core. Quantum physicist Amit Goswami explains:

> Both the world of matter and the world of mental phenomena, such as thought, are determined by consciousness. In addition to the material and mental spheres (which together form the immanent reality, or world of manifestation), idealism posits a transcendent,

> archetypal realm of ideas as the source of material and mental phenomena. It is important to recognize that monistic idealism is, as its name implies, a unitary philosophy; and any subdivision, such as the immanent and the transcendent, are within consciousness. Thus consciousness is the only ultimate reality. [14]

Here Goswami points to the general principle that establishes Consciousness as the ground of being, resonating with both Eastern and Western philosophical schools of monistic idealism (Plato, Hegel, Kant in the West; Vedanta, Tibetan Buddhism, and Patanjali in the East, for example). Of interest, however, and we will return to this argument throughout our explorations, is that the quantum ocean of probability defined by quantum physics, now known as the Unified Zero-Point Quantum Vacuum, may just be another label for pure Consciousness. Through empirical and mathematical analysis physicists have also began to discover that the universe sprang (and springs) forth from a unified substrate, or singularity, therefore postulating a *materialistic* monism in their Unified Field theories. Both aforementioned materialistic and idealistic monistic fields are ultimately human constructs, one inferring pure Objectivity and the other pure Subjectivity, that dissolve as we probe and push deeply into the vast, mysterious, and literally inconceivably infinite nondual nature of this underlying unitive Source. In this vastness, the "two" fields dissolve into the One, the nondual Source of all domains and dimensions.

This argument, as we will soon discover, does not refute the levels approach. On the contrary, it establishes separate, solid, material reality as a direct experience/construction of Consciousness among countless other dimensions, revealing what we call physical reality to be a mere *experience* rather than a reality all unto itself. Were we to tap into the nonlocal quantum signals from David Bohm's implicate order, [15] we would undoubtedly experience a mystical flash revealing everything (more on this later). Lama Govinda illustrates:

> The Buddha himself had already defined the world as that which appears as world within consciousness—without going into the problem of objective reality. Since, however, he rejected the concept of substance, this—even when he spoke

> of material or physical conditions—could not be understood in the sense of an essential contrast to psychic functioning, but rather in the sense of an inner and outer form of appearance of one and the same process, which was of interest to him only in so far as it fell within the realm of *direct experience* [italics mine] and was concerned with the living individual, i.e., the process of consciousness.

Govinda continues:

> In consequence of this psychological attitude, the Buddhist does not inquire into the essence of matter, but only into the essence of the sense-perceptions and experiences which create in us the idea of matter…In this way Buddhism escapes the dilemma of dualism, according to which mind and matter remain accidentally combined units, the relationship of which has to be especially motivated. It is for this reason that we agree with Rosenberg (1924) that the term "*rupa*" in this connection should not be rendered by "matter" or the principle of materiality, but rather as the "sensuous," which includes the concept of matter from a psychological point of view, without establishing a dualistic principle, in which matter becomes the absolute opposite of mind. The external, material world is actually "the world of the senses," as Rosenberg points out, "irrespective of whether we regard it as an object of physics or an object of psychological analysis." [16]

By taking into account the perspectives of many visionary quantum physicists and that of most world mystical traditions, we come to an interesting insight into what is really meant by material or physical reality. The importance of this argument will become apparent as we explore the various levels of reality/

consciousness, particularly level one (material plane, physio-survival) and level eight (causal plane, pure formless Awareness). The traditional materialistic-reductionist view of current science describes consciousness as a mere, unimportant epiphenomena of dead matter; our brain. Yet as we explore the miraculous unfolding of our cosmos, we see how absurd this claim is, for the question becomes: Where do we draw the line between live sentient consciousness and dead matter? Does consciousness jump into existence from unconscious matter in the cell? The organism? The brain? Where is the line between a neuroelectric signal and a conscious thought? It seems much more likely that consciousness is embedded and/ or *identical* to matter, and unfolds in ever more articulated and self-aware modes of self-expression as the cosmos evolves in complexity through time and space. In any case, this exploration would be flat and rather boring if consciousness was believed to be a mere by-product of complex neuronal fireworks in the brain. To postulate that Consciousness, our own being a mere drop in a vast infinite ocean of Cosmic Awareness, is the ground of everything opens up vast and unimaginable possibilities for our species and the unfolding Self-aware cosmos.

Ken Wilber wrote a book titled *Quantum Questions*, [17] where he describes his belief that the quantum realm is at the bottom of the spectrum of consciousness, and that pure Consciousness or the causal plane is at the top. He would undoubtedly call the correlation between pure Consciousness and the Zero-Point Quantum Field the ultimate "pre/trans fallacy," confusing the unconscious ground of matter with the pure Consciousness of the mystics. Yet if what mystics access is truly a universal Ground of Cosmic intelligence, and if physicists are truly uncovering the Unified Field of Everything, then by necessity this Ultimate Field must transcend the human receiving that insight and be *one and the same* Absolute Ground. It seems much more plausible that there is One perennial Ground of Being that is infinite, eternal, and outside of space and time, and, as we will soon explore, we humans have the astonishing capacity to access, explore, and ultimately identify with this vast and infinite Source of all. The perspective in this text suggests that this primordial creative Intelligence (pure Consciousness, Universal Mind, Mind-at-Large, or quantum vacuum) lies on top *and* bottom of the spectrum, is the origin and goal of evolution, the Alpha and the Omega, for as we push deeply into the heights of human experience and the depths of what we call matter, we eventually slip into and intersect that most mysterious abyss of the nondual Void that gives birth to all that is, your Self! Not quantum questions, Ken, quantum *experiences*.

Exercise:

We will conclude this introduction with a simple meditation so as to clear our minds of any mental noise that might inhibit the unbiased Witnessing of the subsequent explorations. First, find a quiet and peaceful space. Next, get into a position that is comfortable and that allows your body to relax. It can be lying down, sitting in a chair, or the lotus position; whatever allows your body to relax. Then bring your awareness to the rise and fall of your breath. Eyes can be shut or half open. I find that when I close my eyes, I am able to focus inward more easily, and external distractions are diminished. Take several deep breaths, releasing any physical, emotional, or mental tension with the out breath. Cultivate the feeling of release, of letting go. Each time a thought, feeling, or sensation arises within your field of awareness, simply notice it and then release with the exhalation.

After your body-mind has quieted down, begin to cultivate that sense of spaciousness that arises as you release the content (thought, sensation, feeling, etc.) within your awareness. At this point turn your attention to that which is Aware. Find within you the part that Witnesses the thoughts, feelings, and sensations, and rest. You will notice that this constant Awareness, Witness, or spaciousness has nothing to do with the ebb and flow of phenomena. It is clear, unbound, empty, and formless. Within the embrace of this pure Awareness or Consciousness, all phenomena, such as physical sensations, emotional currents, thought patterns, memories, plans, images, etc., come and go like the rhythm of the ocean waves. Don't fight the waves, for they will become more agitated. Instead simply allow the natural cycles of your being to slowly come to a calmer and more peaceful rhythm. The more you develop this ability to slow down the rhythmic surfacing of phenomena, the easier it will be to tune in to that aspect of yourself that is motionless, still, and in a harmonious state of equilibrium.

This Witness, Awareness, or pure Consciousness that simply *is,* is the essential background in which all forms arise. As we will soon unfold in the proceeding text, this essence is the source of all being. That contentless essence that exists prior to any form is the primordial ground of all manifestation. It has no space, it does not enter the stream of time, and it has nothing to do with birth and death. It only Witnesses the fluctuating cycles of the moving image that is space-time. Since it lives outside of space-time, we will discover that your inner Witnessing Awareness, right now, is the same eternal-timeless Witness that was present within and throughout our ancestral struggles and strivings. The deepest "I" or "I Am" within you, that formless, unmanifest essence that is pure Consciousness, is the same "I" within all forms of past, present, and future creations.

Thus from within that eternally radiant Emptiness that is Aware, beyond time, space, birth, death, and causality, all of manifest existence arises like a new bud bathed in the fresh sunlight of spring. From this formless foundation of your being, which is one and the same for all beings, our story begins. A mysterious impulse gives birth to form, and the evolutionary dance begins.

(Note to reader: What follows in Part 0 is a physics based exploration of how existence came to be, and is therefore necessarily dense and somewhat technical. Therefore, I encourage the reader to move through it without getting discouraged or stuck, and come back to some of the concepts later as all ideas begin to be woven together into a coherent story toward the end of our journey. The text does get easier as we progress, so move gently and take time to contemplate what is being presented in light of your own creation myths.)

Part 0:

The Void

There was something formless and perfect
before the universe was born. It is serene. Empty.
Solitary. Unchanging. Infinite. Eternally present.
It is the Mother of the universe...[1]

-Tao Te Ching

I am without Form, without limit, beyond space,
beyond time. I am in everything, everything is me.
I am the bliss of the universe, everything Am I.[2]

-Ram Tirtha

In the beginning there was nothing at all....before
the Big Bang there wasn't even any empty space...
and there was no "outside" for the exploding
universe to explode into....[3]

-John Gribbin

The Void

The Unified Field

"Prior" to and beyond the beginning of space and time, Being and non-Being are One; an undifferentiated and seamless totality that stands as the naked, empty vacuum of the Void. Although empty and vacuous in its formlessness, it is pregnant with all possibility and potentiality, as a tiny seed contains the oak or the pine tree. Lying at the core of all existence, the mysterious Singular Source of all rests dormant, awaiting the secret signal for creation. Time rests in this eternity, space exists as a mere "enfolded" potential, and vibrations underlying all universal forces merge as a zero point of stillness. In this spaceless and formless plenum where there is no dimensionality, only an eternal now, an ocean of unmanifest and unrealized possibility and probability extends into the infinite expanse of that which is beyond human conception. A nonlocal (not in a space or time location) unity where consciousness and unconsciousness, inner and outer, subject and object, spirit and matter, are merged as One. Beyond what we call existence and nonexistence, beyond all conceivable and inconceivable dualities and polarities, lies the original substance that gives birth to all that is, was, and will be. We will call this the Ground of Being, the Source of all creation.

Within this vast Void where nothing is, only silence, there is a stirring, what quantum physicists call a "quantum probabilistic fluctuation" that creates a ripple in the fabric of this 'zero-point' field. In an instant, the plenum ceases to be motionless, as it is suddenly disturbed by the spontaneous eruption of a unified force. The unstable nature of this fluctuation makes it collapse back unto itself, thus returning to original perfect symmetry. Due to the uncertainty principle (to be defined), countless of these quantum probabilistic fluctuations have theoretically occurred (and occur) within this primordial creative field "prior" to our Big Bang, but most were (are) reabsorbed due to their inherent instability. Ervin Laszlo speculates that these fluctuations are not lost when reabsorbed, however, but remain recorded holographically as patterned informational codes within the quantum vacuum. This quantum vacuum, also being called the zero-point field (ZPF), or the Akashic Field as Laszlo likes to call it,[4] is conceptualized as the Ground and therefore basis of all space-time-matter.

The word Akasha is derived from the ancient Indian concept of the Akashic records or chronicles, which is a notion that describes an underlying field or medium, the aether, where information of all that has happened and will happen is recorded and conserved as "interference patterns." The Akashic Field is in essence the universal memory bank for all that has and will happen. As we will see, there seems to be an inward moving and outward radiating relationship that actually spins and torques the cosmos into being, as the information that is recorded in the Field is also conveyed to all manifesting structures of the Multiverse (a term that incorporates the possibility of many more universes) in an endless creative feedback loop of information exchange. "Information conveyed through the A-field subtly tunes all things to all other things and accounts for the coherence we find in the cosmos, as well as in living nature." [5]

Infinite quantum fluctuations, resulting in countless possible "bangs" of all shapes and sizes, have theoretically erupted to then collapse back again due to inherent instability. From actuality back to potentiality, the space-time dance explores various modes of existence, leaving the process recorded in this formless, all-pervasive zero-point Ground of Being. After eons of quantum trial and error a quantum fluctuation, or "probability wave function," has enough force to coalesce, rebound and burst into creative radiance with an unimaginable "Big Bang." The liberated force this time transforms the tranquil plenum from an empty formlessness to a dynamic and unstable foaming turbulence. As the newly created, unfolding space-time manifold expands from its formless and timeless Center (which is at every point), a chaotic dance of instantly appearing and disappearing, on and off, energy bits accelerate with inconceivable speed and intensity. The White Light Radiance blasts away from Central Singularity as it simultaneously collapses back upon itself. This sudden, violent movement sets into motion whirling vortices of primal energy; an ocean of vibrating strings. A perfect symmetry of elementary particles and antiparticles emerge to cancel each other out, appearing and disappearing instantly back into the quantum vacuum once they have made contact. This undulating dance of appearing and disappearing particles causes random fluctuations, which generate fleeting emanations called "virtual" particles. These ghostly entities are by-products of the creation/annihilation of particles, and therefore have uncertain existence.

Then, due to a mysterious impulse, desire, or urge from within, the particles gain a slight advantage over the antiparticles. For every one billion pairs of particles and antiparticles, there is one extra particle that survives. Our entire universe is created from these surviving particles. The will to Be transcends the effortless non-dual vacuum of zero, and the dance of this particular space-time existence initiates the unfolding project of self-creation with the first instant in what we call time.

The above creation myth is for the most part aligned with the most current discoveries and theories in astrophysics and quantum physics. It also reflects the ancient mystical teachings of most world wisdom traditions, as we will soon see. And if we personify and call this Ground of Being God, it could align with many of the world monotheistic religious traditions as well. Regardless of what we call this creative Source, the common thread is the notion that our universe, and the whole Multiverse, comes from some Ultimate or Absolute essence that is unified and without differentiation at its core. The difference between the new emerging scientific view and the mystical view is that what science is calling the unified zero-point quantum field, mysticism calls pure formless unmanifest Consciousness, or causal plane. While science arrives at its Ground of Being through advanced mathematics, rational speculation, and observation of empirical (sensory-based) evidence when possible, mysticism explores this Ground experientially and within. Another way of saying this is that physicists have arrived at non-duality through probing the depths of external objective matter and thus theorizing about the underlying Field thus discovered. While the mystic dives deep into the non-dual through the depth exploration of inner-subjective Being, thus *becoming* this Field. The scientific notions are concepts and ideas from the mental-rational level (levels three and four), grounded in the logic of mathematical equations and rational thought, while mystics dissolve into the Absolute in what they call pure Bliss (level eight). We will explore how the Cosmic Unified Field can be directly accessed by an individual human being in level eight, but for now we will equate the Unified Quantum vacuum-Field with pure formless Consciousness. As we shall soon explore, pure Consciousness has no boundaries; is prior to form, time, space, and matter; and transcends subject/object dualities. In fact, the mystical experience of *nirvakalpa Samadhi* in the causal plane makes clear that when one is able to rest in this unbounded pure Awareness, the notions of existence and being vs. nonexistence and nonbeing are seen to be mere constructs; cognitive dualities that dissolve in the radiant White Light of the eternal, pure Consciousness. It is this pure Consciousness that "incarnates" as whirling energy vortices, having its first experience in this particular, increasingly localized universe.

A recent *Scientific American* magazine summarizes four speculative scientific theories that attempt to describe what happened before the Big Bang. [6] Of course, Stephen Hawking reminds us in his playful manner that asking what happens before the Big Bang is like asking what lies north of the terrestrial north pole.[7] Nonetheless, the most common theory among scientist is that the universe of matter, energy, space, and time began suddenly out of nothingness, or a singularity, for no apparent reason, and that nothing existed prior to this Cosmic blast. The next theoretical construct speculates that ordinary space and time develop out of a primeval state described by a yet-to-be-fully-articulated quantum theory of gravity. Physicists continue to search for the unification of gravity, which is ruled by the equations of general relativity, and the other three forces of electromagnetism, strong and weak nuclear forces ruled by quantum mechanics. This has been called the theory of quantum emergence. The third theoretical construct grounds its ideations in the notion that our universe is one of infinite parallel universes in the Metaverse, or Multiverse. In this view, our universe and others bud off from the substrate of the quantum vacuum, all coexisting without connection or interaction, except maybe via speculated wormholes. This theory speculates that each universe contains its own laws and parameters, some hospitable for life, while others alien beyond conception. Ours happens to be finely tuned with what we call universal constants (or, more accurately, evolving habits, as we shall soon explore) so that carbon-based life forms like ourselves can evolve. The fourth scientific theoretical construct describes a single universe that is cyclical. In this scenario our Big Bang is the latest in an eternal cycle of explosion, expansion, contraction, collapse, "Big Crunch," "Big Bounce" back, and renewed expansion; endless cycles of birth and death.

A fifth scenario of how the universe erupted into existence comes from the relatively new field of string theory, super string theory, or M-brane theory, which are all attempts at finding the ultimate equation that unifies all universal forces in what is called a grand Theory of Everything (TOE). According to one of these models, in the beginning the three spatial dimensions and the fourth dimension of time were all tightly curled up to their smallest possible size, called the Planck length (1.62×10^{-35} m). All four dimensions, along with seven others (or twenty-two, depending on the calculations used, for a total of either eleven or twenty-six dimensions), were all curled up in a multidimensional Planck-sized nugget, resting in complete supersymmetry. At about Planck time, three of the spatial dimensions (plus the fourth, time) fall out of symmetry and begin to expand as described by the standard inflationary model, while the others retain their initial Planck-scale size. These multiple minute space-time dimensions provide the geometrical contours that give these theorized "stings" their vibratory signatures.

The so-called strings or superstrings are described by physicist John Hagelin as "one-dimensional closed loops or 'strings' moving in ten or twenty-six space-time dimensions." [8] These superstrings are seen as the ultimate building block of all universes. Hagelin continues, "Within the framework of this theory, the elementary particles and forces which fill the universe are just vibrational states of the superstring. Indeed, the entire universe, with all its diverse and multiform properties (charge, spin, color, flavor, etc.), is just a cosmic symphony—the vibrational states of a single, underlying, universal, unified field of nature's intelligence." [9] All that exists in this material universe, from subatomic matter to the forces that govern their relations, are but manifestations of these vibrating strings, according to this theory. These strings are themselves made out of probabilistic on/off flashing rhythmic signals that create vibrations in the quantum vacuum. Brian Greene speculates that the vibration of the strings may be mediated by the curvature of eleven (or twenty-six) space-time dimensions. [10] In other words, these one-dimensional entities vibrate according to the shape and contour of eleven or twenty-six dimensions. Not only that, but according to the latest version of string theory, called M-theory, there may also be open strings and very large dimensional membranes. In this version, our universe could be only one four-dimensional slice or membrane in a multidimensional Metaverse with a potentially infinite number of parallel universes embedded in their respective membranes. Greene speculates, based on the mathematical constructs, that parallel universes help explain the relative weakness of gravity when compared to the other forces. This could be due to the possibility that gravity may communicate with the other universes, thus losing its strength when measured from our universe.

The various vibrational frequencies of these spinning energy loops, called strings here, underlie the twenty or so universal constants necessary for our current universe to exist. These so called constants are but habits, the collapse of probabilities into actual forms, which define what we are calling the first point of 'reality projection-creation.' Habits conserved and informed by the quantum information embedded in the zero-point vacuum field by means of imprinted interference patterns. Theses "interference" patterns act as the multidimensional molds that dictate the rate of frequency vibration.

According to these views, a number of successful quantum vibrational states emerged with enough stability and coherence so as to remain in existence, becoming our first universal habits, constants, or recorded patterns. These habits have been mathematically formalized as vibrating strings characterized by what physicists call spin. *Spin* here is defined as the angular momentum intrinsic to an elementary particle. Superstring theorist John Hagelin elucidates: "Quantum consistency restricts the vibrational states of the string—the elementary particles and forces—to five fundamental categories, distinguished by their spin." He continues, "This spin is constrained by quantum mechanics to take half integer values: 0, ½, 1, 3/2, or 2 in units of Planck's constant. These spin types collectively comprise the five fundamental categories of matter and energy in nature." [11] According to Hagelin, these five spin ratios vibrate our entire Cosmos into existence, with all subsequent expressions and evolved manifestations emerging from these five basic rhythms. In this scheme, the force fields are defined by even-integer spin particles called bosons, and the matter fields by half-integer spin particles called fermions, such as quarks and leptons. More specifically, John Hagelin reports:

> The spin 2 graviton is responsible for the force of gravity and the field of curved space-time geometry. The spin 3/2 gravitino is the supersymmetric partner of the graviton. The spin 1 force fields are responsible for the strong, weak, and electromagnetic forces in addition to other, super heavy, grand unified force fields. The spin ½ gauginos are the supersymmetric partners of the spin 1 force fields, and the spin ½ matter fields—the quarks and leptons. The spin 0 matter fields include supersymmetric partners of the quarks and leptons (the "sparticles"), plus particles responsible for the spontaneous breaking of symmetries (Higgs bosons).[12]

As we can see, theorists have provided a mathematically elegant description of the underlying rhythms at the base of all creation. Therefore, we can speculate that from the zero point of the vacuum, the first beat of on/off in our universal song produces a break in the perfect symmetry of said vacuum, initiating the spin spiral that unfurls the diverse Cosmos that we so happily inhabit. As the name implies, the unified and formless zero point quantum field rests at zero vibration; absolute zero. The stillness of perfect symmetry is at rest within the Source as zero vibration, which translates as no time, no space, no form, and no manifestation. When zero is signaled into vibration, the songs of creation arise with their unimaginable magnificence, majesty, mystery, and beauty.

The seminal explorer of systems, Ervin Laszlo, has managed to unify most of the above constructs in his masterpiece *Science and the Akashic Field* by postulating that this quantum vacuum field is far from empty. Laszlo explains:

> In the "grand unified theories" (GUTs) developed in the second half of the twentieth century, the concept of the vacuum transformed from empty space into the medium that carries the zero-point field, or ZPF. (The name derives from the fact that in this field energies prove to be present even when all classical forms of energy vanish: at the absolute zero temperature.) In subsequent unified theories, the roots of all of nature's fields and forces were ascribed to the mysterious energy sea known as the "unified vacuum." [13]

Through a series of experiments and discoveries, such as the Casimir effect, physicists are beginning to uncover an ocean of infinite "virtual" energy in what, to our senses and instruments, appears as empty space. When calculated (multiplying the Plank length of the smallest possible wave-length 1.62 X 10^{-35} m times the Plank mass of that wavelength 10^{-5} g times a cubic centimeter) the vacuum appears to contain the unimaginably immense energy, mass, and density of 10^{93} g/cm^3. 10^{93} g/cm^3 is the number of Plank length wavelengths that could fit in 1 cm^3 of vacuum. This unfathomable energy and density is generated by the dance of virtual particles and antiparticles endlessly popping in and out of existence, creating almost infinite energy when added all together. This infinite energy is 'renormalized' by using the Plank units in order to rid the equation of 'infinities' and ascribe a numerical value that physicist can work with.

It is well established that what we call matter is actually 99.9999% empty space, and it now turns out that the space is not actually empty, but seething and foaming with probabilistic quantum zero-point energy. In fact, we are told that the zero-point energy in a unit of quantum vacuum is greater than all the visible energy in our known universe. In other words, if we were to take all of the visible energy and matter of our known universe and squeeze it into 1 cubic centimeter, we would get an energy density of only 10^{55} g/cm^3. From these calculations we see that every cubic centimeter of empty space contains more energy, 10^{35} g/cm^3 *more* to be exact, than the total energy of all matter in our known universe! Again, this vast energy seems to be a product of the briefly appearing and disappearing energy wave functions of the vacuum, which, once added together, give rise to enormous, almost infinite energy. Astrophysicist Bernard Haisch elucidates:

> "Zero-point" refers to the fact that, even though the extent of this energy is huge, it is the lowest possible energy state. All other energy operates over and above the zero-point state. Take any volume of space and take away everything else—in other words, create a vacuum—and what you are left with is the zero-point field full of zero-point energy. We can imagine a true vacuum, devoid of everything, but in the real world, a quantum vacuum is permeated by the zero-point field with its ceaseless electromagnetic waves. [14]

Space is not empty, it is actually *full,* a plenum rather than a true vacuum, and our material universe may be a mere ripple on the surface of a vast Cosmic ocean of unfathomable energy and depth. The Zero Point Field is actually called "zero" because its vast and unpredictable fluctuations are detectable in the absolute zero temperature (0 Kelvin, or -273.15 Celsius), the lowest possible energy state where all matter has been subtracted, leaving "nothing" to vibrate. Yet on the very "surface" of this Ground State Field, there are always going to be some residual probabilistic undulations due to virtual particle exchanges, thus generating the frothing creative energy substrate that gives birth to all of space-time. Beneath this surface, however, where all particles and antiparticles cancel each other out, rests the formless-timeless Void, outside all manifestation, as a true Zero. Here the nondual Mystery stands in its naked purity as total stillness.

Not only is this primordial Ground seething with unimaginable energy, but according to Laszlo it also stores information. In fact, every occurrence, event, or happening in this and all other multiple universes may be recorded in this superconducting, spaceless, nonlocal Field. A superconducting medium means that it is not subject to degradation, resistance, inertia, or the effects of entropy. Information in such a medium is encoded and recorded there practically forever. Waves are natural encoders and carriers of information, so that when they interact they create interference patterns that become imprinted in the Zero Point Field. Since the Field is a fluid medium without resistance, the interference patterns generated by these waves remain imprinted eternally, thus being available as recorded information for future generations of manifesting forms. The underlying substrate interconnects all matter via these information-carrying wave patterns. These waves extend out across all space-time sequences, in-forming and tuning all arising structures, and entangling everything through instantaneous, nonlocal information exchanges.

The image of an ocean is appropriate here. If we had a plane that stretched out across an ocean, concealing its "structure," an above observer would see a smooth, blank, empty surface, except for the probabilistic, indeterminate, uncertain, and random appearance and disappearance of particle points where undulating waves made contact with said plane from below. From above, it would seem like the creation and annihilation of these seemingly separate particles were random and totally unknowable. Now, if we were to peek underneath the "veil" of this imaginary plane, we would realize that each appearing and disappearing separate particle is, in effect, a point where a wave from the underlying ocean rises to briefly touch the plane, to then return to the ocean out of which it came. We would undoubtedly realize that these appearing and disappearing "virtual" particles (the seething probabilistic zero point energy) are not actually random, but a function of interconnected wave patterns that arise from a vast underlying ocean. So each "particle" is actually the tip and expression of a temporary wave that is *one with all other waves.* Not only that, each "particle" would be in direct, instantaneous contact with every other "particle" (the discovered nonlocal entanglement of all matter) because they are brief, separate expressions of One Ocean.

To push the metaphor further, if we were to go down into the depths of the ocean, we would undoubtedly discover that the deeper we went, the stiller and quieter things would be, as all motion ceased in a Ground state of absolutely zero vibration. The motionless oceanic depths that increase in turbulence as we approximate the surface, a surface that fluctuates restlessly in an interconnected self-influencing web of relations, is the place of stillness where all is undifferentiated oneness in a state of total rest. It seems that "prior" to the Big Bang, this ocean was like a still pond, without a single ripple of manifestation, until the Mysterious impulse that blasted creation into being agitated the Field into the restless ocean of ZPE physicists now measure.

So, if we integrate thus far, the emerging view is as follows: our universe is cyclical, as the standard inflationary cosmological theories seem to demonstrate, but is the latest manifestation in an endless chain of universes coming and going, maybe simultaneously with other parallel universes, out of an eternal Field that in-forms and tunes each universe with information/knowledge gained from previous incarnations. This view then holds an eternal succession of evolving universes that sustain themselves through their nonlocal connection to the ever-present, all-pervasive zero-point field. And again, if we equate this Field with pure Consciousness (not to be confused with human consciousness, which is only a fragment of the Cosmic Consciousness behind all phenomena) or pure Intelligence, then we can see how this In-forming of universes is a creative act from a vast Cosmic Imagination. The laws and cosmological constants then appear as dream fragments in an ocean of unlimited potential and probability. Intelligence permeates the Cosmos and is the root of all creation. Now, let's continue our story of how this unlimited Consciousness or Intelligence incarnated into form.

About 10^{-43} seconds after the Big Bang during what is called the Planck era, astrophysicists tell us that the universe is a chaotic radiation of light-energy ten trillion trillion times hotter than the core of our sun. The four universal forces of gravity, electromagnetism, strong, and weak nuclear forces are unified as one Superforce during what has been called the super-GUT (super Grand Unified Theories) era. The heat and energy are so intense that nothing can differentiate. All that is flows and radiates as one energy-force. Whirling with force and power, quantum energy waves begin to interact, creating interference patterns where the energy waves intermingle. Intermingling wave functions or interference patterns come into being as autonomous, spinning mini-vortices of "light chasing itself." [15] The light energy crests onto itself but manages to stay in coherent spinning formation, as the Cosmos develops stability with the freshly created opposing universal habit of resistance.

Due to the restless turbulence of the zero point energy generated by the Big Bang, we witness the birth of inertia, mass, and resistance. In other words, due to the seething energy fluctuations of the Field, the surface of the evolving Cosmos begins to create a stable medium of resistance so that the arising energy-forms can "stick" into manifestation. The newly developed resistance (surface of underlying resistant-less superconducting substrate) gives rise to the property of inertia, which is the tendency of objects to resist acceleration, and later mass. This occurs as the background ocean of energy opposes acceleration by providing a counterforce, the necessary balance needed to create stable forms. [16] This counterforce, as an underlying field of information, begins its career of shaping and forming the sculpture that is our Cosmos. From this perspective, matter and its mass are the product of slowed down light-energy; the slowdown a function of the resistance generated by zero point energy.

Consequently, we see increasing complexity and differentiation on the surface of this evolving, infant space-time matrix. The whirling energy vortices become autonomous on the surface, but remain entangled and interconnected "within." In other words, as expansion and cooling occur, formlessness begins to take form, and an "interior" begins to coevolve with the outer being. The inner or interior of each whirling-spinning energy vortex remains in intimate resonance with the unified singularity of the quantum Void, which continuous to be at rest in timeless stillness from its relative perspective. As form-energy-matter enters the stream of evolution, the internal dimension of subjectivity and inner depth begins to reflect the outer forms as it coevolves with them. The external forms, whirling energy vortices at this point, become localized in four dimensions, as the three dimensions of space and the fourth dimension of time become more defined. Yet the internal domain, though beginning to reflect the spatial and temporal location as an energetic "feel," remains nonlocal and entangled, interconnecting all energy vortices at their core. We will call this rudimentary and limited form of internal subjective consciousness *prehension*. Wilber informs: "Whitehead uses 'prehension' to describe the contact and thus 'feeling' of an object by any subject, no matter how primitive, including atoms." [17] As differentiation occurs during the first nanoseconds of creation, we witness the birth of the first subject/object relationship. The whirling-spinning mini light-energy vortex has an interior subjective experience of prehension, which is one with the timeless nonlocal singularity of all, and is the subject in relation to other light-energy vortices, the space-time-defined objects or "others." The universe has the first experience of itself, and Consciousness is articulated in its most primal form.

These mini-vortices of energy have been mathematically articulated by physicist Nassim Haramein in his Scalar Vortical Model, and are described as the basic fractal templates for all of creation. Nassim calls them Plank Spherical Units (PSUs), which are the minimum size of vacuum energy oscillations that generate minute dual torus-like fields.

Fractals are repeating and recursive self-similar patterns that repeat themselves endlessly up and down dimensional scales, each part reflecting the whole that is also a part that reflects a larger whole, *ad infinitum*. At the center of each mini-vortex is what is called a mini-singularity: the formless and mysterious center that informs, moves, shapes, and manages the whirling energy patterns. *Singularity* is a concept in physics that describes areas in our universe where all our known physical laws, mathematics, and even language break down and cancel each other out. There are singularities at the heart of collapsed stars called black holes, the centers of galaxies have massive singularities, the cores of whirling elementary particles have supra-gravitational mini-black/white holes, and, of course, the ultimate source that gives birth to our universe is called a singularity. We can conceive of the singularity as a portal into the quantum vacuum of the zero-point field. The singularity *may even be* the unified source field, completely still, with zero vibration; the fulcrum point that acts as the solid leverage that torques and moves our Cosmic wheels; the infinite point where inward-moving/outward-radiating energies cancel each other out in the utter stillness of Central Zero.

Singularity is further defined by physics as a point that has infinite curvature, infinite density, and infinite mass so that nothing, not even light, can escape due to unimaginable levels of gravitational collapse. As such, it acts as that unmovable and unshakeable reference point or ground state for all movement and vibration. Since it is One, as the name *Single-arity* implies, we can conceptualize it as the timeless Center that interconnects all points across all space-times through a nonlocal, spaceless common Ground. As quantum theory experimentally verifies through John Bell's nonlocality theorem, every particle of creation seems to be connected, correlated, and entangled with every other particle at its core, for in this core there is no space, time, distance, or form. There is only an ever-present, zero-vibrational Source-singularity of infinite energy and information, resting quietly beyond all human conception.

Physicist Nassim Haramein has noted that the entire universe can be modeled as an inward-moving (black hole) and outward-radiating (white hole) recursive toroidal feedback loop that sustains itself through an endless exchange of energy and information. This image of the universe, reflecting fractally and holographically the mini-vortex of the whirling subatomic particles, is represented by what is called the dual torus. According to physicists studying a new branch of physics called "implosion physics," the torus may represent the sacred geometrical structure that explains and unifies all forces of the universe. For example, as energy radiates outward from singularity, the spacetime curvature immediately begins to act on and pull it back toward the center. Coriolis forces (spin/ torque) act on this space-time-energy as it gravitates back toward singularity. The twist of the spin or torque is caused by an increase in density levels as matter and energy return to the attractor point of the singularity. As this moving space-time-energy approaches the singularity, the increased mass and density draws the energy closer, causing it to spin faster and faster, approaching the speed of light, until it breaks through and reaches the vacuum/ singularity at the center. Once here, massive centrifugal forces radiate the energy back outward again, repeating the process *ad infinitum*.

When the dual torus is geometrically mapped in 2- dimensions we get a perfect honeycomb hexagon, and in 3-dimensions the cubactahedron, where all force vectors are of equal length and of equal angular relationship, resulting in what is called 'vector equilibrium'. This is the only natural geometrical structure that has this perfect vector equilibrium, or singularity at its center, for all forces cancel each other out at the center creating stability in the otherwise chaotic foaming vacuum. This stability appears to us as empty space, pure stillness, as in the eye of a hurricane, for without this stable geometry the force and power of the vacuum energy would completely obliterate all structures. In other words, in order for the immense power and energy of the vacuum to remain stable, each unit (PSU) must cancel its vector forces out at the center, or else the structures would be unstable and collapse. The forces of central singularity, then, radiate and contract simultaneously in perfect balance and synchrony, creating this dual torus structure, with the cubactahedron of vector equilibrium at its center. The creative edge where radiative/ expansive forces balance with the contractive/ attractive forces is called the boundary condition of the event horizon; the sweet spot where the stabilization of energies ultimately give rise to the world of matter.

As lucidly explained by mystic, artist, and close friend Amoraea: "Seen from a viewpoint above looking down the axis of a torus, our awareness (and universe) spins toward an infinite center, and indeed this is where the 'Golden Mean Spiral' is actually birthed from." He continues, "The torus is the mother shape of the spiral and of all the geometric building blocks called the 'platonic solids.' " [18] As the basic universal template, the torus maps a self-sustaining, self-organizing, and self-generating structure that has at its core the empty center into which and out of which all things flow. Through the energy of implosion, the torus is able to generate a radiant and radial spherical field which moves in and out of a singular center.

The torus may even reflect the structure of Consciousness itself in its most primal form. And, as we will soon see, our entire space-time journey across the levels of Consciousness occurs in stages and epochs that reflect the perfect ratios of the Fibonacci Series (0, 1, 1, 2, 3, 5, 8, 13, 21, etc.), which approximates the Golden Mean Spiral of the circulating torus. This unending and infinite Fibonacci sequence is derived by the addition of two sequential numbers to derive a third, *ad infinitum.* If we take any two of the sequential numbers of Fibonacci's sequence and divide the higher by the lower, we will always approximate 1.618, the *divine proportion* known as PHI. This divine proportion is annotated as follows: a/b=(a+b)/a= 1.618. This is the number of the Golden Mean or Golden Ratio, which generates the algorithmic, recursive fractal patterns seen across nature. The Golden Mean Spiral's perfect proportions are evident throughout our cosmos, and, as we will see, in the tapestry of time as well. It seems to reflect the basic underlying mathematical "sacred geometrical" blueprint of creation, and can therefore be seen throughout our macro- and microcosms. In an abstract to his highly technical essay on this topic, found in his website, www.resonanceproject.org, Haramein describes it this way:

> From observational data and our theoretical analysis, we demonstrate that a scaling law can be written for all organized matter utilizing the Schwarzschild condition, describing cosmological to subatomic structures. Of interest are solutions involving torque and Coriolis effects in the field equations. Significant observations have led to theoretical and experimental advancement describing systems undergoing gravitational collapse, including vacuum interactions. The universality of this scaling law suggests an underlying polarizable structured vacuum of mini white holes/black holes. We briefly discuss the manner in which this structured vacuum can be described in terms of resolution of scale analogous to a fractal-like scaling as a means of renormalization at the Planck distance.

In other words, these mini black holes/mini white holes (PSUs) seem to be the basis for all manifest subatomic particles. In essence, these mini structures act as templates recognizable at all levels and scales, from collapsing stars, to galactic formations, to galactic clusters, to the universe as a whole. This so-called scaling law is what we call a fractal, generating a torus-like pattern that repeats itself from the Plank length and PSU to the observable universe, and unfolds along a scale structured by the PHI ratio. Haramein continues:

> Currently we have very strong observational evidence of collapse at stellar, galactic, and quasar scale. Further, the vacuum fluctuation density of the quantum resolution, which has gained great support from theory and experiments, is evidence that collapse may be occurring at the subatomic particle level, producing a polarized structured vacuum. Certainly, if the universal scale emerged from singularity and returns to singularity, and gravitational collapse is found at the star and galactic center resolution, and, finally, if we find that collapse as mini black holes is occurring everywhere in space in a dynamical vacuum, then one can deduce that collapse is not only predicted by the high curvature of the metrical space, but that it is fundamental to the space-time manifold topology as it interacts with matter/energy. [19]

So in the turbulent foaming ocean of the quantum vacuum, constantly appearing and disappearing (virtual) mini black holes and mini white holes create toroidal spinning vortices. These spinning vortices, conceptualized by some as vibrating strings, seem to be energy bits that are trapped by the inward pull of the singularity, but stabilized by their angular momentum, or spin, and the transmitted energy of the ZPF. The vortices' dynamic interactions reinforce their separate existence, and the manifold of the space-time matrix begins to weave itself into existence. At the center of each spinning vortex of energy is, of course, the singularity, which is the portal into (or identical to) the zero point field, or Laszlo's Akashic Field. If so, every speck of space and time is in-formed by the memory and information encoded (as "interference patterns") in the Akashic Field, nonlocally and holographically accessible to all points of all space-time sequences. The whole truly enfolded within each bit of existence, guiding, forming, and shaping the evolving sculpture that is our beautiful universe. And if the unified singularity/ zero point field is equated to nondual, formless Consciousness, the primordial Witness of all, we see that Intelligence is truly the essence and heart of all creation. And thus our story continues.

After the initial "Bang," the infinitely dense singularity begins to inflate and expand its outer surface rapidly, as central singularity simultaneously collapses and pulls all towards itself. Energy and radiation is all there is, smashing, annihilating, and creating a vast range of vibrating-spinning ratios of energy. Some spin ratios manage to gain stability and coherence, and thus begin to differentiate from one another. And then, all of a sudden, a zoo of elementary particles diffract and explode on the scene out of the stabilizing spin ratios (of the strings) via ZPF interactions, and we witness the birth of our first ancestors.

Physicists divide elementary particles into two categories: fermions, which typically carry matter, and bosons, which generally convey forces. Fermions include quarks and leptons, and their antimatter counterparts. As we shall see, quarks (such as up, down, charm, strange, top, and bottom to name a few) are the first autonomous beings, with inner subjective prehension, that eventually come together in the first communities to form protons and neutrons. Leptons later evolve into electrons, neutrinos, muons, and taus. As we saw, the four forces can also be conceptualized as the spinning elementary particles that convey them, such as gluons (strong force), which in effect glue quarks together; intermediate vector bosons, (weak force) responsible for radioactive decay; photons (electromagnetic force), which convey the entire electromagnetic spectrum; and gravitons, which govern the force of gravity.

At around 10^{-35} seconds after the Big Bang, the universe enters what is called the GUT Era, and the force of gravity begins to differentiate from the other three forces, collectively called electronuclear force. The pure radiation is now held together by gravity, but as the momentum from the initial Blast pushes space-tine relentlessly forward, the universe enters the next phase, called the Inflationary Era. As the GUT Era ends, temperature drops past a threshold mark of about 10^{27} degrees Kelvin. So sudden and drastic is this super cool down that the electronuclear force persists as one unified force instead of breaking up. This situation creates an unstable state known as a false vacuum. As the universe continues its expansion, the temperature and energy of individual particles falls drastically. Paradoxically, however, the total energy of the universe continues to increase exponentially. This energy deferential catapults the expansion exponentially by a factor of 10^{50}, as the volume of space continues to balloon. Consequently, the volume of space increases more than a trillion trillion times by the end of this so-called Inflationary Era, 10^{-33} seconds after the Big Bang.

By 10^{-33} seconds after the Big Bang, the inflationary Era ends when the force of gravity begins to slow down the expansion of the universe. With temperatures stabilizing at 10^{26} K, the cosmic density is still great so that a mass equivalent to that of the Earth would have fit into a teaspoon. During this Era, the GUT symmetry begins to break, and the strong force differentiates from the now radiant electroweak force, marking the entrance into the Electroweak Era. Over the next instant, so-called H Higgs bosons appear, dividing the electroweak force into the electromagnetic and weak nuclear forces. This event sets into motion processes that lead leptons and antileptons to develop and evolve into variants such as electrons and positrons, which respond to electromagnetism, and neutrinos and antineutrinos, which are sensitive to the weak nuclear force.

As temperatures fall to about 10^{13} K at around 10^{-6} seconds after the Big Bang, still more than a million times hotter than the core of an average star, the energy slows down enough to allow gluons of the strong force to condense and unite quarks into the building blocks of atomic nuclei, such as protons, neutrons, and their antiparticles. Through this new, unveiled habit made possible by cooling temperatures, the autonomous spinning energy vortices, or quarks, begin to come together to form group structures we call protons and neutrons, with increased autonomy and complexity. The inner Awareness of prehension remains rudimentary, possibly increasing in sensibility as it joins with other quarks to further express itself. Due to the fact that neutrons occasionally decayed into protons, protons gradually come to outnumber neutrons. With few new particle pairs being created, antimatter all but disappears and our world of matter crystalizes into existence.

One minute after the Big Bang and lasting four minutes, the Nucleosynthesis Era begins with conditions that are finally ripe enough for the creation of the first atomic nuclei. The density of the universe is like that of water by three minutes, as temperatures fall to around 600 million degrees Kelvin by the end of the era. Photons begin to slow down and lose more of their energy, and therefore can no longer prevent protons and neutrons from combining into atomic nuclei. Photons due retain sufficient energy at this point, however, to disrupt electrons and keep them from coming into orbit around the newly formed nuclei. As protons and neutrons come together, we witness the birth of a variety of hydrogen and helium nuclei, which account for most of the known matter in the universe today.

The pace of change begins to slow down considerably by the end of the Nucleosynthesis Era at about five minutes after the Big Bang. The universe continues to expand and cool, but no real change occurs until about three hundred thousand to one million years after the Big Bang. The cosmic density becomes like that of air, and the universe becomes transparent to light as outer space becomes black. Temperatures drop from 10^8 K to 3,000 degrees Kelvin, weakening photon interaction so that they no longer disrupt the formation of atoms. Through this development, we finally enter the present Era of Matter, as positively charged nuclei and negatively charged electrons finally come together in stable relationships forming our first atoms. As atomic structures begin to form, the cosmic plasma fog begins to evaporate as free electrons are attracted to and orbit around atomic nuclei. As electrons condense around their respective nuclei, there is a reduction in the random encounters with scattered photons, producing our transparent space. As time goes on, the energy of photons continues to plummet, decreasing over the next thirteen to twenty billion years to the three-degree Kelvin background radiation that permeates our cosmos today.

At around one billion years after the initial Big Blast, hydrogen clouds begin to condense and coagulate under the weight and pressures of their growing gravitational pull, thus fusing and igniting the gas into novel fiery existence as a new Being is born, the Star. Early primal stars, or mother stars, are birthed out of the hydrogen clouds, and a new form expressing the radiant underlying Consciousness emerges in full glory. In their core, the power of the inward moving gravitational force begins to fuse the hydrogen atoms into new, heavier elements, including carbon, oxygen, and calcium. Simultaneous to the inward pull of the gravitational (and strong) force, the outward-moving radiance of the entire electromagnetic spectrum and radioactive decay of the weak force beam out into the cosmos.

As the stars move through their life cycle, they eventually burn out, collapse, and explode as supernovas, spewing the newly created atomic elements into the surrounding space. These elements, star dust, over time begin to come together to reignite as new stars, and/or create planets that eventually find stable orbits around neighboring stars. Five billion years after the Big Birth, there are enough stars so that they begin to attract each other into star communities called galaxies. Galaxies begin forming within the evolving space, as the massive gravitational pull of condensing stars eventually collapse into black holes. The black holes keep the stars in spiraling formation from a central pull, creating a torus energy flow that is but a reflection of the subatomic swirl.

Communities of stars, called galaxies, then begin to interact with one another through vast gravitational fields of curved space-time, coming together to form communities of galaxies called galactic super clusters. One of these galaxies, the Milky Way, forms from star clusters that date back to when the universe was about one billion years old. At around seven billion years, our mother star may have gone supernova, thereby producing the star dust that eventually coagulated into our sun and the surrounding planets.

At about eight billion years, our solar system forms, starting as a disk made of clouds of gas and dust that begin to spin as the clouds collapse into shrinking rotating spheres. Gravity begins to exert its force on clumps of matter in the center of the disk, giving sudden birth to our sun as nuclear fusion begins to burn at the core. The full-spectrum radiance of the sun is the by-product of the fusing of hydrogen into helium, releasing vast amounts of energy. Five hundred million years after the sun began its nuclear fusion, the planets begin to take shape in the outer parts of the spinning disk. Nine planets form from the dust and gas in the disk, bringing the elements together to create stable, orbiting spheres. The third planet from the sun, at first a molten plasma ball, begins to cool, crystallizing into the various heavy elements that set the stage for the next evolutionary leap of form and consciousness. The trend is clear; as the creation of new forms arise, they seek each other, always moving toward the center, yet radiating outwards in a feedback loop of ever-expanding self-creation.

Mysticism: Science of Consciousness

The exploration of where we and our universe came from has been going on for probably as long as humans have been around. The study of this Unified Field in particular is ancient, predating the modern scientific explorations more than tens of thousands of years. Of course, we didn't have massive telescopes, particle accelerators, orbiting satellites, supercomputers, or complicated mathematical equations back then, but we did have that most mysterious inner sense of being called consciousness. The explorers, called mystics, dove deep into the essence of existence through a series of reproducible procedures, techniques, and practices that probed the depths of what it is to be conscious. We will explore some of these techniques at length in the subsequent chapters, but here we note the foundational realizations that mysticism points toward. The parallels between the cosmology of the mystics and that of the new sciences are striking, especially as the myths of Newtonian physics continue to collapse in the face of ongoing discoveries into the nature of quantum reality.

Mysticism will here be defined as the scientific, meaning observations that can be validated systematically through the reproducible techniques to be discussed in later chapters, exploration of the subjective inner domains of Consciousness. One of the fundamental insights of this probe is that as we dive deeper and deeper into what we are calling consciousness, we begin to experience more unitive and deeply connected states of awareness. Again, physicist and longtime meditator Dr. John Hagelin explains:

> Whereas waking consciousness represents a complex form of awareness corresponding to a complex state of neurophysiological functioning, the brain is also capable of sustaining simpler, more integrated states of functioning, which correspond subjectively to more silent and more unified states of awareness. According to direct experience, and to the Vedic science of consciousness from which meditation springs, human intelligence, like nature's intelligence, is hierarchically structured in layers—from gross to subtle, from excited to de-excited, from localized to unlocalized or field like, and from diversified to unified. [20]

As we go deep within, we begin to peel away layer after layer of diversified expressions to finally access realms of experience that seem to transcend even the human vessel that initiates the search. Unity, not just a state of human experience but as a deep universal truth, is tapped and accessed. This revelation again seems to correlate with the discoveries of physics, where the layers of diversified matter and forces are peeled back to reveal a Unified substrate out of which all is created. Both human intelligence and Nature's intelligence seem to be hierarchically structured, one the reflection of the other, having as their ground and foundation a Unified, nondual Field that informs, preserves, sustains, and reabsorbs all manifestations.

In the final mystical flash, the dawning realization that "all is One" emerges as one's separate identity dissolves into a vast ocean that mystics have described as pure, formless Consciousness, although unanimous in qualifying the experience as being utterly beyond words; ineffable. The hallmark of this inner experience is the dissolution of what we call the subject and object duality. Once this occurs, we encounter the fundamental insight with which we began this section: that all emerges out of a unitive Ground of existence, where all dualities merge. If the physicists' Unified Field of Everything is truly what it claims to be, then by necessity it must be accessible by anyone, at any time, given the right key. We will explore various reliable keys in the proceeding sections, with vast amounts of data supporting the wild-eyed claims made throughout history, cross culturally and cross temporally, about the glory and the vastness of what is generally termed spiritual reality.

We can sum up the basic mystical insight with the words of the modern scholar and master W. Y. Evan-Wentz, who spent decades practicing various forms of advanced yoga at the feet of some of the greatest masters of all times. He reports;

> In common with all schools of the Oriental Occult Sciences, The Mahayana (Buddhist) postulates that the One Supra-Mundane Mind, or the Universal All-pervading Consciousness, transcendent over appearances and over every dualistic concept born of the finite or mundane aspect of mind, alone is real. Viewed as the Voidness, it is the Unbecome, the Unborn, the Unmade, the Unformed, the predicateless Primordial Essence, the abstract Cosmic Source whence all concrete or manifested things come and into which they vanish in latency. Being without form, quality, or phenomenal existence, it is the Formless, the Qualityless, the Non-Existent. As such, it is Imperishable, the Transcendent Fullness of the Emptiness, the Dissolver of Space and Time and of *sangsaric* (or mundane) mind, the Brahman of the Rishis, the Dreamer of *Maya,* the weaver of the Web of Appearances, the Outbreather and the Inbreather of infinite universes throughout the endlessness of duration. [21]

This fundamental Core Reality all masters claim is accessible to the evolved Awareness, the one ready to discover its original and true nature behind the hierarchy of manifested forms. Evan-Wentz continues: "Reality, or the Absolute, or Being *per se*, is transcendent over both existence and nonexistence, and over all other dualistic concepts. According to Nagarjuna, it is the Primordial Voidness, beyond mental conception, or definition in terms of human experience." [22] In other words, it is a singularity, or rather *the* Singularity, one with the quantum vacuum and Source of all that is.

In calling this Unified Field of Creation pure Consciousness, a logical confusion arises. Consciousness is typically used to describe subjective, inner states of experience, whereas the quantum vacuum or zero-point field is used to describe the essence of objective, material reality. This final duality was precisely worked out by the ancient Samkhya (complete knowledge) system of philosophy, which is the foundation of Yoga psychology. [23] According to this system of philosophy, there are two fundamental aspects or principles to the universe, two sides of the one universal coin, if you will, responsible for creation. One is *prakriti*, or unconscious noumenon, and is defined as the primordial energy substrate out of which all matter and energy in our material universe come from and are modifications of. *Prakriti* may be equated to the energy of the zero-point field responsible for all force and matter; the unconscious, objective, material shell(s) that unfolds in complexity with the flow of time. The other aspect or principle is called *Purusa*, or conscious noumenon, and is defined as pure intelligence, consciousness, sentience, or the incarnate Self within all forms. It is the subjective experiencer or seer within all evolving forms; the inner radiance of conscious awareness that is housed by the developing shells or structures of *prakriti.* Yoga master Rammurtis Mishra describes them: "*Purusa* is one side which is purely subjective, and *prakriti* is the other side which is purely objective. Samkhya Yoga regards *Purusa* as the Seer and Knower, *Drishta,* and *prakriti* as the seen and known, *drishya.*" [24] In the more poetic Tantras, these two principles are personified as the God Shiva of pure Consciousness and the Goddess Shakti of pure Energy. It is the dance and lovemaking of the two that gives birth to our sentient material universe. Both God and Goddess expressed through and within every form of creation.

The important point made in the Samkhya philosophy, however, is that both *Purusa* and *prakriti* are aspects and manifestations of one fundamental Reality: Brahman, One-Without-a-Second. Objective Energy and subjective Consciousness are both creative emanations of a single, transcendent Source that lies outside of the space-time matrix. Brahman is the eternal placeless place where Shiva and Shakti are merged in ecstatic, loving, orgasmic Unity as the Ultimate Creator-Source of all that is. It is in this transcendent Source where the intellectual distinctions of spirit/matter, inner/outer, subject/object, conscious/unconscious break down and dissolve into that seamless essence out of which our mythic story began. In Brahman, One-Without-a-Second, is where we integrate the "two" Unified Fields, the zero-point quantum vacuum and pure Consciousness, as that single Source.

For the sake of semantic simplicity, this transcendent Source of Brahman will be called the Unified Field of pure Consciousness. As such, the field of pure formless Consciousness will be equated to this transcendent Brahman, and will be seen as the Source of both objective matter and subjective sentience. Of course, as we will explore in level eight, the *experience* of the transcendent Source is best verbalized by the term *pure Consciousness*, for pure Consciousness is empty of objects, yet completely and fully sentient; Void and dark, yet simultaneously radiant and full of Light; having nothingness and nonbeing, but radiantly Being nonetheless; nothing existing in it, yet being pure existence itself. Pure Consciousness transcends consciousness and unconsciousness, as there is nothing to be conscious of, yet consciousness *is*; Pure Being transcends being and nonbeing, as there is nothing to be, yet being itself *is*. In other words, pure Consciousness/ Being transcends all possible dualities, not as a concept but as an actual experience, even though there is no experiencer and no-thing to be experienced. In these paradoxes we are reminded by Wilber that "paradox is simply the way nonduality looks to the mental level." [25] Zen best describes *that* as pure is-ness, total such-ness, or the that-ness of the Mystery. Once one taps into this Essence, all one can say is, "it just IS," and no further "proof" is required.

A basic principle that runs through our text, and that will be elaborated on as we continue with our explorations, is the foundational notion established by quantum mechanics that an observer is required in order to collapse a wave of probability into a particle of reality. In other words, the radical notion, expressed in physicist Erwin Schodinger's probability wave or wave function equations, is that matter exists as a fuzzy and nebulous cloud of probability and potential until an observation, perception, or measurement is made. An electron or light, for instance, is an undefined wave-field that collapses into a particle when an experimental measurement is made. Werner Heisenberg, one of the principal architects of quantum theory, described this phenomenon as the uncertainty principle of indeterminacy, experimentally demonstrating that if one takes a measurement of an electron's position, there is no way of knowing its momentum, and, vice versa, by determining the momentum no position can be observed. In essence, his uncertainty principle describes how from our current level of understanding there is no way of knowing where or when an emerging particle will arise or be, as the ground state field of energy continually interacts with all subatomic particles, keeping them in constant, seemingly random motion. Consequently, the cosmos, thus being utterly unpredictable and uncertain at its base, is found to be stranger and more mysterious then was once supposed. Furthermore, it was found that these subatomic particles manifest only when they are observed!

The logical conclusion from these paradigm-shattering experiments is that an observer, a subject with inherent Awareness, is necessary for any form to arise. The problem that most physicists run into with this notion is based on the materialistic paradigm which states that consciousness arises only with the development of the human brain, and is therefore not present before human life. If we postulate that inner subjective being has been coevolving with external objective matter, as described above, then this problem literally dissolves. The view from this alternate paradigm shows that the observer prehending the world (remember the prehending mini energy vortex) in the initial moments of time is literally helping shape and create the universe. Consciousness is not only present in the beginning of time, but is also the creative observer collapsing the waves of radiation into the diverse and discrete elementary particles thus discussed. The image, then, is that of a web of Consciousness, co-creating itself through the act of becoming aware of itself!

Again, as with most modern "discoveries," the idea of an observer-created universe has been acknowledged and explored by mystics since time immemorial. Buddhists discuss the relationship between form (appearances) and consciousness in their "Interdependent Co-Origination" doctrine. This doctrine describes how the phenomenal world only arises through this intimate relationship. Of course, the Taoist yin/yang symbol also beautifully illustrates this dance: yin Shakti making love to yang Shiva to give birth to our phenomenal world.

Two original thinkers, anesthesiologist and consciousness researcher Stuart Hameroff, MD, and physicist Sir Roger Penrose, PhD, have collaborated to create a persuasive theory that articulates how the above possibility may arise at the quantum mechanical level. Penrose speculates that when a quantum wave function collapses, as in each moment or in the beginning of space-time, there is a parallel result of a moment of consciousness. He argues that consciousness does not cause the wave-function to collapse, but rather suggests that consciousness arises *with* the wave-function collapse. [26] As the quantum probability wave collapses, it gives off a fundamental unit of rudimentary conscious-awareness, just like an electron shift gives off a photon of light. In this scenario, you don't need an outside observer to collapse the wave, for it self-collapses due to a theorized intrinsic, objective threshold in the fabric of the space-time fabric itself. The model states that the conscious moment and the quantum wave-function collapse are one and the same event. This theory then implies that the precursors of a fully articulated consciousness, as in you, the reader, are embedded and built into the universe at the Planck scale, which we recall is the smallest, most primordial unit of quantum space-time at 1.62 X 10^{-35} cm. This proposition describes the primary components of consciousness or awareness as being fundamental, irreducible, and built into the basic fabric of our cosmos. Their model eventually arrives at the same depths that we've been articulating: that there is one common underlying entity, quantum space-time geometry, in their words, that gives rise to both matter and mind. In this view, the fundamental field of proto-conscious experience has been embedded in the Planck scale of space-time geometry all along since the Big Bang. We will return to Hameroff's theories in level eight, as he describes how the evolved consciousness can access the quantum vacuum of its original nature through the instrument of the brain and its trillion microtubule antenna arrays embedded in each neuron (more on this later).

The First Experience

The image thus far is as follows: out of this vast Unified Field of Consciousness, which is eternal and ever-present, a mysterious impulse collapses a probability into actuality, a wave into particle. This new being, our first ancestor, has a co-arising inner subjective proto-awareness that we are calling *prehension*, and the external objective form of a spinning-whirling energy unit, the elementary particle. These elementary particles relate to each other through the four forces, the basic laws that govern their behaviors. The internal view is most elementary; totally unconscious of self and others, but nonetheless 'prehensive' of their environment. This prehension can be reduced to two distinct qualities: that of attracting and that of repulsing. The inner experience is most likely "felt" as pressures and forces, mostly attractive and repulsive, in a chaotic ocean of whirling energy. As we will see, this attract-repulse orientation (habit) remains intact all the way up the ladder of development and evolution. Attract-repulse is the basic psychology of the elementary particle, using the gravitational and strong force fields to attract other members into groups and communities (first as protons, then atoms, then stars, then galaxies, then galactic clusters), and the electromagnetic charge and weak force to radiate out and repel others. Through their evolving relationships, these units of prehending energy begin to weave the fabric of our known space-time universe, "observing" and thus collapsing energy probabilities into actualities that become coherent and stable when in self/ other relations. The dynamic becomes stable and thus a successful habit, held together by the information encoding and resistance creating ZPF, and thus remains in existence to serve as the foundation for the next level of development.

More complex communities of protons and neutrons develop, such as the heavier elements of carbon, nitrogen, oxygen, iron, and phosphorus, which in turn join in massive civilizations called planets. The dance of attraction and repulsion continues, but at much higher levels of chemical complexity and organization. The molten Earth is birthed, growing in size as it is bombarded by meteors. Iron, which is heavier than most other elements, sinks to the center of the Earth and becomes the Earth's crystal core. Earth then cools and forms a hard crust out of the lighter elements that float to the surface. Earth's atmosphere begins to cool, causing hydrogen and oxygen in the air to combine and give birth to yet a new being with unique inner consciousness and spirit: water. And then for about a million years, it rains and rains and rains, covering the planet with water. Mother Earth now develops her hot-water womb, where new forms of complexity begin the explorations that set the stage for the next leap in Consciousness evolution. Consciousness's urge to be and express itself can no longer hold back, as the constricting material world of attract-repulse can no longer keep captive the creative spark inherent in matter. The stage is set for the next spiral of creation to unfold.

Exercises

Before we continue with our journey, let us take a moment and see if we can discover the reality of Source within ourselves through two basic forms of meditation. These two forms or aspects of meditation, often called the two pillars of meditation, are ultimately two sides of the one coin that is meditation practice. Initially, each of these so-called pillars is practiced as a distinct path. Each of the paths, that of mindfulness or insight meditation and that of concentration, has provided sophisticated maps of higher consciousness which will be explored more fully in the last few chapters. As one's practice matures, however, both elements are integrated into an overall technology for self-inquiry and consciousness expansion. Here we introduce the two practices in relation to the concepts in physics just explored.

One-Pointed Concentration Meditation on Singularity

Find a quiet place, and sit comfortably with an aligned spine, neck, and head. Turn attention inward as you bring awareness to the rise and fall of your breath. As your body-mind begins to quiet, bring full attention and focus to the center of your forehead, the traditional third eye or sixth chakra. Now visualize your breath move in and out from that singular point of focus on the center of your forehead. Bring total focus and one-pointed concentration to that point so that when your mind wanders, gently bring it back to that one point. As your awareness begins to focalize into this one point, visualize all energy converging and melting into this one point on the inhale, and release any content that may have arisen as you exhale. So, inhale and center in on one point, exhale and release all content that arises out into formlessness. Inhale into one point, exhale out to formlessness. As thoughts, feelings, sensations, perceptions, images, or memories arise, use your breath to dissolve them back into that singular point, over and over again, using their energy to increase the force, mass, density, and power of this supra-still, laser-like one-pointed consciousness. Now consider this formless one-pointed focalized awareness to be the original singularity. Notice that as mental content dissolves into this singularity, the concepts of space and time also get absorbed into ever-deepening levels of quiet formless depth. As you continue to generate and focus energy on said focal point, a moment will come when the full dissolution of self into formlessness will be experienced, known as *Nirvakalpa Samadhi,* and individuality will merge into a state of total and complete Oneness. Past and future will merge into an eternal now, as the nondual mystical flash of the Source absorbs you complete. See this experienced Oneness as the original Singularity-Source, the ever-present timeless Source out of which all forms arise, and into which they all return.

Mindfulness Insight Meditation on Ocean of Quantum Probabilities

Find a quiet place and, with an aligned spine, neck, and head, bring awareness to the rise and fall of your breath. Allow each slow, deep, rhythmic out breath to relax the body, and each inhale to bring the mind back to breath. Using breath as a centering anchor, allow your awareness to unfold and expand out radially in all directions as an all-embracing field. Notice how your ever-present awareness is like the blue sky; vast, open, luminous, empty, peaceful, and free. As thoughts, images, feelings, sensations, or memories drift into this vast Field, see them as impermanent clouds that come, stay a while, and dissolve back into your ever-present field of awareness. Now, as you sit in total mindfulness and awareness of what arises moment to moment, see this timeless field of your awareness as the Unified Field of all creation. Notice how this field of awareness is not yours or personal, but rather a transpersonal or impersonal empty field in which all phenomena come and go in endless fluctuations. Now correlate this field of open mindful awareness to the quantum vacuum at the base of all creation. First notice its empty, Void, timeless, and spaceless nature. Then, from that empty embrace, notice the endless ripples and fluctuations within this quantum field, at first mere probabilities and potentials, then manifesting as thoughts, mind-stuff, perception, and the material world in general. In this meditation, see your field of pure Awareness as being identical to the nonlocal zero-point Unified field out of which all creation arises, and into which it all disappears after brief flashes of existence. Calmly abide in this spaciousness, allowing all manifesting probability waves to come and go without attachment or judgment, and rest as that primordial Witness that is the primal Field of all that is.

Part 1:
Birth of a World

From the breach to the iron explosion,
from the break in the stone to the highway,
from the quake to the flame, the whirlwind, the river,
that great heart lay still in the
heavenly water and gold,
each seam in the jasper and sulfur,
a motion, a wing,
a dewdrop, a trickle of fire.
Shall the stone live, neither moving nor growing?
Are there lips in the watery agate?
I've no answer to give you, nor power to say it:
Such was the turbulent genesis—
And the stones have lived
Growing and burning in ice ever since. [1]

-Pablo Neruda

The seed moves so slowly and serenely
Moment to moment
That it appears inactive

The garden at sunrise breathing
The quiet breath of twilight
Moment to moment to moment

When we are in tune with this blissful rhythm
The ten thousand forms flourish
Without effort

It is all so simple
Each next moment...
This is it! [2]

-Timothy Leary

Level 1

Physio-survival: Material Plane

Phylogenic Expression

Our story continues in the primal oceans of our early planet. Drifting chemical patterns in a world of water, carbon dioxide, methane, salt, and ammonia mixtures, all molecules with atoms originating in the heart of stars, begin to come together and form simple molecular configurations. Our oceans are hot and energetically unstable. Coalescing, bubbling, and swirling molecular substances come together and dissolve, dancing in a variety of combinations and forms. The seasonal tides, volcanic activity, and geological movements ebb and flow the floating molecules, bringing novel and progressively more complex forms of molecular organization into being. Suddenly, with an electrifying flash from likely electrical storms and atmospheric radiation, a more or less stable molecular pattern is configured and we witness the emergence of a simple amino acid.

Amino acids are molecules composed of carbon, oxygen, hydrogen, and nitrogen. Carbon, due to its four covalent structure, begins to bond and form chains that fold and loop into tiny, slippery bubbles. These become the first membranes separating the primal self from "other," subject from object, in an ocean of chemical chaos. Amino acids combine into twenty different basic patterns, giving rise to a variety of proteins. These twenty amino acids, along with a series of other molecules, such as glucose, fats, sugars, and five nitrogenous molecules, make up what biologists call the twenty-nine characters (or compounds) of the basic alphabet that spells out the story of life on Earth. [3]

The emerging scientific consensus, based on experimental data, suggests the following: as more and more of the twenty-nine compounds formed in the primordial oceans, greater concentrations of these molecules may have chemically reacted with one another to form even more complex molecules. The carbon-based membranes, at first a kind of film on the surface of water composed of molecular chains, spontaneously form. Upon agitation, the film breaks up into globules, which enclose bits of water that abound with floating molecules. Within this microsphere thus created, chemical reactions continue within as the microsphere absorbs materials into the membrane from the surrounding "external" soup. Alice Knight reminds us that "there are no unique atomic elements in living matter: organic material is composed of the same materials as inorganic material."[4] Thus matter, and the mysterious impulse at its core, begins the exploration of novel expressions.

The ability to reproduce is the ultimate definition of life, mainstream biologists tell us. At first, it is believed that these primitive microspheres would grow in size by absorbing external material, thereby reaching a critical size and thus developing buds that would eventually detach and become independent yet identical autonomous microspheres. Eventually, the membranes enclose a chain of molecules called nucleotides, composed of a nucleobase, a phosphate, and a sugar. Nucleobases come in four types and constitute the alphabet in which the polymers (strings of smaller molecules) encode information. Theses nucleotides, now known as DNA and RNA, come into being as spiraling double-helixical chains that imprint in particular stable patterns. In a DNA nucleotide, the four informational codes or nucleobases that dictate the construction of all earthly organisms are now known as adenine, guanine, cytosine, and thymine (A, G, C, and T, respectively). In RNA, which is believed to have been the first polymer to have formed in the primal ocean, uracil (U) replaces thymine (T). Remember that all of these molecules are made from those basic atoms of carbon, hydrogen, oxygen, and nitrogen, cooked in the heart of our ancient mother stars. These nucleobases bind to one another according to simple rules; A pairs with U (or T), and G pairs with C, forming the rungs of DNA's twisted information-encoding ladder —the now familiar double helix. This process allows the exclusive pairing of molecules that is crucial for the faithful copying of information. By these means, a cell can reproduce and pass down its inherited patterns. Meanwhile, the phosphate and sugar molecules form the backbone of each strand of DNA or RNA.

Through this process, the mysterious DNA strand and the inherent Life Force within it begins its career of protein synthesis and production, building itself a floating vessel that serves its replication and continuation programs. The mysterious genetic intelligence designs and constructs itself "a house which protects the replicator molecules from their surroundings."[5] John Reader cites biologist David Usher's theory on how the basic ingredients of the DNA molecule, the nucleotides, could have combined to form the first chains of linked, self-replicating polynucleotides in response to the natural cycle of events on the primitive Earth. Reader explains:

> The daily round of sunrise and sunset created alternations of light and dark, heat and cold, wet and dry, which acted like a very regular switching on and off of energy...This on/off effect, heating

> and cooling, expanding and contracting, would have broken the chemical bonds of many substances and thereby destroyed them, but it may have favored the survival of polynucleotide chains that wrapped round each other to form a double helix. This in effect was the most stable configuration under the prevailing circumstances.

Reader continues:

> Prior to the formation of a double helix the polynucleotides were still random chemical substances, but should two complementary strands meet they would spontaneously form a double helix. Under certain stimuli theses two strands would separate, whereupon the chemical nature of each independent strand would attract the compounds needed to build another double helix, and so there would be two where before there had been one. The first self-replicating molecules—DNA. [6]

Of course, mainstream materialistic-reductionist biology sees this process as a random, mechanical, chance-based accident that happened to bring dead matter together in a specific configuration to suddenly ignite life into being. A more satisfactory view is that Life, here seen as the manifestation of or *identical* to primal Consciousness, was latently embedded in each molecule and atom from the start. From our perspective, Life is seen as that nonlocal source of intelligence and sentience that unfolds and manifests in the diversity of organic forms. There is only One Life, expressing itself in the rich multiplicity of our biosphere, moving and evolving complexity so as to amplify and express itself in ever more magnificent and creative ways.

As we saw, all whirling particles are connected and entangled at their quantum mini-singularity core, as all life is essentially interconnected non-locally at its core. That secret Eros impulse in the heart of matter now releases and frees itself from the confines of matter, entering a new stage of Consciousness known as Life. The inner Consciousness is the force that brings these molecules together to house and create a sophisticated transceiver of information, the DNA molecule. This incredible spiraling structure receives and transmits molecular messages that allow the inner silent

Witnessing Awareness to synthesize proteins that build and repair the evolving vessel, storing the various experiences as informational codes that act as foundational blueprints for subsequent development.

We are told by science that all living things share four fundamental, interrelated characteristics. They are all cellular in structure, their proteins are made up from the same twenty basic amino acids, they all have the same nucleotides in their genes, and all cells use ATP (adenosine triphosphate) as their molecular source of energy. I would add that all living things have inherent life force (a.k.a., spirit) as a fifth fundamental characteristic. This is true of a bacterium, a flower, a blue whale, and every cell in your body. These observations point to the fact that all life has a single, common ancestor, probably very similar to the smallest and simplest organisms alive on Earth today. Therefore, our first Earthly ancestor, living four billion years ago, was likely a single-cell organism with a simple DNA molecule floating freely within its manufactured protein-based membrane. These primitive unicelled beings are known as prokaryotes, characterized by the non-nucleated, free-floating DNA, and can be observed in current times as basic bacteria found in lake beds, marshes, and your digestive tract helping digest your lunch!

In order to keep growing and reproducing copies of itself, the prokaryote bacterium embarks on the mission and program of this first stage of Consciousness: physical self-preservation. These bacteria consumed voraciously, and their food was hydrogen, abundantly present in the oceans and "warm ponds" in which they lived. The ones that could not break apart the hydrogen from the water molecules perished, while those that could lived and split apart exponentially, thus populating our early oceans. As they evolved, their genetic material began recording various techniques and strategies, passing on the successful ones as they split, and dying off when not successful. Some learned to eat iron, others set up camp on the mouths of fiery volcanoes, while others journeyed to polar ice caps. An important development evolved when these bacteria learned the process of photosynthesis. By converting the energy derived from the sun into molecular energy, they were able to to pry the hydrogen from the H^2O of water quite successfully. Wherever bacteria went, they traded and shared information through the evolving global network of the emerging biosphere. They fanned out across the seas, and even onto the developing land, in search of hydrogen and other substances that would aid in their project of self-preservation.

Using the "material-maternal" Mother physiosphere and its floating molecular materials as foundation, the evolving single-celled bacterium began branching out, connecting, linking, sharing, and interacting in growing communities, cities, and civilizations that began to weave the fabric of our planetary nervous system; the biosphere. In the saltwater environment of the oceans, cybernetic communication feedback loops initiated the construction of an infant planetary being, weaving vast networks of information sharing that formed the infant Web of Life. All guided, of course, by that mysterious Essence from within, the Life Force seeking connection, expansion, greater freedom, and increased creative potential.

Around three billion years ago, the light-consuming bacteria become the dominant life forms on earth. Using the light energy from the sun, they consume the two parts hydrogen, to then discard the oxygen into the atmosphere as waste. Millions of years pass, and the photosynthesizers proliferate, releasing vast amounts of oxygen into the evolving atmosphere. The only problem is that oxygen is deadly poisonous to bacteria! With the advent of oxygen, life itself began to literally change and shape the face of the Earth. In other words, life began to co-create its environments and ecological niches, creating a self-referential feedback loop of change and development. Nothing on this planet was a pre-given; all was co-created by the evolving Life-Consciousness within all forms.

The newly released oxygen creates the first planetary mass extinction, forcing the more adaptive bacteria into oxygen-free areas, where they continue to flourish. As oxygen becomes a way of terrestrial life, other cells become oxygen tolerant, while still others add a few molecules of oxygen to the fermentation process that alone had powered life until then. In effect, this innovation held the waste products of fermentation (oxygen) and used it for another round of energy-producing reactions. Thus cellular respiration is born, and oxygen becomes the new fuel that powers the rapidly evolving web of life. At the same time, the single-celled cyanobacteria (basically blue-green algae) inclined to communal life evolves, linking and joining in vast strands of green living material that continues to accelerate oxygen production.

Through the ongoing pressures of change, both geologic and self-created, Life begins to experiment with new forms of energy. Bigger unicelled bacteria begin absorbing the smaller ones, deriving their energy from other single-cells, and a new breed of single-celled organisms evolves: life eaters. These can only survive by eating other living things, and so predators begin their long career on planet Earth. About one billion years later, two battling bacteria trying to turn each other into liquid lunch suddenly merge and create a totally new organism: the eukaryote. A new form of cooperation emerges, and we witness the birth of a symbiotic relationship between two life forms. The bacteria that had learned to turn poisonous oxygen into power, called mitochondria, were at first fierce enemies of other prokaryotes. To escape predators, the mitochondria begin to hide within the cellular walls of larger prokaryotes, mopping up the poisonous oxygen and transforming it into energy that both can use. In exchange, the now eukaryote protects mitochondria from predators in a truly symbiotic, mutually beneficial relationship. Mitochondria, once free-living bacteria, live inside all plant and animal cells, even in yours, burning up oxygen to power your physical vessel.

Eukaryote cells are generally much larger then prokaryotes, with several distinct parts called organelles floating in what is called cytoplasm within their cellular membrane. Their genetic material does not float freely, but is now stored in a nucleus, the heart and brain of the cell, where it is associated with protein structures known as chromosomes. The Eukaryote has about one thousand times more DNA than a prokaryote. This allows for a vast storehouse of information storage and management never before seen, recording the successful experiences of all its organelles so that they may be reproduced within the mother cell. Other bacteria, called flagella and cilia, join the symbiotic community of the eukaryote, linking to the membrane and acting as a sophisticated technology for movement and propulsion. This new partnership brings considerable advantages to both parties, and so the symbiosis becomes hereditary.

At first eukaryotes reproduce the way bacteria do; they split apart and keep going. Then by around one billion years ago, two eukaryotes pair off and fuse, combining their DNA to then have budding offspring that contains half the DNA of each parent. This process initiates the first sexual revolution as sexual reproduction is developed, therefore accelerating change and the production of complexity exponentially. This new development stimulates diversity and life proliferates on our young Earth. The advantage of symbiotic relationships become genetic, and eukaryotes begin to form teams, colonies, communities, and civilizations in what later become multicellular beings.

Inside each colony of eukaryotes, division of labor emerges as each team of cells evolves specific functions that nurture the whole organism. Some colonies specialize in food consumption, others in transforming and distributing the energy derived from the food, others work on disposing waste, others on greater strategies for self-protection and security, while others develop a variety of mobility methods. In coherent concert, all single-cells come together with their specific jobs to form what are to become the first marine animals of our planet. All processes, functions, structures, and experiences of the whole organism are recorded in the codes of every DNA strand, which in turn dispenses messages via messenger RNA to create templates and structures for the organism. The vast production and orchestration of protein assembly lines that fabricate complete organisms and their templated structures is orchestrated by this deep Intelligence-Life, pushing and moving forms forward in the exploration of the now well-established web of Life on Earth. Theoretically, the recorded informational patterns of DNA are also downloaded into that underlying, ever-present, nonlocal, Akashic information Field of the zero-point quantum vacuum as interference wave patterns. It is from this Unified Field that pulsations emanate up the ladder of form, in-forming and giving shape to the unfurling cosmos.

In this brief and oversimplified overview of the emergence of life from the material inorganic matrix, we witness the birth of a self-organizing principle that "transcends and includes" [7] the prior laws of momentum, attraction-repulsion, and bonding found in the material plane. Our fundamental universal forces flower into something new in the universe, but maintain the properties that allow forms to retain their separate autonomous structures. Out of the primal whirling light-energy self-subject, prehending the world of objects and separating itself from the "other" through electrical charge, evolves the single-cell, now "alive" and reactive to its outside environment through rudimentary sensing via the molecular processes of its membrane. The membrane is what separates this new self-subject from the "outside" world of objects.

The basic boundary between self and other, subject and object, is our first "reality creator." It is the basic mechanism, seen across levels, that collapses the unitary state of potential into a discrete entity that exists in relation to an "other." Be it another particle, cell, the environment, or the rest of the universe, the interface between subjective self and objective other is defined by this first projected boundary. The first law of conservation of energy emphasizes this phenomenon by postulating that all energy in a closed system (material matrix) is conserved. In basic language, when a force or energy is applied to or within a system, a necessary reactionary force responds. With every action, there is always an equal opposite or complementary reaction, as energy is never created or destroyed, but rather exists in dynamic states of transformation. [8] As we saw, the most fundamental expression of this law can be seen at the subatomic level where ZPE acts as a counterforce of resistance for subatomic particles, creating the property of inertia and ultimately the solid-heavy world of mass-filled matter. This developed habit becomes foundational, so that when energy is received by any body, the counterforce occurs.

This basic force/counterforce duality is the basis for all form, from the material to the subtle. Again, the Taoist symbolize this fundamental universal principle of creation by the yin/yang symbol, which shows that one side cannot exist without a counterbalance (complementary or opposite force). Buddhism describes this basic necessity of duality for the creation of any form as it pertains to consciousness with its concept of interdependent co-origination. Within the context of our current discussion, we notice that these concepts describe the codependence necessary for the manifestation of all forms and structures, from subatomic particles to organisms to biological ecosystems. All of these insights point to the fact that existence arises through a mutual relationship. Symmetry, and the slight imperfection that breaks said symmetry, must exist in order for anything to arise. This basic duality (negative/positive, in/out, male/female, light/dark, life/death, on/off, etc.) is what I call the first "reality creator." Nothing exists alone. It takes two to dance. In the case of the whirling light-energy, it is its electric charge and inertia that create the resistance and thus sense of solidity and boundary, helping collapse and manifest others like it. In the case of the cell, it is the membrane that reacts to the environment through rudimentary sensing and irritability, separating itself while simultaneously helping shape its environmental niche through its co-creative interactions.

I have called this basic principle of duality the first "reality creator" in that everything manifests in relationship to everything else. In the material plane this happens through a coordinated effort of physical forces and pressures. The inorganic world "experiences" itself and its surroundings as unconscious forces and pressures. These unconscious forces and pressures are experienced by each unit of material form, which in turn help shape and mold the environment (conservation of energy) by emitting their counterforce influence. Other than the pressures and forces "experienced" and prehended in the material plane, each separate form exists in a state of material fusion with the rest of matter with no self-awareness. Thus it is this unconscious ground of solidity that begins to manifest as a reality as life takes on its initial forms.

As Consciousness releases itself from the density and unconscious sleep of matter, enough energy is liberated in the first life forms so as to shed light unto a new world. The world of matter is illuminated by the awakening of Life, thus experienced as the "material plane" in which Life initiates its campaign of self-transformation. Ken Wilber explains that "at each rung in the developmental unfolding there is a different view of the world—a different view of self and other—a different worldview. The world looks different—is different!—at each rung in the developmental unfolding.... Different worldspaces, different worlds, come into being as consciousness evolves." [9]

In summary, unicellular organisms come to life and begin to experience and create their world on this planet. These first vegetative unicellular life forms have no actual perception of the world, but experience it through rudimentary filaments that pick up vibrations. These early units of life have a physiocentric orientation, and thus are concerned only with survival and the acquisition of food. Here we witness the birth of the first primitive instinct and drive: physical self-preservation. Although these early life forms had no self-awareness and could not differentiate between self and other consciously, they nonetheless had the capacity to nurture their physical bodies in order to maintain their individuality and react to others. Fused in what has been called the primary matrix, [10] they drift and float, eating (absorbing at this early stage) whatever is encountered. Building on the attract-repulse orientation of matter, they evolve the approach-avoid strategies inherent in all life forms.

The earliest form of experience at this stage may be conceptualized and reduced to a rudimentary sense of pain versus pleasure. The unicell is attracted to all that is soft, sweet, smooth, moist, nourishing, and avoids the hard, noxious, rough, dry, and irritating. [11] The basic approach-avoid relationship to the environment is developed and is reinforced as life evolves into more complex forms. The unicells begin to form clusters, replicate, and eventually differentiate into the polarity of sexual differences. Multicellular communities form, where autonomous cells come together and are orchestrated by a single Genetic Mind. The unconscious (eternal Conscious Witness at this point is dormant and latent, but eternally present) physiocentric identity concerned with viscerotonic satisfaction is basically driven by the desire for food and security. This level of physio-survival consciousness in the material plane is developed and refined as the evolution of life begins to proliferate in the archaic marine world. Survival is the goal, food is the motivation, approach-avoid is the behavioral strategy, and complete pre-personal dependence on the physiosphere (mother Earth) for nourishment and security is the reality.

Ontogenetic Expression

The various primal mechanisms and strategies of the developing consciousness discussed above are the basis for all life. The fact that ontogeny recapitulates phylogeny is clearly seen as we explore the foundational structures developing in the human embryo. Human life begins as a single cell in the mother's oceanic womb, morphing through all the evolutionary stages of fish, amphibian, reptile, mammal, to then flower as a human embryo. Immersed in the oceanic womb of the mother, the embryo lives in complete unconscious fusion with the material plane. Floating (like its amoeboid ancestors) effortlessly in complete warm security, its physical body is nourished and constructed through the direct umbilical line to the mother's physical body. Here there is no differentiation, only a-dual fusion with the material/maternal plane, as all basic needs are immediately and directly satisfied.

Stanislav Grof has compiled accounts of individuals re-experiencing this primal unitary fusion within the mother's womb. He describes individuals being regressed to the amniotic universe within the womb by various methods inducing non-ordinary states of consciousness. He calls this realm the perinatal matrix and characterizes it as being an oceanic state of blissful and serene intrauterine existence. Grof describes it as "an oceanic state without any boundaries where we do not differentiate between ourselves and the maternal organism or ourselves and the external world." [12]

This mostly unconscious (of self and other, yet radiantly Being) state of material and physical unity within the womb is abruptly and violently terminated as the contractions begin to push the infant through the constricting birth canal. The explosive and bloody birth process is the first separation and is often quite a traumatic experience, as many of Grof's subjects have reported. The traumatic nature of the birth process may be linked to the way in which our modern medical system deals with birth. Nonetheless, after birth there is complete physical separation from the material matrix. The trauma is diminished as the infant is placed on the mother's breast, reconnecting itself physically to the nourishing mother figure. At this point the infant is fully dependent and unconscious of self and other, but nonetheless begins to feel urges and sensations that move it toward the need for nourishment. Not unlike its ancestors at this stage of development, the orientation is viscerotonic and physiocentric, crying when the urges and cravings are painful and being at rest when those instinctual drives are satisfied by the mother's milk. Nursing gives the infant a rudimentary sense of pleasure and security.

Sigmund Freud defined this early level of consciousness as the oral psychosexual stage of development, "when both needs and gratification primarily involve the lips, tongue, and, somewhat later, the teeth." [13] The basic drive at this early stage is to take in nourishment through the sucking and suckling reflex and to relieve the tensions of hunger and thirst. Along with satisfying the physical needs of the infant, the nursing process includes soothing, cuddling, and rocking, giving a sense of security and connectedness to the maternal figure. "The child associates both pleasure and the reduction of tension with the feeding process. The mouth is the first area of the body that the infant can control; most of the libidinal energy available is directed or focused on this one area." [14]

Within Abraham Maslow's hierarchy of needs, this early developmental stage is driven by the need to satisfy the physiological and biological system. [15] These physiological needs include food, drink, oxygen, and sleep. Once these particular needs are met, there is less tension, allowing other drives to surface. If they are not met, a pattern of insecurity emerges, and the person's developmental process remains fixated at this stage.

This early stage of development is foundational in that it creates the most basic pattern of behavioral response to the environment within the evolving personality. Erik Erikson noticed that this stage establishes a basic trusting relationship to the environment if the mother- infant bond and experience is a successful and nurturing one. If the relationship at this stage is unsuccessful (if the infant is not fed or changed when it cries, for example), the sense of basic mistrust is established, or imprinted within the infant's general makeup. [16] A good infant-mother bond will generally imprint a secure, confident, trusting, friendly, and accepting basic survival pattern. A poor mother-infant connection will create an insecure, distrusting, shy, fearful, and paranoid survival pattern as the individual encounters the "external" world.

At this stage of the process (infancy to one year, approximately), the main orientation and reality "receiver-creator" is the sensory-motor apparatus. This first level of information reception is ruled by the senses, programmed to seek pleasurable stimuli and retreat from dangerous and painful ones. The self here identifies with the sensorimotor (material) world to the point where there is no distinction between inside and outside. The physical self and the physical world are fused, the separateness being defined through unconscious impulses and reflexes that are pre-programmed by the inherited experiences of the primordial ancestors. The organism at this point knows its world through the empirical reception of the senses, designed and templated by the evolved DNA. That which "knows" is that familiar essence which we have called pure Consciousness or Spirit, which experiences the world through the various incarnations of evolving forms. Unconscious of itself at this point, but obviously having a sensory experience of the world, Spirit continues its advancement and movement toward higher realms of experience.

Experience of Structure

Q: What do you perceive-project at this level?

A: Things, objects, food, potential threat, danger, bodies, and all sense impressions.

We have just toured the origins of the most basic level of consciousness, physiosurvival, and the reality that it perceives-creates, the material plane or physiosphere. Your body, its sensory-motor system, and all of the instinctual, reflexive, unconscious, and autonomic physiological processes that you now experience are direct expressions of this most foundational first level of being. These processes are mere amplifications of the basic self-preservation drive that evolved primitively four billion years ago. As Ken Wilber illustrates with his concept of "transcend and include," [17] all of the basic structures and programs developed in the early stages of development are included and are part of one's overall makeup, even of the enlightened human being. In fact, your entire organism is composed of specialized single-celled communities whose sole purpose is to keep you alive and preserve your vessel so that you may pass on the best inherited patterns of survival. We are the coherent symbiotic orchestration of trillions of eukaryotes, living in total harmony and unity in order to produce you! Trillions of cells, one intent, as the inherent silent sentient Awareness of each cell combines and joins to create your current experience. A true fractal hologram, where the whole is the magnification and amplification of that which is in each of the parts. Thus Consciousness does not suddenly arise when the right amounts of cells come together in specific ways, but is inherent in each cell, each molecule, and each atom, articulating it-Self in ever expanding complexity and freedom.

Dr. Leary points out, "Throughout human life, when the biosurvival brain flashes danger, all other mental activities cease." [18] Since the first level is concerned with security, identified with the physical body, and motivated by physical self-preservation, any threat will immediately and unconsciously activate the primordial level of retreat and avoid. A simple example is the reflex to immediately move the hand away from the heat of a burning stove burner. Fear and the physiological stress response system are unconsciously and instantaneously activated when threatened, as the body's sensory system is fully in tune and in coordination (i.e., fused) with the environment. Thus our bodies and the various autonomic and automatic response systems will react and activate emergency response systems before we are even conscious of what is going on. Heart and respiration rates increase in order to bring more blood and oxygen to the system, as adrenaline and cortisol floods the system for immediate action. These and other reflexive behavioral responses are pre-programmed since birth to maintain and protect the physical vessel that houses the inner Being.

Fear is the most ancient of emotions, fully connected to the preservation of the organism and its individual existence. It insures that the organism will find a safe space and stay away from danger. Psychologist Frances Vaughan summarizes this level in connection to the Yogic chakra system, which we will use as an archetypal representation of the spectrum of consciousness localized energetically within the body centers (more on the chakra system to follow). She explains:

> The first chakra, the *muladhara*, physiologically localized in the perineum, is associated

> with survival and is represented by the element of earth. Healthy development at this level could mean successful accomplishment of materialistic goals, earning a living, and satisfying basic needs. This can be viewed as the most basic level of self-awareness. The dominant reality material and the self identified with the body. [19]

She continues by stating, "In the world of the first chakra, fear is the dominant emotion. It could manifest as fear or loss of physical health or material possessions." [20]

Before we move on to the next level of consciousness, I would like to discuss why we co-create the world in a very literal way at each stage of development using metaphors from quantum physics and genetics.

At the physical level of consciousness, our world is unconsciously and habitually determined by the sensory-apparatus of our organism as templated (molded) by the DNA code. All creatures have variations to this sensory reception system, and thus live in alternate worlds. Prior to the creation-projection of phenomena by the perceiving-receiving structure, the universe stands as a primordial soup of undulating and pulsating undifferentiated energy; a sea of information waiting to be transceived by an adequate antenna; a chaotic ebb and flow of whirling potential waiting to manifest. As verified by experimental data coming from quantum physics, indeterminate waves of potential and probability at the quantum level collapse into actuality as soon as they are measured, observed, or perceived. In fact, modern physics has completely shattered the notion of discrete, separate, solid material entities floating in empty space. Matter is not solid, they tell us, but the manifest consequence of interacting probabilistic energy waves and patterns within a field of 99.9999 percent "empty space" that is *sensed* as solid by our particular organism. In other words, there is no solid world "out there"; solidity is a mere experience-fabrication of our brain and its senses. Fritjof Capra explains:

> The exploration of the subatomic world in the twentieth century has revealed the intrinsically dynamic nature of matter. It has shown that the constituents of atoms, the subatomic particles, are dynamic patterns which do not exist as isolated entities, but as integral parts of an inseparable network of interactions. These interactions involve

> a ceaseless flow of energy manifesting itself as the exchange of particles; a dynamic interplay in which particles (patterns of energy) are created and destroyed without end in a continual variation of energy patterns. The particle interactions give rise to the stable structures which build up the material world, which again do not remain static, but oscillate in rhythmic movements. [21]

Your sensory-motor transceiver is part of that relationship of patterns, co-creating (collapsing probabilities into actualities) its environments through recursive feedback loops of communication and information exchange.

The structure that receives the energy defines and molds it into a particular form, which is determined by habit. These habits are the basic "reality creators," the first being defined by the law of conservation of energy (every action produces an equal and opposing reaction, as energy can never be created or destroyed because it is always conserved), which is the first boundary separating self from other, and the second by the templated structure of the senses. Each creature is designed and templated by DNA to register, receive, organize, and select various energy frequencies that pertain to the individual survival of that organism. Through the creation of diverse sensory-motor apparatus for each species, it seems clear that "reality" is a relative experience dependent on receiving structure. Each organism selects, filters, receives, perceives, and defines its "external" according to the limits and boundaries of its organic equipment (designed and templated by the DNA code). What we call physical reality is but a fragment of frequencies determined by our five senses and nervous system. Our nervous system and senses have evolved to perceive our current range of physical sensations and perceptions through the ongoing pressures of evolution. What we empirically sense and perceive is nothing more than a habit, a habit that is encoded, determined, and developed by the genetic intelligence within each of our cells.

For example, pit vipers perceive in the infrared (heat to us) frequency range via specialized sense organs (pits) on the side of their head; bats and dolphins perceive soundscapes via sophisticated sonar and echolocation technologies, one in space, the other in water; bees and other insects perceive in the ultraviolet range (invisible to us); fish combine aspects of what we call sound and aspects of what we call touch via what is called the lateral line system to sense their environment; some fish, such as sharks, are capable of experiencing minute electrical fields in the water to detect the motion of prey, who generate electrical activity in their immediate environment; homing pigeons navigate based at least in part on the ability to experience the earth's magnetic field; and many insects have visual receptors on the back of the head for a close to 360-degree view of their world! We can't even begin to imagine what the world looks like from these alternate sensing systems.

What we are calling the genetically templated transceiving structure, our antenna, is of course our central nervous system and the brain. We will explore how this incredibly complex structure formed phylogenetically in the following chapters. Here we will look at how our nervous system organizes external signals in order to facilitate this first level of consciousness: the sensorimotor experience of our physical reality, and our physical survival in it.

Sensory signals, in our human case divided into five modalities, reach the Witness via our five sensory organs. Eyes capture the visible light of the electromagnetic spectrum (a mere fraction of the overall range of electromagnetic frequencies, of which 99.99 percent is completely invisible to us), ears capture a limited range of molecular vibrations in the air, nose and tongue register various chemicals and molecules found in odors and substances, and touch is mediated by the electrical discharge of nerve endings distributed throughout the body. As these diverse frequencies are registered by the various sense organs (what we are calling the second "reality creators"), the waves of probability collapse into specific forms as they are transduced and registered by the senses. After the various nerve endings receive the external signals, they are transmitted via nerve fibers toward the spine. A network of nerves throughout the body transmits billions of signal per second via electrical pulses within an ionized (electrically charged) saline solution within the body. Our brains and entire body are filled with salt water (we carry a bit of the ocean in us, remnants of that first membrane that enclosed the salt water of our primal oceans), which is the medium that allows signals to be carried down our neural pathways. In levels seven and eight, we will learn techniques to work with these raw nerve signals consciously.

A neuron is the sophisticated modern offspring of the eukaryotes, extending and branching out its membrane via what are called dendrites, the receivers of information, and axon branches, the transmitters of that information. The axon is covered with what is called a myelin sheath, which allows nerve impulses to travel at a faster speed. Neurons link up in vast networks of interconnected superhighways of bioelectric information exchange. The nucleus of each neuron is, of course, endowed with the integrator of all information transceived, the DNA, which records said information. These twenty to two hundred billion neurons float in a sea of saline liquid called extracellular fluid, which again reflects the early saltwater oceans in which our early unicelled ancestors floated and intermingled via primal communication systems.

The neuron is the basic unit of the brain. Each of these neurons communicates with as many as a thousand other neurons, thus creating more connections in our brain then there are stars in our known universe. Each neuron has basically two functions: to fire via its excitatory function (on, or 1, in computing language), or to not fire via its inhibitory function (off, or 0). Between the receiving dendrite and the transmitting axon is a space called the synaptic gap. When a signal arrives at the axon terminal, minute chemical messengers called neurotransmitters are released into the synaptic gap. Theses neurotransmitters then bind to their specific dendrite receptor cites. The neurotransmitter then conveys one of two messages: arouse and excite neuron, or depress and inhibit neuronal activity.

The mechanism behind the movement of signals within and across neurons rests in a process of polarization and depolarization of charged ions. The membrane of a neuron is permeable, allowing the passage of small molecules and charged ions from one side of the membrane to the other. The membrane contains a "pump" that expels positively charged sodium ions ($Na+$) and takes in similarly charged potassium ions ($K+$). The net result of the $Na+/K+$ pump and the presence of negatively charged protein molecules inside the cell is an electrical potential (imbalance) between the interior and exterior of the neuron. The shifting potentials move the impulse or signal through the neuron.

A nonactive or resting neuron displays a potential (termed the transmembrane potential) of about – 60 millivolts. If the transmembrane potential is lowered (made less negative) to about – 50 millivolts, the neuron will initiate an "action potential" in its axon. This action potential then initiates a momentary opening of minute "gates" in the axon membrane, first allowing $K+$ ions to rush out, and then allowing the inflow of $Na+$. When the action potential or signal arrives at the axon terminal, it causes the release of some of the packaged neurotransmitters, which in turn bind to the branching dendrites with their excite or inhibit signal. An action potential is initiated through the action of excitatory neurotransmitters at the synapse. Excitatory neurotransmitters lower the transmembrane charge toward the action potential threshold, while inhibitory neurotransmitters raise (make more negative) the transmembrane charge. Rarely is the activity of a single synaptic contact sufficient to trigger an action potential, or spike. Thus several excitatory synaptic inputs must be active more or less simultaneously to raise the transmembrane charge to threshold and fire a spike. In contrast, an active inhibitory synapse on one portion of a dendrite can counteract the effect of an active excitatory synapse on an adjacent portion of the dendritic tree. More excitatory input relative to inhibitory input will trigger a spike, whereas more inhibition than excitation will not.

The basic on/ off chemical messengers produced in all neurons of the brain are called glutamate, the neurotransmitter responsible for the "fire" or go signal, and GABA, the transmitter responsible for the "don't fire" or stop signal. When a glutamate molecule binds to a glutamate receptor, the Na+ ion channel opens and activates a neural chain reaction. If multiple incoming glutamate transmitters bind to a single neuron, the neuron will depolarize and thus fire, pushing the signal down the network. In contrast, a GABA neurotransmitter opens a selective channel for the negatively charged chloride ion (Cl-) in the GABA receptor, which in turn arrest the effects of any incoming positive ions. Thus GABA inhibits and stops the flow of information. So in essence, glutamate and GABA control the flux of voltage potentials across the membrane as they bind at their respective receptor sites.

The more well-known neurotransmitters called monoamines, such as serotonin, dopamine, acytocholine, epinephrine, and norepinephrine, don't cause neurons to fire, but instead tune and tone the spiking rate of neurons. In other words, they act as modulators that facilitate or inhibit the action of both glutamate and GABA, thereby increasing or decreasing their effect at the individual receptor sites. The net effect is that these neuromodulators adjust and fine-tune polarity across the global network of the neural web.

Unlike glutamate and GABA, which are produced in all neurons of the brain, the monoamines are only produced by cells in nuclei found in the primitive brain stem. While produced in the brain stem, these neurotransmitters are distributed up to the higher brain circuits via outreaching axons. Psychedelic researcher James Kent lucidly explains this process:

> The axons from these aminergic clusters reach upward to many areas of the cortex...These neuromodulators produce a one-way bottom-up effect, which means they are switched on and off reflexively and unconsciously by glands in the brain stem and basal forebrain in response to internal conditions or external stimulus. With neuromodulators the brainstem can exert global homeostatic control over organism mood and behavior. [22]

We will return in later chapters to Kent's fascinating model of how the brain produces novelty in response to psychedelic intake, which he calls "psychedelic information theory," with its vast implication for understanding the underpinnings of the "objective" or material aspects of human consciousness, both personal and transpersonal. We will also explore these and other neurotransmitters more fully in subsequent chapters, for their role in many if not all human functions is now coming to light through ground-breaking discoveries in neuroscience.

With this very basic outline of how information flows in our nervous system and brain, we can continue our exploration of how raw external signals are reconstructed to facilitate this first level of consciousness. All signals received throughout our body via our sensory system are networked toward the spinal neuronal cord, our first sensory-motor antenna transceiver. These impulses are then channeled up the spine to the brain stem as somatic input, to then be routed back down the spine as motor and muscular behavioral output after it's been processed, integrated, and interpreted by the higher brain circuits. If bodily sensory signals stop, as in the case of say a spinal cord injury, the body disappears as far as the brain is concerned. Thus our antenna receivers are tuned to our five sensory frequencies. The frequencies are translated and relayed via nerve fibers toward our spinal cord, which then channels all signals up toward the brain stem.

The brain stem, also known as the reptilian brain, is one of the oldest brain structures that evolved to manage this first level of consciousness in multicellular vertebrates. It is the principal brain center that manages and regulates our primal autonomic systems, such as heartbeat, respiration, hormonal fluxes, and bio-survival stress response. This structure is reactive, instinctual, and reflexive to stimuli, as it is barely self-aware, being pre-emotional, pre-verbal, and pre-cognitive.

As the signal from the neuronal cord moves up the spine, it is scanned by a variety of task-specific organs. The sensory signals are first received by probably the oldest brain structure within the brain stem, the medulla oblongata, which is responsible for autonomic physiological processes such as respiration, heartbeat, circulation, stress response, and digestion. In fact, this brain structure may have been the very first vertebrate brain to have evolved millions of years ago. As such, this mini brain networks raw sensory data to and from the brain, scanning external signals for potential danger, with intact involuntary approach-avoid motor responses to threats, pain, loud noises, hunger, warmth, and safety. It is the first "interpretation" of sound, touch, and taste, activating the sympathetic system of the stress response if alarmed, or the parasympathetic system of rest and repair if at rest. Again, this is a totally automatic instinctual brain, finely tuned to the environment so that it may preserve the developing vessel that houses the inner Being.

Crowning over the medulla is a layer of smaller neuronal nuclei, known as the midbrain and pons. This area is associated with the production of neurotransmitters, essential to the functioning of the whole brain. A neural cluster in the pons known as the raphe nuclei appears to be responsible for the production of serotonin, a neurotransmitter essential for mediating appetite, sleep, pain, mood, learning, and emotional processing. In the midbrain area we have what are called the ventral tegmentum and the substantia nigra, responsible for pumping dopamine into the higher brains. Dopamine is a neurotransmitter that mediates motor regulation, reward system, pleasure, smell, concentration, drive, and hormone control. Also in the pons lies the locus coeruleus, responsible for the production of norepinephrine (noradrenaline), a major transmitter that initiates the fight or flight stress response. Norepinephrin is also implicated in CNS sensory processing, sleep, mood, learning, memory, and fear. Another cluster in the pons is known as the cholinergic nuclei, which is responsible for producing acetylcholine, a major player in memory function, sensory processing, motor coordination, cognitive function, and the sleep/dream cycle. As a whole, this primitive brain layer can be seen as a central relay station that is bombarded with raw sense data, to then release the appropriate neurotransmitters that inform the rest of the body and brain as to what is going on. Of course, it is finely tuned to seek pleasurable sensations, which include mating, eating, and reproduction, and to retreat/avoid dangerous and painful ones.

Flowering over the brain stem is a structure known as the thalamus, often described as the grand central switching station of the brain. It filters, screens, interprets, and routes signals up to higher cortical areas, and then back down for an appropriate motor behavioral response after processing. It is a focal point for the transceiving of information, receiving and projecting the co-created world.

Thus far we've explored the antenna transceiver of the first level of consciousness, responsible in main part for the physical survival of the organism. The experience of physical reality is determined by the sensory-motor equipment of each organism at this level of consciousness. The one experiencing the diverse frequency receptions is none other than pure Awareness. It experiences reality according to the limits of this particular stage, felt as urges, instinctual drives, and relative sensory-perceptual information. Nonetheless, it is radiant Spirit that shines through the being and that drives the evolutionary movement toward higher forms of Self-expression.

Exercises:

1.) Take time to feel your body. Witness the various urges, sensations, drives, and reflexes that move you into action. Tune in to the various autonomic physiological processes, such as your heartbeat, your breathing, your digestive system, and all other systems within your body. Feel all of these biological processes working together and contemplate their ancient roots. Look at your skin, feel your bones, and embrace your physical appearance. Take time with each of your senses, contemplating how each of them initially begin as electrical impulses, to then be reconstructed within your brain to represent a particular "external" sensation. Feel the solidity conveyed by the sense of touch, marvel at sound, delight in the limited visual range of your eyes, and attempt to experience the incoming sensory information in its raw, vibratory form before it reaches the organizing tendencies of your brain.

2.) Exercise your body. Take up weight lifting or any sport of your choice and witness the miraculous machinery that is your organism. Good old-fashioned physical work will also put you in touch with and develop your physical vessel. Eat healthy foods and see how this affects your physical state in comparison to eating junk food.

3.) Go to an aquarium and spend time observing fish. Witness their behavior, the suckling reflex, and their approach avoid mechanism. Look under a microscope and watch unicellular organisms interact. Spend time with infants and study their behavior, their relationship to their environment, and their connection to their mother.

4.) Turn on a television and observe how our culture glorifies and identifies with the purely physical aspects of being. Witness people who focus only on physical appearances and observe this tendency within yourself.

5.) Notice how your body reacts, reflexes, and responds whenever you feel threatened or are in a situation of stress. Learn how to manage fear.

6.) Meditate on your first chakra, located in the perineum, and connect with the Earth element. Experience the sense of gravity, solidity, inertia, and hardness within yourself and the environment.

7.) Contemplate the effects of opiates (opium, morphine, heroin, etc.) and the addict's addiction to physical pleasure versus the physical pain of withdrawals. Examine how the drug brings consciousness to an infantile-vegetative state of unconscious impulses and its predominantly physical preoccupations. Consider psychosis, paranoid schizophrenia, senile elders, late-stage Alzheimer's victims, and mentally disabled individuals. Spend time with them, learn about their needs, and see if you can see who lives within those suffering bodies.

Vipassana

Vipassana is a meditation technique originally taught by the Buddha himself to help liberate the mind from suffering and afflictions. Although ultimately a level seven and eight technique designed for total liberation, it works with the sensations of level one in order to purify the impurities of the person at their root: in the body. This technique has been popularized around the world by S. N. Goenka, an Indian man born in Rangoon, Burma. A successful businessman in his youth, he suffered from severe, debilitating migraines that no doctor could cure. He tried all forms of medication, eventually developing an addiction to morphine despite its limited relief. One day a friend invited him to attend a vipassana retreat as taught by meditation master Saiyagi U Ba Khin. Not only did his headaches and addictions go away, but his life was fully and completely transformed. He became completely devoted to the *Dhamma* and began teaching, becoming the world's most influential vipassana teacher.

The practice is as follows: starting at the top of the head, slowly move down the body, observing and witnessing every little sensation as it arises in awareness. The point is to witness the sensation, whether painful or pleasurable, with total spaciousness and equanimity. One is to observe bodily sensations without reaction, judgment, craving, or aversion. Craving for pleasure and aversion from pain being the root of suffering imprinted and conditioned in the body, this practice allows one to develop equanimity, thereby deconditioning our habitual reactivity at its root. Goenka teaches that the unconscious mind is constantly in contact with the body sensations; therefore, in order to purify the mind, he teaches that one must necessarily work with the sensations. He claims that all impurities, or *sankharas,* which are our unconscious and habitual reactions to sensations, can be uprooted by focusing on physical sensations through a meditative body scan, or "sweeping," as Goenka calls it. The ultimate purpose of vipassana meditation is to penetrate the gross, solidified sensations so as to liberate them into subtler vibrational states that finally liberate the mind into ultimate truth. In one of the lectures in a ten-day silent vipassana retreat I attended, I remember him saying, "Whatever external event happens will generate sensations in the body, and you will have trained your mind to have equanimity with those sensations. The sensations are the roots, and if the roots are healthy, then the tree will automatically be healthy."

So, take a few moments, close your eyes, and scan your body, inch by inch, noticing any and all sensations. Notice your programmed reactions, but, without executing the reaction, continue to scan your body. Apply total calmness, indifference, space, compassion, and awareness to all sensations, no matter how intense, extreme, or subtle, and continue the scan. Ultimately, one develops the ability to feel any sensation while remaining in a state of total peace and nonreactive equanimity. This is the state of freedom from the shackles of material existence that we will more fully explore in level eight.

Further Personal Explorations

When exploring and discussing all aspect of consciousness, it seems appropriate to include the "view from within." As such, we follow William James's dictate to take any and all states of consciousness as data. Therefore, at the end of each section I will give brief examples of my development through the stages, my current personal/transpersonal practice that focuses on the relevant level, a brief example of clients from my clinical practice struggling with the stage or level presented, and finally an exploration of psychoactive substances that trigger "altered" states of consciousness within the level discussed. I should mention that there is nothing special about my life, except maybe for the fact that it has been blessed by extraordinary amounts of joy, love, health, and happiness. This incredibly blessed fortune has allowed me to focus on service and giving back, for what else is there to do when life showers you with daily grace?

As mentioned in my opening autobiography, my first stage of development was successfully imprinted due to the love from my family. Particularly relevant to this stage was my relationship to my mother, who provided a loving and nurturing environment where all my physical and biological needs were fully met without struggle. This, of course, provided a trusting and secure foundation for my being, manifesting today as self-confidence and a basic trust in our universe. The fact that all my basic needs were fully attended to also created health not only at the emotional level, but in my body as well. I have been blessed with great health all my life, and I attribute this fundamental health to those crucial early days of development when my body was fully cared for and nurtured with healthy foods and an active lifestyle. Even though we lived in Chile during a time of incredible uncertainty and social unrest, my family provided my growing organism an optimal environment that was safe, consistently happy, and devoid of negativity. Of course, now, as an adult, I've learned that not all was well in those early days, as my father was out of work and my mother struggled to get the basics for survival. My grandmother was instrumental in helping my parents cultivate a healthy home for me, as she would walk blocks after standing in long lines to bring me, her first grandchild, milk, bread, and fresh produce. The stress my parents experienced was thoughtfully hidden from my young development, as I was a source of joy, hope, and stability in a life that was surrounded by social and economic upheaval.

The fact that I am a trusting, secure, and physically healthy individual can be traced to the successful movement through this first stage and level of development. Survival was a given, as fear played a minimal role in my early life. Today, as I approach forty, I attempt to continue with my children the legacy that my parents imprinted in the core of my personality. My wife and I have attempted, and continue to attempt, to provide as healthy and consistently secure an environment for our kids as possible. Meeting their physiological needs unconditionally, I have noticed how their little personalities are also growing from a trusting and secure base. They are happy and healthy kids, which is but a reflection of our efforts to sustain a healthy and loving lifestyle. Of course, every family has sickness, fights, and momentary dysfunction, as the shadow-yang of the system is an ever-present teacher at every turn. Yet these are not problems, only challenges to help us grow.

In order to keep this level healthy, however, it is important to maintain a healthy lifestyle. The foundation of any life is the body, and as with most other people I struggle to find time to keep up physical fitness. Entropy acts constantly in our lives. Therefore, health is not just a given, but something that must be sustained and cultivated through a variety of practices. I have simplified for myself and my clients what it takes to remain physically healthy in what I call the four elements of health. Element one is Earth and is sustained by nutrition. We are what we eat, literally. Without a balanced, healthy diet, no other level or dimension will be able to grow optimally. For our family this means eating local, organic, whole foods. I find no other life investment as important as growing and buying local and organic, not only for the health of my body and family, but for the health of our community and planet. It seems to me that at this point in history it is a moral imperative to not support chemical-spewing practices that kill organisms and the living soil in which they live.

Element two is Water and is related to drinking lots of pure clean water. The Earth is 70 percent water, our bodies are 70 percent water, and every cell in our body is 80 percent water. This means that we are literally beings of water living on a water world; a true fractal. If we don't constantly replenish our water, we will not be healthy.

Element three is Fire and is related to bringing up the heat in our body. This means exercise and an active lifestyle. Like many others, I struggle to keep exercise a part of my daily life. I've taken up running at various points in my life, feeling its vital influence on all parts of my body. Growing up it was mountain biking and rock climbing, and today it is physical work on my land, *asana* postures from my Yoga practice, and occasional runs that keep my physical vessel strong and healthy. I've also jumped into coaching soccer for my kids, which promotes this fire element in their lives and keeps me engaged in some form of physical activity.

And finally we have the element of Air, which corresponds to learning how to breathe correctly, deeply, and consciously. We will explore breath in full depth as we proceed, but here we note its basic contribution to health as a method to release stress, shift the body from the fight-or-flight stress response of the sympathetic nervous system, and activate the rest-and-repair functions of the parasympathetic nervous system. Deep breathing has become an essential part of my health, and the need for clean air for generations to come has become an obvious fact worth fighting for.

Not all people have been as fortunate as I have. Many, if not most, people who struggle in life as adults had issues at this first stage of development. Extreme stress, domestic violence, drug or alcohol addiction, or child abuse during these very early years will unavoidably imprint anxious, frightened, depressed, paranoid, and even psychotic basic personality patterns that persist throughout their lives. Neglect, for instance, will create a sense of worthlessness and insecurity that will eventually manifest as something like Clinical Depression. Yet all of this can be healed through deep work. Regression therapy, trauma-informed therapy, deep psychodynamic exploration, and sometimes psychiatric intervention are all appropriate therapies that may help individuals reconcile with their tormented past.

The problem with working on this level of consciousness in adults is that all experiences of infancy are preverbal. In other words, the infant has no words and/or thoughts about the world, so the impressions captured by the sensory system are mostly energetic and in the body. The only way to get to this trauma is through symbolic work, the body, and psychoanalytic explorations that aim at making conscious the maladaptive programs that run the individual's life from an unconscious source. By providing a safe, nurturing therapeutic environment, a client can initiate a slow process of rewiring the basic survival circuits of the base reptilian brain so that it is not in a constant state of hyper vigilance, eventually learning how to self-regulate and find some peace.

Individuals with the above disorders can for the most part lead normal lives. There is, however, a more basic level of dysfunction that expresses this level of consciousness in its most primal form. Before becoming an actual therapist, I worked for the Nor Cal Day Activity Center in San Rafael, California. This was a place for people with severe physical and mental disabilities. I was the art and garden counselor, which was a great position except for the fact that the participants could barely talk, let alone perform complex tasks. Some were more functional than others, but most suffered from severe paranoia, others could barely care for their personal needs, and all were completely sedated by the medical staff. It was interesting to connect with them, seeing the beautiful shinning Spirit within tormented minds and deformed bodies. Their basic preoccupation, of course, was survival. They were moved and controlled by unconscious inner urges and reflexive impulses, and by intense fear or rage when feeling cornered or threatened. Their lives were completely dependent on the care of others, to the point that without assistance they would probably have died. Individuals here suffered from the full spectrum of acute pathologies, from paranoid schizophrenia, delusional disorders, and psychosis, to mental retardation, severe autism, catatonia, and a variety of organic disorders. The staff's main job was to meet the basic needs of food, hygiene, toilet issues, and restraint when someone "decompensated." Keeping them safe and helping them feel secure through routine and consistency, as in the care of an infant, were the basic therapies that helped individuals imprisoned in such unfortunate bodies lead bearable lives.

As the basic strategy of this stage, approach/craving and avoidance /aversion mark the manner in which individuals relate to their world. These two basic behaviors are, of course, programmed by those most primal perceptions and sensations of pain vs. pleasure. Programmed to seek and crave pleasure, and designed to avoid and retreat from pain through the fear-based stress response, no signal goes past the thalamus unless the brain stem is satisfied. In other words, all other functions are secondary to pleasure and the retreat from danger. This is why addictions to substances that activate the pleasure centers are so hard to break, for we are hardwired to consistently repeat that which gives us pleasure. This has an evolutionary reason, of course, for sex, food, and warmth are pleasurable so that we continue to survive and reproduce. But if we, as Buddhists tell us, are ruled by the basic survival program of craving/aversion, we live in a world of slavery and suffering. According to Buddha's second noble truth, the source of suffering is the mind's tendency to crave pleasure, and to retreat from pain. This structure is essential for survival, but is suffused with suffering if it is the main motivator and preoccupation in life.

This deep suffering, which we all subtly have in the deepest physical roots of our incarnated Being, is most markedly observed in the struggles of opiate addiction. This class of psychoactives, which are derived from the opium poppy to produce opium, heroin, morphine, methadone, codeine, oxycodin, and a variety of other painkillers, contracts Consciousness to level one Consciousness. The opiate family of chemicals activate the pleasure centers so that no pain is experienced, putting consciousness in an "infantile" state of purely physical pleasure with all other cognitive functions numbed. This, of course, is wonderful medicine for extreme pain, but a miserable existence if the brain latches on to it as its main source of pleasure. So intense is the opiate rush that addicts cease to feel pleasure in the simple daily activities of life. Instead, the brain flashes danger and pain when withdrawing, forcing the individual to seek relief by any means possible.

My first encounter with this most devastating addiction occurred while I was still interning for the County Mental Health Department. I was being trained to be an after-hours crisis worker, where my role was to assess people in crisis in the emergency department of our local hospital and determine if they were a danger to self or others. If they were, I had the authority in this role to place them in what is called a 5150 hold, which is the basic code where an individual's rights are taken away from them for seventy-two hours or until safety is determined. My mentor and I walked into the emergency room one late night and found a man in his late forties, shivering, sweating, and moaning in severe pain. His eyes looked like they were about to pop out. Pale and wet from sweat, he pleaded for relief, or "else this life is not worth living," he stated. I immediately thought to myself, "heroin withdrawal." As it turns out, he was withdrawing from Vicodin, a common painkiller prescribed freely by doctors for the most minute of ailments. After assessing him, we decided to place him in a detox facility so that he could cleanse from the grips of this most potent drug.

Over the course of the years I have had many opportunities to work with individuals struggling with opiate addiction. Of course, no true therapy can occur until an individual cleanses from said addiction, for the main preoccupation is that of seeking relief from what is described as extreme muscle and bone pain; a pain that comes from the depths of being. The addict ceases to get high after a while, as the repeated administration is to "maintain and feel normal," and to find relief from extreme pain. Life for these individuals crumbles to the constant seeking of the next fix, and a lack of pleasure in all other life activities slowly erodes any sense of contentment. Consciousness regresses to the purely physio-survival mode, as the addicted brain interprets the lack of opiate in the system as a literal threat to life. Addicts in the throes of withdrawal report feeling like they are dying. The drug temporarily gives relief, as it contracts consciousness to a semiconscious state that "nods" in and out of total unconsciousness. There is little awareness of the environment or of others, as all emotions are sedated into a dreamy, flat, artificial sense of chemical safety and security. The senses are dulled, as can be seen in the contracted pinpoint pupils, and the individual's world is reduced to the mere sensations of pain and pleasure.

Our body is naturally endowed with its own pain-fighting transmitters called endorphins. Endorphins are our endogenous opiates. They bind to opiate receptors distributed throughout the body when pain signals the brain to release them, or when the body experiences pleasure and euphoria. These wonderful molecules allow us to withstand the most extreme pain of major injuries, and also flood our bodies when enjoying chocolate or orgasm, for example. Exogenous opiates such as the ones mentioned above are called endorphin agonists. This means that they bind to and replace the endogenous endorphins at the receptor sites, providing a similar response of analgesia and pleasure. Prolonged use of exogenous opiates will ultimately atrophy the body's natural ability to produce endorphins, therefore inhibiting normal daily pain modulation and the sense of pleasure normally sustained by the release of endorphins.

The effects of opiates, such as analgesia, relaxed euphoria, sedation, sense of tranquility, reduced apprehension, and lack of concern, are also mediated by the dopaminergic, or dopamine-producing, system. Simonato summarizes this process in Julien:

> In the ventral tegmental area, morphine inhibits GABA neurons via mu opioid receptors, thus disinhibiting dopaminergic neurons and increasing dopamine input in the nucleus accumbens and in other areas; this phenomena may be involved in the mechanism of reward, i.e., the positive reinforcer to opioid addiction. [23]

In other words, the reward circuits of the base and limbic brains are also flooded with dopamine, producing euphoric states that are hardly matched by the more regulated releases of day-to-day activities. This in the long run produces the dysfunctional patterns of dependence and addiction. Two other potent stimuli, other than opiates, engage both the dopamine and endorphin complexes: food and sex. Both being crucial for physical survival and self-preservation, it is no wonder that an addiction to a drug that engages this pleasure system is so hard to break. The brain is fooled into believing that without the drug, the organism does not survive.

Of course, we are all addicted to pleasure, for we are supposed to be, but if we aspire to evolve and develop into greater potentials, we must necessarily transcend the limited life ruled by the pain vs. pleasure duality. Just as our unicellular ancestors did, we must leave the free-floating security of oceanic pleasure behind if we are to experience the vast latent richness available to Consciousness. Again, once this stage is successfully managed and integrated, Consciousness is ready to grow into the next spiral of expression in its eternal quest for Self-exploration. The impulse at the heart of creation cannot be held hostage by the constricted materiality and physicality of this level. A deep longing for freedom and expansion pushes and pulls the evolving Spirit forward, as a new dimension unfolds and the next world is birthed in full glory.

Level 2

Emotional-Territorial: Bio-emotional Plane

Phylogenic Expression

This level of consciousness emerged primitively in the marine world of the ocean, but did not fully flower until life left the water, developed backbones, evolved the limbic system, learned to master gravity, control territory, and establish dominance hierarchies.

In the early primal oceans during a time scientists call "Garden of Ediacara" 700 million years ago, eukaryotes were busy experimenting with and forming a multiplicity of soft-bodied beings. These soft-bodied beings were colonies of thousands of eukaryotes working together through specialized functions. The soft (no bones or skeletons present) nature of these primitive multicellular organisms allowed them a flexibility and malleability that increased the creative exploratory potential of Life-Consciousness tenfold. During this time, Life began to experiment wildly with diverse body designs, developing the blueprints for most animal groups during a period scientists call the "Cambrian Explosion" 540 million years ago.

The first hard body parts, such as the exoskeleton found in trilobites, appear during this time. Primitive light-capturing sensors of proto-eyes were developed many times over in different species, but trilobites were among the first to develop actual eyes. The lenses were made out of transparent crystals of calcite, backed by photosynthetic bacteria that sent messages to the trilobite's primitive brain (a cluster of neurons at this stage). Jellyfish developed the first muscles in their twitching tentacles, which were endowed with a network of sensory receptors. Descended from worms, lancelets evolved a "notochord" that would one day evolve into the backbone.

Around the same time, roughly 500 million years ago, Earth changes and continental movements began to initiate climatic shifts all around the globe. The Earth began to cool down and terrestrial environments began to develop, as the climatic changes became favorable for terrestrial life. The proliferation of algae and water plants made possible the production of oxygen, thus initiating the creation of our current atmosphere. Plant life began to migrate to shores at this time, and as John Reader explains, "the land offered many advantages. Both the light and the carbon dioxide needed for photosynthesis were more readily available, and land was unoccupied by competing life forms." [1] These plants, evolved from soft algae, hardened their outside so that they could survive on land without drying out. Primitive plants began to take root in the shifting continents, evolving into groups and clustering into protective niches. Through the process of photosynthesis, plants used the excess carbon dioxide in the air to produce oxygen. As a consequence, the atmosphere surrounding these plant groupings began to change. Fungi also entered the scene at this time, living in the soil and absorbing nitrogen from the organic matter of dead plants and making it available to plants through their root systems. In an intimate symbiotic relationship, these two life forms traded carbon and nitrogen with each other, allowing them to spread across the land by creating fertile soil. With all of these elements in place, the land and atmosphere were fertile for the next evolutionary step.

Four hundred fifty million years ago insects leave the oceans and take to the skies. Arthropods, such as spiders and insects, have a skeleton on the outside, called an exoskeleton, and are the first animals on land as the exoskeleton protects the body from the harshness of the external environment. Today, they make up over 80 percent of the species in the animal kingdom. These creatures also worked out a symbiotic partnership with the plants, providing rich nutrients as the fungi break down their dead bodies, and eventually helping plants reproduce through the process of pollination.

As a consequence to the lowering of the oceans and the drying up of ponds from continental drift and land mass separation, many marine animals were left stranded and exposed to the evolving atmosphere at around 400 million years ago.[2] Eventually, through mutation, natural selection, and the creative ingenuity of the evolving Consciousness itself, marine animals began to develop lungs capable of using the oxygen in the atmosphere. Amphibious creatures, still dependent on mother oceanwater for early years to keep their skin moist and lay their eggs, began to crawl and migrate into terrestrial niches as they developed legs to deal with the force of gravity. Amphibians also developed a different kind of ear, capable of detecting sound traveling through the air.

As further climatic changes and lowering of temperatures conducive to terrestrial life continued to develop, plant and insect life began to rapidly spread across the young continents. Amphibians, mastering gravity and the use of oxygen, began to slowly mutate into purely oxygen-using creatures: reptiles. Unlike their fish and amphibian ancestors, theses new mutants laid eggs that had a protective shell and a yolk that supplied food to the growing embryo. They also evolved scaly, waterproof skins that kept them from drying out, and a penis for internal fertilization so they could breed on land.

Two hundred forty-five million years ago in what is known as the Mesozoic Era, the Earth witnessed the spread of reptiles and dinosaurs across the now separating continents from the original land mass called *Pangaea.* Their new muscular and power technologies, managed by the reptilian brain stem, allowed them to rule the early planet. Territorial dominance and aggressive-submissive strategies began to emerge, as the new frontier required safe spaces in order to insure survival and reproduction.

Further evolution produced birds and mammals from small reptiles, and the biosphere blossomed into a teeming world of colorful ecological niches and diverse biological ecosystems. The first blooming flowers also appeared around 110 million years ago with the development of the encased seed, fruits and nuts, which were packed with food for the young plant. The flower was specifically designed by the plant queendom as a symbiotic strategy to spread and reproduce throughout the land via the process of pollination. Flowering plants and animals evolved together in an intimate symbiotic relationship. Flowers provided fruit and nectar to animals in exchange for the spread of their pollen and seeds by those animals, co-creating and shaping each other through the course of time.

Mammals and birds allowed a further release and expression of energy, as they evolved an internal source of warmth that gave them increased advantages for survival as they no longer depended on the sun as a source of heat. As a consequence, many mammals became nocturnal hunters with increased survival capabilities, especially during the long nights to come at the end of the dinosaur's reign. Birds are direct descendants from dinosaurs and probably survived the cataclysm that eliminated the dinosaurs 65 million years ago due to their feather-covered, warm-blooded skin. Mammals developed hair from scales for keeping warm and had live babies that were nursed by the mother. Since mammal babies were defenseless, blind, bare-skinned newborns that could not survive without maternal protection, mammal parents stayed with their young to nurture and protect them until they were able to fend for themselves. Unlike their reptilian ancestors, mammals began to bond in a deeper (emotional) way than ever before, as their survival depended on it. Cuddling, nursing, liking, and deep emotional bonding became the newest expression of Consciousness, establishing the foundation for this new dimension of Being. These mammalian features are natural outgrowths of a new emotional brain, one wired for warm connections and fuzzy relationships.

With the movement of time, continuing specialization evolved a multiplicity of survival tactics. Dr. Tim Leary describes this development: "survival on land involves control of turf; the strength or cunning to hold territory for food and for breeding.

Complex strategies are developed by various [mammalian] species, muscular power, speed, camouflage, evasion, stealth, shifting flexibility…." [3]

The new gravitational conditions of this new frontier created the need for novel organismic strategies that increased mobility and flexibility. The frontier was now teeming with competition, making necessary the development of novel terrestrial technologies in order to survive. Some animals developed speed, others power; camouflage and a variety of other protective mechanisms also evolved. All features coevolved with the changing environment, as environmental conditions helped shape the morphing bodies. Trees helped sculpt hands for grasping branches, air shaped wings for flight, water molded fins for aquatic propulsion, and land morphed hooves and paws for terrestrial locomotion.

In this ever-creative feedback loop, plants also were shaped and molded through their relationship to animals. One great example of this co-creative partnership is that of grass and horses. Horses were first cat-sized creatures that lived in dense tropical forests. As the planet cooled, the tropical forests shrunk, creating vast plains. The horses moved into these vast plains and ate the plants. The plants developed strong root systems that were strengthened by the consistent grazing of the horses. The horses mowed the grass, strengthening the roots and fertilizing them as they went, growing bigger, and developing hooves to roam the plains more effectively. Grass fed the horses, the horses fed the grass in an intimate relationship that continues to this day.

With the rise of higher mammals, consciousness expanded and survival was not only physiocentric and self-preserving, but was now involved in species and group preservation. Animals, particularly mammals, began to move in packs, groups, and herds, and through this established a new safety mechanism. Dominance hierarchies and precise pecking orders developed as territorial status became the important, even crucial factor of early group survival. Again, Leary describes: "Motor-muscular responses are no longer automatic approach-avoid. Incoming signals are scanned, evaluated, interpreted by the jumpy, nervous Second brain and the appropriate emotional response selected." [4] "Top dog" group leaders with dominant strategies, versus "bottom dog" submissive-passive strategies, began to define grouping structures and territorial dominance. A variety of behavioral-emotional tactics, such as growling, barking, howling, roaring, hissing, purring, or whimpering, for example, were developed, and a complex system of emotional communication was now in place. Body gestures and postures conveyed emotional signals, establishing clear parameters for group structure, turf control, and dominance hierarchy.

The fight-flight stress response fully evolves at this point and becomes the basic strategy for group preservation. The creatures are now biocentric, concerned about group survival, and their reality is an interconnected web of territory, adaptive niches, and emotional communication systems. Consciousness and its organic technologies have developed enough at this stage so that there is an expanded sense of emotional awareness, but still unconscious of self and restricted to biological and instinctual programs.

At this level, newly evolved physiological structures appear to regulate the various sexual-emotional breeding cycles and territoriality of the animal groups. Over the reptilian brain stem, which is the primary primitive physiocentric structure for the fight-flight response, emerges the limbic brain. The limbic brain is the central regulator for the entire limbic system and has currently been associated to most emotional states. Hooper and Teresi point out the connection: "when stimulated by mild electrical currents, specific limbic sites triggered sudden rage, joy, or fear." [5]

Finely coordinated with the endocrine and glandular systems (pituitary, pineal, thyroid, testes/ovaries, adrenal, thymus, etc.), the limbic system helps regulate the release of hormones and pheromones via what is called the "hypothalamic-pituitary axis." This axis is implicated in sexual cycles, emotional states, immune system activity, growth patterns, and other biological processes. The glandular and hormonal secretions produce a variety of emotional states in the animal, and are in full coordination with the seasonal and cyclical movements of the environment. Reproductive periods are triggered by the release of pheromones, chemical signals excreted by animals in various states of arousal, and are picked up by members of the same species. These chemical signals then trigger a series of hormonal responses, and the sexual dances begin. Territory is also regulated in large by pheromones, glandular secretions, and hormonal cycles.

In this stage, Consciousness has developed a series of novel relationships to its environment, biodiversity, and physical territory. Through this emotional web of relationships, a series of ecological niches develop and the biosphere, with its biocentric groupings, flourishes. New physiological structures such as the limbic system, endocrine glands, and the various hormonal systems evolve in complete interdependence with planetary cycles, producing the rhythmic patterns of life. Consciousness expands in this realm, running as the vital life force within all biological systems. The sentience inherent in Consciousness begins to awaken in these new self-organizing natural systems and flows passionately through the veins of our young planetary web of life. In the heart of every living cell pulses the rhythm of Life, Life being the nonlocal, subjective sentience that is essentially One Life-Being expressed through a multiplicity of evolving organic forms. Every living being is made of cells, each of which has a nucleus at its center. In the center of these nuclei spirals the "objective" transceiving brain of Life, DNA, which itself twirls around an empty nonlocal center that absorbs, records, and manages all energies from a quantum Source. This Source, at this stage, revels in the splendor of its flowering creations in young Gaia's web of life.

Ontogenetic Expression

The novel abilities of amphibious creatures learning to crawl in the new frontiers of the terrestrial world are recapitulated in human development as the infant begins to crawl and master gravity at approximately one to three years of age. Leaving the security of the mother figure, the infant begins the exploration of its world. Crawling enables increased mobility, allowing for a sense of territory and familiarity with surroundings. Further along in development, the infant grows into a toddler, a stage known tenderly as the "terrible twos," and initiates its campaign of environmental manipulation. A sense of territory develops and words like "my toys," "my mom," "my bed," etc. develop (language develops at a later stage, but these words are indicative of the emotional-territorial level of consciousness) to convey the newly established territorial boundaries. Like its animal ancestors, the way to get things is through emotional power tactics. Yelling, screaming, crying, cooing, grunting, smiling, laughing, etc., are all human versions of an instinctual mechanism designed to convey messages. Internal urges are now fully expressed in a variety of ways, and the child learns quickly what works and what doesn't work in an increasingly familiar world.

At this stage the child is completely identified with its bio-emotional states and is biocentric in the sense that it is solely concerned with the satisfaction of biological and emotional needs. Ken Wilber describes this aspect of this early stage of development:

> The self is here a purely ecological self, a biospheric self, libidinal self, a natural impulsive self. It is one with, in fusion with, the entire vital-emotional dimension of being, both internal and external. It is pushed and pulled by the currents of its vital life, and it does not differentiate itself from the ecological currents of existence. Its identity is biocentric or ecocentric, fused with the biosphere within and without. [6]

Driven by these bio-vital forces, the child acts according to unconscious internal impulses, displaying any felt emotion without reservation. The child is barely aware of itself, acting from an emotional-instinctual stance. Wilber explains, "Precisely because it cannot differentiate itself from the emotional and vital world around it, the infant self treats the world as an extension of itself—which is the technical meaning of 'narcissism'." [7]

As a toddler, the emotional world is extended and territory and possessions are directly linked to the child's field of identity. Sullivan discusses the radius of significant relationships, and at this particular stage the radius includes both parental persons, a tripolar relationship, as she puts it. [8] Whereas the first stage is unipolar and bipolar, including only the self and the mother figure, the child in this second stage has now the capacity to relate with both parents. Thus "my mommy," "my daddy," become common expressions, and the child's emotional identity becomes inextricably linked to the parents. Again, this is a prepersonal, semi-self-conscious level where the child has not yet developed the ability for self-reflection and self-consciousness.

Freud described this stage in terms of psychosexual development. He called this the anal stage and revealed how the main focus was that of control. He described how between the ages of two and four, children learn to control the sphincter and the bladder. "The rise in physiological control is coupled with the realization that such control is a new source of pleasure. In addition, children quickly learn that the rising level of control brings them attention and praise from their parents." [9] Thus control, along with territory, possessions, and emotional strategies, is the main theme in this stage of development.

Closely related to Freud's anal stage is Erik Erikson's interpretation of this level. He describes the possibility of autonomy if the child is able to develop a sense of control and mastery over environment and physiological processes. Conversely, the possibility of shame or doubt is equally present if the child is not allowed to develop these crucial capacities. This Eriksonian psychosocial stage describes it as follows:

> Autonomy versus shame and doubt occurs at the time of muscular maturation and the accompanying ability to hold on or let go. At this stage, children rapidly acquire a variety of mental and physical abilities. They begin to walk, climb, hold on, and communicate more effectively. The child interacts with the world in new ways—in grasping and dropping objects and in toilet training. The

> child starts to exert control over self and also parts of the outside world. [10]

Family life at this stage in development determines and molds many of the foundational structures of individual personality. If the child has to compete and struggle for attention, space, or control, the child may develop/imprint aggressive, possessive, jealous, protective, dominating, or greedy characteristics and behavioral strategies. If, on the other hand, the child grows up in a loving, egalitarian family structure, he or she may develop/imprint a sharing, welcoming, passive, submissive, giving, and loving personality. Of course, there are many factors involved in shaping the emotional self, and infinite variations on emotional responses to environmental stimuli. The nuclear family unit at this stage, however, is the major influence on the developing being and its emotional identity.

At this point I would like to introduce the third "reality creator," *imprints*. If DNA templates are the hardware, the imprints are the programs that are allowed to run. DNA hardwires the organism and its nervous system to adopt certain environmental strategies. These strategies are stored and passed down the generation if successful, thus becoming a habit. Imprints (the adopted strategies) are more or less permanent neuronal connections that mold and shape an organism's behavior and perception when confronted by given stimuli. These neuronal configurations, or imprints, establish set parameters for interpreting incoming signals. How an organism imprints determines the general worldview and manner in which it relates to its environment. The ramified neuronal connections act as defining patterns for both behavior and perception in a reflexive and unconscious way.

DNA programs brief moments in the developmental life of an organism where there is imprint vulnerability. These genetically programmed periods of imprint vulnerability allow impressions to establish themselves. Once the impression/imprint forms, it acts as a foundational structure for the organism's subsequent life experiences. For example, in a 1930s experiment Dr. Lorenz recorded a case in which a gosling imprinted, in the absence of its mother, a table tennis ball. It followed the ball around, engaged with it, nestled with it, and attempted to mount the ball sexually as an adult. [11] This example demonstrates that during these brief moments of imprint vulnerability, we are capable of imprinting anything. The point is that the imprint will determine subsequent reality perceptions and behaviors.

There are eight major imprint stages (four personal and four transpersonal) as defined by Dr. Timothy Leary in his eight-circuit model of consciousness. [12] Within the personal stages, the first imprints are defined by the infant-mother connection, which establishes a trusting, secure, confident biosurvival imprint or a distrustful, insecure, shy behavioral-perceptual strategy. The second major imprinting occurs as the infant becomes a toddler and begins to interact with the world. Here he or she establishes a dominating, top dog, aggressive, assertive emotional-territorial strategy or a submissive, bottom dog, mellow, passive imprint. The third, intellectual symbol-logic imprint, and fourth, sexual-social role identity imprint, will be discussed in subsequent sections. All of these imprints determine, at the unconscious level, the general underpinnings of personality and the perceptual veils that gloss over and filter the experienced reality.

Within the second level of consciousness, the individual experiences a series of imprint- vulnerable potentials. Toilet training, as was pointed out in Freud's anal stage, is one of many imprint-vulnerable moments. If the child feels that he or she is in control and can take hold of the process successfully, he or she then imprints a sense of autonomy and mastery. If not, shame, doubt, and a sense of powerlessness ensues, impacting all subsequent development. The relationship between the child and its parents is the main force shaping personality, behavior, emotion, and perceptual orientations in reality at this point.

We will conclude this section with Frances Vaughan's interpretation and summary of this level in connection to the chakra system. She explains:

> Second chakra, or *savadhisthana*, is associated with sexuality or general life-expansiveness, and is represented by the element of water. It may be described as "you and me" consciousness in which relationships are given a higher value than material possessions. Motivation at this level is predominantly based on the desire for approval and love from another person.... Relationship issues dominate personal preoccupation at this level. [13]

Experience of Structure

Q: What do you perceive-project from this level?
A: Emotional signals, feelings, relationships, territory, potential mates, and status within a group.

At any given moment we can tap into this most basic second level of consciousness. Our emotions and feelings and the corresponding physiological structures of the limbic system (paleomammalian brain), the endocrine-glandular system, and the hormonal-pheromonal-sexual cycles are fundamental structures inherited from the evolutionary course of life. Reflecting the growing Tree of Life, the evolution of the nervous system, or transceiving antenna, at this stage features the aforementioned limbic brain. An outgrowth from the more primitive and reflexive reptilian brain stem, the limbic brain comes with vastly expanded information-processing capabilities. Its main feature is its ability to facilitate a new dimension in the experience of Consciousness: emotional states and feelings. A deeper, more sentient, and vastly more complex system of communication, perception, and behavioral response emerges as the brain expands. Subjectively, the experience of the world deepens and expands with a felt richness never before explored by the evolving universal Consciousness.

A crucial structure that is *the* main communicator between brain activity and endocrine-hormonal systems (mind and body connection) is the hypothalamus. The hypothalamus has the unique capacity of translating neurotransmitter information into hormonal information via what are called neuropeptides. Neuropeptides are basically twenty amino acid and protein chains that bind to cellular receptors. These peptides are released by the hypothalamus in response to neurotransmitter signals, to then bind with the pituitary and other endocrine glands. Dr. Dharma explains: "The hypothalamus directs the function of the pituitary, and the pituitary in turn governs the function of the entire endocrine system. The endocrine system produces the hormones and neuropeptides that control mood, energy, sexuality, and immunity." [14] These glands then switch on or off to release or inhibit hormonal flow, which activates or inhibits various bodily functions, such as immune responses, growth patterns, sexual-reproduction cycles, etc.

The hypothalamus sits in front of the thalamus, controlling hunger, thirst, body temperature, hormonal cycles, sleep/waking activity, sex drive (id), anger, reward system, and pleasure. Since it is responsible for many of our biological rhythms, such as sleep, mating, hunger, thirst, etc., it is often referred to as our "internal clock." Closely linked to the hypothalamus is the pituitary, or master gland, which helps regulate all other glands via the hypothalamic-pituitary axis, and the pineal gland, which helps regulate sleep cycles via the secretion of the hormone melatonin in the absence of light. Being photosensitive, the pineal gland reacts to sunlight by producing serotonin, thus implicating the link between depression and the absence of light in what is called

SAD, or seasonal affective disorder. We will explore the pineal gland more closely in chapter 7, as there are fascinating speculations on how the pineal gland may be the actual physical structure of the third eye, sixth chakra, or "seat of the soul."

Another fold in the unfolding limbic brain gives rise to the cingulate gyrus, a primitive structure that receives and scans sensory signals routed from the front part of the thalamus so as to influence emotional responses in the limbic system. It is the structure where sensation begins to change into emotion and emotional response. Another main emotion processing-producing structure is the amygdale, located deep in the temporal lobe. This structure is a focal point for fear, aggression, and pleasure, and reacts instinctively and unconsciously prior to further processing. Also intimately woven into these limbic structures is the olfactory cortex, which integrates sense data routed from the nose. Included in the odor data there drift a variety of pheromonal and hormonal scents designed for various biological processes, such as mating, territorial marking, and food location.

Deep in the temporal lobe one also finds the hippocampus, an advanced structure that contextualizes (imprints) emotional information in response to pleasure or pain. This structure is also implicated in the coding and storage of long-term memory, a capacity available only to higher mammals. The entire limbic brain is formatted at the various imprint-vulnerable stages thus discussed, and so establishes enduring patterns that serve as foundation for subsequent development. Once imprinted, these emotional imprints are hard to break, and require deep rewiring to mend if patterns are dysfunctional. This process, being the third "reality creator," imprints and thus filters incoming sensory signals in accordance to the neuronal shape established in those tender imprint-vulnerable developmental years of childhood. These limbic structures then emotionally interpret the signals and either channel them up for higher processing if not threatening, or activate the reflexive/instinctual muscular-motor system if so required. The cerebellum, sitting under the occipital lobe and visual cortex in the back of the head, is the brain structure that helps orchestrate and coordinate movement and fine motor control, an obviously crucial structure for the more flexible mammals.

This layer of the brain can be internally and subjectively felt in each moment acting on our everyday life as emotional currents and reactions, triggered ofcourse by environmental stimuli and our relationships. Our emotions and feelings ebb and flow throughout the day, taking on tones and textures that reflect the environment within the imprinted limits of our emotional programming. These programs are established during our early childhood, mostly in response to our relational experiences with our parents. These emotional programs then color our adult relationships as unconscious patterns of reactivity and emotionality. As Vaughan points out, the main triggers for the emotional self are relational and occur with most intensity as we interact with other people. [15] Since this is a fairly primitive structure of consciousness, it is largely unconscious and reflexive. It exists as instinctive mechanisms that react unconsciously and automatically to stimuli from the environment.

Probably grounded in these brain structures is what Freud called the id, which is described by Frager and Fadiman as such: "The id is the original core out of which the personality emerges. It is biological in nature and contains the reservoir of energy for all parts of the personality." [16] The id represents the aspect of our being that contains the primitive aggressive and sexual impulses of the organism. It lives in our unconscious and acts on our behavior through unobserved influences. Other names for this vital-sexual animalistic force within us are libido, the energy available to the life impulse, and orgone bioenergy, which "functions in the living organism as specific biological energy. As such, it governs the energetic organism; it is expressed in the emotions as well as in the purely biophysical movement of the orgasm." [17]

These structures facilitate the emotional fluidity that binds and connects us to larger social and ecological networks. Our emotional self exists within an interactive web of relationships that moves and flows in a pattern not unlike water. This bio-emotional web of relationships functions from a more or less unconscious level, for it is dictated by imprinted patterns of behavior and reactivity established during early childhood. Many childhood traumas live in adult existence as emotional patterns of reactivity, unconsciously used as coping strategies developed in the early years of development. At this level of consciousness, the emotional patterns are unconscious, and identity is solely attached to the passionate tides of our emotional undercurrents.

Exercises:

1.) Take time to be with your emotions. Feel their ebb and flow. Track how they relate to seasonal, lunar, and astronomical cycles. Witness the various patterns of your emotional responses, reactivity reflexes, and emotional attachments. Tune in to your hormonal and glandular cycles and see how they affect your emotional states. Men have to be especially receptive, for hormonal-glandular movements in men are much more subtle than for women, who are naturally in tune due to their menstrual cycles.

2.) Work on your relationships, both in family and community. Witness how your various relationships produce different emotional responses. See how emotionally connected and attached you are to your various relationships. Pay attention to others' feelings, and witness how many people, including yourself, are driven and identified mostly by and through their emotions. Become acquainted with your different emotions (anger, jealousy, pride, joy, happiness, sadness, etc.) and the stimuli that trigger them.

3.) Go out to a natural environment and experience the biological web of life. Witness the connectivity, symbiosis, and interdependence of all life forms. Marvel at how you are directly connected and in harmonious interdependence with the entire biosphere. Watch animals relate to each other. Watch for their communication styles (verbal and physical) and how they are similar or different to the human emotional world.

4.) Go to a preschool and watch toddlers play. Consider how they form groups and interact. What are their main forms of communication?

5.) Meditate on your second chakra, located near your sexual organ, and connect with the element of water. Experience the fluidity, the life currents, and the emotional system within yourself.

6.) Study the effects of alcohol and see how it affects the emotional body. Consider emotional pathologies, such as mood disorders, adjustment disorders, eating and sexual disorders, and borderline, dependent, narcissistic, and histrionic personality disorders.

Further Personal Explorations

During this second stage of development, my early childhood was blessed by an extraordinary web of familial relations. Until moving to California at the age of seven, I grew up in Santiago, Chile, a land where family is primary. My earliest memories of aunts, uncles, cousins, and grandparents elicit feelings of love and appreciation, as they all contributed to the strong emotional building blocks that form my personality today. Family gatherings and distant laughter still echo in my ability to sustain joy in my day to day life, despite the unavoidable challenges that life brings. As mentioned, my father was central to my development in those early years, as is the case for most kids. In introducing the wonders of the world, he provided the opportunity for the development of confidence and autonomy. I quickly found that I had some control over my environment, as I recall little struggle to get my basic needs met. Life seemed always exciting, as family trips to the Andes Mountains and the rocky coasts of the Pacific Ocean stand out in the depths of my early memory. I was rewarded for my autonomous, creative, curious, and exploratory nature, as shame was a rarely experienced reality. My father seemed always strong, confident, and in control, being my main role model all the way to adulthood.

Of course, like any child, I was often in trouble for my sometimes uncontrollable autonomy, encountering necessary firm boundaries whenever I pushed the limits. My mother reports that I was a bit of a rebel, sometimes defiant, and always "getting into things." I never had to fight for attention, as my parents gave me the necessary unconditional affection that supported the fearless exploration of my world. All in all my emotional limbic brain was successfully formatted toward a generally positive emotional base. I imprinted an open, welcoming, and sharing emotional self that has continued to develop through the course of my life's relationships. Consistent boundaries provided my young organism an unquestioned sense of safety and familiarity, helping shape a deep sense of trust in myself and in my world.

My challenge at this level is to provide the same emotional and environmental stability for my children that my parents did for me, as the importance of this stage of development for the developing personality is monumental. Boundaries are crucial, as they provide limits within which children can safely explore their world. Too rigid, and boundaries inhibit autonomous, confident development, stunting curiosity and the sense of mastery over self and world. Too loose, and no sense of safety and consistency is established, and the child thus becomes either spoiled, the "emotional dictator" of the family, or fearfully over dependent on parental presence. This is a difficult balance to strike and takes some parenting skills not easily acquired. I do a lot of work with parents and their parenting skills, for when a parent comes to my office with, say, a five-year-old struggling with behavioral issues, it is the parent's engagement I focus on the most. The child at this stage is merely imprinting unconsciously the emotional signals of its parents and from its environment, for the limbic brain is in an open state of imprint vulnerability. As mentioned, control must be negotiated with the toddler so that it develops an essential sense of empowerment and control, but not to the point where its emotional tactics dominate the household. I often mimic and role play this negotiation within the therapy hour, working with limit setting while simultaneously respecting the child's natural exploratory and curious nature. Oftentimes I have parents watch, and then have them practice the demonstrated skills with their child within the context of what is known as 'play therapy.'

I find that working with my own kids is much more difficult then working with clients and their kids. Other than the fact that therapy is confined to one hour, my own kids trigger emotional responses in me that were imprinted in my toddler years, thus often being reactive and unconscious. I find that I must work hard to bring to surface my most functional emotional self, but this is not always easy. My kids will elicit the most sublime feelings of love, affection, and tenderness, but also intense feelings of fear, anxiety, worry, and concern when they are sick or in some sort of danger. Anger and even rage can also be triggered in sudden bursts of uncontrollable reactivity as my kids misbehave or fail to listen. I've worked hard to minimize my reactivity and quick temper, as its undeniable damage I have observed in my countless moments of weakness. Anger can be used skillfully and mindfully, but usually there is a kinder and more creative way to handle misbehaviors.

My kids activate my emotional self with most intensity, but all human relationships light-up the emotional circuits throughout the day. As a therapist, I have cultivated a nonreactive, quiet presence that can hold space for most human emotionality. But in my personal relationships, this is not so easy, particularly with my wife. She has the uncanny power to light-up the highest pleasure circuits of love and tenderness, sustaining a joyful and happy state of Being. But within minutes, a tense interaction can trigger an intense flood of anger and resentment that can escalate to a full-blown fight. She and I both have a Basque heritage, thus carrying that highly explosive, quick-tempered gene that came from the Basque country. I can feel my maternal grandfather's Basque rage-gene in my blood in an instant when triggered. My partner and I have both worked hard to make this sometimes uncontrollable anger gene conscious, for if unchecked it can and has created much damage. Whenever anger reaches the "point of no return," no communication is possible. So when we both realize where things are going, we try, as a practice, to first deal with our escalating anger, to then attempt communication.

Much of my work with couples focuses on this underlying level of unconscious emotional reactivity. Without awareness of underlying patterns of reactivity, defense mechanisms, and coping strategies, mostly imprinted between the ages of two and six, no real progress can be observed. In order for the couple to successfully coexist in a mutually respectful relationship, they must necessarily own their emotional baggage and become conscious of the normally unconscious, emotionally reactive patterns. This therapeutic process can eventually lead to the awareness of normally suppressed emotional issues, thereby ultimately decreasing the tendency of each to project his or her internal unrest on the other. Projections normally result in blaming and a reenactment of frustrations experienced during childhood, mostly with parents (of the opposite sex, Freud would add). A basic codependent, dysfunctional interactive pattern can develop if each is not conscious of the underlying emotional issues carried over from early childhood. An abusive, controlling dad will unavoidably produce a controlling, abusive partnership style if this basic personality imprint is not worked with, for example. This is the case for all relational patterns, from dependency on the other to feel OK, to the sense of being a constant "victim," to being emotionally absent due to emotions being a "danger zone," to the need to consistently and jealously control every situation. Self-work is always primary to successful couple's work.

As can be derived from the above paragraph, in order to have healthy relationships in life, one must necessarily work on one's emotional level of consciousness. Being so completely susceptible and vulnerable to environment and parental interaction in those early years, much can go wrong at this stage of development. A family trauma at this stage can remain imprinted for life, as can be seen in the plethora of emotional disorders encountered in adult life. Most emotional issues in life can be traced to these formative years, where emotional stability is determined by the environmental and parental stability of the time. Some psychological disorders that reflect the unsuccessful integration of this level include the mood disorders (such as major depression and bipolar disorder), adjustment disorders, reactive attachment, eating disorders, sexual disorders, and the borderline, dependent, narcissistic, and histrionic personality disorders. There are, of course, many therapeutic modalities that can help individuals struggling with the above disorders. I have found, however, that the ones that address this level most powerfully are the (Freudian) psychoanalytic and psychodynamic techniques that aim at uncovering the unconscious complexes of emotional reactivity often repressed and suppressed from conscious awareness. This uncovering of that which is unconscious gives an individual insight into the nature of his or her hidden emotional patterns, ultimately allowing a conscious rewiring of deep emotional imprints over time. This process often leads to the exploration of the individual's relationship to his or her parents, with reconciliation and forgiveness being the road to eventual healing and emotional stability.

Other therapeutic techniques for this level include regression, which peels away the layers to reveal the raw childhood emotional mess. The mess can ultimately be healed via the rewiring and reimprinting process called structure building. This takes time, as in long-term therapy, but is possible, as I have had the privilege to witness in multiple cases. This requires deep trauma-informed work, but is absolutely doable if the individual is ready to make some fundamental shifts in the deepest portions of his or her psyche. This can only happen with the full development of rapport with the therapist; the complete trust that can at times reenact a healthy relationship with a parental figure, as seen in the well-studied transference phenomena.

Psychodrama is another creative technique that allows individuals to dramatize and enact emotional conflicts (often with parents, but not limited to them) so as to release stored anger, hate, fear, or frustration in a cathartic display. Within the safe confines of the therapeutic space, individuals can act out behaviors without the censorship of the cortical rational mind, thus allowing the limbic emotional brain the opportunity to work things out. One fifty-two-year-old client was allowed to "kill" his abusive father, which was a pillow with his father's face painted on it. He was allowed to express years of hatred and anger without judgment, releasing pent-up toxic emotions that had manifested as years of clinical depression. After forty minutes of stabbing, screaming, crying, and virtually destroying the pillow (father), the client felt a peace and calm well up in his being. He felt freed from emotions he had carried for most of his adult life. By accepting, acknowledging, and ultimately symbolically expressing the repressed rage, he was able to find relief from years of deep depression. He no longer found the need to hate his father, as he realized that he had the power to release such emotional tension. He also found that he had the capacity to forgive, a quality that allowed him to tune in to a healing emotional state previously unknown to him. After months of therapy, he was able to get off his antidepressant medication and has been able to live a healthier life.

The main psychoactive substance that contracts Consciousness to the emotional level of consciousness is alcohol. Alcohol is well known for its ability to numb higher cognitive functions and intensify emotionality. It is also well known that the age an alcoholic starts drinking to self-medicate and cope with emotions is the age when emotional developments stops. This is one of the reasons why alcohol addiction is so devastating, for strong emotions being a part of life one must learn how to work through them. If the organism gets used to dealing with emotions through alcohol, it will take it years to rebuild coping skills that do not include drinking.

My first encounter with alcohol in late high school demonstrated this contraction of awareness in the most succinct and unpleasant way. My older friends planned my "initiation" one weekend when my friend Eddie and I were introduced to the power of tequila. As the buzz started to come on, I proceeded to act in the most silly and manic way. Acting like a complete child, I found incredible joy in falling down or breaking things, thriving on the attention of my friends. Once I caught my friends' social cue, which I was becoming increasingly numb to, that I was not being funny but more of an idiot, my amygdale immediately flashed shame and reacted in uncontrollable rage. I became completely out of control and proceeded to hit, yell, scream, and break things in an embarrassing display of a childish tantrum. After falling flat on my face and noticing my friend's disgust, I entered an inconsolable state of sadness, crying uncontrollably, "You guys don't like me, I am worthless, nobody loves me!" After crying for some time in this fashion, I passed out to wake up the following morning with a pounding headache and a slight sense of shame at some bits and pieces of memory from the night's event. After processing the experience with friends and their unavoidable and humbling humor, I realized that alcohol was a powerful drug not to be messed with. I had never in my life experienced such a loss of emotional control. To this day I have extreme respect for this drug, as my limited experiences have consistently demonstrated its uncanny ability to reduce consciousness to a series of emotional reflexes. We all know the mean drunks, the jealous drunks, the silly, happy ones, or the emotional, sad, crying ones. In all cases, when people get to those levels, the fun of the happy buzz is all but gone. One is left to take care of the released emotionality of oneself or of the other, just like taking care of an irrational toddler. Anger, sadness, jealousy, joy, and fear can all be severely intensified and activated as the rational filters of the adult cortex are all but numbed and sedated by this most popular depressant.

Alcohol produces its powerful effect by disturbing the synaptic activity of various neurotransmitters, particularly the excitatory "go" glutamate and the inhibitory "stop" GABA, as well as other intracellular transduction processes. Julien describes: "Ethanol is a potent inhibitor of the function of the NMDA-subtype of glutamate receptors. Ethanol disrupts glutamatergic neurotransmission by depressing the responsiveness of NMDA receptors to released glutamate." [18] One of the many functions of the glutamate-NMDA receptor system is to activate, excite, and convey signals across ion channels. This allows for the reception and processing of sensory signals and of motor movement activity, among other important cognitive and perceptual processes. Alcohol effectively disrupts the NMDA receptors so that no glutamate can bind, thus inhibiting its activating properties. This is experienced as increased sensory numbness, lack of motor coordination, and a general dulling of all cognition and perceptual function. In other words, it puts your body to sleep.

Julien continues by stating that alcohol/ethanol also "activates the GABA-mediated increase in chloride ion flows, resulting in neuronal inhibition. The behavioral results of this would include sedation, muscle relaxation, and inhibition of cognitive and motor skills." [19] In this sense alcohol acts as a GABA agonist, binding to "a different subunit on the GABA receptor than do other GABA agonists." [20] Being an agonist, ethanol mimics the inhibitory properties of GABA at the receptor site, thus effectively depressing neurotransmission throughout the brain. Briefly, an antagonist drug would replace the neurotransmitter at the receptor site like the agonist, but instead of mimicking activity, the antagonist chemical blocks and inhibits the normal neuronal and physiological action of the transmitter. Most drugs replace endogenous neurotransmitters at the receptor site, but those acting as agonists mimic action, while the ones acting as antagonist inhibit normal transmission.

As rich and exciting as this emotional level of Consciousness is, there is a deep knowing that there are deeper, vaster, and infinitely more refined levels of Awareness waiting to be explored. Emotions have added a dimension to experience that color and intensify it tenfold. Yet as juicy as this emotional level is, Spirit cannot stop there. From this sentient foundation the inner Being pushes relentlessly forward as it begins to break through into a new dimension of reality. Driven by the awakened passion of the life force running through every living cell, Spirit begins to pierce past its emotional identity to discover yet another creative spiral of its own ongoing Self-creation. And so, the journey continues.

Level 3

Mental-Symbolic: Conceptual Plane

Human is nothing but evolution
become conscious of itself.

-Julian Huxley

All tools and engines on earth are
only extensions of man's limbs and
senses.

–Ralph Waldo Emerson

Phylogenic Expression

We continue our journey through time and space, witnessing the miraculous creation of new structures that enable the universe to know itself in novel and creative ways. From the bio-ecological web of early life we witness the emergence of various favorable adaptive strategies that ensure species survival. As we saw, warm-blooded mammals acquire a whole range of novel and more evolved characteristics that place them at the leading edge on our young planet. From evasive techniques to predatorial power to group organization, we witness increasing sophistication in Consciousness's urge to maintain and continue its expressions.

Around 40 million years ago, the primate family branches out from the then-existing species of mammals, and through group organization and cooperation manage to develop a very evolved system of group preservation. Being naturally curious and playful, primates become quite the social beings as they eat in groups and observe each other interact in increasingly varied ways. A variety of signals and communication styles are used, and through this a more complex social system develops, allowing them to become very successful in the competitive archaic world. They learn to articulate feelings of happiness, anger, and love with increasing sophistication through chattering, throwing tantrums, and grooming. Young primates learn from their elders, as the sophisticated social systems increase in complexity as the rapidly growing brain assimilates more information.

So called old-world monkeys, the first primates, develop such complex social systems that it allows them to successfully populate wide areas of Asia and Africa. A further branching occurs at around 9.2 million years ago when the primate family splits into two groups. One group, called pongids, stays in the trees and eventually evolves into our modern apes, such as the gibbon, orangutan, chimpanzee, and gorilla. The second group descends from the trees and becomes the bipedal family known as the hominids.

The quantum leap from emotional animal to self-reflective human is an evolutionary step that still stands as an unknown. Many theories have been proposed, but all fail to convey that most mysterious force that brought forth mental activity from the biological organizations of nature. One such theory describes the early conditions of Earth as playing a crucial role. A rise in continental temperature begins to dry the lush forests of Africa. The tree-dwelling monkeys are forced to the ground and, in increasing frequency, have to migrate from forest patch to forest patch separated by vast spans of dry grasslands. This need for migration forces an increased use of the two hind legs, as the two arms are used to carry the infant primates, gather food, and carry sticks and stones. Through this bipedal adaptation, a whole new branch of primates evolves: the hominids. A series of fossil discoveries in Africa begins to convey the general sequence of hominid evolution. Nelson and Jurmain summarize:

> While considerable evolution occurs during the plio-pleistocene (approximately 3 million years ago), all forms are clearly hominid, as shown by their bipedal adaptation. The time range for this hominid material extends back to nearly 4 million years in East Africa, with the earliest and most primitive hominid now recognized—*Australopithecus afarensis.* Later hominids of a robust lineage are known in E. Africa (*aethiopicus; A. boisei*) and South Africa (*A. robustus*). These groups come on the scene about 2.5 mya and disappear around 1 mya. From these appear the smaller toothed, but larger brained *Homo habillis,* which are believed to have evolved into *H. erectus* and finally into the primitive forms of the *H. sapiens.* [1]

Various anatomical traits, such as an opposable thumb and the bipedal mobility that allows for the increased use of the thumb, are theorized to have played a central role in the development of increased brain capacity. The cortex, having begun its development in early primates, continued to grow in connection to hand-eye coordination and use of tools. Since the hands and arms were liberated with bipedal locomotion, the early hominids went on to the exploration of tools. Hands could grab, throw, carry, shake, hold, lift, twist, poke, pull, fold, carve, and stroke with ever more refined dexterity that sharpened the expanding mind. Sticks, stones, bones, and various other natural artifacts became of interest now that the physiology was capable of handling them.

As noted, we see the rise of the early hominid *Australopithecine* in Eastern and Southern Africa about 4 million years ago. They live in small nomadic bands and develop omnivorous diets. Anthropologists tell us, based on fossil records, that these early hominids split into different branches by 2.5 million years ago. One branch of subspecies, such as the *A. boisei* and *A. robustus*, become extinct, while another branch morphs into families called *Homo habilis*, "handy man," *Homo erectus*, "upright man," and ultimately *Homo sapiens*, "knowing man." *Homo habilis* are the first tool makers initiating the Paleolithic era, or Old Stone Age, 2.5 million years ago. Their descendants, *Homo erectus*, master fire and successfully populate Asia and Europe by about 1.9 million years ago. *Homo sapiens* roam the plains of Africa by 500,000 to one million years ago, and our direct ancestors, *Homo sapiens sapiens,* are believed to have first appeared in Africa by about 200,000 years ago. These larger brained "knowing" hominids become quite successful at adapting to the various climates, eventually migrating up and branching out across the globe by 60 to 90,000 years ago. *Homo erectus* eventually disappears, leaving the *H. sapiens* as the sole survivors of the hominid line.

It is believed based on fossil records that *Homo sapiens* and another branch called *Homo neanderthalis* appear in Europe 35 to 40,000 years ago. The Neanderthals, the first peoples known to bury their dead, become extinct 25 to 30,000 years ago, leaving the larger-brained *sapiens sapiens* as the only surviving branch of hominids on the planet. Estimates suggest that *H. sapiens* reach the Near East by at least 80 to 90,000 years ago, island hoping from New Guinea to Australia by 40 to 50,000 years ago, and reaching the Americas through the theorized ice bridge that is now the Bering Strait connecting Asia to Alaska by 12.5 to 13,000 years ago. Eight hundred years later humans are in the southern tip of South America, as they manage to successfully spread across all corners of the globe. [2]

Although there is wide disagreement amongst anthropologists as to when the modern human mind took shape, archeological data suggest that a major transformation took place during a relatively brief period of evolutionary history. Starting approximately 800,000 years ago in the Paleolithic era and crescendoing around 45,000 to

50,000 years ago, we see for the first time multipart tools, animal bones punctured with holes to create musical instruments, and burials with adornments suggesting sensitivity to aesthetics and the belief in an afterlife. Around this time period we also find cave paintings with rich symbology depicting events of the past and scenes of the perceived future. And control over fire, perhaps one of the central catalysts in the evolutionary development of the brain, is learned and mastered. Fire allows our ancestors to prevail over novel environments by creating warmth, light, and the ability to cook foods to make them edible. Likely discovered on a burning tree after a lightning storm, humans learn to tame the fire by noticing that more fire arises as more wood is put into it.

Another crucial factor aiding the rapid evolution of the brain (cortex) was the flexibility of the changing diet. Early hominids likely expanded their original diet of fruit and small animal kills by including tubers, underground roots, and corms, all accessible through the simple use of digging sticks. According to Terence McKenna, however, these phenomena do little to explain the phenomenal increase in brain size during this relatively short time span. He conveys, "Such a remarkable rate of evolutionary change in the primary organ of a species implies the presence of extraordinary selective pressures." [3] He asserts that bipedalism, binocular vision, the opposable thumb, and the throwing arm are not enough to have accelerated this extraordinary tripling of brain size that allowed these animals to become users of tools, fire, and language. He states, "My contention is that mutation-causing, psychoactive chemical compounds in early human diets directly influenced the rapid reorganization of the brain's information-processing capacities." [4] More specifically, McKenna speculates on the discovery of psilocybin-containing mushrooms (psychedelic in effect; we will explore these chemicals more fully in subsequent sections) growing on herd animal dung by the nomadic hominids. Through the exploration of edible foods, he contends that an encounter with these fungi was inevitable, affecting the evolution of brain size and capacity through a plant-animal symbiosis. In small doses they enhance visual acuity (possibly aiding the hunting process), in larger amounts they stimulate sexual activity (aiding frequency of reproduction), and at psychedelic (mind-manifesting) dosages stimulate mental-imaginal processes within the mind. Clearly these are all evolutionarily favorable traits. The inclusion into the early diets would have stimulated mental activity exponentially, making these psychedelic chemicals a valuable candidate in our search for the missing link of human evolution.

Regardless of the mechanism, the evolution of consciousness brought about a massive reorganization of brain activity and social structure. According to Hooper and

Teresi, "human beings possess an atavistic reptile brain and a paleomammalian brain under the folds of the civilized neocortex. These three brains in one operate like three interconnected bio-computers, each with its own sense of time and space and its own memory." [5] This "three-brained" system, called the triune brain by neuroscientist Paul MacLean, is evolution's pride and joy. It allows for a massive and extremely complex amount of information processing (thought), storing (memory), and transmitting (language). The simple emotional grunts and noises begin to acquire specific meanings, and systems of communication within the nomadic groups begin to flourish. Around crackling fires at night the clans cook hunted game, shouting, grunting, and using simple words to excitedly share stories about the great hunt and the collected berries. The more they try to communicate and express, the more the brain produces symbols and thoughts, and the more they think and symbolize, the more they talk and communicate in an ever-accelerating feedback loop of brain development.

Hunter-gatherer, or foraging, social organization begins to take shape in our early human ancestors. Male hunters and female gatherers in tribal and kinship groups roam the plains, using stones and sticks as tools. The discovery of fire accelerates their consciousness expansion, helping shape the first stage of mind in what German philosopher Jean Gebser calls the *archaic* structure of consciousness, or worldview. [6] It is the earliest form of mental representation, the first true mind, mainly occurring through images captured by the sensorimotor system. The *archaic* worldview is the first developmental stage of mind, defining the Paleolithic tool-/ artifact-using humans. It is believed that at around this time, probably aided by the social use of campfires, the larynx descended to a lower position, carrying the base of the tongue with it. This change allowed the tongue much greater freedom, and the articulation of complex sounds made speech possible for the first time. Leary speculates, "The third circuit emerged phylogenetically when the left hemisphere of the cortex developed its specialized function of mediating dexterity, manipulation of artifacts, and management of the nine muscles of the larynx which perform speech." [7] The laryngeal-manual development at this stage is based on rote repetition and mimicking, thus slowly establishing patterns and habits of language and early culture (birth of Teilhard de Chardin's noosphere).

During the Paleolithic hunter-gatherer epoch, mind begins to expand exponentially (McKenna's mushrooms?), thus evolving from an *archaic* worldview to a *magical* and animistic worldview where everything in nature is perceived as alive and with magical/spiritual powers. [8] The mind at this point begins to conceive the external world in images and early symbolic representations, as seen in the ancient cave paintings in Southern France from 32,000 years ago, for example, but without clear differentiation between the generated symbols and the "external" world. Manipulation of "internal" images changed the world in a very egocentric manner through word magic, as these early humans engaged their environment in increasingly creative and novel ways.

Another factor likely influencing innovation and symbolic thought was the advent of the last ice age, starting roughly 70,000 years ago, peaking 26,000 years ago, and ending by 12,000 years ago. The harsh, icy conditions act as fierce evolutionary pressure, forcing rapid change and adaptation, or extinction. Humans learn to use animal hides for warmth, learn to work tools effectively, and learn to carry the fire so as to keep the tribe from freezing. They experiment wildly with sound and language around the campfire on those long, cold winter nights, eventually expressing the emerging symbolic thought through jewelry, craft, art, dress, and language. This process increases bonding, accelerates the ability to communicate complex thoughts, and eventually leads to the propensity to contemplate the deeper meaning of life.

Through the advancement of language and mental understanding toward the end of the last ice age 12,000 years ago, we enter the Neolithic era (between 10 and 26,000 years ago), where humans (probably women) discover that if they sow seeds in the soil, food eventually grows. On every continent, humans begin to grow their own fruits, grains, and vegetables, as the ice recedes and uncovers fertile soil with an abundance of fresh flowing water. Wheat and barley are grown in the Middle East, rice is planted in Asia, and corn cultivated in the Americas, allowing humans to settle in large communities with free time to pursue other ventures by 8000 years ago. The domestication of animals also begins around this time, where dogs, cats, buffalo, pigs, chickens, cattle, and horses all develop symbiotic, mutually benefiting relationships. Humans protect and feed the animals in exchange for food, clothing, protection, and tools.

Multipart tool making, use of fire, and symbol invention proliferate during the Neolithic era, and the *magical* world begins to shift into what Gebser calls the *mythic* mind structure, or worldview.[9] People begin to settle in specific areas, and villages centered around agriculture develop. Initially, the simple planting and harvesting create horticultural matrifocal societies, which now through a *mythic* worldview begin to worship the Earth Mother Goddess, nurturer of all creatures. The *magical* world of undifferentiated imagery begins to take on more anthropomorphic forms, as the early mind begins to represent the environment and its forces with increasingly concrete *mythological* symbols. As the Earth is understood to be their main source of sustenance, these early humans begin to worship Her and the life-giving power of the feminine principle. Tribes and early villages are governed by a circle of tribal elders, sharing power and leadership equally amongst the tribe in a true partnership social organization. Women and men live in a balanced relationship, as both are honored for the role they play, and a harmonious existence with nature and its abundance is experienced in what most likely was the paradise of the Garden of Eden.

Later, through the creation and invention of more advanced tools and technologies, such as the plow by 6000 B.C., the agricultural work becomes heavy and is taken over by the male strength in a now agrarian society. [10] This development allows for the mass production of food, which frees people to pursue other ventures. The Goddess is slowly replaced by the male God, as strong leaders begin to define their authority in the gradual transition from chief to king. Division of labor becomes necessary and more pronounced in the growing villages, with tool inventors, animal herders, agricultural managers, village and home constructors, clothing weavers, merchants, etc., all developing specialized knowledge and technique in their specific trade. Social stratification begins to take shape, with a hierarchy of social classes defining people's place in the overall system. Central markets develop where people begin trading their milk, bread, vegetables, tools, jewelry, and services in an ever-complexifying system of commerce. To keep track of what is owed, humans mark clay tablets, learning how to count, creating numbers to represent quantity, and inventing simple symbols to represent various things. Simple writing and math begin to emerge, and Consciousness expansion enters hyper speed as the modern brain takes off into the world of mind and thought. In this early *mythic* stage of mind, all processes in nature are viewed as the consequence of supernatural forces and the will of the gods; superstitious symbolism and word magic govern the minds of our early ancestors; and the left-brain hemisphere right-hand dexterity initiates humanity's historical fascination with the world of artifacts.

Ontogenetic Expression

Our exploration of early hominids learning and creating symbol-language systems and using tools is recapitulated during early and middle childhood. Once the child's locomotive abilities and environment manipulating capacities are mastered, the next level of concern emerges (at approximately three to six years of age). The child's young mind is like a sponge at this stage, absorbing as much information as is possible. Initially the mind, like our early hunter-gatherer ancestors, functions through mental "picturing," using only pictorial images. At this stage the worldview is magical as the child populates its world with objects that have mental characteristics. Mind and world are not differentiated yet, as everything that happens is an event directly set up to influence the child's experience. Piaget calls this stage of cognitive development preoperational, and says it is marked by egocentrism—the inability of the child to put himself/herself in the place of another. [11]

Children at this stage of development interpret objects and events not based on definitions or properties, but in terms of how these things relate to them. The preoperational, or representational mind, is concrete and tangible. Children cannot reason outside of what they see, and lack the ability to make generalizations or deductions. Thought at this stage is dominated by what they concretely observe, hear, or experience through their senses. However, they are increasingly able to use language and symbols to represent objects in their environment. Through imaginative magical play, questioning, rote parroting, repetition, copying, modeling, and other interactions, they begin to elaborate concepts and make simple associations of ideas (e.g., the sun needs to go to bed just as they do.)

L. Kohlberg in his observations of moral development revealed this stage to be at what he called a preconventional level of morality. [12] This level of morality has a punishment and obedience orientation and is dictated by "external" forces of authority. It is the initiation of the child into the social and cultural realities of the adult world. Socialization and acculturation forces begin their conditioning project, imprinting the third reality interpreting-creating structures within the early personality (what is good/bad, right/wrong, etc.). Closely related is Erikson's 'initiative versus guilt' stage. "The child experiences greater mobility and inquisitiveness, significant growth in language and imagination…play is the most basic activity of this stage. The child is into everything and its favorite word is 'why'." [13] If the child is given the opportunity and freedom to explore, talk, and question, it will develop initiative and a strong, fast, reflexive, cunning, questioning, witty, resourceful, ingenious, and "smart" intellectual imprint. If this exploratory stage is inhibited or repressed, guilt and a slow, uncreative, dependent, repetitious, unresourceful, and dull intellectual imprint will become established. [14]

Closely related is Freud's phallic psychosexual stage of development. Freud maintained that this third stage is phallic (in his purely male-biased perspective) because the child becomes aware of his/her genitalia and is able to differentiate between sexes. Again, the mind begins its early dualistic training in categorizing, defining, labeling, distinguishing, and judging reality.

Further along in the developmental process (at around six to eleven years of age), the child enters what Piaget called the concrete operational cognitive stage, or rule/role mind, where the individual is able to take on the role of others. [15] It is a mythic worldview where "external" forces and laws run the world, not the individual. At this stage, the mind is able to think with abstract concepts, use rules, learn roles, and run simple operations. Thought becomes increasingly logical and coherent and is able to classify, label, sort, order, differentiate, judge, define, associate, and organize facts about the world and use them in problem solving. They develop a new concept of permanence and conservation, where things and events no longer change in their absence. Reasoning becomes inductive, and thought is less self-centered in an ever-expanding sense of understanding the world through the mental concepts.

At this stage thinking has become socialized, and the child enters Kohlberg's conventional level of morality. [16] In this level the child is concerned with conformity and loyalty, actively maintaining, supporting, and justifying social order. The orientation is toward being a "good boy, nice girl," as children attempt to please authority figures. Rules are understood and for the most part obeyed. In Eriksonian terms, the child develops 'industry or inferiority' (imprints) depending on experience. It is the period in which the child enters a life outside the family structure. School life becomes the dominant shaping and conditioning force, initiating systematic instruction, a shift from play to a sense of work, and the development of practical skills for the socialized world. "Competence, then, is the free exercise of dexterity and intelligence in the completion of tasks, unimpaired by infantile inferiority." [17] At this point the child masters its culture's language and symbol system if industry versus inferiority is established, acquiring the ability to create ideas and concepts.

Freud relayed this stage as the latency period, and is described by Frager and Fadiman as follows:

> Most children seem to modify their attachment to their parents some time after age five and turn to relationships with peers (*villages*) and to school activities, sports, and other skills (*division of labor*). This phase, from age five or six until the onset of puberty, is called the latency period. It is a time when the unresolved sexual desires of the phallic stage are not attended to by the ego and are successfully repressed by the superego. [18] (*Italics in parenthesis mine)*

During this latency period, identification becomes mostly mental, as the two prior structures of physical and emotional consciousness continue to act at an unconscious level. Although becoming exquisitely self-reflective, mental identification is still mostly unconscious at this stage, but begins to acquire self-referencing capabilities that set up the evolving Consciousness for higher forms of expression and self-knowing.

For the sake of continuity, we will conclude this section with Vaughan's interpretation and explanation of the third chakra.

> The third chakra, *manipura,* is associated with power, will, and intentionality, and is represented by the element of fire. It is localized physiologically in the solar plexus, or upper center of the abdomen, under the diaphragm. At this level, a person is likely to have strong opinions and an egocentric investment in being right. Conflict arises when others do not agree with a particular point of view, as one feels threatened by different perspectives and dissenting opinions. The self at this level tends to be identified with a mental egoic self-concept... They tend to place high value on logic and reason and on running things smoothly. Self-esteem is based more on the accumulation of achievements and status symbols (e.g., honors, titles, position of power) than on acquisition of personal possessions or sexual conquests. [19]

Experience of Structure

Q: What do you perceive-project at this level?

A: Beliefs systems, ideologies, symbols, language, thoughts, and artifacts.

The conceptual self, defined by belief systems, ideologies, concepts, thoughts, memories, opinions, symbols, knowledge, labels, and all other forms of mental representation, is the true creator of dualism. Through the advanced information-processing capacity of the neocortex, Being is able to reflect not only about the external world through internal representations, but on self. Self-awareness and self-reflection are thus made possible through the thought-producing capacity of the brain, and a whole new internal reality is created. You can directly experience this mental structure within yourself as the tendency to dissect, categorize, judge, deduce, define, separate, distinguish, and otherwise intellectually conceive the world, others, and yourself. This capacity is egocentric in the sense that it is an identification with personal thought processes, ideas, and beliefs.

When ego/self-consciousness/mind emerges from the bio-emotional realm, it begins to analyze and conceptualize exterior forms through internal imagery, symbol, and conceptual thought. In doing so, a certain sense of power and control emerges, as the modern mind conceives the world through the limiting mental structures of evolving definitions. As the ego's reflecting capacity advances, it gains a certain internal understanding of itself and its territory, consequently developing defense mechanisms that reinforce its identity to those images/symbols/concepts of mind, which is ego. Ego is here defined as the identity to the symbolic representations of the personal mind. With ego's intellectual knowing and understanding, there is a sense of control. Fear that the ego identity may lose control and power (over self and its environment) becomes a major source of concern, thus making necessary the creation of a series of inner defense mechanisms designed to retain control. This fear and its defense mechanisms represses the uncontrollable urges of the emotional-animal self, id, the physiological-sexual body, nature, and eventually the feminine principle, into unconsciousness.

To recapitulate, out of the physical-bio-emotional matrix emerges the mental symbolic representations of the mind, which are eventually identified with (ego) creating a sense of power and control. This sense of power and control represses the prior natural chaotic energies into their unconscious origins out of fear. Through this fear, we find the creation of defense mechanisms that guard the unconscious forces from consciousness. This unconscious repository stores the formative principles of ego, sexual libido, chaotic bio-emotional energies, aggressive animal instincts, and the functions of the physical body. We find this to be a necessary process in order for the "civilized" person to emerge.

The ego is concerned and aware only of itself and its thought processes. It is a duality-creating structure, separating itself from others and the environment through personal associations and the differentiation of everything that is not part of the ego-self. Its structure is defined by the memory of past experiences, associations of self-characteristics, and self-interested ambitions for future goals. The external world is classified according to learned and conditioned (fourth and fifth "reality creators") belief systems, dictated by parents, schools, and culture at large through a constant flow of information. This acculturation, or conditioning process, creates a subjective reality construct that is relative and limited to the individual's experiences and the time and place of birth.

The mechanics of conditioning were elucidated by behaviorist B. F. Skinner.[20] He defined the process of operant conditioning as the reinforcement of behavior through a reward system (positive reinforcement) or the termination of negative stimuli (negative reinforcement). I call conditioning the "fourth reality creator" because it impresses on the nervous system, through repetition, a neurological pattern of response. All belief systems are conditioned, enabling the continuation of certain paradigms and dogmas across the generations. A person with a Marxist-conditioned system of belief will see the world differently than a Capitalist, for example, filtering incoming perceptions through the conditioned networks of associations that were established through constant experience and repetition. Once the foundational imprints (third "reality creator") of the organism's personality are established, environmental influences further fine-tune the behavioral-perceptual filters through the process of conditioning. After each imprint establishes the general strategy, conditioning continues to adjust and shape the organism through repetition of stimuli. These are unconscious processes, thus creating the illusory perception of a set reality. Social realities are first imprinted, then social conditioning adds gender role, identity, status, persona, social role, and classification structures which further define the individual's perception of reality.

Finally there is learning (fifth "reality creator/perceiver"), which is a more flexible and superficial addition for reducing, categorizing, labeling, and defining incoming signals within the perceiving structures. One can learn and unlearn certain task-specific roles, languages, and other systems of belief, but the conditioned birth language, original identity pattern, and foundational family belief systems are much harder to break.

Of course, none of the above would be possible were it not for the development of the self-reflective human cortex. Through this convoluted, ramified, enfolding structure, Consciousness is able to reflect about itself through thoughts and symbols for the first time in our known cosmic history. Consciousness produces thoughts, which reflect the world in evolving capacities, via the vast interconnected circuitry of the human cortex. All cognitive processes, languages, visual imagination, and logic processing occur within the folds of this overgrown organ that has given humans a vast evolutionary edge over all other species on this planet. When most people speak of consciousness, it is this level that they refer to, as it is with the advent of this sophisticated bio-computer that mind emerges to think about itself and others in symbolic terms. Within the context of our explorations, Consciousness only becomes self-reflective in this level, but in it-Self is transcendent of thought, being the subjective witnessing sentience behind all thoughts.

Each fold and turn in the cortex has its specialized function. Each fold coordinates in concert with all other folds in order to establish the gestalt conscious experience that you are having right now. As we saw, signals are first scanned by the nervous reptilian brain to ensure that there is no danger. The thalamus then routes the signals through the emotional limbic brain to further asses the outside stimuli. Once safety is determined, the thalamus proceeds to project said signals into higher cortical regions for advanced computing and interpretation. Each human cortex computes and interprets incoming signals differently, depending on the person's conditioned and learned neural network connections. As a person grows, the neuroplastic (always branching, growing, interconnecting) nature of the cortex allows for a vast array of different neuronal pathways to get established. Therefore, every individual grows completely different neural architectural structures, differing as widely as there are human experiences. This, in turn, allows for the creation of our wildly complex world of diversified philosophies, ideologies, architectures, technologies, music, math, and all other cultural constructs. It is the flexible nature of the branching cortex that makes humans such fast learners, giving them the smart competitive edge over all other beings on this Earth.

The cortex is divided into two hemispheres. The left hemisphere is associated with logic, rationality, language, past/future orientation, and linear/serial processing, which correlates with our third level of consciousness. The right hemisphere is associated with spatial, aesthetic, intuitive, holistic, here/now orientation, and parallel processing, which as we will see correlates with our fifth level of consciousness.

The surface of the cerebral cortex is generally separated into four different sections called lobes. The temporal lobes hang on the underside of each side of the cortex and are responsible for audio processing, olfactory processing, pattern recognition, visual association, emotional processing (coordinated with the limbic system), and long-term memory processing (in coordination with the hippocampus). In addition to being a sophisticated integrator of sense data and patterns, the temporal lobe has been implicated in mystical states via endogenous or artificially induced temporal lobe seizures. Neuroscientist Ramachandran has even called the left temporal lobe the "God module," substantiating his claim with various case studies of patients suffering from brain epilepsy that describe their subjective experiences in mystical terms. Ramachandran suspects that elevated neural activity in the left lobe might contribute to mystical experiences in healthy mystics too. [21] We will return to this and other theorized "objective" brain states that reflect the deeper subjective states of mystical awareness in levels seven and eight.

Another lobe crucial to the transception and reconstruction of information is the occipital lobe, situated on the very back of the cerebral cortex. This lobe comprises what is called the primary visual cortex, which is where we actually "see" the world. In a very literal way, what we "see" is not "out there," but is rather reconstructed (via imprinted, conditioned, and learned neuronal patterns) onto the back wall of the cranial cavity. Light filters through the cornea, to then be projected via the retina to the back of the brain. The image is projected upside down, to then be normalized for the panoramic viewing by Witnessing Awareness. After it is internally conceived, it is projected outward *as if* it literally existed out there in its own terms. Of course, the "out there" we are familiar with does not exist independent of our brain, but is rather co-created through feedback loops with the transceiving structure. If we were able to see what Zen masters call "reality as it really is," we would undoubtedly see a completely different universe; most likely an undifferentiated ocean of whirling potential and chaotic energy waves of probability undulating with primal might (LSD, anyone?). Again, we will explore how to decondition the filters in order to probe the nature of reality in the higher transpersonal levels of consciousness.

The third pair of lobes, called the parietal lobes, are responsible for processing the sensations of touch and all outgoing motor commands. These lobes map spatial data in relation to body awareness, helping the body navigate "outer space" by first interpreting received sense data, to then send motor commands in response to said incoming data. This brain structure provides the "feel" and orientation in time and space of the whole body, and then moves it in relation to its position in space. It establishes a three-dimensional sense of self, creating the boundary between self and non-self in physical space. Another specialized function of the parietal lobes is its logical manipulation of abstract concepts, such as ideas, language, numbers, and other symbols of mathematics. This and other capacities are basically internal representations of our physical world, thereby providing the reasoning behind spatial orientation, our somatic intelligence, and our tactile knowledge of the world.

Finally we have the frontal lobes, which we will fully explore in level four. In relation to this level, however, we have a little module known as Broca's area, which sits underneath the frontal region. Broca's area is where speech originates, both spoken speech, which activates the motor cortex to move the mouth and project meaningful sounds (language), and inner speech, known as thinking, which does not activate motor activity. This brain center is active in all cognitive processes, helping Being think, plan, visualize, contextualize, and ideate about the moment to moment experience of reality. The inner "drunken monkey mind" chatter is most likely centered here, and helps generate the conceptualization of our world.

As we can see, all of these cortical structures are but sophisticated magnifications of earlier brain structures, but have added a whole new dimension to reality. Through thought and concept, Spirit has managed to experience its reality in a completely novel way. All cortical structures, along with the enfolded lower brains, act in harmonious coherence to deliver a real-time interpretation of reality. As we will soon explore, this process seems to function in a holographic fashion, where all holistic data exists in each of the parts. And, of course, if each neuron has inherent Awareness, as was explored in earlier chapters, then each neuron contains the entire human mind in a low resolution form, to then link up with other mini minds for the final product of the fully articulated human mind. Again, in this model mind does not magically manifest once all neurons come together in a specific way, but exists in low resolution form in each of the parts; from particle, to neuron, to brain, in the same way that the pixel contains the whole image in low resolution to then join with other pixels for the fully articulated image.

In this chapter we have examined the discriminating abilities of mind, which accesses past information in order to understand present experiences, all grounded in the complex circuitry of the human cortex. It works by associating learned and conditioned past experiences stored in the hippocampus's memory banks in order to constantly update and refresh its "inner" reconstructions of the "outer." The cortical conceptual mind then acts as a foundation for the creation of culture. With this mental structure in place, the stage is set for the next level of expression.

Exercises:

1.) Take some time and examine your thought patterns. What are you thinking? Where do these thoughts come from, and are there other ways to think about the world? Examine your belief systems, then read about other's beliefs. Find a belief system that you feel a very strong opposition against, such as the Nazi or Ku Klux Klan philosophy, and identify with it. Can you do it? Can you find the logic to it?

2.) Go to a school and witness the teaching process. How does learning take place?

3.) Read and stimulate your intellect. Explore reading material that you would normally stay away from. Learn new symbols and language systems and see how the world looks from those systems' perspectives. Study the logic of mathematics.

4.) Meditate on your third chakra, located in your solar plexus, and connect with the fire element. Feel the power that comes from thought/fire. Sense the connection between the discovery of fire and the ability to think. How has the primordial campfire stimulated the human mind and culture?

5.) Study the effects of psycho stimulants (caffeine, cocaine, amphetamines, methamphetamines, etc.) on brain and thought processes. Do they stimulate the thought-producing capacity of the brain, or is it an illusion of the drug? Consider neurosis and maladaptive mental programs. See how the repression of instinctual impulses-urges-drives-wishes manifest in the person's beliefs and thought patterns.

Further Personal Explorations

My mental level of Consciousness was initially imprinted in the Spanish language, as I attended first grade in Santiago, Chile. I learned how to read and write in Spanish while beginning my Chilean acculturation process at the age of six. The following year, while I was seven, my parents decided to move to California, as the economic and social pressures of a ruthless dictatorship pushed my parents away from their home country. Although sad and difficult for my parents, in hindsight I feel blessed to have been taken away from the Chilean all-Catholic homogenous culture so that my young mind could be exposed to the rich immigrant diversity of Los Angeles, California. My blossoming intellect was exposed to novel peoples, religions, cultures, and customs as we lived in a neighborhood where "Americans" were a minority. My best friends at the time, Ara, Chan, and Jose, were from Iraq, Vietnam, and Mexico, respectively, and our babysitter was from Lebanon. My neighbors were from Scotland, and we would spend some weekends with our Argentine friends. I learned English quickly as I repeated first grade and began the process of mind expansion through the schooling process.

Knowledge was always valued in my family, as I recall lively nightly discussions at the dinner table regarding politics, current events, religion, and philosophy. Questioning was encouraged, and passionate debate was the norm. This love of knowledge mostly stems from my maternal grandfather, the same man that gave us the explosive Basque temper gene. Tata Rodrigo loved books. He would be found late at nights in the dim light looking at his vast library, smelling his books, admiring them, and contemplating as he paced back and forth with a cigarette in one hand and a thick philosophical tome in the other. His love was philosophy, and I remember sitting in front of him mesmerized as he articulated the profundity of Kant, the vastness of

Hegel, the depth of Sartre, and the darkness of Nietzsche. He would pontificate about the art of thinking, while instantly entering an irate rant about the fascist imperialism of the West and the virtues of Marxist philosophy. An existentialist to the extreme and socialist at heart, the love of books and knowledge is a gift my grandfather gave me that has been a cognitive foundation for my entire life.

My whole family inherited this philosophical bent, and as I came of age my uncle Rodrigo and my cousin George continued to stoke my philosophical fire when they too migrated to California years later. We were a close family in those days, and as I matured I began to increasingly enter the mental world and alienate myself from peers at school. Eventually labeled a nerd, I retreated from social friendships and began reading voraciously. I loved philosophy and science, but was not fully initiated into the scientific method until my uncle Rodrigo gave me *God and the New Physics*, by Paul Davis, [22] and *The Rise of Life*, by John Reader. [23] These two books sparked a passion for understanding how the universe worked, where it all came from, and where it was all going.

By eighth grade I was reading books on quantum physics, cosmology, relativity, and evolution, and thought that science answered all of life's questions. I imprinted science's reality maps, and had no need for some supernatural God that managed things from a celestial throne in the gated community of heaven. I identified myself as an atheist and believed that the primal Singularity of physics *was* God. I viewed religion as superstitious and infantile, and saw it as a convoluted ploy to control the masses through fear. Alienated from other kids, I read through recesses and lunches, and happily spent time with my family on the weekends. I learned the language of music and began to play classical guitar at the age of eleven. I romanticized about being a Baroque composer, actually composing three complete concertos for guitar and orchestra. The alchemist's tower full of old manuscripts, innovative inventions, strange potions, and ancient instruments filled my young mental fantasies, providing a deepening fascination for the mysteries of our cosmos.

The love for knowledge and books is something that my partner and I continue to cultivate within our nuclear family. My kids also appear to have inherited this love for books, as every night I peek at my ten- and seven-year-old children to proudly find them immersed in some book. We encourage thought and inspire free thinking as our nightly dinners always include discussion on diverse topics. This love of learning is something I find missing in our standard educational system, as its obsessive focus on the "standard tests" all but kills the natural love for learning that all kids have. The typical "I don't like school" is indeed a sad state of affairs, as school should be the place where the child's mind is sparked with wonder and awe at our mysterious universe. Luckily our kids have us to ignite this love for learning, but others are not so blessed. TV often takes the place of dinner-table discussion, and we find a generation consumed by Beavis and Butthead and the dramas of the latest "reality shows." It is thus every parent's responsibility to supplement what our educational system sadly lacks: an interest and love for learning, and how to think for oneself.

To keep this level strong in myself, I attempt to read new information on a daily basis. Of course, the Internet makes this easy, as any and all info is available at the touch of a key. Interestingly enough, however, I have been less interested in new information and more dedicated to accessing levels of experience *outside* of thought, as I have found thought to be quite limited in scope. Thought never actually arrives anywhere, but produces never-ending loops of rationale and rationalization that actually keeps Awareness trapped in its limited cognitive structures. All thought is relative to each person's culture, time and place of birth, and life experiences, thus never actually revealing anything like Truth; only fragments of relative truths that often clash with other egocentric truths.

From this level of Consciousness, thought does unconsciously create reality, as its defining and labeling properties filter other signals that do not fit its particular reality map. A collection of repeated and habituated thought patterns produces a belief system, and belief systems act as molds that help define reality in its own terms. The limits of this structure are clearly seen in the ideological wars rampant throughout human history. Whether an event is God's will or the function of universal physical laws is dependent on the imprinted cortex perceiving said event. Relative views and paradigms are beautiful in a world rich in diversity, but become pathological when fueled by egocentric and irrational emotion.

Clearly some belief systems and thought patterns are dysfunctional and pathological, evidenced by the suffering they inflict on self or others. Nowhere have I been more privileged to witness the power of thought and belief than in my psychotherapy practice. Dysfunctional thoughts, as simple as "I am worthless" or "my life sucks," have the power to self-fulfill into actual life experiences. The way I describe it to clients is as follows: the more you practice a certain thought, the deeper it is imprinted to eventually become a belief. Thoughts and beliefs trigger feelings and emotions (level two), which in turn have a physical and behavioral response (level one), which feeds back in a self-reinforcing feedback loop into the belief system. The thought "I'm going to die" will generate fear and anxiety, which will trigger the stress response in the body with a racing heart, chest and stomach pain, and shortness of breath, which in turn will feed back and validate the original thought/belief in the augmenting negative spiral of the full-blown panic attack.

For example, a young twenty-five-year-old woman comes to my office presenting with symptoms of depression. Upon examination it is revealed that at the age of eight, she was told by her stepmom that she was unlovable. This thought echoed in her mind for years, becoming an actual belief and unconsciously generating feelings of worthlessness and depression. The depression, of course, had the physiological response of low serotonin levels and the behavioral consequence of fatigue and lethargy. Psychiatry focuses on only the first level, prescribing her a selective serotonin reuptake inhibitor (SSRI), such as Prozac, and sending her home without ever exploring the root cause of her depression. SSRIs block the reuptake of serotonin, therefore allowing more serotonin to be available to stimulate all the postsynaptic receptors for serotonin.

As we probed the foundational belief that stepmom had programmed into her young mind, the young woman eventually was able to see the fallacy in such belief and began the slow process of reprogramming herself with a more positive program. She realized that by believing, at the deepest level, that she is lovable, her depression began to lift. Knowing that she was lovable decreased her depression and gave her enough energy to pursue self-loving activities such as exercise and better nutrition. She was eventually able to get off of her Prozac, as her serotonin levels likely increased due to the new positive programming.

The therapeutic modality used in this case was cognitive-behavioral therapy, which focuses on changing maladaptive thoughts and core schemas (belief systems or programs) so as to change the correlated emotional and behavioral responses. Change your thought, and you change your emotional and physical state, just like changing a computer program will change its output. What becomes apparent is that the human cortex is programmable just like a computer is. This fact makes the school-age years critical in determining subsequent life experiences, as a maladaptive message can have devastating consequences as it lodges into the unconscious mind. A statement such as "you are dumb" can be like a virus, infecting the young mind toward believing and eventually living such reality.

More and more I have come to observe in myself and in my clients that there is a direct correlation between a quiet mind and a healthy state of mental health. The more cluttered the mind is with racing thoughts, the more disconnected the individual seems to be from others and their world. Furthermore, I have noticed that the more time someone spends obsessing about the future, the more anxious they tend to be, and the more time people dwell in the past, the sadder and more depressed they seem to be. Therefore, part of the therapy is to teach clients how to quiet their restless and oftentimes obsessive thinking, and how to refocus awareness in the present moment. This takes a little practice and work, but those who are able to minimize the random and often self-defeating thoughts seem to find more peace in their everyday life.

One class of drugs makes this quieting of the mind practically impossible. The psycho stimulants, which include cocaine, amphetamines, and methamphetamines (variously called meth, crank, or speed), often accelerate mental processes to unmanageable rates. As such, this class of drug appears to stimulate level three Consciousness, as it ramps up thought processes and speeds up the racing mind to uncontrollable levels. Working in the foothills of Northern California, an area rampant with meth addiction, I have had the opportunity to work with many individuals struggling with this devastating addiction. Meth destroys lives, as I have witnessed beautiful young kids transform, in the course of two or three years of abuse, from tender, young, smart, and fit to skinny, pale, scarred, depressed, and confused addicts. With prolonged abuse, many enter psychotic states of mind, lose their teeth, and end up living in trashed environments infested with abuse of all types. Even though this drug activates and accelerates the thinking mind, it actually reduces and contracts Awareness to the contents of the racing mind. Consciousness becomes lost in the never-ending thoughts of the looping mind, reducing any Awareness of and for others, the environment, and life in general. This substance actually numbs the Self from body and emotional states and becomes increasingly imprisoned within the confines of random thoughts. Like the opiates, the addict eventually ceases to really get high, but uses the drug just to feel normal.

Cocaine is less common in the foothills, but has a similar profile. With effects lasting only twenty minutes as opposed to ten hours, and being much more expensive, it seems to circulate in the richer sectors of society. Coke is known as the "ego drug," as it makes people feel powerful and on top of their game. Also extremely physically addictive, when it wears off people often feel tired, depleted, and depressed, often forcing them to seek another line just to take the edge off. Again, by accelerating the thoughts of level three, it tends to decrease awareness of any other levels. Julien explains how cocaine works in the brain: "Cocaine has been known to potentiate the synaptic actions of dopamine, norepinephrine, and serotonin. Such potentiation occurs as a result of cocaine's ability to block the active reuptake of these three transmitters into the presynaptic nerve terminals from which they were released." Specifically, cocaine seems to mostly block the reuptake of dopamine, thus allowing the brain a brief flood of dopamine, resulting in the behavior-reinforcing and psycho stimulant properties of the reward system. Julien continues:

> Increased dopamine levels in the nucleus accumbens and other components of the dopaminergic reward system seem to be responsible for the euphoric/ addictive effects of the drug. Both dopamine and cocaine decrease the discharge rate of neurons located in both the ventral tegmental area and nucleus accumbens, indicating that dopamine exerts inhibitory effects on the postsynaptic receptors. Cocaine markedly potentiates this dopamine-induced decrease in discharge rate: such potentiation occurs secondary to blockade of dopamine reuptake, potentiating its inhibitory action on postsynaptic receptors. [24]

Amphetamines are structurally similar to dopamine, both having as an amine nucleus base the phenylethylamine molecule, and are also called "sympathomimetic agents" due to the fact that they mimic the actions of adrenaline-epinephrine, the main transmitter of our sympathetic "fight-or-flight" nervous system. Julien reports how,

> amphetamines exert virtually all of their CNS effects by causing the release of newly synthesized norepinephrine and dopamine from presynaptic storage sites in nerve terminals....The behavioral stimulation and increased psychomotor activity appear to follow from the resulting stimulation of the dopamine receptors in the mesolimbic system. [25]

As with cocaine, the amphetamines cause their stimulating effect by flooding the brain with dopamine, and thus activating and accelerating many of the brain's functions. The issue with prolonged use of these drugs is that over time they begin to deplete the brain of its essential dopamine (and serotonin) supplies. Julien states how prolonged use can "cause long-lasting decreases in dopamine and serotonin in the brain. These changes appear to be irreversible." [26] If mental health is correlated with a quieter mind and a healthy supply of neurotransmitters, these drugs are not particularly useful in the process of growth, development, and evolution.

As Spirit continues its unfolding process within space and time, it begins to use this level to manifest the next dimension of reality. Thoughts are endlessly interesting, and as they come together to create the self-reflective cognition of the human, Being begins to organize them in order to fabricate the next spiral of evolution. The impulse in the heart of self-awareness continues to relentlessly push forward, as a mysterious Light beckons from beyond, calling the self-aware mind to levels of experience light-years beyond itself. And so Consciousness leaps to its next level of Self-expression.

Level 4

Social Role- Identity: Personality Plane

Phylogenic Expression

With the mental structures now in place, we enter the next phase in the evolution of Consciousness as expressed through the human race. Village systems and division of labor begin to propagate around the continents. As knowledge expands, more tools are invented, thus accelerating the production process and increasing the cultural expansion of the various villages. Civilization is born, group specialization gains momentum, money systems are invented, and we witness an exponential growth in population and cultural expression. Music, art, and engineering systems begin to evolve as an increased dialogue between people expands the development of knowledge.

Historians tell us that the first organized groups initiating the "dawn of civilization" lived in four fertile river valleys around six thousand years ago; the Tigris and Euphrates Rivers in Mesopotamia (Middle East), the Nile River in Egypt, the Indus River in India, and the Huang He or Yellow River in China. In these lush, fertile valleys, people settle and begin constructing villages around their agrarian societies. The earliest towns, such as Jericho and Catal Huyuk, develop near what was known as the fertile crescent of Mesopotamia around 7000 BC. These towns develop through division of labor, as social classes begin to take shape and an efficient mode of production accelerates growth.

The first cities, such as Eridu, Kish, Ur, Uruk, and Sumer, are constructed around five thousand years ago. In Sumer, south Mesopotamia's "land between two rivers," rich farming people build some of the world's first cities, each city part of a city-state ruled by a king. Initially, important family members rule the towns, passing down the developed role to the next generation within the family. These leaders eventually become kings and queens, a monarchy, creating laws that others have to follow, and a taxation system that allows for the construction of massive building projects. In time, the ruling class becomes firmly established with the help of an obedient warrior class, and we witness the birth of government. The ruling class, along with the priest class who can "speak" to the mythic polytheistic deities of the time, begins to manage and distribute the surplus of food and resources as people now begin working for the government.

Around 3100 BC, Sumerians begin to write using picture language, which then develops into a shorter form called cuneiform script using marks on clay. Sumerians also develop fine jewelry, wheel-made pots, and the first wooden-wheeled carts and chariots. The Egyptians begin using picture writing called hieroglyphics, using paper made from papyrus reed, around five thousand one hundred years ago. For the first time humans begin to record events, thus initiating what we call recorded human history.

Through the introduction of social stratification, the "cradle of civilization" gives rise to law-codes, centralized governments, slavery, organized warfare, and empires, as the Neolithic era slowly comes to a close. At around 3000 BC, King Narmer establishes the first known dynasty by uniting Upper and Lower Egypt in one of the first nation-states. By about 2350 BC to 2295 BC, Emperor Sargon attacks and conquers Sumer, thereby establishing the world's first empire. Known as the Akkadian empire, Sargon establishes the world's first standing army with paid soldiers. It appears that Consciousness at this point in history enters a new level of expression; a level self-identified in terms of social roles and governed by the "heroic" and conquering ego. Ego begins to crystallize around the undifferentiated *archaic* and *magical* Awareness of the earlier horticultural and pastoral groups, initiating its vast historical campaign of control, suppression, domination, and power.

Due to these social developments, vast temples and pyramids are able to be constructed around four thousand seven hundred years ago, by mainstream estimates, to acknowledge, worship, and honor the polytheistic mythic gods and goddesses of the *mythic* structure of consciousness. Magnific mythical deities that rule the world like kings and queens. Some human kings and queens are even viewed as godly, giving them supreme power over the over-worked masses as they accumulate vast wealth and resources through taxation and tributaries. Slaves (or possibly lost advanced technologies) are used to build these monolithic structures, taking decades and even centuries to complete. Innovative building techniques, mathematics, and technologies continue to rapidly evolve, helping the city-states grow into emerging empires. The invention of the alphabet and the number system allows for communication over vaster distances. Societies continue to become increasingly stratified, eventually changing their structure of governance from convening circles of tribal elders to the hierarchically organized states. As we saw, this development transforms the groups of Neolithic pastoral-agrarian communities into the vast, archaic empires of Babylonia, Egypt, India, and China.

By around four thousand to five thousand years ago, Near Eastern metalworkers make bronze for the first time by mixing tin and copper. This innovation marks the end of the Stone Age and welcomes in the Bronze Age, which gradually spreads to other parts of the world. Bronze and other precious metals are used as currency, and people begin their historical fascination with jewels and beautiful artifact. The Bronze Age also makes possible the production of a whole new range of tools and weapons. By 2500 BC, Mesopotamian farmers use bronze-tip plows, and standing armies acquire more sophisticated weapons that enable the empires to spread across the lands. By 1500 BC, bronze is widespread from Portugal to China and India, and first appears in the New World by around 900 BC.

It is believed that the Iron Age has its origins with the Hittites of Anatolia, Turkey around three thousand two hundred to three thousand seven hundred years ago. This stronger metal makes sharper, stronger, and more durable blades for tools and weapons, spreading throughout the Middle East and Greece by 1700 BC. This innovation accelerates and refines agricultural production, the building of ships and cities, and the conquering of neighboring states through armed invasions.

Metal and the production of complex agricultural machinery make possible mass production of food, increasingly freeing the masses to pursue other activities. Artifacts are developed and sold, the market place teems with activity, and a vast proliferation of cultural movement begins to expand the collective consciousness. "The Iron Age technologies make possible the mobility of armed bands (traveling in ships constructed by the use of metal tools) which initiates the proto-imperial predator state—male oriented, macho, free booting, warlike, lawless, rapacious." [1] Identifying with mental processes and the power that comes from understanding, and the manipulation of the environment through the use of new tools, male ego begins its campaign of domination over smaller communities, women, and nature. Sophisticated weapons are developed to protect the now established territories and property, and theocratic empires begin to flourish. Monarchy and a ruling class are now firmly in place, using control tactics aided by the mythically-based priest class to govern the masses. The "law" is established and a hierarchical structure of control is set up to rule the people. This hierarchy establishes a series of roles and identity structures that place individuals within a defined social system. Emperors, Kings, Queens, priests, serfs, merchants, soldiers, farmers, slaves, etc., become a reality as individuals begin to identify not only with mental processes, but also with defined social castes and roles. The egocentric structures expand to ethnocentrism. [2] People begin to identify themselves with particular ethnic groups, racial differences, gender roles, and ideological/religious paradigms, as well as the roles played within their society. This mythic, male-dominated, armed empire structure is of course epitomized by the rise of the Roman Empire by 753 BC, spreading, influencing, and "Westernizing" all of Europe until the empire's eventual collapse in 476 AD.

On the shores of the Mediterranean Sea around four thousand years ago, a major leap in Consciousness quietly occurs, as nature philosophers in classical Greece pioneer theories of the world based on observation and reason. This initiates a new structure of consciousness that begins to slowly replace the mythical supernatural gods and goddesses with observable natural laws. Pre-Socratic philosophers evolve and transmute the mythic "heroic mind" of Homer, for example, into the visionary, theoretical, and ultimately rational mind epitomized by Plato and Aristotle. This rationality, along with the advent of quantitative measurement, provides Western civilization with the cognitive tools used to build the modern world of the *rational* structure of consciousness. [3]

Eventually, continuous empires begin to break down and collapse into noncontinuous empires and Feudal-state nations. The Feudal-state era then flourishes with vast architectural progress and rational exploration. Science and philosophy begin flirting with ideas, and the new mental structure of rationality emerges from the mythic power structures of the day.

During the age of classical Greece, around 500 BC, the Greeks lead the world in the development of art, architecture, politics, philosophy, and science as they look for explanations for why humans are the way they are. Schools are set up to teach, educate, and develop knowledge as Herodotus of Halicarnassus writes the first great world history in 450 BC. In 399 BC Socrates is condemned to death for his rational thought and for neglecting the mythical gods and goddesses that were to be worshipped in the ornate and opulent temples of the Greek empire.

Nomadic peoples are historically *archaic, magical*, and early *mythic* polytheistic pagans throughout the Neolithic Era, worshiping Nature, Mother Earth, and spiritual/magical forces that are to be celebrated and honored through tribal ritual, sacrifice, and shamanic technique. After the agricultural revolution, the magical forces of nature begin to get personified as mythic gods and goddesses that control the world through unseen forces, as humans could now control and predict aspects of the once magical natural world. Rationality then eventually emerges and unfolds from the mythic world, analyzing, reducing, and measuring the world into separate parts understandable to the human intellect.

Settled on the Eastern banks of the Mediterranean about 3000 BC, a group of tribal people known as the Hebrews (later becoming the Jews) are the first people in history to abandon the worship of the many gods of Mesopotamia for the worship of a single, all-powerful God. Born in Mesopotamia around 2000 BC, Abraham, known as the founder of Judaism, hears the voice of the One God who instructs him to go west in search of the "promised land" in Canaan. Around 1950 BC God "speaks" to Abraham, stating "I will assign this land to your offspring," and the Jewish people settle in their "holy land."

Some of these Hebrew tribes, known as Semites or Israelites, migrate north to Egypt in search of more fertile lands due to a famine in Canaan. They soon find themselves alienated and enslaved by the Egyptian Pharaohs, who eventually order the drowning of all male Israelite babies as they fear the Israelites might gain power in Egypt. One baby, known as Moses, is sent down the river and is rescued by an Egyptian woman who ends up raising him. As Moses comes of age, he becomes well respected by the Egyptians, eventually convincing the Egyptian Pharaohs to free the Israelites from slavery. The Pharaohs agree and Moses leads his people in 1200 BC to the "promised land" of Canaan in what is known as the Exodus. By this time the Jewish faith is well established, as the Jewish people worship the one God, Yahweh. Moses is reminded by the burning bush that there is only one true God, and that there are Ten Commandments that people must follow in order to lead a moral life as written in their holy book *Torah* and the Old Testament of the *Bible*. The Israelites reach Canaan forty years after the Exodus, and by 1020 BC Saul unites the twelve separate tribes as the ruler of Israel. By 200 BC, Greek rulers outlaw the Jewish religion and force the people to worship the polytheistic Greek gods and goddesses. By the turn of the millennium, Israel comes under the rule of the Roman Empire, which also forces the people to worship their gods.

In 4 BC Jesus Christ is born to the Jewish carpenter Joseph and his wife Mary, so the story goes. A remarkable activist, mystic, and revolutionary, Jesus grows up to eventually threaten the Roman polytheistic rule with his doctrine of the one God, claiming to be the "Son of God" and telling people to love one another. Threatened by this charismatic personality, the Roman Emperor orders the execution of Jesus and destroys Jerusalem by 70 AD. During this time, the Middle Eastern people are ravaged by wars and conquests, unable to organize under some guiding principle due to unending conflict. In 622 AD, the prophet Mohammed arrives and unifies the warring tribes of the Middle East under the one God Allah, bringing to the area the Islamic faith as dictated to him and written in the holy book *Qur'an*.

The monotheistic religions were likely birthed from their prophets' mystical experience. As such, these individuals most likely accessed the higher transpersonal levels of consciousness at a time when people's general stage of development was quite a bit lower. This created the unfortunate consequence of later interpretations of the genuine insights, which were run through the egocentric and ethnocentric mythic filters of the time, creating vast historical consequences. In other words, a direct glimpse into the underlying Unified Field of creation, pure Consciousness, came to be interpreted as the privileged communication from an egoic male God who possessed the human qualities of jealousy, vengeance, judgment, and discrimination; clearly level three (mental-magic) and four (mental-mythic) interpretations of possibly level seven (subtle) and eight (causal) experiences. The male God, clearly reflecting the emerging ego-consciousness of the time, became the dominant deity who ruthlessly ruled the sinning world of creation from His celestial abode.

Buddhism, blossoming around 534 BC from the teachings of the Buddha (the awakened one), formerly Prince Siddhartha Guatama of India, offers a slightly different take on spirituality. Buddha realizes that the Unified Field is the nature of everything and reports that everyone must experience the transcendent for him- or herself, beyond words and dogmas. Therefore, he offers a set of meditation techniques designed to evolve consciousness into nondual realization. Clearly he was a flower before his time. Of course, Buddha was influenced by a much older system, the Vedas, which mean "knowledge," developed in ancient India around the Indus Valley by the Aryan people close to an estimated three thousand five hundred years ago. The Aryan people are believed to have migrated from the North-West, bringing the Vedas, the Sanskrit language, and an advanced system of practices and philosophy to the area. Rooted in shamanic traditions from the native Hindus Valley's tribal past, the Aryans mix and blend their traditions with the natives to create the Hindu religion. Embedded in their religion, these people develop Yoga as a systematic technology for experiencing the Divine. Being a society immersed in the mythic level of consciousness, many of the level seven and eight realities experienced by yoga practitioners, yogis and yoginis, are personified as the pageant of gods and goddesses that color current-day Hinduism.

After the death of Christ, Christianity and the church rise to power when Roman Emperor Constantine changes the state religion to Christianity in 312 AD and uses the teachings of Jesus Christ to begin a global campaign of conversion. The Judeo-Christian-Islamic monotheistic religions all begin their independent campaigns of control, often fighting amongst each other in the name of their respective God as they lose all connection to their mystically-derived origins. The crusaders and missionaries are sent throughout the world to convert the "ignorant and savage" masses, burning the heathen witches and destroying the infidel indigenous cultures throughout the globe.

As Rome adopts Christianity as its main religion, it gives power to the Bishops so that they may manage the various villages and towns as the sole moral authority, and Christianity spreads throughout Europe.

After the fall of the Roman Empire and during the rise of the Byzantine Empire around 476 AD, Christianity begins to make changes to the classical culture and thought of Greece. It adds to the medieval belief system of the time the concept of a world creator who is both the prime mover and the ultimate moral judge of all things. The idea of God is now brought into the light of reason by scholars such as St. Augustine and Thomas Aquinas. Through theirs and others influences, the rationality of the Greeks is conserved but retooled to include the Ultimate Clockmaker: the One who wound up the universal clock at the beginning of time. This belief system becomes grounded in the various technologies of the day, such as the windmill, watermill, clock, horse-drawn carriage, and oxen-drawn agricultural machinery.

Around the sixteenth and seventeenth century, medieval Europe begins to feel further shifts in the collective consciousness, as it embraces the concepts of Giordano Bruno and Galileo Galilei that the universe is a giant machine. Technologies begin to proliferate as the scientific methods and discoveries begin to extract the secrets of Mother Nature in ever more reliable ways. This expansive and prolific era, which begins during the Renaissance, sets the foundation for our modern world.

In1619, Rene Descartes expounds his famous philosophy of dualism. He divides the world into the objective sphere of matter, the domain of science, and the subjective sphere of mind, the domain of religion. [4] Through this Descartes manages to free scientific exploration from the orthodoxy of the all-powerful church reigning over much of Europe. Descartes borrows the idea of objectivity from Aristotle, who expounded the basic notion that objects are independent of and separate from the mind.

Descartes also makes contributions to the laws of physics, which scientifically enshrine his idea that the world is a machine. However, it is Newton (1642–1727) and his contemporaries going into the eighteenth century who solidly establish materialism and its corollary, the principle of causal determinism. This principle is the idea that all motion can be predicted exactly given the laws of motion and the initial conditions of the object. [5] Through the rise of materialism, reductionism, and the mechanistic worldview, the mythic gods begin their slow death as they are replaced by the new scientific/rational paradigm. The world begins to be conceived as an orderly machine, predictable and replaceable when the constituent parts don't work. A writing economy begins to solidify the laws, doctrines, and dogmas, reinforcing social, political, religious, and scientific realities that are learned and accepted by the masses as "truths."

Through the successful progress of rationality and the scientific paradigm, we witness a renaissance in production and creativity. Around 1650 the Age of Reason emerges, ushering in the Enlightenment, where philosophers such as Voltaire, Rousseau, and Thomas Paine argue that society should be organized according to rules based on reason and rational thought, rather then on religious belief. By 1750 in Britain, people begin using steam-powered machines for weaving and spinning clothes, as people flock from farms and villages to work the new machines in buildings called "manufactories." Here we witness the birth of the first industrial towns. Manufacturing factories expand and mass production initiates the industrialization of the world through the Industrial Revolution. In the 1800s the steam engine, the printing press, and later the burning of oil accelerate this process as the mechanical model raises the average standard of living. The once continuous empires are now noncontinuous empires called colonies, federal states, and nations, with machine-mechanical production lines that allow for the mass production of artifacts. Information flow begins to accelerate and planetary connectivity increases in complexity.

This rational stage's later development has been called the modern-industrial era, where justice and civilized, democratic treatment of humans allow a rise in social ethics. Scientific exploration increases the knowledge base of humanity and, through instrumental productivity, manages to liberate much of the slave labor of the times. On the other hand, scientific rationality begins to also slowly kill spirit and nature. It initiates the vast devastation of the ecological system through their influencing repression and control of nature insinuated by their evolving materialistic theories and practices. As Wilber explains:

> The it-domain was growing like a cancer—a pathological hierarchy—invading and colonizing and dominating the I and the we domains. The moral decisions of the culture were rapidly being handed over to science and technical solutions. Science would solve everything.
>
> All problems in the I domain and the we domain were converted to technical problems in the it-domain. And thus science (theoretical and technical) would not only solve all problems, it would decide what was a problem in the first place—It would decide what was real and what was not. [6]

The "It" domain means the empirical objective realm of science, and the "I" and "we" domains mean the subjective realms of mind and religion.

Thus the vast problems of modernity and industrialization emerge from this new structure. The mechanistic worldview, the destruction of nature, the birth of an analytic and fragmented world, the displacement of social cohesion, the collapse of religious sensibility, the rise of male domination, and the cancer of the military-industrial complex dictating the lives of the masses begin to rule the planet. Although these problems are vast and have currently reached a critical point within our planetary system, Wilber reminds us that this stage also importantly brought what he calls the "dignities of modernity," which include "the liberation of slaves, of women, of the untouchables." [7]

The mechanical, rational, law-and-order, mathematical, and logical worldview begins to reach its limit as the undeniable destruction of the biological systems and the rampant social and ethnic wars roam the planet. This fragmented and unsustainable world of industrialized pollution and military male aggression reaches disproportionate levels in the First and Second World Wars of the twentieth century. The realization that planetary resources are limited dawns in the minds of the very few, as the eroding toxins of the industrialized pollution begin to sicken populations living in crowded cities.

From this dawning reality, we witness the emergence of a collective existential crisis. The dark existential philosophies of Sartre and Nietzsche, for example, begin to haunt the minds of the collectivity. The apparent collapse of the world and the "preoccupation with death overshadow any transient joy. Hence the stereotype of an existential realist is morose rather than jovial." [8] Four main themes run through existentialist thought, namely subjectivity, meaning, freedom, and free will. [9] Existentialists maintain that each individual human being has the birthright to choose his or her attitudes, purposes, values, and actions. Friedrich Nietzsche argued, "Since God is dead (i.e., the illusion of religious mythic beliefs have now been replaced by the cold, heartless sciences), we will have to rethink the whole foundation of our lives and find our meaning and purpose in human terms alone" (parenthesis mine). [10]

From the existential dissatisfaction with conformity to the sad, war-ridden social realities of the day, we witness a movement into postmodernist thought. Surrealism, cubism, nihilism, jazz, and the beat generation begin to deconstruct the rational paradigm into culture-context-bound, relative interpretations of reality. All is perceived as relative, empty, and consequently all arguments loosing their intrinsic meaning. No view is better than the other, but rather is bound to the experiences of each individual.

With meaning being a relative construct of each individual and each culture, a generation wanders in existential despair, searching for something that would free them from the empty void of reality and its lack of meaning.

This collective existential crisis lays the foundation for a new model of reality: a paradigm shift that would change the constricting, cement-bound rationality of the domesticated culture. The existentialists and beats, unable to integrate due to their obsession with the deconstruction of the industrial-rational paradigm, express their urge for change through art (surrealist, cubist, etc.), poetry, and music (jazz). Tim Leary describes this shift in music:

> Jazz suddenly popped up at the height of the industrial age, eroding its linear values and noninteractive styles. A factory society demands regularity, dependability, replicability, predictability, conformity. There is no room for improvisation or syncopated individuality on a Newtonian assembly line; so it was left to the African American, who never really bought the factory culture, to get us boogying into the postindustrial quantum age. [11]

The limits of linear rational thought, cause and effect mechanical determinacy, three-dimensional Euclidean geometry, and Newtonian solidity begin to come to surface during this time, as the Einsteinian relativistic formulas and quantum interconnectivity, nonlocality, and indeterminacy are birthed. The sciences, paralleling the arts and the social movements of the time, begin to uncover the notion that the world is much stranger then the rational mind originally conceived. Relativistic physics shows that reality is relative to position, velocity, and frame of reference, and that mass is really bound-up energy as expressed in the immortal $E=mc^2$ equation. Quantum mechanics paves the way to a subjective, observer-created universe, as light is discovered to be a particle (photon) or frequency (wave), depending on the instrument (extension of human perceptors) used to observe it. The uncertainty behind the position of an electron if momentum is measured, or the uncertainty of momentum if position is measured, defined in Heisenberg's Uncertainty principle, further relays the observer dependence of actualities. [12] Reality, at the quantum subatomic level in physics, is experimentally shown to be composed out of probability waves that collapse as soon as an observation, measurement, or perception is made. [13, 14]

These paradigm-shattering discoveries and concepts begin to leak into the collectivity, as they are backed by the new electronic technologies of the day: radios, telegraphs, and eventually black-and-white television sets and the telephone. The world is ready for something new. The old war mentality and the industrial pollutants are seen for what they are, and the people are ready for change.

Ontogenetic Expression

Recapitulating the rise of civilization, the industrialized age, and modernity, children mature into adolescents (approximately twelve to nineteen years of age) with more or less capacity for rational thought. Symbols and language are fully mastered and the adolescent begins the exploration of self-identity and that of social roles within the larger society. Piaget describes the cognitive abilities of this stage, calling it formal operational, where the individual develops the capacity for deductive and abstract reasoning. [15] Here the individual can think not only about the world, but think about thinking. Also, the ability for hypothetical, deductive, or propositional reasoning (if *a,* then *b* logic) arises, which gives the individual the ability to apprehend higher and more complex relationships. Formal operational thought is characterized by adaptability and flexibility. Adolescents can think in abstract terms, use abstract symbols, and draw logical conclusions from a set of observations. Personal realizations, theories, opinions, concepts, and ideas are now developed as the individual grows more independent from parents and the family unit.

In Kohlberg's terms, the adolescent enters the postconventional, or principled, level of moral development. [16] The individual at this stage of development can now hold values and principles that are valid and applicable outside the authority of the groups and persons enforcing those principles. He described this level as having a "social-contract" orientation, where correct behavior is defined by basic individual rights and social standards that have been agreed upon by the entire society. Acculturation and socializing forces come in full force at this stage, for hormonal, sexual, and other developmental changes unleash a series of creative and rebellious forces within the individual. In a conflicting drama between social conformity and the young, idealistic pursuit for freedom, adolescence is marked by confusion. [17]

In the midst of this confusion, while intense hormonal and physiological changes are occurring, the adolescent searches for a sense of identity. How to act, who to be, and where to fit in become dominant themes in the youth's mind. [18] Role models are sought, and media and popular culture begin to play a central role in the individual's search for who he or she is. Erikson described this psychosocial stage as 'identity versus identity confusion.' [19] The adolescent begins to question old role models and identifications from childhood and begins experimenting with new and more "hip" roles. The fundamental question of "who am I" unleashes a series of provocative modes of being, self-expression, and self-image. Purple hair and pierced eyebrows, for example, mark this search for an authentic way to be. "The sense of ego identity, then, is the accrued confidence that the inner sameness and continuity prepared in the past are matched by the sameness and continuity of one's meaning for others, as evidenced in the tangible promise of a 'career'." [20] The pressures from society begin to impinge on the developing personality career decisions and tangible social roles, many times producing the identity confusion that is common throughout adolescence.

A sense of identity and belonging then begins to develop, and the individual begins to identify who he or she is in relation to others like himself or herself. Maslow articulated this stage as having the need for belonging; defining one's self through a sense of identity with others like oneself. [21] Teens reach out, trying to fit in and feel like they belong, as they seek close relationships with others to feel part of a group. Social groups (e.g., jocks, nerds, goths, mods, punks, gangs, etc.), sports teams, ethnicity groups, gender identification, and racial classes begin to differentiate themselves, creating an ethnocentric identification process reflecting our early human history of social stratification.

Personality patterns begin to acquire specific characteristics of self-definition and self-worth, forming a strong self-esteem if successfully developed or poor self-esteem if not. Maslow's fourth need for esteem develops concurrently with the sense of belonging, as the teen identifies his or her self-worth and self-esteem through his or her sense of belonging. [22] This need for esteem manifests as a desire for status, appreciation, popularity, fame, recognition, and respect from others. When these needs are not met, the adolescent tends to feel inferior, weak, or helpless. These patterns can remain throughout life, but are established at this stage. They are inextricably linked to the various ethnocentric, group-centric, image and role identities thus explored. If the first level, physio-survival, is physical self-preservation, then the third level, mental-egocentric, is "mental self-preservation." Similarly, the second emotional level is physical group preservation, as the fourth, social role ethnocentrism, is "mental group preservation."

The main event triggering these processes within the individual's life is the emergence of the biological program to procreate. Sexuality and the instinctual drive to mate are responsible for the individual's preoccupation with image, looks, identity, and courting rituals. Dr. Leary describes: "During this stage the sexual imprint is laid down, the fourth reality defined, and a sexual-impersonation role selected. Sex-role experimentation is passionately experimented with. Contelligence is obsessed with courting rituals, display, sexual exploration…." [23]

Accordingly, Freud called this level the genital stage of psychosexual development, which occurs at the onset of puberty with the maturation of the reproductive system and the production of sex hormones. He describes how the libidinal energy returns to the sexual organs, making the genitals the main source of sexual tension and pleasure. Also at this stage, energies are invested in forming friendships and preparing for marriage.

The foundations for the social role, identity structure, and personality patterns are thus established at puberty. Social morals and the ethics of society are conditioned into the behavior of the individual, "civilizing" him/her into a sense of loyalty to society, state, and nation. As the adolescent grows into a young adult, marriage and careers placing them snugly into an accepted social context become of focal importance. Responsibilities to the "system," taxes, and living within the whole of bureaucratic institutions define the various social realities, reinforced by the daily news and television.

This shift from experimental adolescent to conforming young adult is in large part dictated by physiological processes, specifically triggered by mating. Leary explains, "At the time of impregnation, powerful biochemical and neurological changes occur which produce nesting and child-protecting responses." [23] These physiological-neurological changes that occur through the mating process domesticate the individual into law-abiding citizens of the state, with political, religious, and occupational identities that define their place within the social fabric. Status and social prestige become a major goal, and a variety of personas, or social masks, are developed for various social and cultural situations. These are all motivated by the desire to maintain and support a family.

After adolescence, the individual goes through a series of stages that mainly strengthen, integrate, and develop the identity-personality structure. Erikson described the 'intimacy versus isolation' stage, where health is defined by the ability of the individual to develop intimate relationships, and isolation by the inability to do so. [24] If successfully developed, this stage marks a successful marriage-family life. The person is well accepted and integrated into the overall matrix of society. 'Generative versus self-absorption' describes the level of contribution, or lack of, to the whole of society. And finally, in Erikson's final stage, we have 'ego integrity versus despair.' This is the point where the individual comes to terms with his or her life and faces the end years with either wisdom and compassion, or despair and a fear of death. Despair and the contemplation of death can also happen, however, at any point in the individual's life. This marks what has been called the existential crisis.

It should be mentioned that the highest level discussed by the Western psychology pioneers of consciousness is that of the integrated identity-personality within an orderly societal structure. The early fathers of Western psychology had no experience of transcendent states, usually labeling them pathologic or dysfunctional. Consequently, it is at this point that we depart from the personal, independent, and rational Being in order to explore the transpersonal, interdependent, and transrational levels of who we are.

At some point in the development of the individual, the idea or experience of death is unavoidably encountered. This inevitably puts the individual face to face with the harsh reality of Buddha's first noble truth: the existence of suffering, impermanence, old age, sickness, and death. [25] These realities, inherent in a separate existence, bring about what has been called the existential crisis, and a sense of despair, angst, and the futile meaninglessness of all actions is confronted. How can one enjoy life knowing that all is temporary and will soon end some day? In Vaughan's words:

> In the face of meaningless the existentialist attempts to create meaning through individual action in the world, but even the most heroic efforts cannot overcome ontological anxiety. From this perspective there is no way to overcome existential dread. The separate self is always eventually overcome by death. [26]

Thus we come to the end of the personal road. Death, being unavoidable, must be confronted and made friends with. This can only happen through a progressive expansion and shift of identity. An identity that is no longer defined by external forces but by internal intuitive factors, as we will see, is the only way out of the ontological horror of complete termination and annihilation. Spirit's journey has only just begun, for now it begins to awaken from its dream, uncovering the various layers that conceal its original Essence.

Experience of Structure

Q: What do you perceive-project from this level?
A: Personalities, identities, roles, scripts, social groups, ethnicity, and the entire social world.

This level or structure of consciousness has been defined as that which identifies with various social roles and culturally sanctioned identities. This is the world of doctors, police officers, politicians, lawyers, fathers, nurses, philosophers, Americans, Muslims, Socialists, Chileans, Republicans, driver's license holders, etc. The list goes on, for it is the structure that creates our social world of psychodynamic associations and relationships, never before witnessed in cosmic history. Ethnocentric in nature, where identity defines itself in relationship to groups, this psychological structure lives in a world full of internal divisions. These divisions are expressed in our current world as national, religious, economic, and political boundaries. The lines drawn on our globe are the direct expression of our internal biases, classifications, identifications, and judgmental divisions. This internal structure is naturally expressed in our societal structures, our cities, stratified bureaucracies, class systems, and the thousands of institutions that govern our world.

With an understanding of this level of consciousness/reality, we can continue with our story of how the personal unconscious came to be. With the rise of civilization and then modernity, the rational heroic ego needed to suppress the animal-instinctual id into unconsciousness in order to "civilize" and create order in society. The creation of the superego, which is the internalized collective socializing-conditioning forces that make sure that kids through schooling develop the mental-rational faculties and later an ego-role personality, begins to suppress the sexual-animal-emotional-instinctual wishes, urges, impulses, and drives that are not "civilized." Thus the superego, an internal structure reflecting the norms of the consensus that form an orderly society, comes into being.

The rational mind and ego are shaped by culture, which insists on the repression of the uncontrollably chaotic wild impulses and desires of the id into the unconscious (this being the root of neurosis in the individual and society, according to Freud). This process consequently creates much fear and myth about the unknown, nature, and the inner contents of the psyche. Through the development of this prudish, self-conscious, thinking mind, much of modernity's "dignities" flourish: democracy, human morality, ethics, etc., which transcended the animal "kill or fuck" instinctual impulses, as Wilber puts it. [27] Instead of acknowledging and channeling said "irrational" energies, however, such as through adolescent rites of passage or vision quests practiced by diverse aboriginal groups, they are repressed into the shadows of the unconscious. Here they eat away at people through diverse neurotic pathologies and destructive practices.

Frager and Fadiman describe the superego as such:

> The superego serves as a judge or censor over the activities and thoughts of the ego. It is the repository of moral codes, standards of conduct, and those constructs that form the inhibitions for the personality...As conscience, the superego acts to restrict, prohibit, or judge conscious activity, but it also acts unconsciously. [28]

It is clear that this process develops over time as society and culture conditions young minds into the consensual values of the group. Only through this structure are we able to have the "dignities of modernity" in a civilized world. [29] This civilized world enables an infinite variety of personality structures to relate and live in relative harmony, functioning productively and moving toward economic and material progress. Since superego (social conscience or identity—level 4) represses physiological forces (material—level 1), the id (bio-emotional instincts—level 2), and ego (some mental processes—level 3), the individual mostly identifies with this surface personality, leaving all prior structures buried within the personal unconscious. Identity and reality at this level are purely defined in terms of roles, nationalities, races, ethnicity, class, and gender, leaving the realms of nature, sexuality, and deeper mental structures repressed.

The newest part of the brain, believed to have developed around forty thousand years ago, is of course implicated in this role-identity structure. The neocortex, and more specifically the prefrontal cortex (PFC), which is in the front part of the frontal lobes, emerged to process and create self-identity. This structure is implicated in conscious identity, working short-term memory, learning, long-term planning, attention, focus, and what is called the executive self. The executive self (PFC) is responsible for integrating and contextualizing sense data and making appropriate voluntary motor decisions based on said data. It communicates with other parts of the brain via feedback loops to control both voluntary and involuntary behavioral output. The main feature is the PFC's ability to contextualize self in relation to others and make decisions, a crucial capacity for the "civilized" life. It defines and differentiates itself from others by creating associated networks of associations, integrating memories of past habits, and running self-referential feedback loops that reinforce and shape personality structures. This is the seat of the "decision maker," the ego-personality that acts in an increasingly complex world of other ego-personalities. Called by many the "fourth brain," the PFC can only develop after birth, and then only to the extent that the foundational triune system has successfully formed.

As we saw in the phylogenic and ontogenetic expressions of this level, the limits of this "small self" become clear in the face of the universal truth of impermanence. Separate existence will always come to an end. Pure identification with this transient structure, which creates the non-sustainable social realities of our industrialized culture, will unavoidably cause neurosis, pathology, and suffering. We have reached the limits of the non-sustainable sense of permanence rooted in short sighted, profit-driven economic growth and polluting practices as a collectivity, reflected in the many novel pathologies, diseases, and sufferings of our present era. The new generation feels the evolutionary drive to change and transform itself into something new, as a deep Light beckons and whispers the promise of a new possible world.

Exercises:

1.) Contemplate your social roles, personas, and various cultural identities. How identified are you with your ethnic background, your race, your gender role, or your political/ religious belief systems? Take time to observe yourself, your personality traits and patterns. How do society and culture affect your behaviors, actions, and perceptions?

2.) Go to a busy city and observe the reality created by all of the interacting personalities and the hierarchy of social positions. Contemplate the structure of our institutions, our stratified bureaucracies, and the current boundaries of our world.

3.) Watch television and amuse yourself with the infinite dramas of personality games. How does TV convince us of the "reality of the world"?

4.) Study the culturally accepted drugs. See how nicotine defines a person's image (observe the hundreds of billboards and magazine ads) and how it contributes to the consuming mass-production mentality. Contemplate the coffee break and how it stimulates the "production line." Consider television as a cultural drug. How does Prozac contribute to the creation of an "authorized, normal" reality? Contemplate script/identity pathologies and existential despair.

Further Personal Explorations

Starting in high school, I remember this structure come on-line quite clearly, as I began noticing who is who and how I fit in. Although labeled a nerd by peers, I identified myself as a scientist, a philosopher, and seeker of truth. I felt proud to be a Chilean male and often differentiated myself from others by feeling "more worldly." Of course, these were all attempts by my teenage brain to find some sort of identity that was unique, different, and cool. Other identities included musician, rock climber, agnostic Chilean, son, brother, and friend. I looked to my father and mother as role models and was content to be the "intellectual kid."

As mentioned earlier, junior year came around along with the topic of girls. No longer content to be the nerd, I began to pay more attention to how I looked, what I wore, what I said, and how I acted. What others thought of me became much more crucial, and fitting in seemed more important than ever before. Luckily I had big muscles from rock climbing, weight lifting, and mountain biking, and was able to use them to enhance my budding sense of self and self-image. The need to belong and be a part of a social group became strong in those days, as the sense of not belonging could no longer be overlooked by my blossoming prefrontal cortex. I was not quite in the "popular group," but no longer was I a mere nerd. I hung out with a group of seniors who took Eddie and me into their clique, inviting us to parties and initiating our naïve minds into the socially disinhibiting properties of alcohol. My intellectual interests waned, as freedom and having fun took center stage in my life.

As time progressed, I matured and realized that who we are is deeper than a mere set of labels. Yet with college and the study of psychology, I nonetheless began to subtly identify myself as a social scientist, and with the advent of some life-changing experiences to be explored in the following chapters, my identity once again changed to that of a mystic, activist, psychonaut, yogi, and shaman. These identity structures defining my early twenties, unknown to me at the time, fed my ego in subtle ways, even though I prided myself on being "egoless." I found much power with these identities, even though they were based on experiences from far beyond the ego-personality. Maturing from those identities toward my thirties, I eventually shifted and began to identify myself as a psychotherapist, meditation teacher, husband, and father. Of course, I continue to use all of these identities at different points in my day-to-day life, as I use my body to navigate time-space, but no longer am I truly identified with any of them. In other words, they are mere masks used to navigate the social realities of our culture. At stage four of development, we identify completely with the identity labels, as in my teen years, but as we grow beyond these stale mental constructs we can begin to access deeper identities barely imagined by those who are merely their social roles.

I witness the formation of this level most clearly as I work with teenagers in my psychotherapy practice. Their main preoccupation seems to always revolve around self-image, self-worth, self-esteem, and belonging, as they try to define who they are in relation to their peers. Today's cliques, such as the jocks, nerds, stoners, goths, emos, gangsters, punks, and rockers, to name a few, tend to define the clothing style and their general way of being. Once a teen enters one of these cliques, their entire demeanor changes as they anxiously try to emulate and be like the others in the group. No longer fully influenced by parents, teens follow peer pressures as if their very survival depended on it. The work in therapy, if focused on this level and not the earlier stages, is about strengthening the ego, helping build a strong sense of self and a healthy identity. The balance is to support their exploratory nature and drive to be unique, while providing guidance so that they don't get too lost in the drama. This is an important stage of development, as the brain is in a state of exponential growth. Providing a positive and exploratory environment of acceptance sometimes is all a teen needs in order to process and move through these years successfully. Engagement in extracurricular activities such as sports, band, or youth groups can be quite valuable, as it provides the budding personality a healthy and secure social group to which they can belong. Positive influences are essential to the building of a healthy sense of self and personality.

When things don't go well and a teen is alienated, abused, picked on, or bullied, a general maladaptive personality pattern can develop. All personality and identity patterns are in essence story lines that minds unconsciously repeat to themselves, creating a script that either supports the healthy adult personality or an unhealthy one. Unhealthy patterns, if not addressed, can over time develop into what are called personality disorders, where the basic personality traits are what create problems for people in their life. For instance, dependent personalities, narcissistic personalities, histrionic personalities, and borderline personalities all have faulty scripts that continually generate conflictive relationships and problematic life experiences. The extreme disorder of split personality is one in which a person will shift between two completely different identity patterns, oftentimes creating much confusion and suffering for those who love them. These personality disorders are hard to work with in therapy. They often require the long-term relationship of consistent psychotherapy in order to rewire the neocortex toward healthier life scripts.

One twenty-eight-year-old woman has been in therapy with me for close to five years. When she initially came to me, she had tried all sorts of antianxiety and antidepressant medications with no symptom relief. Even though she suffered from the above-stated symptoms, it became quite clear early on that it was her personality that was creating conflict and suffering in her life. She would rage on people at the drop of a hat and blame everyone for being "stupid." Her life was a series of tragedies, and she was always the victim of life's unfairness. She often felt alone and alienated, yet she consistently pushed people away despite her need for their attention. As she continued to attend therapy, she eventually developed enough trust so as to be able to look at her life scripts and storylines as pathological. Slowly she opened to the possibility that she played a major role in her life's misfortunes. With gradually increasing insight, she eventually dropped all medication, as she came to the realization that it was the way she dealt with people and who she identified herself to be that generated most of her angst. She realized that she did not have to be the "victim" of life, and that she could begin to work with an alternate identity and storyline. She still struggles, but is now able to lead a normal life as she pursues a nursing degree and parents her two kids. When I first met her she had just come out of suicide watch from an inpatient facility. Everyone "hated" her, people went out of their way to make her life miserable, and people were always talking behind her back. Today she is able to ignore frustration, let go of angry feelings, and own her part in conflict. She feels more empowered to make choices and now realizes that she can be the co-creator of her life, and not just a victim. She uses therapy as her place for release, and I provide the mirroring necessary to bring insight into her often unconscious faulty perceptions and maladaptive interpretations of social cues.

Therapy at this level involves a deep script analysis, an exploration of personality patterns, a review of unconscious story lines, and an evaluation of the general sense of identity. Script analysis, transactional analysis, reality therapy, REBT, and basic cognitive therapy are all appropriate modalities that address this level of Consciousness. Gender identity confusion also falls into this category, as today gender is not limited to black or white, gay or straight, but spans a spectrum of possibilities. Again, by exploring the basic patterns of identity and personality in a safe and nurturing space, the individual has the opportunity to evaluate his or her life script and make changes so as to maximize his or her life experience. One does not have to be a victim to life, but can become the author of one's chosen life script. Only then can a person enter his or her social world with confidence and a strong self-esteem, thus adding and contributing to society in a healthy way. A healthy sense of identity eventually results in intimacy with others, generativity in society, and integrity in self. Social roles can be embodied with confidence, allowing the individual entrance into society as a productive and contributing member.

As mentioned, being a strong ego, productively and obediently working the social game within the consensually accepted social role identity, has built-in limits. It produces divisions, hierarchies, and institutionalized realities that have turned out to be unsustainable. The bureaucratic social games are just that, and the social roles are but mere masks that conspire to believe in their associated labels. Ultimately all social roles and personality patterns are cognitive constructs, fabricating a social world full of dramatic personalities. Turn on the TV and you can see this structure in full bloom. Endless personalities caught in the most absurd dramas, all believing this to be "reality." The illusion that we are doctors, politicians, Democrats, Muslims, Chileans, therapists, seekers, etc., all but veils a most salient fact: that we are mere mammals whirling on a rock ball around an average star in an incomprehensibly large multiverse. Our complex social games, overwhelmingly absurd when viewed after spending some time in the jungle with indigenous cultures, for instance, would be fine if they were not creating such havoc on our planet and wielding misery to all other living beings living on it.

Our unsustainable social realities, completely unconscious of the natural biosphere which organically supports them, are quickly taking our species toward ruin. Our ego-personalities have unconsciously created a fragmented world, so that if you are a banker, you do not see the humanity of the homeless man, but only the rising numbers on your bank account. The world appears as a fragmented "kill-or-be-killed," heartless race toward personal monetary wealth. Supporting this illusion of personal wealth at the expense of others is the endless factory production of stuff, which feeds an increasingly numbed ocean of consumers a barrage of plastic junk. The "economy," measured by how much crap people are buying, has become the all-important measure of how we are doing as a people. The 1 percent gets rich while the rest of the population works endless hours to barely pay their health insurance, let alone have time and money to pursue other activities. Corporations have become living entities, rooted in an egoic sense of separateness that turns a blind eye to the environmental and social devastations it creates by pursuing its bottom line. Fueled by the dirty energy of the industrial revolution, mega-corporations continue to rape the planet of its fossil fuels so as to power their outdated assembly-line machinations of mass production while polluting their very life supports.

The level of unconsciousness is amazing at a time when information is so widely available and when alternative energy sources clamor to be recognized. Of course, while the ego-corporations continue to benefit and perpetuate the illusion of "economic growth," the cries and protests of the 99 percent will remain mere distractions on their path toward economic monopoly. Having the mass media in their pocket, corporations control the programming of the "matrix" by keeping people entertained, amused, and numbed by increasingly violent and meaningless electronic imagery. The top executives decide what people need to think, buy, and pay attention to, while the military and politicians create unfair international foreign policies that support the executives' rising wealth. The ego and its corporate expression are fundamentally rooted in the Newtonian paradigm that views the world as a series of separate, isolated entities that only influence each other through direct, local contact. If the CEO in his mansion does not think about the war that rages to support his oil stock, or the countless ten-year-olds in sweat shops producing junk at a wage that barely supports them, or the vast ancient jungles that are being cut down for profit, or the selling of mind- and body-polluting substances that eventually kill people, he lives happily surrounded by his false plastic paradise.

No substance represents the unsustainable aspect of this level and its industrialized expression more than does the cigarette. The smoke, a clear reflection of the polluting furnaces of coal stacks and oil-fueled industries, perpetuates the mass consuming mentality by hooking individual brains to its devastatingly addictive properties. A product designed for mere profit, the cigarette is engineered to keep consumers consuming, locking the nervous system to an agent that has been proven to kill while making its producers billionaires. Despite the evidence, the hooked brain cannot rest until it has its "smoke break," repeatedly ingesting psychoactive chemicals that do nothing to contribute to growth and evolution, but rather keep people in a conditioned pattern of reinforced use. The endless ads and billboard advertisements condition people, at a young age, to believe that by smoking you will look and be cool, enhancing your personality and self-image tenfold if you hold a cig while "striking a pose." These ads target level four adolescent Consciousness that strives to look cool, fit in to hip social scenes, and express an increasingly orchestrated "glamorous" image. So in order to fit in, the teen (or teen-minded adult) uses this "image-enhancing" drug to first create a "cooler" identity, but later finds it becomes a necessity due to its addictive properties. Julien explains how this chemical works in the brain:

> Nicotine exerts virtually all of its CNS and peripheral effects by activating certain specific acetylcholine receptors (nicotine receptors).... In the CNS, the nicotine-sensitive acetylcholine receptors are widely distributed and may be located on the presynaptic nerve terminals of dopamine, acetylcholine, and glutamine-secreting neurons. Activation of nicotinic receptors by nicotine facilitates the release of these transmitters and increases their action in the brain. Nicotine increases

> dopamine levels in the mesocortico-limbic system involving the ventral tegmentum, nucleus accumbens, and fore-brain. This accounts for the behavioral reinforcement, stimulant, antidepressant, and addictive properties of the drug. [30]

Another drug that perpetuates and sustains the predictable assembly line of the eight-to-six office-job reality is caffeine. A psychoactive stimulant, it reinforces the level four social reality by keeping the various parts of the machine, a.k.a. people, lubricated and efficiently producing for "the Man." The coffee break, fully integrated into the busiest of work schedules, keeps the workforce obediently mass producing to support the owner's profit margin. Caffeine works to stimulate a person's social role by blocking the action of adenosine, a neuromodulator that influences the release of various neurotransmitters. Julien describes how "adenosine appears to exert sedative, depressant, and anticonvulsant actions; and blockade of adenosine receptors produces actions considered to be stimulating or anxiogenic." [31] In other words, caffeine is an adenosine antagonist, therefore replacing it and thus inhibiting its neural action. Julien continues, "Adenosine receptors decrease the discharge rate of many central neurons, increasing the activity of dopaminergic, cholinergic, glutaminergic, and noradrenergic neurons....Blockade of these receptors accounts for the modest reward and increased vigilance and mental acuity actions of caffeine." Interestingly enough, caffeine "leads to a release of dopamine in the prefrontal cortex, which is consistent with caffeine reinforcing properties." [32] Caffeine is a great social, ego-reinforcing agent that keeps the social games going until a fabled retirement is reached and the person can *then* pursue self-actualizing activities.

Another common social drug that perpetuates consumption through addiction via dopamine excitation is sugar. Even though the evidence that shows links to childhood obesity, diabetes, heart conditions, and possibly cancer has flooded the medical journals in recent years, the mega-corporations continue to sell their junk sodas and candy bars at schools, hospitals, and in every service station throughout the country. High fructose corn syrup is in everything that most people eat due to one salient fact: it is a cheap filler that fattens the pockets of the industry while it fattens the belly of the masses. As it directly activates the pleasure centers of the dopamine circuit, it has become the most common of addictions, producing mass un-health and disease. A society based on consciousness and compassion would never feed its children poison, knowing well that the dangers to a growing organism are vast and devastating in the long run.

So here we stand at the evolutionary threshold, where "breakthrough or breakdown" are the only two choices, for business as usual does not seem possible given the state of the planet and its dwindling limited resources. Yet as Einstein so wisely proclaimed, we cannot fix the problems from the same level of consciousness that created them. So the imperative of our age, individually and collectively, is evolve or die. And nothing less than a death, ego death, or the end of materialism/consumption-based capitalism/ sense of separateness will help us spiral into the birth of a new world. We can feel the birth contractions of a new Consciousness, and we see hints of its life around us, yet it will take nothing less than a radical collective awakening if we are to midwife the birth of the next dimension of Consciousness. A new world awaits, shiny with the promise of humanity's deepest aspirations.

Part 2:

Back Toward the Light

Spirituality is a progressive awakening to the inner reality of our being, to a spirit, self, soul which is other than our mind, life, and body. It is an inner aspiration to know, to enter into contact and union with the greater Reality beyond, which also pervades the universe and dwells in us, and, as a result of that aspiration, that contact and that union, a turning, a conversion, a birth into a new being. [1]

-Aurobindo

Our original Buddha-nature is, in highest truth, devoid of any atom of objectivity. It is void, omnipresent, silent, and pure. It is glorious and mysterious peaceful joy—and that is all.

-Zen Master Huang-po, ninth century

Evolution is the ongoing expression of Creation in our experience of Time and Space; and Christian Love manifests itself as the most real of cosmic energies. God, the Creator, is the God ahead of us drawing all things toward a unity of love in Christ at the Omega point. [2]

-Alice Knight

Level 5

Mind-Body Centaur: Holistic Plane

Phylogenic Expression

At this point in our phylogenic explorations we will depart from conventional thought, for these higher structures and levels of consciousness have not been reached by most of humanity. However, the fact that certain individuals and groups have reached higher levels of being and identity brings us to the supposition that, as a collectivity, we might, someday, reach the visionary aspirations of history. As we will explore, there were and are some collective movements who express genuine integral values and a more expanded sense of holistic understanding, revealing the fact that the evolution of consciousness continues toward greater complexity, integration, and wholeness. The forces involved in this transformation are many, and I will attempt to touch on some relevant aspects of this metamorphosis of Consciousness. Most importantly, however, is the consideration of technology and its catalytic function in cultural evolution. In fact, through our technologies, which are ultimately extensions of ourselves, we are once again quantum leaping into new experiences, perceptions, and understandings of reality and ourselves. Again, there are no "facts" at this level of the game; therefore, I encourage the reader to enjoy the explorations with an open mind, and to consider personal scenarios and connections to this most mysterious unfolding stream of Time.

As the wise Aurobindo puts it, "Reason cannot arrive at any final truth because it can neither get to the root of things nor embrace their totality. It deals with the finite, the separate, and has no measure for the all and the infinite." [3] This profound realization marks a historical shift in consciousness where the rational-industrial paradigm is seen for what it is: limited and ultimately unsustainable. As was seen in the last section, the collective existentialist crisis reaches a high during the late fifties as a generation attempts to reconcile with the inherited wars of the twentieth century. The Beat Generation, for example, begins its vast deconstruction of the "traditional values," questioning all the major premises of the modern world. They lay the counter-cultural foundation for what is to become one of the greatest movements into consciousness since the discovery of fire. As Leary conveys:

> In the 1950s in America there appeared such a
> group of free people who created a counter-culture

> which was to change history. They were called the Beat Generation. Their spokesperson was poet Allen Ginsberg. Their philosopher hero was William Burroughs. They were anarchist artists and writers. They hung out with avant garde painters and jazz musicians. They stood for the ecstatic vision and for individual freedom in revolt against all bureaucratic, close-minded systems. They saw themselves as citizens of the world. They met with Russian poets to denounce the Cold War. They practiced oriental yoga. They experimented, as artists have for centuries, with mind-opening foods, drugs, sexual freedom. [4]

This counter-cultural ("cultural" meaning the rational-industrial materialistic paradigm of the day at this point) movement began to bubble from beneath the folds of consensus society, as "it was the end of the 1950s—a decade defined by conformity, consumerism, political paranoia, and the just-discovered nightmare of global nuclear annihilation." [5] The movement did not fully flower until the early sixties, as the United States entered yet another war in the name of Democracy. The war in Vietnam was the final pressure to burst the social fabric of conformity, as the new generation openly revolted against this political aggression. The war led to the antiwar movements, the peace movements, protests, and the "dropping out" of an entire generation.

Many social groups at this time became empowered, for the times were ripe for change. The civil rights movement defending all human rights, regardless of race, color, ethnicity, or social class (divisions based on the ethnocentric level of consciousness), began its campaign in 1955 in the midst of segregation and social chaos. African Americans, led by Martin Luther King, among others, loudly and peacefully demanded their rights for freedom and equal treatment. The women's liberation movement also flowered as thousands of empowered young women threw their bras into burning fires. The development of the birth control pill in the early '60s gave women reproductive freedom, empowering control over their own bodies and initiating the sexual revolution of "free love." Social segregation and oppression were openly questioned as thousands began to move into a new level of awareness; world-centrism. From the ethnocentric-rational worldview, collective consciousness began its slow unfoldment into a more humane world-centric perspective where all of humanity was seen as citizens of the one planet, with the right to fulfill the same basic needs.

Supporting and helping shape this profound shift in consciousness is humanities move into space. In 1957 the Russians send the first satellite, Sputnik I, into space. Orbiting around the planet Earth, Sputnik I begins to send the first images of our one planet, capturing an image that defines the emerging world-centric structure of consciousness of a new generation. It no longer makes sense to kill each other and the natural world, as people for the first time see with their own eyes that we are truly one world, one planet, interconnected and interdependent. In 1961, Russian Yuri Gagarin becomes the first person in space, and by 1969 Americans Buzz Aldrin and Neil Armstrong walk on the moon.

This new world-centric awareness begins to transcend the existentialist, nihilistic, deconstructionist, a-perspectival "all views are relative" perspective into what has been called universal pluralism, green meme, or integral-aperspectivalism. [6] This new structure and perspective accepted all culture/context-bound points of view as relative, but embraced them as the product of a common, universal humanity that shares all basic needs. This world-centric universal pluralism is itself a higher level of embrace and *experience,* thus a "truer," more compassionate and humane attitude that deserves the label of "higher level of consciousness." It is a higher value system of acceptance and tolerance that cherishes the equal treatment of all peoples and sentient beings on planet Earth.

This level of conscious world-centric embrace naturally led to the blossoming of the environmental and ecological green movements. The industrial-military society left a polluted planet for the new generation, which was now wise enough to take action and initiate a global restoration program. For the first time we had people standing up against the cutting of the old-growth forests, the mindless destruction of the jungles, and the polluting of the oceans. Back to the earth movements, Gaia web of life models, eco-feminism, eco-psychology, systems theory, and holistic thinking all came to surface as people began to realize how interconnected all life systems were. Contrary to what Wilber seems to suggest, [7] the back-to-the-earth movement was not a regression into level two consciousness (bio-emotional identity), but was rather an actual ascendance into a world-sensitive perspective—level five. This new level five perspective is holistic in that it integrates the prior levels of being, such as the physiosphere, biosphere, egocentric-mental sphere, and ethnocentric-social sphere, into what we are calling the world-centric-holistic sphere. Mind (ethno- and ego-mental) and body (physio- and bio-emotional) are integrated at this level. In the prior level four of ethnocentric social-bound perspective, the physiosphere (earth, body), the biosphere (nature, bio-emotional id, sex), and the ego-sphere (unauthorized mental processes) are repressed into an unconscious repository of formative forces. Through the collective awakening (or at least initiation) of the sixties, there is, for the first time in Western history, a *conscious* universal acknowledgment of the interdependence of all life, thus a conscious movement toward restoring the original harmony between humans and nature. This original harmony, which existed prior to the rise of rational ego-identities and the industrial boundaries created from that worldview, was sought in nature and in the body. The new perspective treated all aspects of being as part of a living network of interdependent relationships, none of which could be repressed without damaging the whole.

This new generation was anti-technology, however, and rejected most of the products produced by society. Paradoxically, while rejecting the materialism of their culture, the new generation could not have created the revolution that it did without technology. Radio, electronic rock 'n' roll, television, and novel chemistry all played a catalytic role in helping reorganize the thinking of the day. The technologies that were rejected were the same instruments that helped establish the infrastructure for the next level of consciousness. With the state of the planet during those days, it is easy to see why technology and all that is "man made" was looked upon with vast skepticism. The choice to them was clear: culture either changes its addictive materialistic habits, or depletes and pollutes all of Earth's life support systems so that no life is able to subsist. The message today is the same, perhaps with an exponential urgency.

The ones leading this change were the youth, as is the case in every generation. The so-called "hippies" emerged on the scene, with world-centric values of peace, love, and harmony for all beings. Their overt rejection of material gains, power struggles, technology, and male world domination immediately produced a heated civil war between the establishment values and the new "hippie" ideals. They experimented with mind-altering drugs such as LSD, psilocybin mushrooms, mescaline, marijuana, and a variety of other substances expressing their new lifestyle choice of artistic and sexual freedom. Through Rock and Roll, many cultural icons came to the stage to profess the "new consciousness," as kids all over the globe chanted "make love, not war." Many initiated unsuccessful nature communes that attempted to live the "back-to-the-earth" sustainable philosophy. Due to property taxes and busts of illegal drug activity, the authorities quickly terminated many of these innocent projects that aspired for a more holistic and sustainable way of life.

In 1938, Swiss chemist Dr. Albert Hofmann of Sandoz Pharmaceutical Company synthesizes for the first time a chemical he calls LSD-25. Not knowing its nature, Dr. Hofmann shelves this new chemical until he decides to revisit its properties five years later. It is 1943, two years before the United States drops two nuclear bombs in Hiroshima and Nagasaki, ending World War II, when Dr. Hofmann unknowingly absorbs some of his potion through his fingertips. Feeling its powerful and mind-melting effects, the Swiss Doctor has the world's first acid trip, as he rides his bicycle home to a glowing and undulating garden. Three days later he takes the first intentional dose, discovering the vast mind-blowing properties of a substance active in the microgram range. LSD is said to be like a nuclear explosion in the subjective mind. The synchronicity of its simultaneous discovery during the time the nuclear bombs are dropped in the objective material world implies a deep coherence and intelligence at work behind the observable. Right when humans unleash the destructive forces within the nucleus of the atom, with the potential to destroy the entire planet, this substance is birthed with the potential to shift consciousness toward a more holistic embrace and with the promise of healing the violent cognitive divide between people.

Psychedelics played a major role in redefining social and environmental values, as the drug was said to "expand consciousness" to religious heights by literally dissolving internal boundaries. [8] This kind of consciousness exploration opened the doors to Eastern philosophy, mysticism, meditation, yoga, and the multitude of gurus that managed to spiritualize the West. Old church-based religions (mythic structures) were quickly outdated as kids "turned on" with psychedelics to directly experience the God within. Nature mysticism blossomed, neo-paganism was back in the West, and the techniques of Eastern spirituality were widely practiced and acknowledged.

The colorful explosion of creativity marking this era managed to reach all corners of society. Literature, art, music, philosophy, science, political/social thought, film, technology, and fashion design all came alive as new energy was being released in all areas of human life. The human potential movement, new-age thinkers, transpersonal and humanistic psychologies, breakthroughs in quantum physics, nuclear fusion, a man on the moon, space exploration, genetic discoveries, holistic medicine, health foods, personal computers, etc., are all aspects of a monumental shift of energy toward some higher, more complete ideal. Breakthroughs in all fields began to hint at this evolutionary unfoldment and liberation of creative energy. Consciousness was collectively waking up to clearer reflections of itself, its predicament in history, and its myriad manifestations.

Ontogenetic Expression

Breakthrough into this higher structure of consciousness can occur at any time within the chronological life span of an individual. There is no defined time marking the transition into higher realms of experience. It can happen spontaneously at any moment as a "peak experience" or an "altered state." The first four foundational levels must be in a healthy state of functioning, however, if one is to advance into the higher stages and *live* from those perspectives with their "enduring traits." Physical good health, balanced emotions and relationships, a healthy mind, and an integrated personality-identity structure set the foundation for the exploration of expanded energies and self-identities that "transcend and include" [9] the previous structures of development.

The main characteristic and drive of this level is focused on healing the mind-body split established by Descartes, who we remember helped solidify the Cartesian-modern era of rationality and duality. As was explored in the level four section, the rise of the social-rational "civilized" identity structure was made possible through the successful taming and repression of physiological instinctual urges, sexual bio-emotional id impulses, and various unauthorized mental processes into an unconscious. The individual at the level four developmental stage identified himself/herself purely with the personality and its various associated identifications. Through the existential crisis, the limits of this impermanent separate identity were seen and a new mode of being was sought.

Level five is concerned with reestablishing a connection with the roots of our being. Healing the mind-body split means a conscious integration of body, emotion, thought, and identity into a "whole organism" mode of functioning. Fritz Perls was pivotal in establishing a psychology for the whole organism, where the mind-body connection was directly worked with through Gestalt therapy. [10] Gestalt therapy is mind-body work in that the whole organism is taken into account. "The chief principle of the Gestalt approach is that the analysis of parts can never provide an understanding of the whole, because the whole consists of the parts *plus* the interactions and interdependencies of the parts." [11] In short, Perls believed that the organism as a whole has an innate wisdom that selects what is of interest to it at each moment. Thus once we stop over intellectualizing things and tune into what our body-mind system is doing-sensing-feeling-thinking, then we can understand the predicament of the organism. The whole is more than the sum of its parts; it is a gestalt and is in full expression at each moment and interaction.

Wilhelm Reich, founder of Somatic Psychology, was another explorer to encounter the deep, undeniable connection between body and mental-emotional states. He believed that the principle vehicle for expressing internal states was the body. He saw the body as an essential dynamic in all psychological functioning, where an individual's actions and behavioral patterns were determined by that person's character and character armoring. "Character armoring includes all repressive defensive forces, which form a coherent pattern within ego." [12] This character armoring, or emotional blocks and psychological knots, manifests in muscular tensions within the body as body armoring. (Eckhart Tolle calls this contracted body-mind state the pain-body). Reich contended that only through direct body work could someone release these stored complexes and patterns.

Ken Wilber has called level five the Centaur: "the great mythological being with animal body and human mind existing in a perfect state of atonement." He explains:

> As consciousness begins to transcend the verbal ego-mind, it can—for the first time—integrate the ego-mind with all the lower levels. That is, because consciousness is no longer identified with any of these elements to the exclusion of any others, all of them can be integrated: the body, the persona, the shadow, the ego—all can be brought into a higher-order integration…All in all, this is the stage variously described as one of autonomy, of integration, of authenticity, or of self-actualization—the ideal of humanistic/existential therapies, the highest stage to which orthodox Western psychology aspires. [13]

In an attempt to expand into this new, integrative, whole-person experience, many groups have arisen professing the necessity to get back to our roots, to get in touch with our bodies and emotions. The inability to be present with these aspects of being occurs through an over identification with social and mental processes conditioned and learned throughout our development. The work in level five is a reversal, so to speak; a gradual de-conditioning and unlearning of our habitual ways of experiencing our world and ourselves through the process of quieting down our purely mental orientation. This quieting down or transcendence of the conditioned ego structure allows Awareness to tune in to what has up to this point been unconscious processes, physiological and bio-emotional.

Once this level of awareness has been reached, a new world is birthed, full of wonders previously only glimpsed. Habitual identification with conditioned social and mental structures now quieted (i.e., ego death), the mind-body is free to become an integrated unit of experience. The Being can now tune in to the direct experience and wisdom of the senses, body, emotional streams, thought patterns, and environment in the here and now. The moment awakens the fresh experience of a sensual world of vast beauty and sensory enjoyment. Previously limited to unconscious processing and reactivity to sensory signals, at this stage the sensory world comes alive as Consciousness expands into a receptive embrace of all frequencies and vibrations.

Dr. Leary calls this level the Neurosomatic, fifth circuit of consciousness where, "the body freed from the neuro-umbilical imprints is ready for zero-gravity existence…this is called being 'high,'…sensory-somatic signals are consciously received. Sensory consumerism emerges." [14] At this level the Being has reached a state of aesthetic and hedonic connection to the world, a higher vibratory state of presence within the body and with the surrounding environment. Art, music, and poetry can bring about this "high" by directly activating the nervous system into an open receiver for here-and-now information. Dance and other artistic expressions also trigger this sensitized state of awareness. Many of these creative processes and holistic perspectives have been attributed to the right hemisphere of the brain. Psychologist Charles Tart explains: "The type of thinking associated with the right hemisphere seems holistic rather than analytical, atemporal rather than sequential in time, more concerned with patterns than with details." [15]

Also called a "hedonic engineer" by Leary, [16] the person at this level is freed from conditioned norms, mundane survival imprints, and social morals and takes the liberty to self-explore the wondrous vessel that houses the inner Being and the world around it. The "hippie" has become the stereotyped hedonic engineer, exploring novel sexual-sensual experiences (reclaiming formerly unconscious id/libido), "far-out" artistic and musical expressions, and the highs and sensory magnification felt from marijuana use. Arthur Hastings describes some of the researched psychological effects of marijuana: "visual scenes often have more depth, sounds are heard with more dimensions; so too with time—there is an expansion of the fabric of time so there is a feeling of depth instead of the usual two-dimensional flow." [17] This and other studies have provided evidence that marijuana initiates an altered (new) level of awareness where all sense impressions are greatly intensified, physiological processes made conscious, here and now awareness of environmental vibrations magnified and made available, and an overall hedonic enjoyment of the moment experienced. As will soon be explored, marijuana only opens a door to a transitory state, albeit "higher," to soon wane after the chemical has been metabolized. The trick is to open to that higher state of presence, by techniques to be discussed, and thereby live from that expanded space.

Since Consciousness reclaims the body in stage five (with marijuana or "naturally"), all that is sensed and perceived takes on a new luminosity, a new richness, and an appreciation for beauty never before experienced arises. Except for the elite of cultures throughout history, who, being materially secure, could explore hedonistic and aesthetic endeavors, along with some artists, sensualists, and hedonists, this level can now be accessed by all who venture beyond the confines of the consensus mind. The Ramsdales speak of this level in terms of the new sexuality:

> There is a new sexual revolution, authentic, spontaneous, natural, free to all, not in conflict with morality itself, unanticipated by those in favor of sex without love or love without sex; this new sexual revolution is happening now; this evolutionary revolution simply helps make making love a statement of fact; enjoy now the new intimacy "sexualove," a vibrant blending of sexual energy [*body*] and love [*mind*] in a marriage of happy intelligence [*italics mine*]. [18]

Sensual awareness of the body, enjoyment of all sensory frequencies, and an expanded appreciation for that which is beautiful naturally brings the individual into a direct sense of connectedness with nature. Establishing nature communes and sustainable communities are natural consequences to this more aesthetically world-sensitive perspective. Nature mysticism, worship of Gaia, and neo-pagan rituals all express this most organic experience of being alive, in this moment, fully in touch with nature and the body that embraces the multiplicity and diversity of the world.

The new mental structure arising from the mind-body integration is that of vision-logic. [19] Whereas the formal mind articulates higher relationships and concepts, vision-logic comprehends the interwoven tapestries of those relationships and concepts. This high mental level has a panoramic apprehension of mass networks of ideas, systems, associations, and relationships, and how they influence each other and interrelate. It is thus the beginning of a truly holistic and integral mind, with higher-order synthesizing capacity. It makes connections, weaves memes, relates truths, coordinates ideas, integrates concepts, and thinks holistically about the world.

Systems thinking and the mind-body-based *experience* of the interconnectedness of all things help arouse compassion, a higher-level emotion based on insight. The individual is world-centric, being able to conceive of the interrelated relationships through vision-logic, thus identifying with all sentient life on planet Earth. Brotherly/sisterly love and compassion are established within the context of this stage, as the opening of the fourth chakra enables the ideal conception of a one-world village, one human family. Vaughan describes this level in connection to the fourth chakra:

> (In) the region of the heart lies the fourth chakra, or *anahata,* symbolized by the element of air. At this level one becomes aware of the subtle energies of spirit, symbolized by air or wind or breath, as inspiration. Emotions are associated to the heart center, namely love and compassion. In order to complete the process of body/mind integration at this level, one must die to former identification, i.e., one must accept ego death. The oneness of all beings is intuited, and values shift accordingly in the direction of compassion, cooperation, and selfless service. [20]

Experience of Structure

Q: What do you perceive-project at this level?
A: Human beings, environment in the moment, simultaneous symphony of sensory frequencies, beauty, systems, and the interconnected planet.

Yoga and Tai Chi, ancient practices evolved in India and China, have proven themselves to be exceptional mind-body integrators. Level five awareness can emerge spontaneously, but generally must be sought through conscious self-work. Through the systematic practice of yogic techniques, one is able to directly access and consciously work with the various levels of being thus discussed. There are literally hundreds of physical postures, called *asanas,* that work with breath, mental focus, and spiritual energy in a process of self-healing, cleansing, and integration. Since Yoga is an integral approach to healing, it works directly with the physical body, emotional currents, mental energy, and Spiritual essence or Awareness so as to optimize the system's functioning. [21]

Through the practice of Yoga, one brings Awareness into what previously was unconscious and reflexive. Being an incredible form of physical therapy, the various postures, in concert with the related breathing, help move vital energy throughout the body and its many subsystems. Muscles are strengthened and a toning of the ligaments, joints, and tendons is felt as the increased flexibility and agility creates a sense of well being. The various *asanas* open channels, increasing circulation and allowing increased oxygenation of tissues, cells, muscles, and brain. Prolonged practice eventually speeds up metabolism, making the body more efficient and giving it more energy. Some particular postures squeeze out stagnant fluids, air, and energies, allowing the free flow of fresh vitality. Tensions, knots, body armor, and stress are also released through the developed *asanas*. Ultimately, the practice of conscious (mind) stretching (body) gives an expanded awareness of body states, and thus allows complete control over most physiologic functions. [22]

Through Yoga the body becomes increasingly sensitive, acting as an integrated sensing unit that is able to pick up signals previously unnoticed due to mental noise from the prior levels of development. *Asanas* liberate much organismic energy, fine-tuning the receptive nerve endings of the sensory system. The conditioned ego-mind is quieted enough so that a greater sensitivity to energy is experienced. One tunes into the spine and the various energy currents, channels, and nervous-electric activity moving up and down the spine through an act of conscious focus. The practice gives access to internal frequencies too subtle to have been recognized in previous levels. This increased nerve sensitivity is also experienced at the sensory-perceptual nerve ending receptors, where depth of external sensations is vastly amplified. Ultimately the yogi (advanced practitioner of Yoga) is able to consciously control the internal energy currents and the influx of external frequencies before they are interpreted by the various levels of the brain.

In the introduction I talked about the purifying and cleansing of the receiving mechanism necessary for the perception, reception, and experience of a wider range of frequencies, both internal and external. Yoga provides advanced techniques for this kind of perceptual refining so that energy may be consciously managed. Through the practice, the "doors of perception" are opened so that the surrounding sensory information comes in clearly and is experienced as a display of raw harmonic energy. This energy is consumed by the sensory system joyously, consciously, and at times ecstatically.

Along with increased inner sensitivity to nerve activity, glandular regulation, and muscular states, emotional currents and psychological tensions stored within the body can also be released and brought to the surface. Many repressed emotions from childhood or traumatic experiences stored in the body armor can be directly accessed, and thus allowed to exist as part of the overall being, but with Awareness. Yoga accesses these stored patterns, brings awareness and vitality to them, and aids in the process of releasing them so that the organism may find freedom from their constricting rigidity. Level six deals with techniques that directly address all of the previously unconscious material that begins to surface as our field of Consciousness and identity begins to expand.

Another practice that links the unconscious autonomic physiology of the body with the Light of Conscious Awareness is Patanjali's fourth limb, *pranayama,* or breath control exercises. *Asanas*, the third limb or step, and *pranayama* are part of an eight-limbed system of Raja "royal road" Yoga developed by sage Patanjali. It is not known when Patanjali lived, or even if he was indeed a single person rather than several authors using the same name. Estimates for the date of *Patanjala Yoga Sutras,* the primary text for Raja Yoga, range from 5000 BC to 300 AD. [23] Patanjali did not invent Raja Yoga, but rather systemized it and integrated the already existing ideas and practices of Yoga. Since that time, he has been considered the "Father of Yoga," with his *Sutras* as the basis for all other types of meditation and yoga which flourish today in their myriad forms.

The first limb in Raja Yoga is called *yama* (restraint), and is a world-centric vision-logic dictate on the ethical and moral principles that underlie the spiritual life. These principles include non-stealing, nonviolence, non-injury, truthfulness, sharing, loving-kindness, non-killing, chastity, and non-receiving of gifts. *Yama* underlies the basic understanding of our oneness, our interconnections that establish "do unto others as you would like done to you" as a deeply felt reality. All world spiritual traditions have a version of such commandments, revealing the felt experience of a compassionate and loving embrace of all sentient beings as the awakening recognition that we are all truly part of One Being.

The second step or limb is called *niyama* (observances/discipline), and consists of cleansing and purifying practices that prepare the vessel for expanded states of consciousness. Cleanliness of body, purity of mind, contentment, austerities without going to extremes that weaken the body-mind, study of spiritual wisdom, and devotion to God, also known as Bahkti (devotional) Yoga, are all parts of this limb. These practices cleanse, purify, heal, and refine the organic vessel and its transceiving apparatus in preparation for optimal flight into higher, deeper, and more expansive dimensions of Being. Without a pure, clear, and refined vessel, the released energies run the risk of being blocked, and thus manifesting in a variety of potentially negative and harmful ways.

The third limb is *asanas* (postures, also known as Hatha Yoga), developed to unlock, release, and open the body and its many systems. The postures facilitate the opening of the various channels in the body, allowing the free flow of bioelectric currents, oxygen, blood, hormones, and neurotransmitters unhindered by the normally accumulated unconscious knots, tensions, blocks, and body armor. This practice also begins to reveal to Awareness a deeper energy system within the body, called the subtle or ethereal energy system, which is too subtle and refined to be detected by our current medical instruments. Nonetheless, this energy system exists, as experienced directly by the yogi, and reflects the denser bioelectric circuits of the nervous system. The channels through which the subtle energy travels are called nadis or meridians. Dr. Dharma explains: "The human body has seventy-two thousand nadis, nonphysical energy channels analogous to nerves. Prana travels through theses nadis and energizes the entire system, particularly the chakras. Three central nadis are the *ida* and *pingala,* which are on each side of the spine, and the *shushmana*, which runs up the center of the spine to the head."[24]

The chakra system, which we've been using to summarize each level of consciousness as it relates to its correlated chakra, has seven (up to twelve or more chakras can be experienced above the head as overtone harmonic octaves) ethereal centers along the spine where this subtle energy can be transceived. Chakras, meaning wheels, are said to spin at various rates of vibration as tiny vortices. When there is a block, these chakras slow down or stop, creating imbalance in the whole system. Again, modern instruments cannot detect these centers, but it has become apparent that each chakra can be correlated to the glands of the denser endocrine system, and to the nerve plexus or nodal points of the nervous system focalized along the spine. [25] *Asanas* release and liberate physiological and subtle energy, helping cleanse, heal, and make conscious the organism that houses the inner Being.

Prana is the *Sanskrit* word used to describe the life-force energy responsible for the motion of the entire Cosmos. It is this cosmic energy principle that orbits the planets around the sun, expands and contracts the universe, and controls the fluctuation of social and ecological systems, the pulsation of the heart, and the inhalation and exhalation of the breath. In effect, *prana* is Cosmic energy manifesting itself in various fractal forms. Within the human body however, one is able to directly manipulate and control this cosmic energy through the use of various techniques. The breath is one of many forms of *prana*, consequently being our individual connection to the larger universal forces, for, in essence, Yoga tells us that they are one and the same force.

For most people breathing is an unconscious, autonomic, physiological process that just happens, as does the beating of the heart or the crashing of the ocean waves. The beauty of breath, however, is that it can also be a conscious process. We have the choice to take a breath or not, unlike our heart or the ocean waves. Thus the breath is literally the link between the unconscious, involuntary system and the conscious, voluntary system, between body and mind, individual and universal, internal and external, unconscious and conscious, and finally between life and death. In other words, breath is the center of our practice. *Pranayama,* then, are exercises that work directly with the breath/*prana* and its control. Once the energy is liberated through *asanas,* one can consciously direct, control, focus, and manage said energy via *pranayama.* Patanjali tells us that all of these practices are designed solely for the purpose of preparing the whole system for meditation.[26]

Breath, then, is our direct link between the body and the mind, between the conscious and the unconscious. For example, one can witness this link by noticing the direct relationship between breath and mental-emotional states. How one breathes—the depth, frequency, rhythm, and speed—directly correlates with how one feels and thinks. For instance, shallow, quick breaths often indicate poor health and a low, anxious, agitated state of being. Holding one's breath often indicates angry, constricted states, whereas deep, slow, rhythmic breathing correlates with relaxed states and physical well-being. The whole autonomic body listens to the breath, so that when the breath is fast and shallow, the entire organism shifts into the sympathetic nervous system's stress "fight or flight" response, restricting circulation to vital organs, taking the cortex offline so that thinking and remembering are impaired for faster reaction time, speeding up the heart to increase blood supply to the endangered body, tightening muscles as adrenaline and cortisol are secreted by the adrenal gland to fuel the system, and elevating blood pressure to prepare the organism to deal with the pending emergency. In contrast, slow, deep, rhythmic breathing will inform the autonomic body that there are no threats. This allows the body to activate the parasympathetic "rest and repair" nervous system, allowing muscles to relax, improving circulation and oxygenation to the rest of the body, improving digestion, slowing down the heart, lowering blood pressure, improving cognitive functions, increasing the production of endorphins and other neurotransmitters, and allowing the immune system to initiate its healing functions as it uses the excess energy to heal the body. In other words, by consciously working with our breath we can engage our entire organism, creating a direct line of communication to a physiology that was, up to this stage, completely unconscious and automatic. Through breath, we make the body and all its states conscious, thus healing the so-called mind/body split.

As we saw, the brain structure that helps facilitate communication between mind and body is the hypothalamus. The hypothalamus receives direct messages from higher cortical centers via neurotransmitters, which are then translated and relayed to the pituitary or "master" gland via neuropeptides. The pituitary gland then communicates with the rest of the endocrine system, instigating the various functions of the endocrine glands. It is the hypothalamus that calls up for more adrenaline when the thought "I'm in danger" is received, or more thyroid hormone, or testosterone, etc., when respective mental messages are encountered.

So in this sense, not only can we engage our entire physiology via breath, but thoughts also have a powerful influence over the entire body. Again, Dr. Dharma elucidates:

> The mind—consisting of thoughts in the brain—can heal. It does so primarily through the phenomenon of psychoneuroimmunology. Thoughts (originating in the cortex) trigger responses in the hypothalamus and pituitary....The hypothalamus and pituitary act as links between the mind and the body. For example, positive, calming thoughts can heighten immunity, by causing the nervous system to shift into its healing, rest-and-repair branch (parasympathetic Branch). [27]

What we think, how we think, and what we believe (mostly unconscious up to this stage) directly influences our body states and perceptions. In stage five we begin to awaken to our mind's influence over our body, and can initiate the practices that will allow us to manage this mind-brain-endocrine-body feedback loop communication system consciously.

As we begin to discover the potentials latent within the mind-body connection, the prospect of "spontaneous healing" [28] or "quantum healing" [29] becomes a reality. Both Dr. Chopra and Dr. Weil, leaders in the holistic health movement, have accumulated a plethora of case studies demonstrating the power of psychosomatic healing, proving that the state of mind of the individual greatly affects immune system activity, immune response, and overall healing. Negative belief systems or programs will self-fulfill into actual physical manifestations, as positive beliefs will measurably increase overall health and well-being. For example, a strong set of negative beliefs appears as imprinted, conditioned, and/or learned networks of biochemical reflexes in the cortex of the brain. Since communication exists between parts of the brain, and between the brain and other systems, these negative beliefs are transduced into biochemical reflexes of the organism as a whole. Specifically, the "belief" reflexes in the cortex get transduced into neurochemical and hormonal processes when they pass through the hypothalamus, the ancient part of the back brain which regulates and/or influences many body programs, including the immune response.

Among the chemicals regulated by the hypothalamus and transduced to the immune system are a variety of neuropeptides, including endorphins. Within the brain, neuropeptides act as neurotransmitters, chemical messengers conveying information across the synaptic cleft, naturally reactive to mental activity such as thoughts and beliefs. These neuropeptides also act as hormones. They can trigger immune responses within the endocrine and limbic systems, as they are directly affected by the brain's mental activities since neuropeptides have the dual identity of being a neurotransmitter (brain/mind) and/or a hormone (immune system/body).[30]

Other approaches to direct body-mind communication exist with technologies concerning biofeedback. Biofeedback is a means to monitor biological and physiological processes so that a person may learn to regulate them through various techniques, such as breath control and visualization. Screens and similar devices monitoring physiological states such as heart rate, brain wave frequency, skin temperature, and blood pressure allow for the possibility of conscious alteration of said processes through direct observation and willful changing of those biorhythms. Almost any bodily process that can be observed can be consciously modified and controlled via the information feedback loop facilitated by biofeedback monitors. Biofeedback devices provide direct lines of communication between mind and body states, giving Being yet another way to reconnect with that which has been unconscious up to this point.

Tai chi is another mind-body integrating practice from the Taoist tradition that specifically works with the movement of *chi* (the Taoist version of *prana*). Elias and Ketcham describe *chi* energy as follows:

> *Chi* is the energy in the atmosphere that moved the flag. *Chi* is the force that enabled the observer to perceive that the flag moved. *Chi* was the force that prompted the observer to ask whether it was the flag or the wind that moved.

> *Chi* is the wisdom that understood that the flag and the wind moved only when the mind moved. *Chi* is simply a name for the dynamic pattern of interactions that occur between the individual and her environment. [31]

As we saw, *chi* or *prana* is the name given to Cosmic energy as it manifests in various forms. As it is also the energy found within the body, one can tune into it and either control it (*pranayama*) or move with it (Tai chi), thus becoming conscious of a normally unconscious creative force and process.

Faith healing, hypnosis, holistic medicine, acupuncture, naturopathy, homeopathy, Chinese and Ayurvedic medicine, massage therapy, and health food awareness are all indications that Consciousness is moving toward a more holistic approach to the human condition. The deep wisdom inherent in our bodies and our cells once known to the ancient masters is becoming clearer and stronger, as Spirit pushes forward in its drive to evolve. The above healing practices work with the bodies' natural tendency toward healing and wholeness. The work, then, is to dissolve the accumulated tensions that block the pure flow of energy inherent in our organism, across all levels and dimensions, so that one may come into conscious integration with the whole of individual being. As a fully integrated human being, the division between self and nature begins to fall away. Compassion naturally blossoms in the heart center, and Consciousness experiences a depth of experience and a sense of connectedness never before seen in our known Cosmos. Greater connectivity, deeper integration, and fuller compassion set the stage for the next unfolding of Being.

Exercises:

1.) Attempt stretching with the coordinated use of breath and mental focus. As you attempt the stretches of your choice, close your eyes and "listen" to your body. Try to establish a direct line of communication between your mind and your body, as you gently focus your attention on the area being stretched in accordance with the inhalation and exhalation of your breath. Feel the rushes of energy, loosening of tensions, and the release of stress as you breathe out stagnation and let vitality back in. Learn and practice Yoga. A continuous practice will bring innumerable time-tested benefits to body-mind-spirit health. Also learn about and try other mind-body practices, particularly the various oriental martial arts.

2.) Close your eyes in a standing position. Feel your inner flow of energy and follow it. Move to the rhythm dictated by internal forces. Experience the Tao/flow moving through you and the rest of nature. Learn about and practice Tai chi.

3.) Go out to Nature and meditate on its sounds, forces, and interconnected energies that embrace your very existence. Create a ritual atmosphere in Nature and make offerings to the Great Mother Earth Goddess. Feel Gaia running through your veins. Make an offering to the four directions and connect with the various elements of manifestation.

4.) Go to a museum and become one with the art.

5.) Meditate on your fourth chakra, located in your heart center, and connect with the air element. Breathe deeply, and feel the air as it connects your internal being with the external world, your body with your mind. Feel your heart chakra open, and experience the compassion and unconditional love that resides within that center.

6.) Create and design a sustainable, regenerative intentional community that harmonizes nature and culture. Research bio-regionally based local economies, permaculture, biodynamics, and renewable energy sources.

7.) Study the effects of marijuana. Contemplate case studies on MDMA (variously called ecstasy, "E," "X," or Adam) users, and its current use in psychotherapeutic settings. Investigate why it has been called a fourth chakra drug. Is there a connection between these drugs and the mind-body state of being?

Further Transpersonal Explorations

The first time I glimpsed a state of consciousness that seemed to lie outside the social realities surrounding me and reflect an identity larger than my ego-personality was toward the end of my senior year in high school. I'm visiting Chile on spring break when a few older friends invite me to the back of my uncle's farmhouse. They pull out a strange-smelling cigarette and proceed to pass it around the circle. With a sense of apprehension, curiosity, fear, and excitement, I try it. Not feeling anything at first, I continue to inhale until suddenly I feel a complete shift in consciousness. I feel my thoughts fade into the background as waves of sensory information begin to overshadow and overwhelm their feeble attempt to understand. Colors all of a sudden explode with brilliance, sounds appear deep and mysterious, and my sense of smell seems more powerful than ever. My body and skin seem to open to textures and tactile sensations of an intensity never before imagined. As one friend passes some chocolate around the circle, I am amazed by the depth and richness in my sense of taste. Eating food becomes an ecstatic experience, as we sample multiple delectable munchies. All of this sensory augmentation and magnification would have been terrifying if it all didn't seem so funny and ridiculous. I found myself immersed in a hilarious new world of sensory signals never before consumed in such a conscious way. The vast richness of my sensory world, and the new sensitized awareness of and in my body, in the here and now, all pointed to a new mode of consciousness that existed right around my developmental corner.

Back in the States I discover that my friend Eddie has also discovered marijuana, and we dive deep into the new dimension it temporarily bestows on our bewildered Awareness. Our philosophic discussions take on a whole new level, so we believe, and we begin to *experience* the physics of vibration as revealed to our opened senses. However, even though the marijuana experience was positive for me at the time in the sense that it awakened a new possibility in Consciousness, I feel fortunate to have discovered it late in my adolescence. I was in a good, happy place in my life, as my sense of identity was strong and healthy with a clear sense of direction and goals. I had already been accepted to the University of California, Davis, my grades were in good standing, and my family life was healthy and happy. I had no *need* to use pot; it was only an interesting, occasional experience that provided my curious mind with an alternate mode of operation.

Despite my experience, I have consistently found that kids who experiment with pot, or any other substance for that matter, in the early teen years encounter more problems and cause more damage in their lives than good. As we have been exploring, adolescence is marked by an often confusing exploration of identity and a consequent development of coping strategies for budding hormonal emotions. One learns how to deal with strong feelings and emotions in adolescence, and if one of the strategies developed is to use a substance to cope, dependence and addiction inevitably follow. Emotional development stops, as the drug masks feelings and keeps them suppressed in the unconscious, later to cause psychological and clinical symptoms.

Drug experimentation among youths is common, as teens are hardwired to seek adventure, danger, and thrills, often at the expense of academic success and other life responsibilities. This natural drive was addressed in tribal cultures by the socially sanctioned vision quest and rites of passage ordeal. In the absence of such cultural context, teens are forced to channel this natural drive in dangerous and often destructive ways. As a psychotherapist, I have come to the conclusion that drugs and alcohol are negative and often damaging to a teenager's natural development. My standard line to teens as I work with them is as follows: Your brain is in exponential growth up until age eighteen or nineteen. As such, any contaminant will necessarily interfere with optimal neural development. Memory, ability to focus, emotional coping skills, self-regulation, goals, motivation, sense of self, and social development are all being fueled exponentially by an avalanche of hormones and neurotransmitters. Thus, any foreign chemical can disrupt said development, ultimately causing problems down the developmental line.

A typical scenario is outlined by a fourteen-year-old boy client I worked with while working for the County Mental Health Department. Dealing with a dysfunctional family, this boy found relief and escape by smoking pot. Without it, his anger and depression overwhelmed him. All the mental health system wanted to do was replace his pot with another socially accepted antidepressant drug. He struggled in school, lost all motivation, couldn't focus, and all he thought about was getting high. Over time we worked on anger management skills and other methods for coping with strong emotions so that he wouldn't be so dependent on pot, but it wasn't until he got in trouble with the law and landed on probation that he tried to stop smoking marijuana. He struggled to stay clean and remained on probation throughout his teenage years, as he was completely psychologically dependent on the pot high, unable to remain clean for more than a couple of days. The dangers of using drugs at a young age are clear, as their powerful biochemical effects overshadow the subtleties of sober highs brought about by everyday life. A young brain introduced to the powerful chemical states of mind produced by drugs will most likely fail to recognize the richness that life has to offer without external chemical agents. Add to that the legal persecution of the person's struggle with drugs, and you have an inevitably challenged existence.

As a side note, it seems worthwhile to denounce the so-called "war on drugs" as the most immoral and destructive social program yet devised by the powers that be. Clearly a neurological, physiological, psychological, social, and health-related issue, the laws have instead criminalized a sector of the population for their choice of what to put into their bodies. By criminalizing drug use, the legal system has created a whole criminal class that sustains itself by unavoidably criminal means. Who are these drug-using criminals? Your kids, uncles, grandmas, and community members who either use recreationally or are chemically addicted and, as a result, suffer tremendously. The fact that the two most dangerous drugs on the planet, causing more deaths than all other "illicit" drugs put together, are legal, shows that the laws are not based on medical research and scientific understanding, but rather on profit-making margins and politically motivated reasons. The alcohol and tobacco multibillion-dollar lobbying industries keep the politicians' pockets full, as they turn a blind eye to their products' fatal long-term effects while demonizing the substances that they deem dangerous. Not only that, but the criminalization of certain chemicals has inadvertently created a money-making industry that cold-bloodedly persecutes and destroys lives while sustaining its "war on drugs" propaganda machine. The war on drugs is a war on people's birthright to choose what to do with their body and their consciousness. I tell people before they experiment, "Just say *know*" in a world of unlimited information. If you are going to put a substance into your body, learn about it, see what it does to your brain, inform yourself of its possible side effects, and make an informed decision based on your research. Drugs are not a criminal issue; they are a health issue and should be treated as such. Criminalize anything, and you create criminals. Simple as that.

Our interest in exploring various substances is purely scientific and spiritual, as they reveal and trigger aspects of Consciousness. Through my own research, I found that only one class of drug has any benefits beyond mere entertainment, medication, and fun. This class of substances is known as hallucinogens, entheogens, or psychedelics. All other drugs seem to actually contract Awareness with diverse negative, adverse side effects, while psychedelics seem to provide access to expanded states of Consciousness hinting at evolutionary modes of Being available to humanity in future states of development. Psychedelics provide a peek into expanded states of Consciousness, soon to wane after the drug is metabolized. In other words, they provide a temporary "altered" state of Consciousness. As useful as this may be, I have found that it is through conscious self-work and discipline that one is able to integrate and thus live from these higher states. At some point one gets tired of getting high and pursues disciplines that allow one to *be* high as a permanent state of Being.

Marijuana revealed a sensory world of wonder, a delicious sensual body awareness, and an expanded state of mind, but it wasn't until I discovered Yoga that I was actually able to live in said state. The pot high lasts for about two hours, to then degrade into a tired, burned-out, spaced-out afterglow. As pleasurable as this may be, I eventually found it to be ultimately limited in its ability to help Consciousness evolve. As my consciousness was beginning to change once in college, I started studying various forms of Yoga through UC Davis's experimental college. Through the practice of Yoga I began to experience an opening of the senses light-years clearer, more refined, and acutely more tuned in than any marijuana experience. As I deepened my Yoga practice, I found pot actually *decreased* my level of sensitivity to the sensory world around me. Yoga helped me tune into my body, allowing my Awareness to discover worlds of psychosomatic beauty within and without. My thoughts and ego began to quiet, as the vast electromagnetic networks of nervous and ethereal energy systems became available to my Witnessing Awareness. My body states, its emotional currents, and the vast complex of body armor I had developed over the years became completely conscious, as I awakened to a totally new mode of existence. Focused in the here and now, my eyes opened to a beautiful world of natural wonder and sensory enjoyment. Well, this was the intent and practice, for cycles from the not-so-pure influences, shall we say, were also present in those days with their relentless teachings.

Consequentially to my transformation in Consciousness, sustained by an ever-deepening discipline of Yoga practice, my views and experiences of the world began to change. I began to feel a much deeper connection to the Natural world around me, as the mental noise quieted enough to allow communion with the deeper frequencies of Nature. Nature, I noticed, was a literal extension of my body and Soul. The need to take care of Her became so obvious that anything but that seemed absurd. I began to gravitate toward other "conscious" individuals, joining a cooperative, agriculturally focused, intentional community called the Domes, or 'Baggin's End.'

'The Domes' are twelve dome structures resting on beautiful permaculture gardens, with fruit trees, organic vegetables, and herb and flower gardens lining the interconnected pathways. Being a part of the UC Davis housing department, the twenty-four of us "starving students" were able to stay for $120 per month. We grew our food, had nightly musical jam sessions around the fire, had monthly sweats (a sweat that was taken down by the University two years later for safety concerns), and danced barefoot during the full moons to the funky psychedelic tunes of friends' bands. It was a kind of sixties revival in the early nineties, connecting us to the environmental movement, ecological and feminist ideals, and social activism in its various forms through a budding world-centric, vision-logic perspective. We were all educated college students, transformed by shared communal living and the bubbling passion of inspired young ideals. Initiated into the Green meme, we all learned how to live in more sustainable ways, creating rituals around seasonal and lunar cycles and learning how to build soil.

The Domes were actually designed in the early '70s by UCD engineering students, who collaborated with the agricultural and art departments to install these twelve energy-efficient white domes by 1971. Since then, the Domes have witnessed an evolution of communal living, as countless groups of students have come together to experience what our ancestors once lived: a sense of tribal community, living in harmony with nature and each other. Currently, the Domes are powered by solar panels and grow enough food to sustain their members and beyond. As an energy-producing entity, I believe it to stand as a great model for future system redesign. It is clear that our current design of "energy-consuming entities," the modern home and city, is not sustainable, as evidenced by the environmental degradation and mass animal extinction under way. By contrast, if we use permacultural techniques for edible regenerative landscapes, rooftop gardening, and community farming, we could wipe out hunger and feed a healthy community, worldwide.

What in effect happened to me, at both the individual level and the communal level, was an integration of body and mind, psyche and nature. This healing has allowed me to live, or at least pursue, a more holistic and organic way of life. If we are fractals, when I heal my mind-body split, the planet's mind-body split can also begin to heal through my everyday choices. Healing the mind-body split of the planet means taking a green stance on all human issues, as the bios is the body that feeds our life. Healing the mind-body split personally means putting aside time and space for reconnecting with my body and the inner Being. Yoga has become an essential part of my life, especially as a mostly sitting psychotherapist, as it infuses me with fresh vitality, a clear, focused mind, and an open state of receptivity (gardening seems to do the same). It allows me to sit for long hours in complete comfort and presence, Witnessing my and my clients' energy currents as they fluctuate. I experience my whole Being as I Witness my client's whole Being. This connection creates a resonance where healing can occur.

Working with the whole person is crucial, of course, as all levels play a role in a person's moment-to-moment experience. When I do initial assessments in my practice, for example, I ask questions regarding all aspects of the person's life. From food choices to medical problems to all psychosocial stressors to spiritual belief systems, the person is a gestalt of all these forces. Being more than the sum of all forces, the person can learn to access awareness of all that was previously unconscious, following the ancient dictum to "know thyself." By becoming aware of body states, as happens by simply asking something like "where in your body do you feel that anger, or guilt, or sadness," one can bring awareness to where the person holds the pattern. This is revealing in therapy and can often lead to psychosomatic healing. Somatic psychology, bioenergetic analysis, Gestalt therapy, and Rogerian therapy are all modalities used to help individuals heal the mind-body split; not just one symptom or part, but the whole person. This process can eventually lead to the self-realizing quest available to the individuated personality.

I am currently working with a twenty-year-old young man who has been able to heal from his grief around his dad's sudden death four years ago. He tells me he is ready to "develop mastery over mind and body." He was taken at first by a breathing technique I taught him to manage his anxiety. So much success did he achieve with said breathing technique that he was curious as to what other technologies existed to manage emotional storms. A child of the sci-fi fantasy gaming world, he viewed said techniques as means for mastering the "Force." Using his terminology, I taught him various forms of *pranayama* to excite or calm his nervous system, and a deep meditation technique so that he could "become aware of and master the Force." I equated the "Force" with basic underlying Awareness, which my client was eventually able to connect with. From being depressed and lost, he now beams confidence and excitement, as he has adopted a Tai chi practice and continues to meditate on a daily basis. Still not quite sure what he "wants to do with his life," he reports finding a center within that allows him to be happy no matter what he does. He is writing and illustrating his first book, and appears to have individuated from his familial pain.

As we close this section, we will look at the mechanism of action of two substances that appear to reunite, if not enhance temporarily, the mind-body connection. The first is marijuana, cannabis, or pot, which has in recent years been legalized for medicinal and recreational use in certain states and countries. Both patients and their doctors have been loudly reporting the beneficial effects of THC, or tetrahydrocannabinol, marijuana's active ingredient, for both physical as well as psychological ailments. A plethora of studies, reports, and testimonials have made clear that the THC containing herb has effects that help relieve everything from nausea, stomach irritation, nervousness, tics, tremors, pain, glaucoma, asthma, arthritis, migraine headaches, premenstrual syndrome, and general physical discomfort (body) to anxiety, depression, ADHD, PTSD, and psychological distress (mind), to name just a few. [32] Despite the overwhelming evidence and the voters' will, the federal government continues to invade private property and arrest patients, taking away their right to choose the best medical course of action for themselves. The herb has been used as medicine and sacrament throughout the world for thousands of years, thus the absurdity of its recent six-decade old illegality. Let's look at how THC can affect both bodily as well as psychological aspects of Being.

TCH has a complicated psychopharmacological profile, as what are now known as cannabinoid "G-protein-coupled" receptors, which THC is partial agonist to, are widely distributed throughout the human body. Julien reports, "There are huge numbers of cannabinoid receptors in the brain, perhaps ten to twenty times as many as there are opioid receptors, perhaps more than any other type of receptor. Anandamide, as a partial agonist, activates perhaps only 50 percent of available receptors; THC activates only about 20 percent." Anandamides are "naturally occurring ligands that bind to the cannabinoid receptors and thus...function as a natural THC." [33] *Ananda* means bliss in *Sanskrit*, inferring that the endogenous anandamide molecule may be responsible for modulating various mind-body states naturally, possibly facilitating euphoric states. Julien continues:

> Cannabinoid receptors are primarily found on presynaptic nerve terminals and act to inhibit calcium ion flux and facilitate potassium channels. As a result, stimulation of cannabinoid receptors inhibits the release of other neurotransmitters from presynaptic nerve terminals. It is thought that this presynaptic inhibition at nerve terminals accounts for the psychoactive effects of cannabinoids... THC acts as a partial agonist at hippocampal glutamate-releasing neurons to 'reduce, but not totally block, excitatory transmission'....THC is probably effective not because of any inherent efficacy but because of the tremendous number of receptors for it in the brain. [34]

Therefore, THC seems to mimic naturally occurring endogenous molecules within our body, affecting almost all known functions of the mind-body system due to the ubiquitous distribution of receptors. Whether perceived as good or bad, the cannabinoids have an inhibitory function that slows down the nervous system, having the effect of "mellowing" people down by calming the mind and relaxing the body. Not what you want at school or work, but a welcome medicine when in the throes of cancer or AIDS.

One last group of substances, worth mentioning in relation to the mind-body connection, are sometimes called empathogens due to their ability to allegedly generate empathy in its users. A series of "research chemicals," such as DOM (or STP), MDA, DMA, MDE, TMA, 2-CB, 2-CI, and, most popularly, MDMA (known as ecstasy, "X" or "E" in the underground) grew quickly in popularity during the early seventies and eighties due to their supposed psychosomatic effects. Ecstasy in particular is a synthetic compound that was developed in 1914 as a potential dietary aid. Its psychoactive effects were discovered in the mid seventies by Bay Area alchemist Alexander Shulgin, who synthesized it and many other novel empathogens and psychedelic 'research' chemicals, some of which are listed above. Due to its apparent heart-opening properties, MDMA gained wide popularity within the psychotherapeutic communities, as therapists used this substance successfully to help individuals and couples heal from intra-psychic, psychosomatic, and relational afflictions. Word got out about its heart-opening, sensuality-activating properties, and youths began to use it for dancing in all-night underground parties called raves. The authorities quickly got wind of these ecstasy-fueled parties and, by 1985, completely made illegal the use and research of these promising therapeutic tools.

As of today, a number of studies have been authorized to study the use of MDMA in the treatment of PTSD in war veterans. Those interested should check out MAPS.org (Multidisciplinary Association of Psychedelic Studies) for ongoing updates into the incredible new research being done on MDMA-assisted psychotherapy, along with a plethora of other studies related to the use of psychedelics in medicinal, therapeutic, and healing capacities. The doors have apparently once again opened to the research of these mind-manifesting (psychedelic) substances, which promise potentials not only for healing, but for helping humanity find more enlightened and compassionate modes of existence.

MDMA's chemical name is 3,4 methylenedioxymethamphetamine, and it belongs to the phenethylamine hallucinogen family of substances, of which mescaline is a part. These substances are cousins of the tryptamine family, to be discussed in level seven. Phenethylamines are structurally similar to both catecholamine neurotransmitters dopamine and norepinephrine, and the amphetamine molecule, thus acting as an agonist in the related receptor site. Julien explains, "Structurally, the catecholamine psychedelics resemble norepinephrine, dopamine, and the amphetamines in that they contain the basic phenyl ring, a ethyl side chain with an attached nitrogen or amine ring." He continues:

> Phenelthylamine psychedelics exert amphetamine-like psychostimulant actions, presumably on dopaminergic neurons. However, their psychedelic actions are probably ultimately exerted by augmentation of serotonin neurotransmission; they are probably full agonists at postsynaptic serotonin 5-HT2A receptors…These psychedelics can therefore be safely classified as mixed dopamine and serotonin agonists. [35]

Phenylthylamines, and more specifically the empathogens, seem to have a global effect on the brain and body by activating the "somatic" circuits of both dopamine and serotonin pathways, thus "turning on the senses." Of course, due to their illegality, it is impossible to know whether one is taking pure MDMA when buying something called ecstasy from the street. Due to this reality and its determined neurotoxic effects over prolonged, excessive use, extreme caution is advised when thinking about experimenting with this chemical.

As it turns out, my journey eventually led me to one of those infamous raves in 1992, my freshman year in college. This experience was to shift me even beyond the psychosomatic green body-mind integration described in this section. While beginning to feel grounded in the organic Earthy community of sustainable living, this experience opened my Consciousness up to what seemed like a new dimension of reality altogether, beyond the body. Transformation and initiations were now happening at a quickening pace, as the electronic trance dance scene was gaining momentum in what appeared to be a global movement of change. Something new was emerging from the reincarnated "peace and love" consciousness of the sixties, once again fueled by the modern version of ancient psychedelic medicines, but now interconnected by the new information technologies taking hold of culture in the early nineties. The Spirit within all things once again demonstrated that evolution continues its relentless push toward higher, more integrated, and ever-more novel forms of Self-expression.

Level 6

Awareness of Mind: Psychic Plane

Do what thou wilt shall be the whole of the Law.
Love is the law, love under will. [1]

-Aleister Crowley

Phylogenic Expression

As Spirit moves toward higher, more integrated forms of Self-expression, we witness its manifestations as greater connectivity, faster communication, and a gradual dissolution of boundaries between its manifest parts. What we are talking about is the '90s, the information revolution, and the new planetary cyber culture that is emerging as a consequence to the new technologies. Even though in this section I will be talking about the higher aspects and implications of our current technological leap, the fact that most of humanity still functions in level four awareness, ethnocentric-egoic identity, should not be forgotten. What the Internet and the World Wide Web represent is an infrastructure with the potential to completely transform our culture, our lives, and ultimately the evolutionary destiny of our species, if applied consciously toward those ends. Since most of the collective awareness is still focused on the lower levels of consciousness, the new technologies have been primarily used for consumerism, business, self-promotion, divisiveness, and a variety of other socially related exchanges. Current events in 2017 actually seem to point toward dissolution rather then breakthrough, but we will soon explore how this collapse is actually necessary for the transformation to unfold; a transformation that will increasingly rely on the informational web now firmly in place. Once we transcend our money-material-gaining motivations, as is starting to happen through the Open Source and Peer-to-Peer networks where sharing and community is actually practiced, we can begin to use our technologies to heal and reconnect our fragmented planet.

During the roaring twentieth century, the equations of quantum physics led to the development of quantum appliances that allowed humans to receive, process, and transmit electronic images. Telephone, cinema, radio, television, computers, compact discs, fax machines; suddenly humans

> were creating digital realities that were accessed
> on living-room screens. [2]

The slow Newtonian-mechanical world is gradually changing, along with the related mental structures, into a quantum light-speed world of electrons and information. As the human brain contains vast latent potentials not yet realized by the collectivity, so does the global network now firmly embedded amongst our cultures. To learn and master our brain technology means to learn and master its extensions, the computer and cyberspace. Marshall McLuhan established in his first Law of Communication that "the medium is the message," where the technology used to package, store, and communicate thoughts defines the limits of those thoughts. [3] In the industrial age, thoughts and ideas were bound and recorded in static books. Now ideas, thoughts, and concepts flash light speed around the globe, merging, fusing, synthesizing, and fluidly changing as they interact with other thought-forms. All that is currently known by the human race has been digitized, quantisized, and packaged into bits of data that exist in a spaceless, timeless dimension called "cyberspace." This cyberspace seems to represent the emergence and expression of the collective human unconscious, the extent of which is not fully understood at the current moment due to its infant stage. Nonetheless, the human race has extended the information transceiving dendrite-axon nerve endings of the brain through the personal computer, creating a global web of interlinked information systems that communicate with all points, at any time, throughout the globe, simultaneously at the press of a key. These vast networks of information are accelerating our cultural evolution exponentially, for memes (bits or units of mental information that, like genes, are subject to evolutionary pressures) are interacting and mutating at a rate formerly not possible due to the absence of the new digitizing appliances. Just like thought was not possible until the emergence of the cortex, this level of planetary integration was not possible until humans learned and mastered the laws of electricity.

Boundaries appear to be dissolving due to this new, increasingly integrated, planetary nervous system. National boundaries, language barriers, spatial divisions, linear time, separate identities, and even sexual differences are all becoming irrelevant in the web, as we exist as beings of pure information in cyberspace. Inevitably this will begin to mutate consciousness, as our experience of reality is becoming more mystical in nature. People have access to an almost infinite variety of ideas, opinions, points of view, and ideologies, for the vision-logic mentation is now *witnessed* (as opposed to being identified with) as patterns of light and configurations of electrons. We are literally entering each other's minds, as "we are soon to stroll the virtual labyrinths of each other's digitized imaginations." [4] The world is slowly being "uploaded" into this new info-space where everything is made of on/off, 0/1, yin/yang codes of information that manifest as electronic realities on our screens, iPods, and wireless smart phones.

Human-computer interface is now making possible the empowerment of the individual. People can now create and express subjective realities on their screens, and then share with the entire globe what formerly was limited to their private imagination. Passive consumption of information created by the television networks is slowly becoming uninteresting, as individuals have the power now to create their own digitized movies, CDs, and cyber playgrounds on the new continent some call "Cyberia." Creativity has found a new realm for expression, and is now the driving force behind most human endeavor. As McKenna points out:

> Out of these connections will come an unexpected and radical redesign of culture. The disparate human family is in the act of undergoing a true metamorphosis into something which more nearly resembles a single thinking, reacting, and planning super organism; the necessary partner with the larger Gaian Mind in the humbling task of healing and wisely managing the planet. [5]

What we are witnessing is the "Planetarization of Consciousness", [6] what Jesuit priest and palanteologist Teihard de Chardin called the Noosphere in his 1938 classic, *The Phenomena of Man.* [7] *Noos* is the Greek word for mind, and *noosphere* refers to a "sphere of thought or mind" enveloping the Earth. De Chardin envisioned the world moving toward greater levels of connectivity and complexity as the human mind and its cultures developed faster modes of information exchange. He believed that this movement would eventually produce a single global mind, which he called the Noosphere. He explains, "No one can deny that a world network of economic and psychic affiliations is being woven at ever-increasing speed which envelops and constantly penetrates more deeply within each of us. With every day that passes it becomes a little more impossible for us to act and think otherwise than collectively." [8]

This Noosphere is clearly seen in our self-regulating global market, as well as in all other areas of endeavor taking place within the awakening collective mind. Social networks are interweaving memes that reach all corners of the globe, initiating movements and practices that shape environmental and social realities of the material plane at ever accelerating rates. This, of course, reflects how a thought in our networked brain can move an arm or leg. The computer-based information networks of the Internet and World Wide Web seem to be the material brain or objective "shell," the Technosphere, of the subjective Noosphere, the nonlocal mind of the collective human unconscious.

Being birthed in level three, when thought, language, and culture began to first develop, the Noosphere has now reached a level of maturity where it is becoming self-aware. Within cyberspace, cybernetic communication close to light speed is making possible a self-organizing system of information exchange that is slowly becoming self-referencing and autonomous. In other words, the collective unconscious of humanity is becoming conscious in a single, thinking, information-processing super organism. It is truly the emergence of a new level of collective consciousness that is reshaping our educational, economic, political, scientific, social, and artistic modes of expression. We now have the technological infrastructures that will allow, *if* human consciousness catches up with its technologies, a true planetary consciousness to emerge. Just as billions of separate neurons link up collectively to support and transceive a single human mind, all humans interacting via the Web are creating the gestalt of a single species mind that seems poised toward self-awareness in the Noosphere. Again, the highly networked electronic systems represent the nervous system and brain of the Noospheric mind, supporting through local routers a nonlocal sphere of collective human imagination.

Jose Arguelles in an excerpt from his last work, *Manifesto for the Noosphere: The Next Stage in the Evolution of Human Consciousness*, writes:

> Just as the biosphere is the unified field of life and its support systems—the region for the transformation of cosmic energy on Earth, to use Vernadsky's phrase—so the noosphere is the unified field of the mind, the psychic reflection of the biosphere. Because we as a species, the aggregate of consciousness-bearing cells of the evolving Earth, are not yet awake to our role as a planetary organism, so too the noosphere is not yet fully conscious. When humanity becomes conscious of itself as a single organism and unites to activate the noosphere, we will find the collective resolve and will to reconstruct the biosphere and divert the energy of the human race from a path of destruction based

> on a mechanized abstraction from nature to a new harmonic order of super-organic reality based on an entirely different state of consciousness than has yet existed on Earth. [9]

Before we can master these technologies and cause some truly evolutionary changes, we must first learn how to use, understand, and ultimately master our own brains. If level five's focus was the mastering of the body-organism, level six is the mastering of the brain. Dr. Leary describes: "The human brain has a hundred billion neurons, and each neuron has the knowledge-processing capacity of a powerful computer. The human brain has more connections than there are atoms in the universe. The human brain can process more than a hundred million signals a second, and counting." [10] This ecstatic statement reveals the immense complexity that is our brain, and at this level of evolution we are students of such complexity.

Both Dr. Leary [11] and Dr. Lilly [12] have described the human brain as a massive biocomputer which runs multiple programs simultaneously through a hierarchy of information-processing systems (i.e., the "triune" brain). These programs we are familiar with by now, for we have been discussing them throughout our explorations. Our human existence up to this point has been dictated by physio-survival imprints/programs processed and executed mainly through the reptilian brain stem; mating-emotional-territorial strategy imprints/programs run through the paleomammalian limbic brain structures; and mental-symbolic belief-system programs and social-identity programs conditioned and encoded within the neocortex. All structures act in harmonious, coherent coordination, dictating the reflexive behavioral and perceptual activities of the human organism. At level six (I will discuss some techniques and strategies in the Ontogenetic section), we can master these arbitrary programs by becoming the "meta-programmer" (Lilly) of our neuronal wiring through "serial re-imprinting" (Leary). This means that our brain/mind must become aware of itself through the act of deep introspection (i.e., meditation), and can then begin to play with the relativistic possibilities of alternate programming/imprinting sequences.

Serial re-imprinting was proposed by Dr. Leary to be the mechanism for establishing novel perceptual-behavioral programs within the nervous system. Through various methods, such as neurotransmitter drug intake, sleep deprivation, sensory deprivation, prolonged fasting, giving birth, near-death experience, shock, spontaneous mystical experience, hypnosis, deep meditation, or systematic yogic techniques, old imprints can be temporarily suspended. "The only way to rewire neural patterns is to interfere with the neurotransmitter sequence at the synapse, thus retracting the old imprint and allowing for a new one." [13] As the old imprints/programs are suspended through the disruption of habituated biochemical neural bonds at the synapse, new imprints can be established to replace the old reflexive programs with novel behavioral-perceptual strategies that can take over earthly functions consciously. "Neurologic is the science of selective re-imprinting. The use of the nervous system as a motion-picture camera. The conscious creation of a sequence of realities." [14] In each moment there are billions of signals drifting through the ether. In level six Awareness we can learn to de-imprint/de-condition/dis-attach our frequency receivers from the narrow four lower reality channels, making available a vast ocean of alternate information signals. We can become master surfers in this electromagnetic ocean of information, tuning into any frequency we so choose through the act of Will. Leary elucidates: "Although the brain receives one hundred million impulses a second, mundane consciousness is limited to signals which have been conditioned to one of the four imprinted game boards." [15]

A modern term backed by extraordinary new findings in neuroscience that describes the individual's ability to re-imprint, meta-program, or rewire neural pathways is called *self-directed neuroplasticity*. Psychiatrist Dr. Jeffrey Schwartz has been studying the brain's capacity to heal and rewire itself via mindfulness meditation, a technique that we will be talking about at length in the "Experience of Structure" section. In particular, Dr. Schwartz worked extensively with OCD (Obsessive-Compulsive Disorder) patients, taking state-of-the-art images of the brain via MRI (Magnetic Resonance Imaging) technology prior to and after mindfulness training. Dr. Shwartz found that the observable abnormalities associated with OCD, namely "pathologically overactive orbital-frontal cortex-anterior cingulated gyrus-caudate nucleus circuitry," [16] were almost completely healed after only six months of mindfulness meditation practice. This practice allowed a strengthening of the prefrontal cortex's ability to consciously self-regulate reflexive limbic patterns. Dr. Swartz states in www.ocdcentre.com, "Studies using state-of-the-art brain imaging demonstrate that mindfulness-based treatments are associated with significant changes in brain abnormalities. Of particular interest, research shows that people are capable of rewiring brain circuitry associated with Obsessive Compulsive Disorder." [17] In other words, using mindfulness techniques, the subjective minds of patients were literally able to reshape and rewire objective brain structures that were dysfunctional and maladaptive. This is possible due to the fact that the brain is always moving, changing, growing branches, making connections, and creating novel neural pathways. The brain in effect is a fluid, "plastic," ever-branching structure that is sensitive to both external and internal stimuli. At this level of consciousness, we can use this neuroplasticity of the brain consciously to reprogram, rewire, and heal the brain. Here we see how the subjective aspect of the universe is becoming more central than the objective structures, as awareness in this level can directly shape the perceptual filters that up to this point have been unconsciously built by the slow-moving streams of evolutionary time. The reshaping occurs by mindfully harnessing the fluid nature of brain growth and channeling said growth toward desired self-programming outcomes.

Mindfulness, bare attention, or simply self-observation is the capacity of an individual to be aware of the mind. It is a conscious act of self-witnessing that allows awareness to dis-attach and dis-identify from the fluctuating phenomena of mind (which include perceptions, sensations, emotions, thoughts, images, etc.). This practice allows awareness to witness, without reacting or judging, the repetitive patterns of mind, thus inhibiting the unconscious and reflexive execution of said patterns. So instead of acting on internal mind stuff, through mindfulness we merely witness it, and thus cultivate a spaciousness that over time allows us to make alternate choices, which translate into alternate neural pathways. We can see that through this process we can begin to break the habituations of mind, the extreme of which is OCD, and begin to master the workings of our brain/mind system. "The use of mindful awareness is the practical key that opens up the human capacity for self-regulation. The application of bare attention to one's own mental processes is the activity that leads to the development of the human mind's full potential. And as advances in scientific understanding have demonstrated, it is an act of the mind that is capable of rewiring the brain." [18]

Only at this level of consciousness can we begin to understand and *experience* "external" reality as an "internal" event. As stated, the objective universe is slipping into the background as subjectivity is becoming more central to Spirit's journey of awakening. In fact, at this stage there is the peak realization that what we call the "objective universe" is ultimately a subjective event, a mere state of *Being*. As we have been exploring, external frequencies (originally chaotic and indeterminate) are filtered through the genetically templated receptive nerve endings of our sensory system. The senses pick up the signals (light, sound, smell, etc.) relevant to the organism and its level of awareness. These sensory signals are converted into bioelectrical impulses that travel via nerve fibers to the spinal cord and eventually to the brain. The brain then receives the bioelectrical information and proceeds to organize, filter, categorize, and interpret it within the limits of its ramified and imprinted neural branches. The bioelectrical impulses from the "external" stimuli trigger the release of chemical messengers, our neurotransmitters, that encode the bioelectrical, on/off information within their chemical constitution as inhibitory or excitatory binary (0/1) functions. These neurotransmitters bond to specific receptor sites signaling either "fire" or "don't fire" to the next neuron. In real-time motion, the dynamic process at the synapse can be seen as oscillations or vibrations resonating at various frequencies. The many vibrating neurotransmitters, with their respective inhibiting and/or exciting functions, produce waves of information that interact with one another, producing interference patterns that encode the external signals. These interference patterns seem to hold holographic representations, limited to imprints, programs, or neural connections, of "external" reality. They manifest as 3-D images within the mind when Consciousness shines its activating rays on it. In other words, a web of interacting frequencies in the brain creates global gestalt states that reflect the outer experiences within programmed parameters. Thousands of wave-interference patterns crisscross the synaptic fields constantly, effectively deconstructing "external" signals into standing wave-interference patterns. The Witnessing Light of Awareness is what gives the interference patterns captured by the brain the luminous 3-D quality that we experience as reality.

Writer David Aaron Holmes has described this notion brilliantly in his Neurobioluminescence theory. He articulates his theory by postulating that the quantum field itself, in this case, "the minute quantum electromagnetic field effects produced by the firings of presentation neurons within the brain—are the foundational source of a basic proto-awareness from which our own highly articulated conscious awareness is formed" [19] (remember Sir Roger Penrose's theory—when a quantum wave collapses, it emits a unit of conscious awareness). He continues by stating that "the ultimate biological function of the sentient brain is to organize and amplify the minute, proto-conscious electromagnetic field effects of its firing neurons into the very scene that manifests each moment before our eyes." [20] He further describes how the neurons collectively form a *neural resonance chamber* that creates a "brilliant sound and light show, which is projected directly upon the convoluted surfaces of the cerebral cortex, a crumpled two-dimensional surface, overlaid with a wide variety of sensory cortical maps, which function as a brightly lit, constantly refreshed presentation screens for the primary sense modalities." [21] The Witness is thus presented with a "three-dimensionally superimposed, multisensory presentation that effectively re-creates an entirely credible view of the surrounding world within the dome of the skull." The inner "holographic" sensorium field presentation that reconstructs the outer world is "experienced by the awareness inherent within the very quantum electromagnetic field that comprises the presentation itself!" [22] As stated, the internal resonant multisensory gestalt representations produced by the interaction of oscillating neural pulses seem to be holographic in nature. In fact, many neuroscientists are beginning to suspect that the brain may organize all information holographically.

A hologram is a three-dimensional photograph made from light beams. Holography is a method of lensless photography in which a wave field of light scattered by an object is recorded on a plate as an interference pattern. When a coherent light beam such as a laser is directed toward the photographic record, the original wave pattern is regenerated and a three-dimensional holographic image appears. The phenomenon of interest, however, is the fact that if the photographic record is divided into two, a laser beam shining through one of the halves will still generate the *whole* image. If we further break down the recorded image, say into one hundred pieces, each piece will regenerate the *whole* original record with less intensity. Thus each piece or part contains the information of the whole.

Karl Pribram used this general principle to describe the brain and its functions after stumbling across the newly developed techniques of holography in the late 1960s. [23] He noticed some basic correlations between how holograms are generated and how the brain works. In his early research, Pribram had the opportunity to join colleague Karl Lashley in 1946 to research the nature of memory in rats. Theses rats were trained to run mazes so that they would memorize the route. The team then surgically removed portions of their brain, areas where the memory might be stored, and put the rats back in the maze. To their surprise, they found that no matter how much of the brain was abstracted, they could not eliminate the memory of the route. This and other experiments revealed that when certain parts of a rat's brain where removed, overall behavior continued more or less in a normal fashion. While intensity of recall was found to be relative to the mass of the brain, nothing short of removal of the entire brain would interrupt overall recall. This led Pribram to propose that most brain functions seem to be distributed equally and ubiquitously throughout the neural matrix, such that any part of the brain embodies the whole of its functions. The whole of behavior more or less remained, no matter how much of the rat's brain was removed.

Not only may memory function in a holographic fashion, but it seems plausible that all functions, including perception, work this way. The senses receive external data, and the data from "objective" reality is then sent to the brain, which mathematically deconstructs said data into wave-frequency patterns that are scattered throughout the distributed networks of the brain. Perceptions (and memory) are coded and stored as interference patterns. The brain then interprets the information to generate a holographic "internal" representation/interpretation of the "external" world. These internal holographic representations of the "external" world are then displayed within the context of the Witness, pure Consciousness, or inner Being. The internal frequencies and wave patterns are then projected "outward" and experienced as "external" events. Even what we call solidity is nothing but the interpretation of bioelectrical signals within the brain, but through habit we have mistakenly externalized what in reality is an internal affair. In other words, our experience of reality is really a *psychic experience*: i.e., an experience of the psyche. Internal signals, such as thoughts, emotions, feelings, memories, plans, images, imaginings, or dreams can also be observed as biochemical electrical impulses that are registered and interpreted by the organizing tendencies of the brain, holographically displayed to the Witnessing Awareness. Pribram elucidates this process in an old *Scientific American* magazine:

> How can interference effects be produced in the brain? One can imagine that when nerve impulses arrive at synapses, they produce electrical events on the other side of the synapse that take the form of momentary standing wave fronts. Typically the junctions made by a nerve fiber number in the dozens, if not hundreds. The patterns set up by arriving nerve impulses presumably form a microstructure of wave forms that can interact with similar microstructures arising in overlapping junctional contacts. These other microstructures are derived from spontaneous changes in electrical potential that ceaselessly occur in nerve tissue, and from other sources within the brain. Immediate cross correlations result, and these can add in turn to produce new patterns of nerve impulses. The hypothesis presented here is that the totality of this process has a more or less lasting effect on protein molecules and perhaps other macromolecules at the synaptic junctions and can serve as a neural hologram from which, given the appropriate input, an image can be reconstructed. [24]

Pribram speculates that these wave forms create the pictorial images, neural holograms, in our brain. He believes that perception arises not in the neuron, but in the synaptic fields distributed throughout the brain. Like television antennas, the dendrite branches are tuned to receive certain frequencies, dependent on the reality sequence being selected and transceived.

The illusion of an "external" world exists as a function of the ignorant grasping of the Eternal Consciousness onto the structures and holographic creations of the brain, which arise moment to moment as a product of resonating frequencies that interact holistically to reflect what it interprets as "out there." We can then propose that what we call mind, grounded in the neural architecture of the brain, is a hologram of the external world, illuminated by the Light of conscious awareness emanating from the holo-field itself. As has been seen, the ramified neural patterns get connected/imprinted/conditioned/programmed in particular ways that reflect the organism's experiences in the world. An infant comes into the world as a "blank slate," but through the course of its development, its tender dendrites-axons get wired in particular configurations that program subsequent behavioral-perceptual strategies in and through life. The unmanifest pure Consciousness, Spirit, or Self, being incarnated in physical bodies, is presented with all these neuro-electro-chemical information patterns that holographically display thoughts, images, perceptions, emotions, and sensations. At the lower levels, Consciousness grasps and identifies with this information, condensing its limitless boundless Identity into space-time bound forms. In level six, Consciousness begins to awaken to its true creative participation in the process of moment to moment creation.

The holographic metaphor can be taken further, for as we have been exploring, the Witness resides silently in every neuron (and every wave function!). As such, the neuron contains, or rather transceives the whole human mind. Just as the entire Internet is available from one router, so is the entire mind from a single neuron. Again, the image is that of a nonlocal field of information (a single human mind or the Noosphere) that is transceived and transduced by interconnected antenna arrays that simultaneously communicate with each other at all times. Specialized brain structures, such as the hippocampus for memory, for example, contain the high-density memory networks, but as the neural web fully interconnects every point with every other point, the memory is also distributed throughout the neural net. Just like Google has its main headquarters somewhere in local space-time, its programs are transceived throughout the Web. You pull one corner of the Web, and the whole Web feels the tug. Information flows, and at this stage of Consciousness we begin to awaken to the fact that we have unlimited access to all information, *if* we learn how to surf.

With this elementary interpretation of brain/mind activity we can begin to understand the workings and, ultimately, how to operate our bio-computer, the brain.

Timothy Leary calls this level of Awareness the Neuroelectric Circuit and describes it as such:

> The Sixth Circuit emerges when the nervous system begins to understand and control its own functioning as a bioelectric transceiver. We have noted that each new evolving circuit of the nervous system includes and interconnects with those that precede it. The Sixth Circuit is the central bio-computer. It receives signals from the other five circuits. These signals, regardless of their original sensory location, reach the brain as electro-chemical on/off "bleeps." [25]

As a bioelectric transceiver, the brain and its extension, the computer, creates and organizes patterns of information that display realities. The content of these reality constructions can be seen in terms of programs which, once made available to Consciousness, can be manipulated and managed by our higher Self, i.e., the metaprogrammer.

Ontogenetic Expression

In level six we are becoming masters of our reality. What we are doing in essence is bringing what has been traditionally called the personal unconscious into consciousness. The Freudian psychoanalytic movement began shining a light on this most mysterious realm of the unconscious mind at the beginning of the twentieth century. Through the methods of psychoanalytic examination, dream interpretation, and free association, the doors to the unconscious were briefly opened, revealing the basic primal programs from the previous stages of evolution thus discussed. To the externally oriented West, the personal unconscious appeared as a dark, chaotic, frightening world that could overwhelm the fragile "civilized" ego at any moment. This limited view reflects the shallow identification with the surface ethnocentric ego that defines the early 1900s of Sigmund Freud. In stage six of development, we turn to the sophisticated inner maps of the East, for the oriental sages and mystics had been developing a systematic approach to self-observation and self-inquiry for millennia.

The psychic level of consciousness can happen spontaneously in rare cases, but in the absence of such grace there exists a technology that moves awareness directly into those psychic realms of experience. This technology provides navigating techniques for any person wishing to explore deeply the nature of their own Being, and ultimately the nature of Reality. The master technology is Meditation. We will explore both Buddhist and Yogic methods of meditation so that we can gain some necessary tools to do some of the deeper explorations that can unfold, with some practice and discipline, the psychic level of Awareness.

Lama Yeshe in his *Becoming Your Own Therapist*, describes how the practice of meditation enables a conscious exploration of that which has been historically unconscious. [26] John Engler, among others, has brought awareness to the contraindications of meditation for people who have not yet developed an integrated ego-personality structure. [27] But for those who have more or less integrated the previous levels of Consciousness development, and are ready to confront deeper aspects of their Being, meditation stands as the most advanced technology for this kind of work.

Basically, what happens in meditation is that the person contacts what we have been calling the Witness, the inner Presence, or pure Awareness. This sounds like an easy task, but as any meditator will reveal, the Witness is constantly pulled into the phenomena being witnessed. In other words, our habitual identification and attachment to our sensations, emotions, thoughts, personality, and individuality as a whole is so great that it constantly pulls pure Awareness into an involvement and identification with those arising forms. After some practice, however, it becomes easier to contact and rest in that Witness, allowing phenomena to come and go in impermanent waves.

One of the main insights realized through meditation, and specifically discussed in Buddhist circles, is that of the impermanent nature of all phenomena. "Since nothing perceptible to the senses is static, but always at the stage of becoming, waxing, waning, or ceasing to be what it was, it is reasonable to deduce that the same holds true of what is neither measurable nor perceptible." [28] This insight can be either extremely liberating or ontologically horrifying, for in the moving stream of phenomena one realizes that there is nothing to hold on to. Even what we up to this point had identified as being real, solid, separate, and permanent is seen as "empty" and "void," as the components that made up our individuality are inevitably seen to be in a state of flux. Our bodies are growing old day by day, our moods and emotions change moment to moment, our thoughts move like a stream, and even our personality is in a state of constant change as is described in the Buddhist doctrine of "no-self." Bonfel explains; "The seeming individuality of each is a bundle of transient qualities, all ephemeral and unstable, all dependent for their fleeting existence on innumerable interlocking factors to which billions of causes, prior and concurrent, have contributed." [29] This observation reveals that the personality construct (levels one through four) is an ever-changing conglomeration of transient qualities that have no individual, separate, solid reality, thus the small self being ultimately an illusion. Useful for navigating the 3-D world, the ego-personality is fundamentally an ephemeral mirage with no intrinsic reality unto itself.

Once we have stabilized our witnessing capacity we begin to observe our sensations, emotions, thought patterns, images, plans, memories, fantasies, ego or small self, and all other phenomena that arise *within* Awareness. In other words, we come to the same realization that our neuroscience counterpart came to: all experience of the "external" world exists *within* the Empty embrace of Consciousness. All phenomena, from physical sensations to outward perceptions to internal mind stuff, are in existence only as they are directly apprehended and conceived by Awareness. All experience, internal or external, physical or mental, is *psychic* in essence. By dis-identifying with our body-mind system we can establish contact with the Witness, and only then can we acquire the ability to experience reality from a psychic space.

Once you have gone deep enough, you begin to access deeper levels of insight. You eventually enter a "place" that is behind all your habitual patterns of personal being, and you witness all of the fluctuating information within your field of Awareness as a multiplicity of vibrations and frequencies. You enter into a truly trans-mental, transpersonal realm where identification has broken its attachment to the components making up the individuality. From this spaciousness, a space that is behind it all, Awareness calmly and mindfully observes the never-ending input-output, rise-fall, on-off, birth-death, yin-yang cycles of the phenomenal world. In this state we perceive reality as nothing more than bits of information that enter and exit our Consciousness in infinite forms and variations, but ultimately being configurations of mental energy existing within the psychic space. Like being in front of the Internet, in meditation you surf the various channels of your being, with an infinite variety of informational forms directly and spontaneously available to the inspection of Conscious Awareness.

Once you have practiced long enough, that which was previously unconscious begins to rise into conscious awareness. [30] The entire geography of the unconscious psyche is potentially available once the grosser aspects of being, such as body sensations, emotions, and mental noise, are brought to a quieter rhythm. Id impulses, childhood memories, repressed traumatic events, conditioned patterns of thought, imprinted networks of associations, impressions, compulsions, tendencies, complexes, drives, reflexive thought, desires, fears, addictions, shadows, repressed content, anima and animus, and the entire display of behavioral-perceptual programs can be seen in their raw form. One is able to stand far enough from their personal history to examine all of the various causative forces that form their current expression, as identity expands to reclaim all that was previously unconscious. Behind the mosaic of individuality one can directly become aware of the unconscious underpinnings of personality—the wiring under the board, so to speak—and bring into consciousness, and thus master, what until this point was reflexive and automatic.

As this level is an "internal" experience, one can become aware of the hidden structures and mechanisms behind thought, perception, and behavior. No longer dictated by unconscious forces and reflexive imprints, the individual at this level can re-imprint or meta-program the various structures that to this point dictated all action. From this level all action is a conscious decision of will, rather than a robotic conditioned reflex, and the person becomes a conscious creator of their reality and their experience within it. The relativity of all realities is perceived, as the meta-programmer within becomes a master in designing, shifting, writing, and implementing alternative perceptual-behavioral programs. The more basic programs/imprints of physio-survival (level one), emotional-territorial strategy (level two), patterns of belief, language, symbols (level three), social identity-personality (level four), organism as a whole (level five), and ultimately perceptions of the external world can be shifted and rewritten as many sages and yogis have done throughout the ages. Reality is thus viewed as the reception-projection that emanates from a hierarchy of programs. But one realizes that these programs are a necessary part of mundane existence and have their relevance in the consensus everyday world. The trick is to make these programs effective, functional, life enriching, healthy, productive, and ultimately conducive to a positive life experience. Many humans, if not most, live life with dysfunctional traumatized programming, thus living and creating mass suffering for themselves and others. Psychotherapy is designed, when it works, to help individuals reprogram those faulty perceptions and behaviors. At this level, however, we become our own therapist, and through mindful awareness of these programs can begin to empower ourselves to shape our life by choosing the programming that works best for us.

As the name seems to suggest, the psychic plane is often the home of various forms of ESPs, extrasensory perceptions, such as telepathy, clairvoyance, and precognition. Yogis have called these psychic powers *siddhis,* which are acquired through the mastery of internal forces. Mishra explains: "The process of the psychic mechanism consists of the law of the mind, how the mind operates. These mental laws are not corporeal. They are incorporeal, but they move the entire body." [31]

According to Patanjali's Yoga Sutras, supernatural powers, *siddhis,* arise from the coordinated focus of mental/psychic energy through the advanced development of concentration. This deep state of concentration can be intentionally guided through the use of Will, focusing enough mental energy on the desired outcome so as to acquire the sought after result. The spiritual traditions warn practitioners against the seduction of these powers, for even though they are road marks signaling progress, they can also become obstacles inhibiting further spiritual development. So not only can we shape and rewire our own brains, but at this level we can even go beyond our individual brain to access information that is not personal. Synchronicities, where external events correlate with internal processes, and telepathic knowing become deeply established realities as Awareness begins to awaken to the inner unity of all things.

Since at this level Being resides behind the brain-displayed phenomenal world of electromagnetic spectrums of reality, the Witness can access signals that are not of a personal nature. Others' thoughts, as in telepathy, can be picked up as one's personal informational flux comes to rest. Frequencies and resonances from distant events in time or space can be accessed through what has been called the "sixth sense," which is the intuitive ability to access frequencies of a non-personal nature; i.e., transpersonal information. Being behind the phenomenal display of the world, one has a panoramic view of an ocean of potential information, since all is seen as a shimmering sea of vibration. By dis-identifying and dis-attaching our-Self from our personal mundane signals, we can potentially access infinite alternate frequencies.

A friend of mine once said, "The Internet is training wheels for humanity, to remind them of their original abilities and powers." She meant that we can all be telepathically linked beyond time and space, we can all access information in distant places at different times, and we can access our collective archives of information regarding the entire human race naturally and within. We have only forgotten these abilities through our obsessive over identification with our individuality and our time-space-bound bodies. If we go deep enough, into what was called the personal unconscious, we may find links to what we are currently accessing through the Internet. This seems like a far-out speculation, but if nature and our brain are holographically structured, then it is only logical to assume that all information is "here now." Nonlocality is a function of a holographic universe, where all information resides in the very fabric of our being, in each neuron, in each particle.

The above speculation can give us a hint of what it will "feel" like when and if the planetary human Noosphere is activated into an actual, single collective consciousness. When and if the Noosphere becomes self-aware, subjectively we will become psychic. We will have telepathic abilities, we will know instantly what happens on the other side of the globe, we will be immersed in synchronicities, and we will have access to the archives of all human knowledge as individual awareness becomes truly global in nature. An internal global telepathic and synchronous guidance will allow us to make decision for the collective interest, as opposed to past decisions based on self-interest; a self that is seen to be temporary and ultimately illusory. Of course some individual consciousness will remain; just as body consciousness remains after entering emotional consciousness, or emotional awareness remains once mental consciousness is activated, so will a strand of space-time-bound awareness remain as we simultaneously access the collective human mind of the Noosphere.

We can also consider what is called Magik as an expression of the psychic level. Aleister Crowley was one the most controversial modern practitioner of this ancient art. He claimed that by mastering Will and becoming aware of the level of mind that interprets the perceptions of reality (unconscious imprints and conditioned neural patterns) we can directly manipulate (re-imprint or meta-program) our nervous system and those of others. In this way a "glitch" in the space-time matrix shifts an occurrence that is normally dictated by the laws of cause and effect, and an a-causal event is displayed in phenomenal reality. He contended that at the psychic level of awareness we can play with information and alter signals so as to shift perception. "Do what thou wilt shall be the whole of the law. Love is the law, love under will." [32] Will then is the ability to focus and concentrate Awareness to achieve specific tasks, from rewiring our own brain to accessing information at a distance to ultimately altering the occurrence of events in the space-time continuum.

We will conclude with Vaughan's synthesis of this level:

> The fifth chakra, *vissuddha*, is the ether center which penetrates everywhere and yet can be found nowhere, and is not matter but concept. At this level we enter a world of psychical reality. When control of the mind and emotions is achieved, peace of mind ensues. At this level, material reality is perceived to be a world of appearances or illusions, while abstract ideas and values become palpably real as the source of experience. [33]

Experience of Structure

Q: What do you perceive-project from this level?
A: Energy in different forms, patterns of information, mind-stuff, flux of phenomena, psychic phenomena.

Techniques to achieve this level of expanded awareness are many, but I will focus on Buddhist mindfulness insight meditation and Yogic concentration practices due to their millennia-old origins. After the preliminary moral and ethical foundations of *yama* and *niyama* are established, and the physical and mental purification through *asanas* and *pranayama* completed, the yogi is ready for the more advanced practices of meditation. The fifth limb in Patanjali's Yoga system is *pratyahara* (withdrawal), and involves sitting and gathering the forces of the mind. "When all senses renounce their respective objects and the psychic energy of the thinking mind, along with the energy of all senses, transforms into *chittam* (mental body) for the time being—that is to say, when the individual 'I am' transforms into impersonal 'I am' (witness)—that is called *pratyahara*, the fifth step of the Yoga of stillness or complete psychic rest." [34] In *pratyahara* one turns inward and withdraws conscious awareness from the senses. The individual traditionally sits in the meditative posture (cross-legged with an aligned back, neck, and head) and slowly turns attention away from sensory stimuli and focuses it inward toward an object of meditation. This limb allows Awareness to extricate and dis-attach it-Self from the sensory world of matter, thereby freeing up conscious energy, otherwise used to experience the external world, so that it may be directed inwardly. Once this has been accomplished, the individual enters the sixth step or limb called *dharana* (concentration).

With Awareness now freed from worldly signals, it can now be directed and managed through the faculty of Will. In *dharana*, the person fixes the mind upon one point, channeling the freed conscious energy to the desired object of concentration. The object of concentration can vary greatly, but the point of this step is to still the mind by concentrating the psychic energy on one object. The object of meditation can be a candle flame, a chosen Deity, God Herself, an internal image, the breath, or a *mantra*. The different chakra centers are also points suitable for concentration, particularly the higher heart, throat, forehead, and crown centers. So once our attention has been directed inwardly, attenuating external signals through *pratyahara,* it is then focalized like a laser beam through *dharana.*

The seventh limb is called *dhyana* (meditation) and is the continuous flow of attention without break on the object of meditation. At this point the meditator experiences one-pointed focus on the object, with the outcome of stilling the body, senses, mind, and ego. The practitioner ceases to identify with the lower complexes of Being and begins to experience the Witness as a freed locus of concentrated Awareness. Thus anchored in *dharana* through the continuous flow of one-pointed focused Awareness, one then undergoes the final act of Will: the complete relinquishing of attachment, identity, and imprinted habit to the lower structures and frequencies of Being.

Within the Buddhist path of concentration, various levels or states called *jhanas* have been mapped out to describe the ascending subtleties of mind as one deepens the concentration upon the chosen object. The summit of the psychic stage occurs in the fourth "material" *jhana*, where "equanimity, one-pointedness, bliss, and feeling of bodily pleasure cease." [35] In these ultra subtle meditative states, Awareness begins to access deeper realms of experience outside the personal domain. Before entering the fourth *jhana* of the psychic plane, one first enters the Access state, where one experiences brief moments of absorption. This then leads to the first *jhana,* where "hindering thoughts, sensory perceptions, and awareness of painful bodily states all cease." [36] This leads to the second and third *jhana,* which are deepening degrees of one-pointedness and bliss, to finally flower in the last "material" fourth *jhana* as deep equanimity, spaciousness, and bliss.

The reason why one would even want to pursue such an inwardly-directed quest is outlined in Buddha's four noble truths. Truth number One: there is vast suffering in the world due to the realities of impermanence, old age, sickness, and death. Truth number Two: the cause of this suffering is based on our ignorant clinging, grasping, and attachment to that which is impermanent, eliciting craving for the pleasures, and aversion to the pains of this world. Truth number Three: the end of suffering can be reached by all who explore the nature of their being and reality, thereby ultimately realizing the impermanence of everything and thus extinguishing the conditioned craving/aversion tensions of the mind. This leads to true peace. And truth number Four outlines the Middle Way and the Noble Eightfold Path used to achieve freedom, peace, and liberation from the suffering inherent in the wheels of birth and death.

The Noble Eightfold Path, grounded in deep mindfulness, was outlined by Buddha as a means to reprogram the Being so that it diminishes its tendency to get trapped by the clutches of the material world. The Eightfold Path delineates the world-centric course of conduct for those seeking liberation, and includes right understanding, right thought, right speech, right action, right livelihood, right effort, right mindfulness, and right concentration. "Right" means acting in a way that does not cause harm, cuts through delusion and ignorance, and expresses a balanced mindful approach for working with these eight factors so as to reprogram the nervous system toward a more peaceful, balanced, compassionate, wise, and sustainable expression. Within the context of our current discussion, we see that suffering is inevitable in the lower five stages of consciousness. Only in level six can we begin to deprogram and decondition our habitual reflexes to the fluctuations of the world so that we may experience reality "as it is," without clinging and attachment. Only then can we flow through life as a truly free being, master of our own reality, ready to pursue the evolutionary aspirations of the Spirit that is awakening in such individuals.

Mindfulness as discussed is a crucial practice for this level, as it allows us to be aware of fluctuations, patterns, attachments, cravings, and aversions moment to moment without reaction or judgment. This practice keeps Spirit from becoming fully trapped and entangled with that which is witnessed, which as we saw produces suffering. The constant centering of mind (Crowley's Will) is the basis of mindfulness meditation. The essence of mindfulness is centering the mind, usually using the breath, on the present moment. When the mind begins to wander, the person is to notice mindfully where the mind has gone, and then gently bring it back to the breath, or any other object being used for centering. With this practice one establishes the Witnessing capacity through the mindful observation of what arises within Awareness from a cultivated center of observation. Govinda emphasizes the centrality of breath in mindfulness meditation: "The simple observation of the process of breathing, without mental interference, without compulsion, without violation of the natural functions of the body. Hereby breathing becomes conscious." [37] He continues by stating, "The next step is the stilling of all the functions of the body through the conscious rhythm of the breath…the breathing becomes a vehicle of spiritual experience." [38] Breath then becomes our vehicle, being the central attractor for our wandering mind.

Through mindfulness, achieved by the constant centering of mind, one begins to access various levels of insight. The highest insight within the psychic plane on the Buddhist Path of Insight is called Pseudonirvana: "clear perception of the arising and passing of each successive mind moment, accompanied by various phenomena such as brilliant light, rapturous feelings, tranquility, devotion, energy, happiness, strong mindfulness, equanimity toward objects of contemplation, quick and clear perception, and attachment to these newly arisen states." [39] This deep state of insight arises after a process of deepening awareness that begins as Bare Attention, progresses to Mindfulness, to then flower in the stage of Reflection as the "experience of *dukkha,* unsatisfactoriness...these processes are seen to arise and pass away at every moment of contemplation; experience of *annica,* impermanence…these dual processes are seen as devoid of self; experience of *anatta,* no-self....awareness and its objects are perceived at every moment as distinct and separate processes." [40] As the grosser levels of our Being quiet down, we become mindful of deeper information fields that lead to ever deepening states of transpersonal insight. Here we find peace, tranquility, space, and ultimately freedom.

Reciting *mantras* is another powerful method for suspending old imprints and bringing the mind into deeper states of Being beyond the conditioned reflexes of the psyche. A *mantra* is a word or phrase that is repeated internally or verbally. The repetition of these particular syllables creates a pattern of focus within by bringing the mind into center over and over again. The *mantra* develops its own momentum by establishing itself deeply within the psyche of the individual, thus overriding the habitual loops of mind. Ram Dass says in regards to *mantras*: "you identify with this new thought you have added, until you and that thought become one and all other thoughts are passing just like clouds in the sky." [41] *Mantras* were developed in ancient times in order to create certain internal vibratory patterns that change the content and nature of internal events. This happens through a constant centering and pulling of the mind into the vibrations emitted by the *mantra.*

As we explore these deepening stages of Consciousness from within, empirical neuroscience looks at the brain states from the "outside" to see if in fact there are functional changes in the material brain. What has been revealed from reading brain wave activity as recorded by EEG technology is that in fact the organic brain, the *neural resonance chamber,* resonates at various frequencies that reflect and correlate with inner states of consciousness. As it turns out, the brain of the average person goes through these brain-wave changes every night through the wake-dream-dreamless sleep cycle. As we will see, at night we move through the entire spectrum of consciousness, yet most people have not developed their Awareness sufficiently to remain conscious through theses progressive states. Waking everyday states of people who live from levels one through four, basically the busy, thinking, rational mind of the typical ego-personality, vibrates in what is called the Beta Brain Wave range of 13 to 40 Hz (cycles per second). The Beta state reflects the thinking "monkey mind" of the average human today. In levels five and six we begin to experience slower brain waves as we begin to quiet the surface structures of body and mind. This marks the entrance into the Alpha Brain Wave state that reflects an alert, yet fully relaxed meditative state of awareness many times experienced naturally as one begins to fall asleep at night in the hypnagogic state. The hypnagogic state arises as a discrete moment of consciousness between wakefulness and sleep. This relaxed, alert, meditative Alpha Brain Wave state accessed by meditators has been measured at 18 to 13 Hz. This slowdown allows access into mindfulness and the states of deep insight (level six) thus explored. As one deepens the meditation, or as one enters REM dream states, the brain slows down to the Theta Brain Wave range of 8 to 3.5 Hz. As we will soon explore, this allows an entrance into deep trance, visionary, and shamanic states of Consciousness (subtle level seven). And finally, as all surface activity diminishes to 3 to .5 Hz in the Delta Brain Wave range, one enters deep states of mystical formlessness, experienced by all at night in deep dreamless sleep (causal level eight).

A technological method has been developed to help people enter these various states of Consciousness. This technology in effect produces light and sound pulsations that entrain the brain into the desired brain wave frequency. These so-called 'light-sound brain machines' can be programmed to pulsate at specific rates, thereby entraining or resonating with the brain waves to elicit corresponding inner realms. By producing binaural beats via headphone and light emanations from LED light-producing glasses, the individual brain gets "played" like an instrument to produce the desired state. Through sound and light pulsation, the entire brain can be tuned to the desired frequency: from highly effective problem-solving states of Beta, to relaxed meditative states of Alpha, to visionary journeys in Theta, to mystical fusion in Delta. Again, Consciousness has devised technologies through human ingenuity that aid it in its deepening explorations of its deepest nature. Of course, one can consciously slow down brain wave activity through breath, as in meditation, for breath is the conductor of the entire symphony of body-mind frequencies. Slow, deep, rhythmic breathing eventually entrains the brain toward Alpha, Theta, and Delta resonant states of Consciousness.

What in essence is happening at this level of Consciousness development is that Spirit, Awareness, Being, or Self is beginning to untangle it-Self from the constrictive gravitational hold of the typical space-time-bound locus of our body-mind-personality. This stage is the beginning of a gradual departure from our limited personal identities in focused time and space. The work at this level is to develop non-attachment to the transient phenomena of our individuality by letting go. This letting go of limited fixations to the personal mind enables Spirit to further release itself from boundaries, and thus begin to access vaster aspects of itself barely conceivable to the human imagination. In other words, Spirit is finally awakening to its omnipresent, omnipotent, and omniscient identity. Spirit is beginning to remember who it really is.

Exercises:

1.) Sit in a relaxed position. Close your eyes and tune in to the rise and fall of your breath. Place your Awareness on the gentle inner rhythm of your breathing. If a thought, sensation, feeling, or any other phenomenon arises, simply notice it, let it go, and then gently bring your attention back to the rise and fall of your breath. Notice the ebb and flow of all phenomena, and notice how you are not them. Become acquainted with that which witnesses within you. Notice and say to yourself "I have a body, but I am not my body. I can see and feel my body, and what can be seen and felt is not the true Seer. I have thoughts, desires, and emotions. I can know my desires, feel my emotions, and intuit my thoughts. What can be known, felt, or intuited is not the true Knower, Feeler, or Intuitor." Who is that which knows, feels, and intuits? Who is it that Witnesses the entire display that is your individuality?

2.) Practice centering your mind through the repetition of *Ma* with the inhale, and *Om* with the exhale. Try repeating this *mantra* as much as possible and see how it changes your inner states.

3.) Get on the Internet and surf the many info worlds created in cyberspace.

4.) Meditate on your throat chakra, the *visuddha,* and notice the vibratory and creative nature of all reality. Feel the ether element and sense how it interpenetrates all things.

5.) Study the effect of LSD. Research the vast literature on the clinical studies of LSD-assisted psychotherapy. Can LSD produce psychic states of awareness and open the unconscious to conscious inspection? If so, what are the implications for the therapy community if such a tool where to exist?

Further Transpersonal Explorations

It was the early '90s when I entered college, a time when change appeared to be accelerating like a rising techno beat. When I entered UC Davis in 1992, no one had e-mails or cell phones, and the Internet was a concept that was only talked about. I find it amazing that I got through my four years of college without ever having an e-mail account, something that today is as essential as having pencil and paper. The first time I surfed the net was in 1993. Entering it with a sense of wonder and amazement, I began to discover a whole new dimension of possibility. By working the mouse, I began to navigate info worlds that seemed endless and without limit. The minds of others were explicitly available for exploration, and a social web of instantaneous communication was swiftly networking a new planetary consciousness. I would spend hours mesmerized by the digitized multimedia productions of dedicated pioneers, amused by the boundary-dissolving capabilities of what was basically an extension of our own brains. Fascinated by what this meant for our collective evolution, I spent countless hours discussing its promises and dangers with peers who were also experimenting with its electronic buzz. Change, so it seemed, had entered a new spiral of development, catalyzed by these emerging technologies to proceed at exponential, light-speed rates. Life as we knew it would never be the same, again.

As previously mentioned, concurrent with the information revolution of the times, a new "raver- cyber punk" subculture was taking root in the debris of the regressive money-fueled ego materialism of the 1980s. Electronic music in its various forms, such as techno, trance, house, acid, dub, industrial, goa, psytrance, and ambient, to name just a few, was beginning to reawaken a deep desire in people to connect with community and the inner Spirit. In the late '80s and early '90s, renegade DJs would break into abandoned warehouses with generators, light and laser installations, and pounding record-based beats to initiate a whole new young generation hungering for authentic contact into the ancient mysteries of tribal trance. Fueled and connected by a renaissance in psychedelic use, a techno-tribe emerged, reinventing the ancient shamanic techniques of trance, dance, and inner spiritual illumination. Through the ancient technology of recursive, never-ending beats, the techno-shamans guided the multitudes of multicultural humans through inner worlds of light, love, and revelation. Your skin package did not matter, as people from all walks of life and cultures celebrated their divinity while tapping into an ocean of boundary-dissolved consciousness.

My first rave in 1992, already described in my brief autobiography, actually catapulted my budding Consciousness to level eight, pure Awareness, as I merged into an ecstatic mystical Oneness beyond all dualities. But as I reflect back on those initiatory days, I notice that it was this level, six, that I was being introduced to. Prior to raves, my Awareness had always focused on the "external" world, thoughts being a part of this "external" world. Other than at night before going to sleep, I had never really spent much time looking inward. Closing my eyes to witness the contents of my own psyche seemed foreign and weird, as nowhere in my (mainstream) culture was I encouraged to look within. This all changed as I began to explore the rave scene, and the catalyst that completely changed the nature of my inner Being.

In those days, pure LSD was sold at the entrance of every rave, as people of all ages ingested and trance-danced throughout the night. After my first rave, I established the ritual and habit of dancing all night long with eyes closed as the optimal way to access transcendent states, a practice I continued throughout my rave years. To me, this became a spiritual practice leading to actual spiritual experiences, which for an initial skeptical atheist was quite worldview shattering. I would basically spend the entire night traversing the inner corridors of my mind, guided by the ever-ascending trance beats of the techno-shaman DJ. Held in motion by the heartbeat "from whence it all came from," every particle of my body resonated with the bass-pounding pulse, in full Awareness that everyone around me was also swayed by the same Single beat. LSD is now well known for its ability to expand consciousness and reveal inner dimensions of mind; no other way to describe it. Known for its "boundary-dissolving" properties, once it is taken, the user's Awareness is able to explore transpersonal dimensions barely imagined by those uninitiated. Set and setting, the person's inner disposition and the environment in which the chemical is taken, are crucial factors that help shape the person's experience. The mind becomes completely vulnerable and open, so that any minor influence can send the mind spinning.

Raves in those early days were, for me, the perfect setting for this kind of exploration, as I felt safe in these warehouses that were transformed specifically to catalyze the "tripper's" experience. The feeling was that we were all in it together, and the communal love that was unleashed was something I had never experienced before. I felt safe and supported, the music guided my trips, and a feeling that we were the pioneers of a new planetary cyber-culture was the emerging philosophical underpinning of our tribe. The revelations into the nature of my mind and reality during one night's journey surpassed anything I had ever experienced, compressing years of learning, studying, and psychotherapy into one night. For endless, rhythmic hours I would explore the labyrinths of my mind, accessing grids of light that interconnected the souls of all living beings. While my body moved without any conscious effort, my mind would explore the corridors of inner Being with a fluidity and lucidity that was at once revealing and ecstatic. I would park my physical being in some strategic location, let the rhythm take control, and ride the visionary wave into inner imaginal realms of expanded Mind space. Mostly working through personal material, I sometimes glimpsed astral realms far beyond my personal being. Realms of undulating, ethereal, spiritual entities made of light, intuiting a whole higher order of reality (level seven, it turns out) peeked at while dancing with my new found "global tribe."

I learned more about the mind in one night's journey then I did in the four years of studying psychology in college. In the course of one night, I would have mini life reviews, where all of my childhood memories and experiences would be displayed holographically, helping me work out issues and traumas within the context of an ocean of Consciousness and Love. My mind would become crystal clear, lucid, and laser like in its ability to penetrate the Mystery, as I peeled away layer after layer of conditioned thought, imprinted belief, and addictive behavioral pattern. The rational mind and its ruling ego were deconstructed beat by beat, as "I" peered into the abyss of the gap found between two thoughts. I discovered complete inner freedom, as the shackles of conditioned personality and imprinted thought patterns were dissolved within the merging color, sound, rhythm, and strobing light. There was no time, or separate self, only Consciousness.

Unfortunately, the rave scene was short lived, as the same fate that killed the hippie movement in the early '70s began to erode the naïve purity of the rave culture. By 1995 raves where the rage, and everybody knew about these "drug" parties. Raves became huge money-making events, while all other drugs began to infiltrate the once purely psychedelic events. Alcohol, meth, and cocaine entered the scene, completely contaminating the love and peace consciousness triggered by psychedelics. The setting no longer felt safe for this all-out mind expansion, as aggression, lust, and the "meat-market" mentality of the male ego began to replace the purely sensual, feminine openness explored by early ravers.

Set and setting are crucial factors for a positive psychedelic experience, as they can also be the factors that produce very negative or unpleasant experiences for users. Psychedelics have been demonstrated to be physically nonaddictive and minimally damaging to the brain and body. Their main danger lies in the user's potential reckless and uninformed use, for if consciousness is opened in a negative environment, a negative experience is almost guaranteed. I witnessed many "freak-outs," as people ingested in less than optimal settings with little if any preparation and knowledge about the power of these tools. Add to that the fact that pure LSD all but vanished by 1998 as the main producers and distributers were busted, at least in the San Francisco Bay Area, and you have the end of a beautiful era. House and techno became mainstream, played in most alcohol-selling clubs, and the "true rave" receded into the memory of those lucky enough to have been initiated.

However, the Spirit of the early rave days does continue today, as the more "conscious" events continue to initiate those minds ready for transformation. The ecstatic dance scene, with a focus on the mind-expanding practice of dancing without any chemical aid, is now becoming a worldwide movement. The tribal trance dance scene seems to be alive and well today, touching people's lives around the globe as the organizers have morphed mere parties into actual spiritual-experience facilitating events. The global electronic dance culture and the transformational festivals continue their relentless call toward transformation, and even though I no longer go to many of these events, their early influence on my life will forever be viewed as pivotal in my life's journey.

So what was it that raves and LSD showed me that was so special? My inner Being, the Self, a Consciousness that is so deep that we as beings are barely beginning to uncover its true magnitude. LSD is to the psychologist what the microscope is to the biologist, or the telescope to the astronomer, as it magnifies all aspects of mind to the *n*th degree. A psychology that does not utilize this powerful tool is like an astronomer that does not utilize the telescope. Over time I stopped going to raves for the above reasons, but continued to use the mind-expanding properties of the drug in the safety of my own home to continue the exploration of my psyche. My method was to use LSD by myself, at night, in complete, silent darkness, for I found external distractions and influences took away from the richness of the purely inner voyage. To report the nature of these experiences would be rather pointless, for the intensity, brilliance, magnitude, and vastness is truly beyond words. I stopped taking these substances in social and recreational situations, as I treated them with utmost respect. They became serious tools for introspection, unveiling a spiritual dimension to the Cosmos that is summed up in the pages of this text.

After being introduced to the inner worlds of mind, initially accessed by the LSD-fueled raves, I joined a Mahayana Buddhist group of meditators in 1993, learning the basic techniques of concentration and mindfulness meditation. LSD showed me the way; now I had to walk the path. I began to meditate regularly, exploring the nature of my consciousness on a daily basis without chemical help. I began to integrate and ground my ecstatic revelations into my day-to-day life, as I found Awareness to be the Ground of all Being. As I cultivated mindfulness through practice, my life began to change. Every thought, emotion, sensation, and perception was viewed as an impermanent, "illusory" phenomenon that came and went on its own accord within the vast, empty Field of my ever-present sky like Awareness. I learned that the ego-personality, or small self, was a mental construct; a conglomerate of thought-forms temporarily assembled to ultimately vanish back into their Source. I became acquainted with the Witness, and mindfully observed the tides of the external world from that inner place of stillness that seemed eternal and to lie outside the space-time continuum. As I became more proficient at accessing the inner dimensions of Being through meditation practice, I began to have less need or interest in blowing my mind with LSD. LSD showed me the terrain in full, multidimensional, holographic splendor, but it was the disciplined and sustained meditation practice that allowed me to *live* from the higher perspectives accessed. My inner technology shifted to meditation, and today it is through my meditation practice that I access and traverse the inner terrains of my psyche.

Meditation has become more than a mere vehicle for exploring Consciousness. It has become a way of life, keeping me connected to Source while helping keep my mind focused on the present moment. Yoga liberates the energy, *pratyahara* withdraws it from the senses, *dharana* focalizes it, and *dhyana* blooms in a state of full mindful Awareness. The mental mind begins to quiet, as one becomes aware of the vast ocean of information, electromagnetic in nature, that can be Witnessed without attachment. I usually try to meditate before providing psychotherapy sessions, centering my mind and helping it tune to the entire spectrum of my client's Being. When I am very still and internally quiet, I can gather much data from merely observing body postures, facial gestures, emotional currents as revealed by changing skin color or level of agitation, eye contact, as well as the more overt mental messages, symbolic talk, "Freudian slips," and general maladaptive programming. In order to teach others how to reprogram and rewire their brain, I find it essential to function from a place outside of my and their programming. In other words, to be effective I feel I must be free from inner constraints in order to best help others free themselves of theirs. Sometime I view the therapy session as a meditation, mindfully observing whatever comes up from a calm, compassionate but detached center. I attempt to cultivate presence and a Witnessing awareness, reflecting each person's own ultimate capacity for mindful living. I basically function as their conscious Witness, modeling an innate capacity latent in all human beings. I notice things as they come up, to then report on what I see. This noticing is meant to awaken awareness, hopefully shedding light on the usually unconscious habits and repressed content, which can help liberate blocked energy as people become conscious of that which is normally unconscious.

Meditation practice has had such a deep and profound impact on my life that I have become a chief proponent of its physiological, emotional, psychological, and spiritual benefits in my community. When I first moved to my small foothill community, there were no meditation groups or teachers available. As I deepened my community involvement and presence, eventually I felt moved to start a meditation class/group that attracted very few at first. Over time, word got out that this meditation group was literally transforming and healing people from within, and interest started to rise. Eight years later and my meditation group continues to hold the space for countless individuals ready to dive into their deeper selves. Group after group, I am amazed at how individual consciousness immediately slips into resonance with the larger Field of pure Consciousness when allowed, guided, and re-minded. My approach is simple: with the basic mindfulness and concentration practices, we work to quiet the mind so as to be able to recognize the underlying Presence or Awareness that is inherent in all beings. The recognition that basic Awareness and Presence *are* peace, joy, healing, Spirit, or enlightened mind gives people the direct, authentic contact to Ground that stops all searching and seeking. The premise is that "you are what you are seeking," and that to seek keeps one away from finding. I am amazed how fast people can enter this enlightened space when it is presented to them simply and without religious baggage. The practice then becomes one of quieting the "drunken monkey mind" in order to "hear" the ever-present Field in which all phenomena arise, and to which they all return.

Another observation that I have made in myself and others is how, when the surface mind is trained to quiet, the deeper structures of the unconscious tend to surface. Many of my meditation students have over the years pursued psychotherapy after some initial meditation practice, as the need to resolve intrapsychic issues becomes glaringly apparent as repetitive habituated patterns surface over and over during the course of their meditations. For them, unresolved emotional and psychological issues disturb their meditations so that no progress can be obtained until said issues are resolved. Much can be resolved on one's own, but the more persistent blocks and traumas sometimes require guidance and outside professional help. Facing deeply buried, repressed, or unconscious material can be frightening and overwhelming for most people. Therefore, working things out within a psychotherapeutic environment becomes indicated, often helping people move deeper into the meditative states as they resolve or dissolve their maladaptive programming. I have found meditation, in concert with psychotherapy, to be an optimal approach to self-healing, psychic growth, and personal evolution.

What meditation seems to have in common with LSD is that it helps open the doors to the unconscious psyche. They both give access to the psychic plane of reality by taking one beyond physical sensation, emotional imprints, mental conditioning, and habituated identifications. Meditation, of course, takes time, discipline, and practice and is gentler and safer, while LSD literally dissolves the neural connections and imprints of the surface mind to reveal deep dimensions of Mind. It is unfortunate that the reactionary, uninformed legal restrictions have prohibited the legitimate research of and with this powerful psychological tool.

Before prohibition in the late 1960s, researchers were reporting almost miraculous results for treating alcoholism, depression, PTSD, and a spectrum of other emotional and psychological disorders. One such researcher, Dr. Stanislav Grof, has accumulated literally thousands of case studies utilizing LSD to treat various traumas and psycho-emotional ailments. His work is summarized in his *LSD Psychotherapy*, which goes over the history of LSD-assisted psychotherapy and his results utilizing this tool. [42] As mentioned in the last section, in recent years psychedelic research has once again attained legitimacy, as newly approved studies utilizing LSD and other psychedelics have been approved in the United States and Europe. Again, those interested can check out MAPS.org for updates in the ongoing research.

So how does a molecule, active in the microgram range, have such a powerful effect on human consciousness? This question has been slowly researched due to legal constraints, but consensus is now emerging as to how it seems to work in the brain. More maverick theories will be explored in the proceeding chapters, but the basic idea here is that LSD (Lysergic Acid Diethylamide-25) is what is called an indoleamine, or tryptamine, the dual-ring family that includes neurotransmitters serotonin and melatonin. As such, LSD's resemblance to serotonin allows it to be a partial or full agonist at the 5-HT (serotonin) receptor sites distributed throughout the brain, thus facilitating a new pattern of neurotransmission. Julien summarizes the research:

> Almaula and co-workers mapped the binding site for LSD on the 5-HT2A receptor and correlated the binding with receptor activation. Penington and Fox claim that LSD exerts a spectrum of agonist-antagonist effects on a variety of 5-HT receptor subtypes, but they think that the best candidate appears to be agonist action on 5-HT1C receptors. Egan and co-workers…argue for an agonist action at both 5-HT2A and 5-HT2C receptors. Giacomelli and colleagues argue for a complex interaction between serotoninergic system and the dopaminergic system….Finally, Marek and Aghajanian argue for an agonist action at 5-HT2A receptors.[43]

Psychedelic researcher James Kent elucidates, "Visual hallucinogenic effect is associated with 5-HT2A and 5-HT2C receptor interaction." He continues by stating that "agonistic interference at 5-HT subtypes promotes disinhibition and cross-excitability between feedback-coupled assemblies in the brain. Excitation and loss of feedback inhibition in the circuits responsible for processing sensations and perception lead to spontaneous self-sustaining feedback hallucinations." [44] Kent's general premise is that human perception and consciousness are linear, cause-effect processes of bottom-up perception and top-bottom behavioral output. Psychedelics effectively disrupt and destabilize said linear dynamical system toward a chaotic, nonlinear mode of operation. This happens by exciting circuits while simultaneously disinhibiting neural feedback loops, which is experienced as the layered kaleidoscopic fractal imagery of the trip. Kent describes his psychedelic information theory: "psychedelics destabilize linear perception of space and time to produce fractal states of frame layering, bifurcation, and infinite frame recursion." He continues by stating, "Psychedelic perception presents a progressive nonlinear bifurcation of recursive self-similar information corresponding to both internal and external perceptual space." [45] He contends that through this process, the human mind can produce novel information through the complexified, cross-layered, and nonlinear interaction of multiple cortical circuits. He specifies, as a self-proclaimed system materialist, that the brain is what produces the vast and novel visual information, transpersonal or otherwise. I argue that the destabilizing properties of psychedelics do put the brain-mind into a chaotic, nonlinear state, but rather then produce novel information, I believe it makes the instrument of the brain hypersensitive so that it can *receive* truly transpersonal information beyond the brain. Psychedelics decrystallize neural bonds and suspend imprints at the receptor site, particularly in the control centers of the pre-frontal cortex, allowing the instrument (the brain) to become so sensitive so as to be able to transceive the deeper energy matrices of creation (more on this later).

As we bring all of this together, the information revolution of the internet, cyberpunks, LSD, Buddhist meditation, and the "telepathic" global electronic dance culture, we notice a movement into an entirely different level of Consciousness. Something is waking up in all of us, and the interconnections made available through the wireless electronic highways are making it possible for the collective to wake up as a single thinking organism. The Noospheric Mind of the collective human Consciousness has finally constructed itself the material means to transceive as a single Mind. Yet this Noosphere, and the psychic plane that supports it, is only the tip of the Consciousness iceberg. As we continue to dive deep into the oceans of Awareness, Spirit begins to uncover its original substrate, and there awaken as the Source of all that is.

Level 7

Soul: Subtle Plane

Phylogenic Expression

At this point in our phylogenic explorations, we ride the edge of pure speculation, for we can barely imagine what the future will bring due to our collective acceleration into novelty. It does seem clear, however, that if we do not join the Natural Intelligence that preceded the brain-powered human cleverness by billions of years, we may not make the next spiral of Consciousness evolution. The exclusive identification to mind and its artificial products has alienated aspects of Consciousness "encased" in the pre-frontal cortex human identity from the deeper Awareness underlying the natural world for at least the last six thousand years, but specifically for the last couple of hundred industrialized years. The linear egoic mind, intoxicated by its power and held hostage by the patriarchal testosterone-infused male strength, managed to divide Awareness into "little" self and the "unconscious." The "unconscious" can be thought of as the underlying, interconnected, causative forces of the body, the feminine principle (which has been suppressed by the dominator cultures of history), and the natural world. This has inadvertently made a cancer out of our species, despite our arrogant so-called intelligence. Even the higher self-aware Noosphere is a dead end without the more organic support of its Mother; the Planetary Intelligence, or Gaian Mind. It is my sense that level seven Consciousness can only arise if we heal ourselves and the planet by dissolving the dualistic barriers of the ego. Only then will we transform our cancerous selves into the evolutionary agents that we were meant to be.

Gaia, the Earth Goddess of ancient Greece, is the name British scientist James Lovelock gave in 1969 to the living organism that is Planet Earth. He noticed what the archaic tribal elders have known all along: that the Earth is a living organism, finely tuned with itself through interlocking, self-regulating webs of information exchange. The "Gaia hypothesis" states that all living and nonliving systems of the Earth are part of a single interactive organism, regulating itself via cybernetic feedback loops that keep homeostatic balance so that the *whole* may thrive. Like all levels discussed thus far, Gaia has an "outer" objective manifestation and an "inner" domain of sentience. As we will see, this sentience can be directly experienced, and ultimately identified with, as our deeper planetary identity.

It should be clear by now that Nature, and the entire Cosmos, is structured as a fractal. Remember that fractals are self-similar, recursive patterns that repeat across scales and dimensions. The part reflects the whole. Part atoms come together to form whole cells, part cells join to form whole organisms, part organisms come together to form whole ecosystems, and part ecosystems link across the globe to form Gaia. Thus Gaia as an organism reflects our very own mind-body system. And, of course, Her evolution reflects our own as a larger fractal harmonic of the process we have been exploring thus far. So, in essence, Her story is our story, and it unfolds through the same progressive levels and stages. Level one is, of course, the Physiosphere; the blood, flesh and bones of Her material body. As the ancient tribal elders knew, the living planet has four basic elements that are reflected in the four basic material spheres that make up planet Earth. The deep Magmasphere (fire) oozes like blood below the thin crust, the Lithosphere (earth). These two spheres interact to shape continents with undulating mountains and deepening valleys. Caressing the material surface as it flows is the Hydrosphere (water), further shaping the landscape and preparing the Earth for the fertile emergence of Life. And the atmosphere and stratosphere (air) encircle the planet and provide yet another means of interplanetary communication and self-regulation.

All these subspheres, which compose and are collectively called the Physiosphere, interact in ways that sets the stage for the second major sphere (stage or level) of development: life and the Biosphere. The biosphere has been evolving for over 3.5 billion years and has been developing an internal sentience for at least that time. It is not certain how self-aware the entire planet is. It seems likely, however, that if humans *consciously* join the collective awareness of the biosphere, then it would likely expand its level of sentience considerably. The planetary awareness predates humanity by billions of years. At this level, we wake up to the underlying intelligence that created us in the first place.

Out of the Biosphere emerges the human Noosphere, not fully self-aware but apparently poised in that direction. Like the ego mind separating itself and being unaware of the body in level four, the Noosphere is separate and currently not sustainably integrating with the biosphere. In level seven, it seems logical that the split dissolves and the Noosphere (the collective human intent) joins the natural communities of the Biosphere, resulting in a sustainable and enlightened culture; possibly the full activation of the Gaian Mind, healthy, vibrant, and self-aware through all life. The experiences of those who have regular contact with the Planetary Intelligence, called shamans, report that this vast Intelligence has been there before humans ever entered the scene. We at this level can consciously align with the underlying sentience of our natural world in ways that make our actions harmonious with our environments. As we will soon explore, the Gaian Mind is an actual inner realm that can be accessed and explored through various techniques and technologies, and a consensus is developing around what the Planet is telling us: "clean up, humans, or die."

But as each level transcends and includes the prior, the move forward in evolution necessarily involves an integration of the prior levels. Just as in level five the conscious mind reconnected with the unconscious body for higher integration, so, at level seven, the noospheric mind consciously reconnects with the ancient wisdom of the Gaian body-mind system. In a practical sense, this may mean that through the implementation of the Internet we should be able to work, go to school, shop, vote, and access all sorts of entertainment in the Global Mind Network of the Noosphere (eventually psychically and within!). When not engaged and hooked-up to the Global intent, we would be putting our energies into our local families, communities, and the Earth, with a renewed conscious reconnection to the planetary ecosystems that support all life. Working, playing, shopping, and educating ourselves electronically could vastly reduce fossil fuel consumption, resource depletion, pollution, material obsession, and traffic jams, freeing the living planet from the polluted constraints of the industrialized world system that is rapidly killing our green foundation. If evolution is to continue to unfold into greater creative potentials, at this stage the human race and its emergent Noosphere must rejoin the rest of the living planet in a renewed symbiotic partnership. This may unfold, if successful, as the next expression of Consciousness on planet Earth.

A trend in that direction seems to be reflected in the miniaturization of technology and the emergence of green renewable energy systems. Everything we think we need in the mental level—entertainment, information, culture, art, music, communication, commerce, education, etc.—will ultimately exist in cyberspace, accessed by gadgets that can fit into our back pockets. This miniaturizing trend will probably continue until technology disappears from material space. We will eventually create access through implanted chips and nanotechnology: miniaturized atom-sized transmitters whizzing through our neural networks, transmitting the Collective Mind wirelessly as these "nanobots" link up to our receptors in the synaptic cleft, for example. What will inevitably dawn on humanity, however—soon I hope—is that all of these imaginative dreams and futuristic potentials depend ultimately on how we treat the land we live on, the soil we build, the water we honor, and the air we breathe. The awakening at this level would ultimately entail a total redesign of our homes, communities, cities, and international relations; a new system modeled after the perfect designs of Mother Nature. Each home could be a self-sustained, energy-independent, permacultural mini farm that produces all the basic needs for its inhabitants. Excess produce, often the case in small yard-sized vegetable gardens, can be abundantly shared and bartered amongst the larger communities, as the various communities interact with each other in mutually beneficial networks of bioregionally based relations.

As we've seen, this is the way it's been done for at least the last fourteen billion years. Vast networks of self-organizing relations have linked to form emergent fractals of themselves in ever-ascending dimensions of complexity and interconnectedness. I will be discussing in more detail what I foresee as the only way out of our planetary crisis, with a proposed design, in the final chapter. But, in essence, all energy, power, food, and water must be decentralized and locally produced and owned. Energy is everywhere, and at this level we learn to work with and cultivate the local, bioregional elements to support ourselves and our local, bioregionally centered communities. Power must be decentralized politically as well, as each community should work together through its own strengths and resources in a process of self-governance. As seen throughout our cosmos, all structures are ultimately self-organized from internal sources of power and intelligence. Our societies have fallen into top-heavy pathological hierarchical structures of dependency and control, resulting in vast inequality and unfair distribution of resources. A poor woman from South Africa, for example, should have the same access to all resources as the tycoon from Beverly Hills does, for it is every living being's birthright to breathe clean air, drink pure water, eat whole foods, live on land, and be free to pursue its greatest creative potential.

In order for this communal self-governance and self-reliance to work, all world communities, at this theoretical level of enlightened evolution, would have to share the same global vision of unity, peace, and equitable self-sustainability for all. In essence, this means no multinational corporations raping the natural world, enslaving kids in other countries for cheap labor, and selling trash to the mindless in the pursuit of the mighty profit, all, of course, in the guise of "free trade" and "globalization." Entering a partnership society where we work together to maximize the whole of creation, not just ourselves, our corporations, or our countries, would entail a literal breakthrough into a new dimension of Consciousness: a "planetcentric" civilization, rooted in the fertile soil, yet flowering into the deeply creative cyberspaces of humanity's most aesthetic imagination.

If "the medium is the message," then technology could be an indicator that reveals the potential direction of the collective evolution of humanity as it moves into other orders of Being. [1] Like my friend so wisely exclaimed, "The Internet is like training wheels for humanity, supporting an already innate ability." The technologies that I will discuss next as representing the seventh level of Consciousness are only external surface forms of internal potentials that reveal deeper, more expansive aspects of the whole of creation and of who we are. But as we have been exploring, the inner Awareness must evolve alongside its technologies, or else high technology has the potential to totally wipe out the organic matrix that gave it birth.

As mentioned in the above paragraphs, we already possess a technology that can allow us to do many of the time-money-resource-energy consuming tasks of today electronically and virtually. We already have virtual (existing in cyberspace) cities where people can telecommute to work environments, go to virtual shopping malls, sit in virtual classrooms with other students and a cyber-professor, and cyberspaces for meeting and even having "cybersex" with other people. And this is only the tip of the iceberg, since this technology is a relatively new invention.

Currently, however, we are witnessing more of the shadow side of our technological age, as people have developed addictions to their screens, actually disconnecting them from 3D life and each other. This is natural, I believe, as we are like children trying to figure out a powerful new tool. The pressures of our shifting world will, no doubt, force humanity to use and repurpose what it has developed to save itself from the social and environmental catastrophe now underway. The tools, technology, knowledge, and infrastructure are all in place to help humanity move into a higher level of existence. The problem lies in the old outdated power structures of the elite, still holding on to the old paradigms of domination, profit, dirty energy, war, and monetary control. Either that system collapses, or we act collectively toward a peaceful global awakening, the fact remains that it is time for change.

Virtual cities in cyberspace are nothing compared to some of the work being done with Virtual Reality, where you can actually walk, see, hear, touch, and interact in electronic alternate worlds. We seem to be literally migrating into the new frontiers of cyberspace, and there creating virtual worlds that are limited only to the extent that there are limits within the human imagination. Headgear with audiovisual output, gloves with motion-detecting sensors, and ultimately entire suits will allow us to actually navigate and temporarily live in worlds ranging from Mars simulations to infinite imaginal universes conceived by the human mind. Of course, the VR (virtual reality) suit will also become old technology when wireless implants and nanotechnology enter the scene. Terence McKenna illustrates:

> It is only a short step from fighter simulations to simulations of architectural models that you can literally "fly the clients into," and it is only a slightly longer step from 3-D blueprints of an imaginary office to the simulation of the Taj Mahal on a moonlight-flooded summer night—in virtual reality. [2]

We have evolved into information-producing-consuming organisms that hurl bits of meaning light-speed around the globe, enriching and transforming the old definitions of who we are. In cyberspace we find each other not as separate organic creatures, but as bits of personal consciousness trying to figure itself out. We meet in these cyberspaces and ultimately realize that our thoughts, ideas, and all that is expressed by the human mind are made of light and not bound by space or time. This insight into the nature of our mind, magnified and extended through computers, will empower individuals to design and fabricate their own realities. Our subjective reality creations will then be shared with anyone interested, not only on screens, but in actual virtual landscapes that one can move around in and explore. It's as if our imagination, traditionally expressed in art, music, poetry, and literature, can now be "downloaded" as a manifest multimedia, multimodal, and ultimately multi-dimensional reality that can be interacted with and explored via cybersuits (and/or nanotechnology, which we will further explore in level eight). In cyberspace we are virtual wizards, magically creating worlds of light that are inhabited by imaginative beings of information that interact for the sheer joy of expressing themselves.

The implications of Virtual Reality are vast, for not only is it allowing the space for the unfoldment of humanity's deepest inner creativity, but it seems to be completely redefining the nature of reality and our place in it. "The Internet approach to identity makes it clear that we put on personae the way that we once put on clothing; different costumes are appropriate in different situations." [3] Since we are beings of light-information within these realms, we can travel from personality to personality in unlimited virtual worlds that arise at our command through the right set of informational codes.

From a slightly different angle, but with a similar underlying theme, are the implications from the breakthroughs in Genetic Engineering. Scientists are finally beginning to crack the genetic code contained within the DNA double helix. Within the spiraling strands of the amino acids guanine, adenine, cytosine, and thymine is the encoded information for the entire history of organic evolution on planet Earth. DNA is information. Within the nucleus of every living cell lives the Brain of Life, sending out chemical instructions via RNA to fabricate the mobile sensory organs we call organisms. "Every living creature, from a bacterium to an astronaut, is a robot—designed, constructed, and programmed by DNA to perform specific functions in the evolving web of life." [4] In other words, the DNA strand contains within its spiraling matrix the blueprints to construct jungles, forests, brains, ants, flowers, lions, New York City, and the entirety of human dramas. This tiny molecule stores more information than our largest computers could ever hold, and apparently the intelligence to manage and coordinate trillions of protein production lines that manifest as our biospheric-noospheric planet.

Just like our brain is the localized center for the nonlocal (not found in a space-time location) human mind, or the hardware of a computer the localized center for the nonlocal software programs of the Internet, the DNA molecule can be seen as the localized center for the nonlocal Gaian Mind. Within the nucleus of each living cell lives the mini brain of the entire Gaian entelechy, with vast memory banks containing the entire evolutionary sequence of organisms, ecosystems, organic forms, and events occurring on planet Earth. As we've seen, the entire Planetary Mind can be stored within the tiny DNA molecule, *if* our universe is holographic in nature. Remember, the part reflects and embodies the whole in a holographic universe.

Physicist David Bohm proposed a general holographic theory for the entire universe, where he conceived the space-time continuum to be a holographic manifestation, the unfolded or explicate realm, of interacting wave forms stored in the enfolded or implicate domain. [5] The subatomic wave forms interact to form interference patterns, which produce oscillating patterns called particles, which further interact in a dynamic exchange, creating the moving image Bohm called "holomovement." He envisioned the implicate, or enfolded, nonlocal quantum order as containing and encoding the information of the entire space-time sequence. He deduced, based on the experimental data coming from quantum mechanics, that underlying our diversified space-time matrix is wholeness. Bohm believes that this underlying wholeness is how nonlocal and entangled effects can be explained. Of course, his implicate order is equivalent to Laszlo's Akashic Field, where all information is stored and recorded in a nonlocal, frictionless, spaceless, timeless plenum, which is everywhere and everywhen.

British biologist Rupert Sheldrake coined the term "mophogenetic field" to describe the invisible organizing principle around all natural systems. [6] He described these fields as being nonlocal, yet containing the information and memory necessary to shape and mold everything from crystals to organisms to social systems to galaxies. He theorizes that all self-organizing natural systems take their respective shape and form based on built-in memories recorded in invisible "morphic fields," which are evolving habits that emanate influences via "morphic resonance." Each form draws on the memory of past forms for its shape and function, while adding something entirely new. The new comes from the inherent evolutionary Eros impulse that strives toward novelty from within said form.

From this perspective, Laszlo's Akashic Field is the Mother Mophogenetic Field out of which all other morphic fields draw their energy and information. These nonlocal morphogenetic fields theoretically provide the information and blueprint for the manifesting local forms. The material plane of the cosmos manifests from the first morphic field that emerges from the nonmaterial Akashic Field. From that foundational cosmic morphic field arises Earth, with its own developing morphogenetic field which we've called the Physiosphere. This field of information and its expressed material forms provides the mineral and elemental foundations for the biosphere. The biosphere as a whole is also regulated and in-formed by its own evolving morphogenetic field, which is composed of endless organic forms with their respective interacting morphic fields. Out of that emerges the noosphere, which again is the morphic field of humanities collective mental expressions. All of these fields do not appear to have been fully conscious until the emergence of these last three levels (six through eight), where the inherent Awareness in all forms begins to awaken to the underlying causative information fields that mold, shape, and guide said forms. These fields can be conceptualized as being made of what we call mind: full of nonlocal information, yet needing Awareness for it to be activated and illuminated, and not becoming self-aware until mind (individual and collective) matures toward complete self-reflection. In level seven, Gaia theoretically becomes fully self-aware as humans tap into and become conscious of the six morphogenetic fields that comprise the Gaian superorganism discussed thus far.

In connection to DNA, we can see how in a holographic universe the informational morphogenetic field containing the blueprint and recorded history of Gaia's organic evolutionary development, the whole (i.e., the Gaian Mind), can be recorded and stored within the nucleus of every living cell, the part. Each creature contains the whole of organic history on planet Earth within the fabric of its own being. That fabric is made of cells, each of which contains the information of the whole. It becomes apparent that there is a fractal pattern of holarchical (hierarchy of nested wholes) self-similar organizational patterns that repeat themselves throughout the levels. The McKennas elucidate:

> The DNA from one cell theoretically contains all the information necessary to regenerate the entire organism. It is due to the presence of certain "inductors" (notably RNA) that DNA makes cells into skin, others into nerves, and still others into muscles, and so on. Thus, on the organismic level, also, we note the ubiquity of genetic information, but also that each cell "reads" only some part of the DNA-hologram, though the entire message is there. [7]

Modern Genetic Engineering is concerned with the manipulation of genetic information for the mutation, splicing, replication, and cloning of various organisms. Obviously, we as a species have tapped into an energy level that is so powerful that we would need to acquire god-consciousness to be able to handle these forces without completely destroying the delicate web of life. The consequence of GMOs (genetically modifies organisms) on the planetary gene-pool could be disastrous if we do not proceed cautiously. As mentioned, these technologies are external manifestations of inner potentials, and if human consciousness doesn't catch up with its technologies, the ignorant misuse of these powerful creative energies could potentially kill Gaia as a whole.

What the hard sciences of Genetic Engineering are failing to realize, according to Dr. Leary, is that Genetic Engineers at Level Seven Consciousness "will use as their basic instrument their own brains, open to and conscious of Neurogenetic signals. Only the DNA neuron link-up can produce the immortality and symbiotic linkage with other species." [8] According to Leary, the McKenna brothers, [9] anthropologist Jeremy Narby, [10] and, as we will explore shortly, some shamanic and yogic traditions, we at this level of Consciousness can directly access the information contained within the DNA code. Leary explains this vast possibility:

> The nervous system continually receives DNA and RNA signals. Inside the nucleus of every neuron, there "lives" a DNA master plan which contains a record of the chain of bodily reincarnations back to the origin of life on this planet... When the Seventh Circuit of the nervous system is activated, the signals from DNA become

> conscious—thousands of genetic memories flash by, the molecular picture-album of species consciousness and evolution. This experience provides glimpses and samples of the broad design of the multibillion-year-old genetic panorama. [11]

If the information stored within DNA could be consciously accessed and experienced, we would potentially have access to an energy level of such vast evolutionary magnitude and intelligence that it would truly represent a "transpersonal" level of experience. If Consciousness were to theoretically become Aware/Witness to the DNA information field, it would seem that the Gaian Mind would immediately be activated and planet Earth as a whole would become self-conscious. Not an anthropocentric intelligence as was proposed in the previous level (six) of the Noosphere, but an ancient, old-wise, genetic-Gaian awareness that transcends brain-guided human awareness by billions of years.

The Gaian Mind is expressed in the self-organizing principles at all levels of manifestation discussed thus far, and at some point the process must lead to an actual planetary Awareness that finds itself embedded within a Galactic community of inconceivable fractal levels of alien intelligent existence. In this context, DNA can be seen as the "objective" molecular transceiver for an experience of Consciousness that completely transcends the human-personal domain. DNA fabricates brains, which produce personal consciousness. But as the incarnated Awareness evolves into higher levels of intelligence, it begins to tap into the informational displays of those higher minds, genetic/Gaian in this case, that create all life forms on Earth.

One possible mechanism for this kind of internal DNA receptivity has been proposed by the McKenna brothers in conjunction to psychedelic ingestion, and should hopefully illustrate neurologically how a shaman is able to link up to the Gaian Mind, or World Soul. [12] It should be of no surprise that shamans throughout history have used plant-based psychoactive chemicals as symbiotic keys to access the Gaian Mind, for in Her wisdom Gaia has provided chemicals specifically designed to fit primate neurology. These psychedelic molecules found throughout nature are so structurally similar to our very own neurotransmitters that the inevitable conclusion is that they were specifically designed for communication across species lines, specifically between evolved primates and the vegetable Queendom. Psychedelic plants and mushrooms may have not only catapulted Consciousness from animal instinct into language producing self-aware humans, [13] or been the source of humanity's religious sensibility,

[14] but they may in fact be the very key to our next evolutionary unfoldment. If these "plant-teachers" are in fact chemical messengers from our Gaian Mother, as shamans worldwide exclaim, then we may be able to open up direct lines of communication and guidance between us and the rest of the Natural world. As McKenna points out, "reestablishing channels of direct communication with the planetary Other, the mind behind nature, through the use of hallucinogenic plants is the last best hope for dissolving the steep walls of cultural inflexibility that appear to be channeling us toward true ruin." [15] He continues,

> The closer a human group is to the gnosis of the vegetable mind—the Gaian collectivity of organic life—the closer their connection to the archetype of the Goddess and hence to the partnership style of social organization...Without such a relationship to psychedelic exopheromones regulating our symbiotic relationship with the plant kingdom, we stand outside of an understanding of planetary purpose. And an understanding of planetary purpose may be the major contribution that we can make to the evolutionary process. Returning to the bosom of the planetary partnership means trading the point of view of the history-created ego for a more maternal and intuitional style. [16]

These "exopheromones," molecules that allow for the transception of alternate informational signals distributed ubiquitously throughout nature, may indeed be Gaia's way of communicating with us and self-regulating its living systems toward sustainability.

As discussed, all perceptual, mental, behavioral, and emotional processes have a corresponding neurological correlate. Through the neuronal firing of chemical messengers called neurotransmitters, encoded vibratory patterns (on/off sequences) are conveyed at receptor sites specific to a variety of neurotransmitters. Remember some of the common neurotransmitters: serotonin, dopamine, norepinephrine, endorphin, melatonin, acetylcholine, glutamic acid, glycine, histamine, GABA, Glutamate, and a variety of neuropeptides, to name a few. Each of these neurotransmitters has specific receptor sites that are designed to accommodate only their molecular structure. Like a specific key is required for a specific lock, particular neurotransmitters fit snuggly into their designated receptor site. One class of psychedelic substances called tryptamines, which include DMT (N-dimethyltryptamine), 5-MeO-DMT, "magic" mushrooms (psilocybin and psilocin), Ibogaine, and LSD-25, have such a similar molecular structure to serotonin that they fit and thus replace serotonin at the receptor site. These tryptamines are called serotonin agonists. In fact, most hallucinogens are structurally similar to the modulators that regulate firing sequences throughout the brain.

As stated, serotonin is structurally similar to the above mentioned tryptamines (indoleamines). Dopamine and norepinephrine (catecholamines) are structurally similar to what are called phenethylamines, which include hallucinogens (and empathogens) such as mescaline, and synthetically produced "research chemicals" 2-CB, MDA, MDMA, and STP, to name a few. We will explore the precise pharmacodynamics of these substances in the "Further Transpersonal Explorations" section, but for our current discussion we will look at the specific role that naturally occurring DMT (specifically in the Amazonian plant admixture called ayahuasca) and psilocybin (in mushrooms) may play in allowing awareness to view holographic readouts from the nucleated DNA.

The McKennas explain their theory:

> The tryptamines offer an informational readout through molecular intercalation into neural nucleic acids and molecular broadcast of the ESR (electron spin resonance) waveform of information hypothetically stored in the neural nucleus. In the case of serotonin, this ESR signal represents the electrochemical basis for consciousness as it is typically experienced....During the application of these techniques *(the replacement of serotonin with exogenous tryptamines)*, the owner of the DNA so treated will spontaneously produce ever more complete analogical descriptions of the configuration and interrelation of the energy patterns stored in the structure of DNA, patterns that imbue life with its characteristically performative, actually atemporal, teleology. [17] *(italics in parenthesis mine).*

In other words, when serotonin is replaced at the receptor site by the psychedelic tryptamine, the McKennas speculate that a different (higher) vibratory rate in the

ESR is generated due to the hallucinogen's greater affinity and ability to intercalate (bond and oscillate) with neural DNA. The Mckennas explain: "The rapid bonding and debonding of intercalators causes a rapid twisting and untwisting of the helix, and this gives rise to a vibratory oscillation of the macromolecule. This oscillation, occurring within the electrical field at the synapse, has the effect of generating an electromagnetic waveform." [18] This alternate frequency vibration at the serotonin receptor site apparently creates a resonance with the neural DNA, generating an electromagnetic waveform at the synapse that hypothetically contains stored genetic information. Normally, serotonin and other neurotransmitters create frequency wave patterns throughout the brain that resonate with one another to make available mundane perceptions, thoughts, etc., holographically to Awareness. When these molecules are replaced by the psychedelic neurotransmitters, a different rate of vibration occurs through this direct molecular intercalation within neuronal DNA, generating an ESR waveform that displays genetic information to the witnessing Awareness. Again, the McKennas elucidate their fascinating theory:

> When a hallucinogen...is introduced into the system, either from an endogenous source or from the external environment, it may show greater affinity for the DNA than serotonin and bond in place of it; a stronger charge-transfer reaction may result and may produce an amplified ESR signal, facilitating greater access to stored memories and subconscious content. Thus, a population using harmine or similar compounds in shamanic and religious practices might well be afforded a tremendous evolutionary advantage, as it would possess an enhanced access to the informational *gestalten* of its own holographic genetic storage system. [19]

This neuron-DNA resonance circuit generating a standing waveform of information throughout the brain would theoretically display a holographic informational readout of the encoded genetic structures, thus allowing Awareness to view multiple panoramic evolutionary reincarnation vistas and sequences of life on Earth (or memories beyond Earth existence if DNA was seeded by an Alien Intelligence!).

Anthropologist Jeremy Narby, fascinated by the organic, information-rich imagery described by shamans and other users of DMT-containing ayahuasca, also explores the possible connection between these shamanic visuals and the stored information in DNA. [20] His first clue arises when he discovers the ubiquity of transcultural claims of snake imagery in the shamanic quests. Snakes, spiraling like the double helix, turn out to be the most common visual on ayahuasca. The connection to the snake is, of course, historical, from the biblical snake that tempted Eve to eat the apple from the tree of knowledge; to the Divine Kundalini-Shakti serpent in Yoga, coiled at the base of our spine, awaiting its awakening; to the spiraling snakes of the caduceus symbol symbolizing healing in the medical professions, to name just a few. Narby speculates that these may be symbolic expressions of a true witnessing of the genetic spirals within our very own cells.

Narby encounters a second clue when he discovers Fritz-Albert Popp's research demonstrating that DNA consistently emits highly coherent photons in the visible light range. [21] Popp and colleagues developed an instrument that was sensitive enough to detect the ultra weak emissions radiating from all living things. Through this and a series of other experiments, Popp began to see that all organic systems radiated light, including the DNA molecule. He called this radiation "biophoton emissions" and noticed that DNA was capable of emanating a large range of frequencies, including but not limited to those within the visible light range. Due to the fact that waves store and convey information, he reasoned that biophotons must be the means for communication between cells, organs, organisms, and the environment as a whole. Popp showed in his experiments that these light emissions could carry enough encoded information to coherently regulate the entire body, and even coordinate it within the interconnected web of the entire biosphere.

Narby contends that the hallucinogens at their respective receptor sites "set off a cascade of electrochemical reactions inside the neurons, leading to the stimulation of DNA and, more particularly, to its emission of visible waves, which shamans perceive as 'hallucination'." [22] In his work, Narby reiterates how the DNA-generated biophotons, shown to be a form of cellular language, allow cells, organs, organisms, and ecosystems to communicate with one other in a living web of intercommunication. The image then is that of a global "Internet" of bioelectromagnetic information, transceived and maintained by every DNA molecule antenna at the heart of every living cell, creating an entangled web of coherent interconnections that help correlate all parts of the biosphere to all other parts. The DNA strands act like localized antenna points, broadcasting and receiving radio-like signals that interweave and interpenetrate our planet. This creates an oceanic matrix of signals that interact to create the collective Gaian Network: a self-organizing entelechy that is self-referencing and aware of itself.

The many genetic points can be seen as the local neurons of the planetary brain, which is but the localized external aspect of the nonlocal intelligence that is the Gaian Mind.

Narby states his hypothesis as follows:

> What if DNA, stimulated by...DMT, activates not only its emission of photons (which inundate our consciousness in the form of hallucinations), but also its capacity to pick up the photons emitted by the global network of DNA-based life? This would mean that the biosphere itself, which can be considered "as a more or less fully interlinked unit," is the source of the images. [23]

He continues by stating: "according to my hypothesis, shamans take their consciousness down to the molecular level and gain access to biomolecular information." [24] So if every DNA molecule is the localized "objective" material antenna, transceving the nonlocal "subjective" sentience of the entire planetary mind, then we, at this stage of consciousness development, can learn to access the planetary Web and become conscious participants in its ancient dialogue. These photonic bioemissions may provide the means for the morphogenetic field of the Gaian Mind, facilitating the self-regulating "thoughts" of the planet that may eventually lead to the development of a planetary self-awareness. These nonmaterial, nonlocal thoughts of Gaia are thus networked through every DNA, which maintains the living field that is our planet, just as neurons network and maintain the personal human mind. So in this scheme all DNA molecules, distributed throughout our web of life, are literally the neurons of the biospheric brain, linking together across the globe via fields of electromagnetic emissions to create the living hologram that is the Gaian Mind.

Shaman, artist, and friend Amoraea sums it up beautifully:

> All living cells emit both photons of light and phonons of sound. These are called biophotons, and it is how cells of the human body communicate. They are released and stored from within the helix of the DNA molecule. The helix structure serves as an antenna to both receive and emit this light. On the receiving end, DNA has the unique property of attracting these photons into itself that causes the light to spiral through the molecule.

> As the light spirals, it gains charge and momentum and actually implodes through a virtual "zero point," exactly like a black hole. Energy and information passing through the helical tunnel literally becomes superconductive. When energy is superconductive, it has zero resistance and travels superliminally beyond light speed. Light in general is a bridge to higher dimensional space and the gateway to the overall Mind-field of consciousness. Light, as biophotons in the body, IS consciousness itself—our beingness is made of pure consciousness![25]

Here Amoraea brings it back to the Source, as he points to that formless "zero-point" center into which all energy and information converge, and out of which information and energy pulse. This energetic pulse travels out through the spiraling DNA blueprint lattice. The molecular lattice then channels and guides the emitted energy to construct our planetary body-mind through imprinted morpho-genetic blueprints. In this way we can speculate how the DNA may act as a superconducting antenna that channels energy/information into and out of the Akashic zero-point Field Source, in-forming the evolving structures of Nature with the inherent morphogenetic designs stored in said Field. DNA may be the molecular structure that translates and transduces the Cosmic information of the Akashic Field into the organic terrestrial designs of planet Earth. And as Amoraea reminds us, the Source and the emanating Light that interpenetrates, permeates, and informs our entire body (and all of creation) is pure Consciousness. Amoraea continues; "through our human architecture, our DNA unites us with the infinite creation matrix wherein all information and energy is accessible. This is the physics translation of the Akashic Field…." [26]

If the above speculations are anywhere near true, then the vast memory banks of the planet (and cosmos!) can be directly accessed, as well as future designs, within and through our very own DNA. Indeed, through modern and ancient shamanic pharmacological tools called entheogens (revealing the Divine within), we can create a direct link to the Gaian Mind, eventually mastering the realm, merging with it, and ultimately identifying it as our deeper, wiser, intuitive, evolutionary Mind. As we will explore, we can enter this realm, the subtle plane, through other methods. But these take practice, discipline, and a specific character type. Psychedelics are ancient tools that have been used historically for moving into other worlds, and deliver the intense experience with practice or not.

Ontogenetic Expression

The shaman is an ancient figure in indigenous cultures who "specializes in a trance during which his soul is believed to leave his body and ascend to the sky or descend to the underworld." [27] Shamans have existed since the twilight of human history and are believed to be the originators of all world religions. Through archaic techniques for accessing other worlds, what they call the Spirit World, the shamans have been the historical healers of tribal cultures around the world. Through various techniques, such as chanting, drumming, fasting, dancing, ritual, and psychoactive plant ingestion, the shaman enters trance states. Through these trance states, the shaman goes on what are called shamanic journeys where he/she works with various animal spirits, spirit helpers, inner guides, and ancestral presences to cure and heal souls. Their basic function in indigenous societies is that of doctor, psychotherapist, philosopher, and priest. "The shaman is a master of spirit entities, a venturer on different cosmic planes." [28] Through this interdimensional mastery, shamans are able to not only work miracles, but to access information regarding future events. Often called curanderos or medicine wo/men, the shamans have vast knowledge of the natural world and the various kingdoms. Their knowledge of medicinal plants and herbs surpasses that of any modern pharmacologist, for unlike the two-century-old Western use of chemicals, shamans have been using vegetable medicines for as far back as we have records.

Of interest to our explorations, however, is that realm variously called by shamans the Spirit World, or intermediate realm, inhabited by animal spirits, past and future ancestors, disincarnate souls, entities, angelic and demonic beings, spirit helpers, and a vast array of mythological representations of hyperdimensional forces. The shamans report that the world has a center, located inside every one of us, and running through that center is a vertical axis known as the "*Axis Mundi*" that allows one to travel up or down. The upper worlds unfold into celestial and paradisiacal dimensions, and the lower worlds lead to infernal and hellish realms. All of these dimensions are inhabited by their respective entities and can be accessed by various shamanic means. Terence McKenna describes the shamanic role:

> The shaman has been the agent of evolution, because the shaman learns techniques to go between ordinary reality and the domain of the

> Ideas: This higher dimensional continuum that is somewhat parallel to us, available to us, yet ordinarily occluded to us by cultural convention out of fear of the mystery...shamans are people who have been able to de-condition themselves from the community's instinctual distrust of the mystery, and go into this bewildering higher dimension, and gain knowledge, recover the jewel lost at the beginning of time, save souls, cure, commune with the ancestors....[29]

Even though methods vary greatly among the various tribal shamans of the world, the most potent has been recognized to be the psychedelic trance. Native North American Indigenous people, currently organized as the Native American Church, have been known to use a cactus plant called peyote, whose psychoactive chemical is currently known to be mescaline. Unlike our materialistically biased Western conception of these chemicals being just "drugs," the Indigenous North American's conception of peyote is that of a medicine, purifier, teacher, and an actual spirit plant helper called "Mescalito." [30]

Mexican Mazatec curanderos have been known to use teonanacatal, "flesh of the gods," currently known as psilocybin-containing mushrooms, to access the Spirit World for divination and healing purposes. South American jungle shamans are known to produce a visionary brew called *ayahuasca or yage,* which is an admixture of a MAO inhibitor called harmine, found in the plant *Banisteriopsis caapi,* and of various DMT containing plants. DMT is also used amongst the tribal healers in the form of a snuff, which produces the short-acting hallucinogenic effects often attributed to DMT. By mixing the DMT with the harmine alkaloid, however, the effects of DMT are prolonged due to the inhibition of its metabolism by the MAO-inhibiting properties of harmine. Iboga root in Africa and the mushroom called *Amanita muscaria* used in some Eastern shamanic cultures are other examples of the historical relationship between the human world and the vegetable gnosis of Nature. It seems that through the symbiotic plant-human relationship, a door is literally opened between our ordinary Newtonian world and that of the gods. There is ample evidence that these ancient modalities are being brought back to the global village once again, at this time, in order to help humanity heal in what my friend Rak Razam is calling a *shamanic resurgence* in his new documentary, *Shamans of the Global Village* (2017).

Australian Aborigines have created a different shamanic tool called the dijeridoo, which is a wind instrument that produces a deep resonant vibration. This vibration supposedly brings the entire organism into a state of harmonic resonance, thus healing the discordant patterns within the organism. The Aborigines call the "other worlds" DreamTime, which is a higher-order manifold in which our linear space-time flow is embedded. They believe that the DreamTime, accessed at night through dreams and/or other shamanic techniques, is a valid reality that is "more real," revealing normally hidden aspects of creation. Other methods used for accessing the DreamTime or Spirit World are trance dancing, hypnotic drumming, fasting, and social isolation in the form of a "vision quest."

This vast realm accessed and experienced by shamans was first brought to the attention of the Western psyche through the work of Carl Gustav Jung.

> Jung identified the collective, or transpersonal, unconscious as the center of all psychic material that does not come from personal experience. Its contents and images appear to be shared with people of all time periods and cultures…the collective unconscious is common to all people and is therefore one. [31]

Jung conceived this collective unconscious to be the repository of universal patterns and structures inherited throughout our species's history. These basic patterns shared by all of humanity, he called Archetypes. By analyzing dream content, world myths, world religions, and folk "fairy" tales he noticed reoccurring themes that to him were indicative of deep psychic structures existing within all people. To him, many actions and behaviors of people cross-culturally were seen as expressions of underlying mythic scenes that have occurred in many forms throughout history.

The Jungian collective unconscious with its array of Archetypes is only the surface of what we have been calling the Gaian mind. As we go deep into our "unconscious," we first encounter personal, unconscious material. As we go deeper yet, the Jungian collective unconscious of humanity is accessed, where the various mythical Archetypal patterns of the ages that stand as deep psychic imprints are revealed in the form of images, scenes, and archetypal beings. It seems that this racial mind is really an anthropocentric filtering of deeper energies from a vaster mind; i.e., the Gaian Mind. The Gaian Mind contains stored blueprint Archetypal patterns and complexes not only of the human race, but of the entire planetary drama. These patterns are the fundamental and primordial Archetypal seed Forms out of which the lower manifestations draw their characteristics. As McKenna explains, "The Logos is perfect and, therefore, partakes of no quality other than itself. I am here using the word Logos in the sense in which Philo Judaeus uses it—that of the Divine reason that embraces the archetypal complex of Platonic Ideas that serve as the models of creation." [32]

The Platonic Idea, conceived by Plato as the first place into form from the Divine imagination, is the most basic foundational pattern out of which all of creation is derived. Russell explains the Platonic conception of this higher, more essential plane as it pertains to cats. "The word 'cat' means a certain ideal cat, '*the* cat,' created by God, and unique. Particular cats partake of the nature of *the* cat, but more or less imperfectly; it is owing to this imperfection that there can be many of them." [33] Russell emphasizes that this original Platonic Idea exists for all forms of manifest existence. The Idea behind form, the perfected source and mold for the imperfect reflections existing in material reality, can be correlated to and conceived as that morphogenetic field out of which forms derive their structure. Russell continues: "*the* cat is real, particular cats are only apparent." [34] Ken Wilber describes and synthesizes various traditions describing the subtle plane thus:

> From the Neoplatonic traditions in the West, to the Vedanta and Mahayana and Trikaya traditions in the East, the real archetypes are subtle seed-forms upon which all of manifestation depends... the first Forms that emerge out of this Emptiness are the basic Forms upon which all lesser forms depend for their being...you are looking at the basic forms and foundations of the entire manifest world. [35]

In order to enter the inner subtle planes of creation, one must completely transcend individuality and embrace the universal forms of underlying energies that shape being and reality. The Platonic Archetypes encountered in the subtle plane are creative/chaotic ethereal energy dances that stand as elemental patterns and original molds for the manifest world. This hyperdimension, Spirit World, collective unconscious, Gaian Mind, Aurobindo's Overmind, Mind-at-Large, DreamTime, or subtle plane is an oceanic world of interacting patterns, entities, and ethereal energy dances that live in a sort of eternal, transdimensional hyperspace. Wilber, in defining the subtle plane, states: " 'Subtle' simply means processes that are subtler than gross, ordinary, waking consciousness. These include interior luminosities and sounds, archetypal forms and patterns, extremely subtle bliss currents and cognitions (shabd, nada), expansive affective states of love and compassion, as well as subtler *pathological* states of what can only be called Kosmic terror, Kosmic evil, Kosmic horror." [36] The latter reflect the underworlds of shamanic cosmology.

The so-called Spirit World of shamans is really the articulation of internal, subjective experiences, thus lying beyond the realm of empirical materialistic science. As discussed above, DNA may be as close as science can get to an "objective" material structure containing such vast information. It does seem evident that the animal spirits, the ancestors, and the vast array of spiritual forces encountered in the depths of the human experience are but descriptive metaphors for this underlying genetic photonic field of information emanating from every DNA antenna in Nature. Narby poses the question: "What if these spirits were none other than the biophotons emitted by all the cells of the world and were picked up, amplified, and transmitted... This would mean that spirits are beings of pure light—as has always been claimed." [37] The DNA-sustained morphogenetic field, or Spirit World, can therefore be seen as the nonlocal repository of memories and patterns that in-form material reality in a series of incarnations that imbue the material "shells" with the subjective sentience (a.k.a. spirit) inherent in the underlying matrix of creation. The evolving cosmos then has this coevolving underlying causative morphogenetic field, the Spirit World, which continually gives life, intelligence, creativity, spirit, meaning, and sentience to the evolving forms. In the higher reaches of evolution, the sentience begins to fully awaken to it-Self, enfolding the three-dimensional "material" reality of time-space in its higher dimensional fold. In other words, in the higher levels our material world is experienced as a minute subset of Reality, existing *within* the higher hyper-dimension that is Consciousness and the Spirit World. But who or what are we if we enter into these vast realms?

Various traditions have their interpretations. They all agree that to enter these inner, higher-dimensional planes, one must temporarily leave the body in what has been historically called an "out-of-body" experience. Once the localized, space-time-bound body-mind system is left behind, one is said to be a soul, a "light body," or an astral being that can travel through a transpersonal realm of infinite possibilities. Multiple worlds are possible, as the astral/virtual/imaginal/subtle realm is really a deeper and more basic identity of Consciousness. Other beings are said to inhabit this subtle plane (other aspects of our Self?). They have variously been called angels, disincarnate souls, ancestors, aliens, fairies, Dakinis, Deities, Dhyani-Buddhas, peaceful and wrathful beings, gods, self-transforming machine elves, and a variety of other names representing these mysterious otherworldly forces that influence physical reality in inconceivable ways.

If this underlying, immaterial, morphogenetic Akashic Field sustains and in-forms all structures in our cosmos with information, including us humans, then it seems logical that the energies that are injected into the forms to give them life and consciousness return to the underlying field upon completion of their respective lifecycle in the material plane. Thus informational units, spirits or souls or other entities, can incarnate in the material world until evolving to the point where they realize their oneness with the One Consciousness out of which all emerges and returns.

Of course, there must be a hierarchy of fields, ascending worlds of subtlety and depth, inhabited by alien intelligences beyond most mundane human's wildest imagination. The field relevant to most humans is that of the Gaian Mind, containing the informational "morphic fields" of our human and animal ancestors. As we move deeper and beyond earth-based existence, we begin to potentially access galactic informational fields possibly inhabited by alien intelligences. Psychiatrist Dr. Rick Strassman and others have compiled a number of research essays written by serious researchers that describe different subjects' experiences of alien entities in alien worlds as contacted through the use of naturally occurring tryptamines. [38] These stories and their related theories are covered in Strassman's book, *Inner Paths to Outer Space: Journeys to Alien Worlds through Psychedelics and Other Spiritual Technologies.* Some subjective "tryp" reports from these realms will be explored in the following sections. The deepest field, the Universal Akashic Field, of course, contains the holographic blueprint for the entire Multiverse, and is thus the ultimate Spirit World that houses the information for all Being(s). This Ultimate Field is, let us remember, made of the One (White) Light where all merges into One. It is the Source that creates the material forms inhabited by the subjective sentience that expresses itself through the multiplicity of forms as aspects of that One.

Experience of Structure

Q: What do you perceive/project from this level?

A: Archetypes, souls, color-sound-form synesthesia, Eternal patterns, Ideas behind form, entities, spirit worlds.

When Spirit or Awareness untangles it-Self from the time-space confines created by the various imprinted-conditioned attachments to the lower levels, it is able to pick up genetic frequencies—Gaian thoughts, so to speak—amongst an ocean of signals and frequencies. The practice at this level becomes one of consciously quieting the grosser realms of Being so that one can "hear" the underlying harmonies of creation. These underlying harmonies, Platonic Ideas, Archetypal Forms, or Eternal patterns are the basic Laws and principles that govern the hierarchical condensation of Spirit into the denser planes. A flash flood of images, beings, essences, spirits, genetic memories, reincarnation vistas, and ethereal energy patterns all come rushing in as one quietly transcends the limits imposed by time, space, and matter.

In the deeper levels of experience and mastery within the subtle plane, one begins to de-template OneSelf from the Genetic programs of organic design. Frequency reception at this level of Consciousness is no longer limited and defined by the sensory organs of the organism. The soul or "light body" is liberated from the localized body-mind and drifts in a dream like astral realm. Since time is largely transcended in this realm, ancestors from past and future may be encountered, along with a plethora of archetypal beings. The soul, or "light body," inhabits various archetypal patterns, which in turn inhabit a mental body (level six), an organism (level five), a personality (level four), a thought (level three), an emotion (level two), and a material body (level one).

When one is able to de-template from the typically differentiated sensory modalities of sound, smell, taste, color, or touch, the various diffracted frequencies collapse into a unitive flow called synesthesia. "A cross-wiring of the senses in which one sense evokes another, the most common form of synesthesia is *audition coloree,* or colored hearing." [39] Synesthesia is a perceived energy flow of combined modalities (i.e. sound, color, tact, geometry, meaning, etc.) that seems to be what this other plane is made out of. This more fundamental undifferentiated energy of an archetypal/primordial nature lies behind all form as what is traditionally called spiritual energy. It seems to be the energy out of which the hologram of reality is made. The energy is experienced as harmonic, spectral, overtonal spirals of color-sound-meaning-feeling-etc. that coagulate into coherent patterns of being, a sort of Radiance from the Source that interacts with itself to manifest individual souls, worlds made of synesthetic light, and astral/virtual universes that can be explored once the "light body" is mastered. Through this mastery, navigation is made possible. This means that Awareness awakens to its more fundamental substrate, and there encounters other aspects of itself, outside the constraints of the material shells, as beings made of synesthetic light.

The realm I have been painfully trying to articulate in two-dimensional words is so vast that only direct *experience* can reveal the peaks and valleys of its wondrous landscapes. Being the level right before the complete merging into infinite formlessness (level eight), it also seems to exist as an infinite/eternal substrate with unimaginable possibilities. This realm seems to be multidimensional, thus the limits, if indeed there are any, are not possible to discern with our limited brain-minds. Only through a transcendence of the brain-mind can we tap into these heavenly realms of infinite potential.

One can access these higher levels of intelligence with techniques other than the discussed shamanic methods. These techniques are the deeper practices from the Yogic and Buddhist traditions. Lama Govinda explains:

> Through the power of concentration and other yogic practices, we are able to raise the subconscious into the realm of discriminative consciousness and thus draw upon the unlimited treasures of subconscious memory, in which not only our own past lives but the past of our race, humanity and of all prehuman forms of life is stored up. [40]

Within Patanjali's Yoga system, the eighth limb, after the meditator has achieved *dhyana*, is *samadhi.* There exist various levels of *samadhi,* but the one that corresponds to the subtle plane is called *nirvichara or savikalpa samadhi.* Here the individual's mind finds identity with the Supreme principle, or the highest Archetypal Deity. One identitfies with God or Goddess without any other awareness, or nondual absorption with the object of meditation. [41] In this ultra subtle state of consciousness, the meditator begins to merge with the underlying Platonic Archetypal patterns, historically conceived as deities, gods, and goddesses, and the realization dawns that we, at the deepest level, are divine and perfect. In the subtle plains of creation, accessed through the deepest stillness of the concentrated meditative mind, the traditions claim that we have access to a panoply of beings and deities, Dakinis and Devas, that guide, protect, and support our spiritual evolution through invisible forces.

Sarvikalpa samadhi can be seen manifested in the Buddhist path of Insight as 'Effortless Insight,' where "contemplation is quick, effortless, indefatigable. Instantaneous knowledge of anatta, anicca, dukkha. Cessation of pain, pervasive equanimity." [42] Within the path of Buddhist concentration, in level seven we begin to enter the formless states of the fifth *jhana.* The fifth *jhana* is defined by "consciousness of infinite space, equanimity, and one-pointedness," [43] and is called the first formless state as the meditator goes beyond all perception of form and experiences a sense of infinite space. According to Buddhist scriptures, this is when the meditator begins to access other worlds. Buddhist scholar Edward Conze describes:

> The horizon of Buddhists is not bounded by the limits of the sensory world, and their true interests lie beyond it. Not all forms of life fall within the range of the five senses. There are in addition the heavens and hells, in which people are rewarded and punished for their deeds, the "intermediary state" in which they pass the interval between death and rebirth, and the "Pure Lands" of the cosmic Buddhas. The "gods" are in a way really "angels," and their "heavens" might also be called "paradises." Buddhist theology knows of about thirty kinds of gods, but the higher grades have a constitution so refined and a mode of life so unfamiliar that we could not easily form a concrete idea of their mode of existence. [44]

In this description of Buddhists' other realms, we find correlation to the shamanic upper, middle, and lower worlds. Of course, all world religions have versions for these alternate worlds, historically using them to control the human masses that have not yet found direct personal inner access to these realms in their lifetime. The point in Buddhism, however, is to get acquainted with these inner realms before death. They tell us that at the moment of death all of these realms are displayed panoramically in the intermediate realm, or in what Tibetans call the Bardo of Dharmata. Through practice and evolution, the Awareness may choose to incarnate into the higher heavenly realms of the gods, or as a human for another round in the earthly planes. If the Awareness has not evolved, or has created suffering in its incarnated round on Earth, it enters-creates hellish realms of pain and suffering. As we will see in the next chapter, once Awareness realizes that all realms and beings are emanations-creations of its own Radiance, it frees itself from all form and finds liberation from the rounds of birth and death in time and space.

"*Bar* means 'in between,' and *do* means 'suspended' or 'thrown', " so that the Bardos are the "in-between" dimensions available to Awareness after death and before rebirth. [45] These Bardos have been beautifully articulated in the famous *Tibetan Book of the Dead,* describing the subtle realms in exquisite detail. According to Tibetan master Sogyal Rimpoche, there are four basic Bardos: "the 'natural' bardo of this life, the 'painful' bardo of dying, the 'luminous' bardo of dharmata, and the 'karmic' bardo of becoming." [46] The after-death bardo of dharmata correlates with the subtle realm we've been exploring, and according to Rimpoche, has four basic phases which the soul or light body goes through after the death of the physical vessel.

The first phase is called *Luminosity—the Landscape of Light,* where the departed light body or soul enters a realm where "space dissolves into luminosity."[47] Suddenly one is aware of a flowing, vibrant world of sound, light, and color, which is the first place in which the formless Clear White Light (nature of one's mind) takes on a subtle form. From its infinite radiance, the Source comes into manifestation as light-sound-color (synesthetic) energy. If the person fails to recognize this awesome heavenly display as the brilliant nature and projection of his or her own mind, then the second phase of the Dharmata Bardo, *Union—the Deities,* comes into being. In this phase the radiating color-light-sound energy condenses and coagulates into spheres of light, taking on personified autonomous characteristics in what are called "tikles," which express themselves as the "peaceful and wrathful deities" of this realm. Again, if the person fails to recognize these phenomena as playful expressions of his or her own mind, then the third phase, *Wisdom,* unfolds. In this third phase, the being has the ability to "perceive" multiple universes, past and future lives, and has the view of the entire evolutionary sequence of reincarnations. Finally, if by this point the being has not realized that the entire display is a projection-creation from the nature of his or her own mind, he or she enters the fourth and final phase of the Dharmata Bardo, *Spontaneous Presence.* In this phase, "the whole of reality presents itself in one tremendous display," [48] and every possibility, from wisdom and liberation to confusion and rebirth, is presented. From this higher-dimensional plane one perceives all the lower realms and of the physical world, and is the final opportunity for liberation if the being is able to recognize the display as the projection of pure Consciousness. Buddhists claim that in order to have these liberating recognitions after death, one must prepare in this lifetime by investigating the nature of one's mind through the deep meditation methods thus discussed.

Both of the above-mentioned meditation methods, concentration and mindfulness, are designed to quiet the mind-body system and the information coming from the personal unconscious so that Consciousness can "hear" the subtler energy currents of creation. These subtle spiritual energies, whether biophotonic frequencies from the

DNA molecule, messages from hyperspace, emanations from the dharmata bardo, or signals from the spirit world, are felt as sublime rushes of bliss, internal luminosities, inner illuminations, and/or visionary glimpses. In the Tibetan tradition, this realm is also referred to as the *Sambhogakaya,* "the creative expression or formulation of this universal principle in the realm of inner vision; the 'Body of Bliss' (rapture or spiritual enjoyment), from which all true inspiration is born." [49] This realm, often called the intermediate state between the witnessed material world and the formless Witness, is the home of true spiritual vision and insight. Again, the Tibetan sage Govinda illuminates the *Sambhogakaya* state: "the body of pure Form; which is extremely perfect, pure, eternal and universal, which is boundless and posses true attributes, due to the effects of immeasurable virtue and knowledge… It will always experience within itself the bliss of Dharma." [50]

Of interest in these deep levels is the contemplation of *nada,* or inner sound. Through deep meditation one is able to quiet the grosser levels of manifest existence to the point where inner frequencies and sounds are audible. There exists a hierarchy of ever more subtle inner sounds (actually discovered to be synesthetic in nature) that represent the vibration of subtle aspects of creation. We will explore the nature of these eternal sounds in Level eight, but in connection to the subtle plane, we can speculate that beyond the vibration of the nerves (one level of nada) is the vibration of the cellular structures (another level of nada). Beyond the cellular we potentially can "hear" the photonic-phononic frequency (holographic-synesthetic) emissions of DNA at the heart of all life. If we can tune into these subtle sounds, merge with them, and identify with them, bliss currents, illuminations, luminosities, and all sorts of spiritual visions unfold revealing the deeper aspects of creation.

As mentioned in the previous chapter, when a brain is hooked up to an EEG machine during deep shamanic trance states, or deep meditative subtle states, or REM dreaming, the recorded frequency is within the Theta range, 8 to 3.5 Hz. This shows a true slowdown of neural activity, theoretically giving the Witnessing Awareness access to the deeper harmonic *nada* frequencies from within the nucleus of cells. We naturally enter these inner subtle (intermediate) realms at night as our minds unfold elaborate dream sequences infused with archetypal symbology, beings, ancestors, and signals from that deeper well of universal wisdom. We rarely remember even a fraction of our dreams, but as the Australian aboriginal people tell us, we should learn to pay attention to the DreamTime, for our lives and this material world are but mere 3-D shadows of that deeper realm of higher dimensional Light. Every night, as our body-minds enter a hibernation-like state of suspended animation, our Essence is liberated from its constricted attachments to the Earthly world and its physical laws. Here in the "field beyond ideas" our Essence unfolds into self-created epic archetypal journeys, free to wander in worlds limited to the extent that there are limits in the imagination. Of course, imagination is just another word for that transpersonal realm of infinite possibilities, and at this stage our individual self learns to access and make use of the imaginal realms for the pursuit of evolution itself. Becoming aware that you are the dreamer in a dream by practicing the art of lucid dreaming, cultivated by special techniques that allow one to become aware of the fact that one is dreaming while still dreaming, is another excellent method for exploring the subtle world as expressed in dreams. The possibilities inherent in "waking up" in your dreamscape are endless.

Frances Vaughan summarizes level seven in connection to the sixth chakra, or third eye:

> The sixth chakra, the *ajna,* physiologically localized in the region of the third eye, represents the realm of ideal perception. The God that was dormant in the lower chakras is fully awake. This center is the place of union with the deity, where one knows the Self as psyche. Mind at this level is more subtle; more spiritual gifts are bestowed as it awakens. Control of imagination allows the discovery that all experiences are the creation of mind. [51]

A final historical doorway into the visionary realm of the subtle plane needs to be explored. This doorway is the "third eye" of the sixth chakra, *ajna,* and serves as an unparalleled focal point for meditation. This is the traditional center for in-sight, inner vision, and intuitive access into other worlds. A fascinating correlation with the pineal gland, called "seat of the soul" by the ancient Greeks interestingly enough, is that this gland sits directly in the location of the third eye in the center of the brain. One of the many functions of the pineal gland is to excrete various hormones, neuropeptides, enzymes, and neurotransmitters that help regulate biorhythms, such as the sleep/wake cycle. One such excreted enzyme is called tryptophan hydroxylase, a crucial amino acid for life, which serves as the raw indole foundation for the production of other neurotransmitters. The pineal, as it turns out is photosensitive, which means that in the presence of sun light, it synthesizes the tryptophan into the neurotransmitter serotonin for daily activity. In the absence of light, as in nightly, the pineal converts serotonin via the HIOMT enzyme into another tryptamine, called melatonin, the "hormone of darkness." Melatonin is a hormone that helps the body-mind go to sleep at night. We can see this phenomenon at work in SAD (Seasonal Affective Disorder) cases, where people become clinically depressed without the daily exposure to sunlight that tends to happen during the long dark winters of the higher Northern latitudes. Without sun, the pineal does not produce much serotonin. Without serotonin, low moods are inevitable.

Dr. Strassman presents compelling research that has found traces of DMT in the pineal gland, as it is also made from the same basic tryptophan indole ring that serotonin and melatonin are made out of. He reports, "The unique enzymes that convert serotonin, melatonin, or tryptamine into psychedelic compounds also are present in extraordinarily high concentrations in the pineal." [52] This has led him and others to suspect that maybe in the depths of deep REM dreaming and deep dreamless sleep, the pineal gland begins to secrete and synthesize DMT, thereby producing visionary archetypal dreams, and a possible connection to the spirit world of ancestors.

A potential metabolic sequence could be as follows: Tryptophan, which is modified into serotonin in the presence sunlight, is converted into the "sleeping hormone" melatonin in the absence of light as we go to sleep at night. In prolonged darkness, as in deep sleep into the night, sensory-deprivation, dark cave meditation, prolonged silent meditation, or ascetic isolation, the melatonin is converted into 5MeO-tryptamine via the HIOMT enzyme. The 5MeO-tryptamine molecule is one or two atomic shifts away from the hallucinogenic N, N DMT and 5MeO-DMT molecules, and is likely converted into them by INMT and other enzymes in the depths of sleep or deep meditation. As DMT is quickly metabolized by the body, an endogenous MAO inhibitor would be necessary to potentiate these transmitters. In fact, it has been discovered that the pineal gland does produce such MAOIs, such as the pinole enzyme, and potentially harmaline and harmine. Therefore, during the day we function with serotonin (levels 1 -4); as we fall asleep we enter the relaxed alpha hypnagogic state via melatonin (levels 5 and 6); as we enter the deep trance of theta REM dreaming, the melatonin may shift into N, N DMT (level 7); and finally, as mental activity is reduced to the deep dreamless sleep of mystical delta, the DMT may convert into the 5MeO-DMT molecule where one returns to the Source (level 8- more on this next chapter).

As we saw and in correspondence to our current level, the released endogenous DMT could bind to and "intercalate" with the neural DNA, stimulating the biophotonic emissions (ESR) and providing the illuminating light for our nightly dreams. In other words, this could explain why we "see" dreams in full light in the darkness of the night. The pineal may store photons from daylight, which may also be released at night through the DMT-mediated pineal-DNA link-up.

Dr. Strassman calls DMT the spirit molecule, and believes that it can also be produced at "extraordinary times in our life." He speculates:

> When our individual life force enters our fetal body, the moment in which we become fully human, it passes through the pineal and triggers the first primordial flood of DMT. Later at birth, the pineal releases more DMT. In some of us, pineal DMT mediates the pivotal experiences of deep meditation, psychosis, and near-death experiences. As we die, the life-force leaves the body through the pineal gland, releasing another flood of this psychedelic spirit molecule. [53]

This could be how the reported life review at the moment of death flashes across Awareness. A flood of DMT, illuminating every circuit, every memory network, simultaneously and at once, making the entire neural web glow one last time, could theoretically allow one to view every event-feeling-thought of one's life instantaneously. As that final glow faded, the life-force essence would theoretically retreat from the neural web and into the nucleus of the neuronal cells. There Awareness would hypothetically return to the Gaian-genetic imagination, the subtle spirit world of our ancestors. As the life-force essence continued to spiral through the tunneling dimensions/bardos of the dying process, it would eventually recede from the cellular DNA back into the White Light/Black Hole Singularity of the vacuum-Void within each particle. If the essence recognizes this Singularity as its very own nature, pure Consciousness, it is liberated from the rounds of birth and death. If not, it is pushed back down thorough the spiraling tunnels of the Bardos, to then be birthed into the many possible worlds, universes, dimensions, and rebirths available to Consciousness.

Deep, concentrated, one-pointed meditation on the third eye could also theoretically lead to the conscious secretion of endogenous DMT, as the laser-like focalized energy of conscious-awareness through *Dharna-Dhyana-Samadhi (Samyama)* could be potent enough to stimulate its release. This could be a possible neurochemical basis for the mystical experience of inner vision, illumination, enlightenment, or encounter with the inherent Clear White Light within all things.

One way to conceptualize the transceiving qualities of the sixth chakra pineal is to visualize it as the top of the antenna of Consciousness. Each chakra represents a circuit of Consciousness, the dimensions and levels we have been exploring up to this point. The chakras are the computational centers that transceive, transduce, and co-create the various planes of reality. From the sixth chakra, we have dominion and mastery over the lower five centers, as they are seen as ultimately being spectral light emanations from the subtle realm of *ajna.* The chakras transduce the subtle light energies of the subtle body (the morphogenetic biophotonic emissions of our individual genetic makeup, or light body) into the grosser manifestations of the physiology, and vise versa. The material body is in turn encoded into the informationl morphogenetic field of the biophotonic subtle field generated by DNA, thus recording physical activity in the vibratory plenum of the karmic subtle realm.

The McKennas illustrate the antenna like nature of the pineal:

> The pineal gland is sensitive to sound, photic stimuli, temperature, and X-rays. We suggest that the pineal could also function as a transducer for the detection of ESR in a feedback-type mechanism; the pineal could act as an antenna by detecting a modulated electromagnetic carrier-wave and converting it to a modulated spatiotemporal pattern of nerve impulses, much as a radio converts electromagnetic waves into sound. …In this way this feedback mechanism could give rise to self-propagating, evolving neural process that we experience as thought, memory, or perception. It is also conceivable that the pineal may be receptive to the ESR signals of *other* organisms…it could act as a receptor for the ESR "strum" of the biotic community and function to effectively integrate an organism into its ecology. [54]

As an antenna, our pineal is sensitive to many forms of energy, such as light, sound, temperature, X-rays, and a variety of hormones, pheromones, and neurotransmitters. Being photosensitive, it is specially tuned to light. If DNA augments its biophoton emissions through the discussed methods, it seems likely that the pineal would pick up those subtle biophotonic signals emanating throughout the brain. The entire

DNA architectural grid of electromagnetic information, likely sustaining holographic information, may be received by the pineal and translated into neurochemical information computable by the neuronal brain. As a transmitter, the pineal would then send out signals via hormones and neurotransmitters (such as melatonin and serotonin) to the rest of the body and brain, informing and regulating them within the context of the environmental stimuli. So in this way the pineal may act as a transducer or transformer, translating signals from DNA, the ecosystem, or from other dimensions into neurotransmitter information that the brain can interpret and reconstruct in terms understandable to the human mind.

To summarize, our pineal antenna may be the visionary gateway into other dimensional worlds. Through the awakening of our inner vision, via entheogens or meditation, we can tune in to the deeper intelligence within our cells. The organic wisdom of our Mother lives in each pixel of our being, quietly guiding our life's journey. At this level we illuminate our connections to this Gaian Mind, possibly via stimulation of neural DNA or through emanating photons from our pineal antenna, and consciously align with Her greater evolutionary intent. We become humble servants to the Goddess of life by creating a direct line of respectful communication with all of Her creatures. Only through a conscious human-Gaian alliance can we even begin to dream of an evolutionary potential higher than the one we just explored, initiating us into a true global shamanic resurgence. Once this conscious partnership has been made however, Consciousness will be ready to spiral into its final octave of Self-realization in a blazing flash of Awakening.

Exercises:

1.) Find a comfortable position, either lying down or sitting up right, and close your eyes. Feel your body-mind relax as you tune into the rhythm of your breath. Begin by visualizing your body. Within that physical body, contact the Witness or Presence that inhabits your body. Slowly and gently visualize that Essence rising from your body. Direct the Essence to a place that you feel is beautiful, comforting, and peaceful. Once the scene has manifested within your inner eye, begin to explore it. What is the imagery made of? What objects appear, and who is the one moving around in your imaginal place? If you have a question or a problem, seek the answer in this inner place.

2.) Find some percussive or evocative music and listen to it with eyes closed. Allow yourself to journey with the music to wherever your mind wants to take you.

3.) Focus your mental energy on the sixth chakra, located between your eyebrows. In coordination with your breath, begin the calming of your body-mind. Tune in to the inner sounds. Can you hear them? If your environment is noisy, try ear plugs and repeat the exercise. You will find that the more you practice, the louder these inner sounds will be. Once you hear them, focus on them to the point where "you" and the sound become one. What insights arise?

4.) Contemplate the connection between Virtual Reality and the Subtle realm. Is there one? Are there two different forms of light, or is it the same essential light source that creates all realities?

5.) Learn about the ancient shamanic healing practices. Contemplate their traditional use of peyote, mushrooms, Ibogaine, and *ayuhuasca* and why our society so blindly and violently prohibits their use.

Further Transpersonal Explorations

One early morning in 1999 I awoke suddenly from a very intense and vivid dream. In this dream I encountered a large, undulating snake, the context of which I now forget. Surprisingly, the snake was not menacing, threatening, or frightening, but rather seemed to be trying to communicate something to me. Upon awakening, I laid in my bed contemplating this unusual dream, as I had never before dreamed about snakes, as far as I could remember. Not thinking much of it, I continued with my day, completely forgetting about this dream. That evening as I was working in my garden, I had what I feel was my first true vivid hallucination. I hallucinated that a snake came rushing toward me! This time with fear, as there are many rattlesnakes that live in my area, I jumped up and actually ran back away from this large onward-rushing snake. When far enough, I looked back to see the snake, and to my surprise no snake was there. I sat for a moment, shaken and slightly confused, wondering if the snake from my dream the night before still lingered in my subconscious. Moments passed, and I continued with my evening, not thinking much of it.

Later that night I get a call from my friend Amoraea, who proceeds to blow my mind by asking, "Do you want to participate in an ayahuasca ceremony this weekend, only three hours away from your house?" Shocked by what seemed to be a direct invitation from the serpent power of the sacred "vine of the soul" Herself, I felt no choice but to accept. Up until that date, I had never had an ayahuasca experience. I had read much about it, thus knowing about its connection to the snake, but the opportunity had never before presented itself. The synchronicity (or whatever the dream and the subsequent hallucination were) was a sure sign that it was time for me to finally meet the Mother of all plant teachers.

The ceremony was set on some beautiful land in the foothills of Nevada City. Twelve of us gathered, many of whom were mature professionals, psychotherapists, and MDs, to my surprise, within a diamond-shaped structure that felt like an actual spaceship. The shaman, Christina, was a vibrant young Peruvian woman who apparently had trained with many native indigenous Amazonian shamans after she was recognized as a healer at an early age. We arrived early in the day and helped her prepare the brew by smashing the harmine-containing *Banisteriopsis caapi* vine and plucking the DMT-containing *Psychotria viridis* leaves. After the initial preparation, I took some time for myself, did some yoga and meditation to prepare the body-mind system for what was to come, and finally settled on my spot where I would sit for the rest of the night.

As the sun sets, all twelve of us settle in our chosen spots and await the distribution of the medicine. Christina enters the space and, to my amazement, has transformed from a playful young woman to an older-looking, wise being, emanating an almost supernatural energy. As she distributes the thick, syrupy substance, I take two shots and return to my seat to await the unexpected. As I feel the goop move through my system, the shaman begins to sing the most beautiful songs in her native language. These songs, called *icaros,* I later find out have an ancient lineage and carry the power to lead the journey. They end up being a precise technology for navigating the DMT space, and she uses them masterfully and systematically to activate visions that I later find have a deep morphogenetic heritage. As the journey unfolds, the first experience is one of unease and restlessness. Suddenly I feel a deep wave of nausea arise from deep within, forcing me to get up from my seat and go outside to relieve this most uncomfortable feeling. I proceed to throw up the entire contents of my stomach, which isn't much since I had fasted for the whole day prior to the ceremony. But this is no ordinary vomit; it literally feels and sounds like every cell of my being is releasing years of stored toxins in what I later call a "fractal throw-up." Every part that made up my whole released simultaneously layers of pain, armor, conditioning, trauma, toxins, and false beliefs that had apparently weighed me down for years.

Feeling relieved, light, and healed, I return to my seat to discover that my Awareness has opened, now that the channels are clear, into a dimension of Light so vast and rich that it humbles me complete. And who is there to greet me? The Snake! Fully alive, intelligent, with worlds and universes spinning within the patterns of Her skin. That night She (the presence was undeniably feminine) took me on a journey that can barely be described, but left me with a very basic gnosis: the planet is alive and sentient, and Ayahuasca is the messenger that is helping humanity wake up to its fundamental connection to the planet. She taught me that my awareness is part of a planetary Gaian Consciousness that is so deep, so profound, and so vastly beautiful that nothing in our human world can compare to its majestic mysterious Reality. Hours of organic wisdom and undulating beauty were downloaded into my visual cortex, as various beings made of light, possibly animal spirits, guides, souls, or ancestors, reminded me that what I called me was a mere strand in an interconnected web of relations that span evolutionary time. In the deepest stillness of the experience, I seemed to slip beyond planetary Consciousness into dimensions that were truly alien, possibly Galactic in scope. At one point I peeked, as if coming out of a wormhole, at a civilization that seemed to lie on some planet light-years away. Angelic or extraterrestrial beings guided me, showing me magical feats and teaching about love. They said that I was here on Earth to help heal Her, and that humanity's egocentric ignorance and greed was destroying the living Web at frightening rates. I witnessed, in the course of six hours, the entire evolutionary sequence of organic life on Earth, and saw that I was the inheritor of countless incarnations of this Life-Force. In this deep trance, I somehow reconnected with the One Intelligence of Gaia that is what we call Life, and that "I" was One with this Intelligence in my deepest Identity.

At some point in the journey, the *icaros* changed and began to skillfully bring me back to my body and the temple in which the ceremony was taking place. Within minutes Christina brought us back, and I found to my amazement that I had a body in this particular space-time location, and that "I" was back in my personal being. I felt a healing in the deepest part of my soul, as I had reconnected to the Mother of all Life. My Awareness was clear, empty of thoughts and emotions, except for a deep love for all the brothers and sisters in the group, and for the beautiful planet I was blessed to be a part of. My body also felt healed, as every cell felt cleansed and devoid of toxic patterns. I felt light, enlightened, and fully connected to the Web of Life that I was now poised to help save and heal.

All changed, once again, after that experience, as I truly understood at a cellular level how we are merely parts of One Body, One Planetary Mind. I took two more ayahuasca journeys in the course of two years after that, which served mainly to reinforce my growing relationship to the Earth Goddess, and to fuel my unwavering determination to be an agent for Her ultimate plan of global healing. Today, I find no need to access the Mother plant-teacher (this may change, of course, as time goes on) as I work with the subtle teachings of other plants. I now find that I can communicate and learn from my tomato plants, my peach trees, lavender and rosemary, the various mints and herbs, the changing seasons, and the living bios that I care-take on a regular basis. I now feel that the channels have been opened, and that communion is an ever-present guidance that becomes clearer the more I quiet my mental-mind and its consistent noise. Plant teachers are everywhere; we need only listen to their subtle frequencies that interweave across the planet.

I was further initiated into the wisdom of the ancestors and the plant medicines in 2004, as I worked for a Native American clinic as a psychotherapist. The elder Miwoks invited me to participate in their biweekly sweat ceremonies, teaching me how to connect with the Spirit World of the ancestors through songs, drums, and the guidance of the "fire and rock people." In the "womb of the Mother," the spirits emerged from the darkness during the traditional four rounds inside the sweat lodge. Their aim seemed to be to reconnect us to the Central Fire that unites all Life. I was taught how to use white sage, sweet grass, wormwood, deer bush, elderberry, mullen, yarrow, ginger root, angelica root, opal, and a variety of other local herbs, salvias, and plants to heal and commune with the spirits. The Miwok elders taught me that the Spirit World is not somewhere else, but that it is all around us. Plant teachers like ayahuasca, peyote, and the magic mushroom are for those who are not open to the spiritual realm, they told me. Once one has opened, the Miwok elders explained, one can have an ever-present relationship of guidance and communion. The spiritual worldview of the subtle plane can be a sustained Awareness, allowing one to see beyond the sensory boundaries of the meat world. They taught me to respect the elder oak trees, the grandfather sky, the water spirits, the rock guardians, the four-legged cousins, and the winged sisters all around us. The Elders taught me to work with the five elements, the seven directions, and to harmonize with the changing seasons. I began to integrate their medicines and worldview with my evolving transpersonal psychotherapy practice, as the dysfunctional Native community was receptive to the "Red Road" and methods from the "White Bison." Working with the feather, the crystal, the stone, sage, and the clapper stick, I facilitated talking circles that activated the healing response amongst the members, as the issues of alcoholism, drug addiction, trans-generational trauma, PTSD, abuse, and diabetes were worked with in a communal setting.

Unfortunately, the funding for the mental health program of the clinic ran out, and they could no longer sustain my position. I continue to attend occasional sweats, but have since lost some of my contact with the Miwok community. I have carried the teachings, however, into my garden, growing vegetables, herbs, fruits, and flowers to sustain my family and community. I continue to learn from these more subtle plant teachers, becoming the steward of the land my family and I currently live on. I have since adopted the spiritual worldview, seeing the ancestors, working with the spirits, honoring Mother Earth, and finding Great Spirit in everyone and everything.

On auspicious dates, full moons, and planetary alignments, I sometimes create ritual space to journey into visionary realms so as to access information, find guidance, acquire strength, and heal myself. I use the subtle medicines of white sage and sweet grass, while integrating yogic technologies to transcend the personal being. My current technology for accessing the visionary space of the subtle plane is yogic. After a long session of *asana, pranayama,* and *pratyahara,* I focus my free-flowing Awareness and *prana* on the third eye, *ajna.* I focus all my attention there, and proceed to use various breathing techniques to activate the pineal. This, I have found, gives me entrance into the deep, subtle, spiritual realm once accessed by entheogens. There I find strength, guidance, healing, and a connection to a much larger matrix of information. A literal doorway seems to open, as I blissfully ride a current of rising Consciousness into realms of sublime beauty and light. There I ask questions, pray, and commune with the higher minds beyond form, or just silently listen to the deep *nada* of creation. After a ritual session, I find that I see that inner Light in all beings and things, as the intuitive eye of inner vision opens. The Spirit World and the material plane seem to become superimposed, and the notion that we are "spirit beings having a material experience" becomes a living reality. The archetypal nature of all beings and events becomes apparent, as I pierce through the mundane social perceptions of "business as usual." Deep synchronistic meaning is found in every interaction, as I see the One Spirit moving through all beings.

From this shifted worldview, everyone is seen as an archetype, playing out a Cosmic role in the Archetypal story that is creation. The healer, the warrior, the teacher, the fool, the wise one, the Mother, the miserable one, the evil one, the lover, the philosopher, the king, the trickster, etc., all existing in their various forms as basic archetypal characters playing their perfect role in the mythic drama that we call our life. Most people embody and accentuate one of these particular archetypes, but ultimately we all have *every one* of these archetypes existing latently within, awaiting activation from life's synchronized events. The unity of all these archetypes, both from the light side and the shadow side, Jung would say is the Whole; the integrated Higher Self of Pure Consciousness (level eight) often expressed as the God-Deity in all world religions. In level seven we work with the archetypal level, helping make that level of the game conscious so as to help heal, integrate, understand, and evolve.

Working with the archetypal level of the psyche can be incredibly therapeutic, as one explores deep intra-psychic and relational patterns that are often expressed symbolically from an unconscious source. Jungian analytical psychology specifically addresses this level as it utilizes dream interpretation, art and play therapy, guided imagery, visualization, and free association to tease out the deep symbolic structures of the psyche that reflect collective or archetypal patterns. This work helps the individual access these deeper energies for the purpose of greater psychic integration. The goal of course is full integration in Self-actualization, making the unconscious, collective and individual, fully conscious. I use sand tray and art therapy, even with adult clients, so as to access and activate this level of exploration. I am often amazed by the richness of information that can arise when the person is allowed to use symbols and play to express often unconscious issues. By exploring their creative expressions, individuals gain access to what is going on in their life often hidden from their consciousness by the overly mental thinking surface mind.

In my current psychotherapy practice I have had the honor of working with an elderly woman who seems to work and live from this seventh level, spiritual universe. When doing her initial assessment I asked her for three goals for her therapy. She looked at me with a sparkle in her eye and exclaimed, "I just want to reach enlightenment, what else?" Currently age eighty-seven, she has a wealth of wisdom that makes me feel like I am the one receiving the therapy. One of her more remarkable attributes is her ability to receive guidance from "the Groupies," who she claims to be "a group of nonphysical beings that are more evolved than most humans and are there to help me ascend." She has struggled most of her life, as the conventional mental health system has labeled her at best manic, at worst psychotic. Within a transpersonal framework and approach, we have been working with her "Groupies," examining their messages and guidance. The wisdom, gnosis, and otherworldly perspectives that this conglomerate of beings poses are astonishing, and I feel humbled by their explanation of what's to come. My client's practice is to ask a question in front of her computer, sit quietly in meditation, and start writing the answers given as they are channeled by these disembodied, disincarnate entities. The question of whether they are real or not seems pointless, as the information coming from whatever source seems wise beyond human conception. Clearly there are other dimensions coexisting with our own, somehow accessible to those with instruments tuned to said frequencies. In these realms there is clearly a non-dual interaction between personal imagination and the Other, just as we are at once individual entities and part of the One Consciousness. My client is well aware of her archetypal journey toward wholeness, and in our sessions we work to integrate the vast amounts of information coming to and from her. She explores her shadow side with amusement, while embracing her light without attachment. She is truly a remarkable being with a clear teaching role on this planet at this time.

Why do some have access to alternate dimensions, hyperspace, or the Spirit World while others don't? One reason is clearly cultural, such that in a materialistic culture such as our own we view these perceptions and experiences as pathological and schizophrenic. Our empirical material world has no need for spirit entities. In other cultures, such as that of the indigenous, the Spirit World is a living fact, experienced on a daily basis.

The other more speculative possibility may be that a brain with higher levels of DMT, the "spirit molecule," could be better tuned to the deeper, subtler frequencies behind 3-D sensory-based empirical reality. We have already explored how DMT may possibly activate bioemissions from nucleated DNA, transmitting the holographic visuals of the Gaian Mind. The more standard description of mechanism of action is that like all other tryptamines, such as LSD and psilocybin, DMT (N, N-Dimethyltryptamine) is a full serotonin agonist at the 5-HT2A and 5-HT1A receptor sites. The difference between DMT and the other tryptamines is that it is almost instantly metabolized by the monoamine oxidases (MAOs) found in the gut, the same enzymes that metabolize serotonin, when taken orally. When smoked or injected, it has a chance to actively cross the blood-brain barrier. Like glucose and certain amino acids, the brain expends energy to acquire DMT via active transport across the blood-brain barrier. This barrier is the brain's protection against foreign blood-borne chemicals that may be harmful. The fact that DMT so easily passes this blood-brain barrier infers that DMT may somehow be an essential molecule for consciousness and brain function, as the brain appears to be so comfortable with said molecule. This notion is further substantiated by the fact that "dozens of studies cite that DMT has been found in human blood, urine, and spinal fluid." [55]

Recent brain-imaging studies done in the UK and at John's Hopkins University using psilocybin mushrooms (and recently with advanced meditators, interestingly enough) have shown a marked decrease in neural activity in the pre-frontal cortex regions (particularly the mPFC- medial prefrontal cortex, and PCC- posterior cingulate cortex) of the brain after ingestion, an area known as the Default Mode Network (DMN) of the brain responsible for ego-consciousness, mental rumination, and the filtering of non-essential information. In other words, the "reducing valves" of Huxley's doors of perception that block out the energies of "Mind-at-Large." The brain imaging studies showed a marked decrease in mPFC and PCC activity, structures responsible for self-referential and self-directed processing. The experience of "ego-loss," often accompanied by the more mystical of psychedelic experiences, seems to be mediated by this decreased Default Mode Network activity, allowing Awareness an experience that is not filtered by ego-consciousness. As the Default Mode Network of ego-self shuts down, Awareness expands to access information that was previously unconscious and filtered out, to ultimately merge in the deep states of egoless unity Consciousness of Mind-at-Large.

A fascinating mystery still exists: how did the indigenous shamans of the Amazon basin discover that by mixing plants containing DMT with other plants containing digestive enzyme blockers the DMT becomes orally active for up to six hours? These enzyme blockers are called monoamine oxidase inhibitors (MAOIs), and are found specifically in plants containing beta-carboline compounds such as harmine, harmaline, and tetra-hydro-harmine. When asked this question, the shamans usually answer quite casually, "the plant spirits told us, of course."

Dr. Rick Strassman was one of the first researches to be granted permission by the US government to study the effects of the short acting N, N-DMT in a clinical setting. To his utter surprise, the most common experience reported was that of contact with extraterrestrial entities that appeared to inhabit alternate dimensions. The shamans, of course, know all about these disincarnate beings, and have reported their historical relationship to what they call the spirit world for millennia. For the modern human subjects, however, the experience was not so simply explained. The overt alien and extraterrestrial themes were more like the typical sci-fi alien abduction phenomena than the more organic nature spirits of the shaman. One of Strassman's subjects reports:

> ...an insect-like thing got right into my face, hovering over me as the DMT was going on. This thing sucked me out of my head into outer space... a black sky with millions of stars. I was in a very large waiting room, observed by the insect-thing and others like it. We were aware of each other. Then they lost interest. They have an agenda. It's like walking into a different neighborhood. [56]

Another subject describes his experience:

> ...a space station below me, and to my right. Presences were guiding me to a platform. I was

> also aware of many entities inside the space station—automatons, android like creatures that looked like a cross between crash-test dummies and Empire troops for *Star Wars*, except that they were living beings, not robots. They had checkerboard patterns on parts of their bodies, especially their upper arms. They were doing some kind of routine technological work, and paid little attention to me. [57]

And finally, a more "typical" DMT experience:

> Millions of brilliantly colored little "skull clowns" swarmed me in a most visionary way while emitting crickling, tinging sounds which looked like violet sparks coming out of their mouths. These tiny skull clowns were laughing most musically as I died in the light. Melt down—feels like drowning and being electrocuted at the same time. Some fear is good though, and pretty soon the skull clown swarm had laughed me through death to a place of jeweled coiling roots and capillaries, swaying endlessly in a gem sea...The glowing, ember-like afterimage instantly swirls and shatters into blue and red sizzling domes that pinwheel ecstatically into a Creative, God-thing with a trillion jeweled eyes that dissolves into an atomic ocean. This is the multieyed God that is my Creator, Master, Destroyer. [58]

These three reports represent the now commonly known experience of DMT, as the Internet is full of reported contact with what Terence McKenna called "self-transforming machine elves." The common perception among users is that the DMT space is not a hallucination or even psychedelic as is commonly understood, but rather represents an alternate, parallel hyperdimension that is inhabited by intelligent alien entities. These entities, aliens, elves, angels, demons, fairies, deities, or spirits seem to be playfully instructing humans on the nature of reality. These sound like my client's

"Groupies" (my client has never had a psychedelic experience, let alone a DMT trip), and can be found throughout the fairytales and mythologies of human history. These trickster allies seem to be presently expressing themselves in high-tech guises, notably reflecting our cultural level of technological obsession.

So who or what are these tykes? Some believe it is us in a future, more evolved form. In level seven of Consciousness evolution, we have the potential to tap a planetary Consciousness that is vast and ancient. Conceivably, if the Gaian Mind were to become fully self-aware, it could wake up to a Galactic network of advanced civilizations. The Gaian Mind fully awakened could eventually join a larger network of higher planetary minds, to eventually join a Galactic citizenship that defies even humanity's loftiest of imaginings. Ultimately, all higher minds joining together could form an intelligent alliance, Galactic in scope, to ultimately join other galactic intelligences for the final awakening into and as Cosmic Source. Evolution seems to be rapidly moving toward some, if not this, full awakening into its original creational Source. To All our relations!

Level 8

Pure Spirit: Causal Plane

Phylogenic Expression

"Human history represents such a radical break with the natural systems of biological organization that precede it that it must be the response to a kind of attractor or dwell-point that lies ahead in the temporal dimension." [1] As McKenna illustrates in this provocative line, we seem to be embedded within a Cosmic unfolding process that has apparently focused its intent on the human species. As the perceptive reader might have noticed, a general trend toward the acceleration of change runs through all the levels. Each level of complexity occurs and unfolds at a faster rate than the preceding one. Peter Russell puts all the pieces together:

> The creation of the Earth was preceded by approximately ten billion years of stellar evolution. The evolution of simple life forms took place over a couple of billion years. And multicellular life appeared a billion or so years ago. The evolution of complex nervous systems, made possible by the emergence of vertebrates, began several hundred million years ago. Mammals appeared tens of millions years ago. A few million years ago the genus *Homo* first stood on the planet. Our species, *Homo sapiens,* appeared several thousand years ago. The shift to *Homo sapiens sapiens* that was triggered by the emergence of language and tool use, and that resulted in the Agricultural Revolution, began tens of thousands of years ago. The movement into towns and cities started several thousand years ago. The Industrial Revolution began a few centuries ago. And the Information Revolution is but a few decades old. [2]

Each stage produces an emergent property, something completely novel in the universe, and develops at an accelerated rate compared to the preceding stages. When we compare successive stages, we find that each new development occurs in about a tenth the time of the previous stage; thus, the shape of evolution can be visualized as an inward-turning spiral in which each successive circuit is accomplished in a shorter time period. When graphed, it turns out that this inward-moving spiral of evolutionary time fits precisely the proportions of the Golden Mean Spiral. These proportions, seen throughout nature from spiraling seashells to exfoliating trees to our bodily proportions to whirling galaxies, we recall follow variations to what has been called the *golden proportion, divine ratio,* or the *golden ratio.* This ratio is known in mathematics as *Phi,* 1.618, and its close relative *phi,* .618. Both are a form of the golden ratio and describe a special relationship between two parts of a whole. For instance, if we divide a line by this golden ratio, the relationship of the smaller section to the larger one will always approximate 1.618, while the larger to the smaller will approximate .618, all the way up and down dimensional scales. So when we look at the spirals of a seashell, we are literally peering into the actual shape of our space-time continuum.

French statistician George Anderla calculated just how much the rate of information flow and exchange has accelerated in recent times by converting various historical events and inventions into mathematical equivalents in binary units. He calculated that the rate of information flow doubled between Christ and Leonardo da Vinci (1,500 years). Between Leonardo and the steam engine, the flow of information doubled again (250 years). It doubled again between the steam engine and quantum theory (150 years). Doubling again between 1900 and 1950 (50 years), and again between 1968 and 1973 (5 years). Mathematician Jacques Vallee calculates that information flow now doubles every eighteen months, and accelerating. [3] Robert Anton Wilson quoted the above mathematicians in 1983. Currently (year 2012), it seems likely that the information flow is doubling now in the course of weeks, and rapidly accelerating with the Smartphone revolution.

This general tendency of exponential acceleration toward novelty and change is something we can all relate to. Each day that passes, we intuit that "time is speeding up," especially in today's accelerated information age, where more happens in a couple of hours than did in a couple of years in the eighteenth century, for example. Terence McKenna has taken this general tendency of acceleration to be an actual property of time built into the physical laws of the universe. [4] He describes this universal principle in his Novelty Theory, where he speculates based on a mathematical model derived from the King Wen sequence of the *I Ching Book of Changes* that time is not some homogeneous substrate of pure duration, but an actual fractal spiral which he calls "timewave." This timewave maps the 'ingression of novelty' into the universal flow of events, which, according to McKenna, happens at an accelerated rate as time goes on due to the shorter and shorter intervals that repeat the larger patterns that precede them. Novelty is here defined as that creative emergent property that arises from existing forms of organization, such as life arising from matter or mind arising from life. Furthermore, McKenna believes that the entire evolutionary process is being pulled into a teleological object at the end of time, which he calls the "Transcendental Object at the end of history." "There is both the forward-flowing casuistry of being, causal determinism, and the interference pattern that is formed against that by the backward-flowing fact of this eschatological hyperobject throwing its shadow across the temporal landscape." [5] Thus time is conceived as a process spiraling at ever-faster rates, in self-repeating fractal patterns, that moves toward this Transcendental object, which is novelty itself. He continues:

> What is happening to our world is ingression of novelty toward what Whitehead called "concrescence," a tightening gyre. Everything is flowing together. The "autopoetic lapis," the alchemical stone at the end of time, coalesces when everything flows together. When the laws of physics are obviated, the universe disappears, and what is left is the tightly bound plenum, the monad, able to express itself for itself, rather than only able to cast a shadow into *physis* as its reflection…As one closes distance with the eschatological object, the reflections it is throwing off resemble more and more the thing itself. In the final moment the Unspeakable stands revealed. There are no more reflections of the Mystery. The Mystery in all its nakedness is seen, and nothing else exists. [6]

Teilhard de Chardin in 1938 came up with a similar conception almost fifty years before Terence, and called this culminating event which evolution seems to be moving toward "the Omega Point." [7] He envisioned the purpose of universal evolution to be the complete fusion of all souls into the eternally radiant Love-Light of God. "In the world's ascent to the Omega Point, the goal of evolution, Teilhard believes that physical and psychic energy flows out from Omega toward mankind, empowering, illuminating, and leading it forward." [8]

As we will soon explore, this Omega Point is actually a level of Consciousness which can be achieved by each individual through deep spiritual practice. As a collectivity, however, many are skeptical as to whether we will ever reach this universal awakening, for human ignorance is vast. If this accelerating principle which McKenna believes is part of the overall structure of space-time is true, however, and all past and present circumstances of evolution seem to support this claim, then we might indeed be closing in on a truly Cosmic event. The quickening of information flow has undoubtedly accelerated, and if the rate of acceleration continues to increase, McKenna calculates that on December 21, 2012, we will witness the end of time as we know it as the human species quantum leaps into a higher octave of existence (you, the reader, are likely reading these words post- 12/21/2012, therefore can judge for yourself whether we are indeed in the act of transformation or not. We have clearly not quantum leaped into a higher octave of existence, but as of 2017 seem to be actually devolving into chaos and collapse. But, before any rebirth can occur, the collapse of the old must take place, which seems to more accurately describe our current predicament).

The notion that all of evolution is being pulled by a teleological "Hyper Object at the end of time," the Omega Point, is not new. It effectively describes an actual future state of completion that acts as a "Chaos Attractor" that pulls all forms toward its unifying ends. In Chaos theory, Attractors are future states of equilibrium that pull processes toward said states. In McKenna and de Chardin's vision, this Attractor is an actual Unified Singularity that is infinite and eternal, existing outside of space-time, and, as such, orchestrating all events in time toward the final realization of it-Self. The Attractor-Singularity is, of course, trans-time, therefore lying at the beginning, present, *and* end of time. Not only is it the Omega, but the Alpha and the Present as well.

What the actual Omega will look like on a collective scale is hard to envision, but inventor and philosopher Ray Kurzweil believes that it will inevitably be the product of a human-machine symbiosis that accelerates intelligence increase exponentially. In his book *The Singularity is Near,* Kurzweil outlines what he believes will be the inevitable future given the rate of modern-day technological breakthroughs. [9] He believes that nanobot implants will allow humans to increase their abilities to levels barely imagined. Not only that, but he believes that machines will wake up one day, and artificial intelligence will supersede that of humans tenfold. He explains in an interview with David Jay Brown: "I think machines will match the subtlety and range of human pattern recognition and human intelligence in general. And once a machine achieves human levels of intelligence, it will necessarily soar past it....They'll be able to go on the Web and read and master essentially all of the human-machine civilization's knowledge." [10] He does not think that our artificial intelligence will take over our planet, however, but rather believes that "we're going to merge with our machines." He continues: "if you talk to somebody in 2035, you're going to be talking to somebody that really is a hybrid of biological and non-biological intelligence." [11] Through nanotechnology, genetic engineering, artificial intelligence, computer implants, and ultimately space migration, humans are poised to spread intelligence throughout the universe. Kurzweil believes that this force of intelligence will beat entropy and "can spread (at the speed of light, and possibly even faster through wormholes) through the universe. Ultimately the entire universe will be suffused with our human-derived intelligence." [12] As we join forces with the speed, storage capacity, and information-processing capabilities of computers, our intelligence will begin to expand exponentially through an accelerating, recursive, self-reinforcing feedback loop, thereby creating a singularity: an infinite curve of novelty and interconnected complexity.

When this will happen is unknown. McKenna calculated with his TimeWave Zero software that something like this would occur on December 21, 2012. (I wrote these words in real time on September 24, 2012, and excitedly awaited the promises of this end-date. Now, five years later, it is quite clear that the shift and transformation will be much subtler than the speculations of this section. Even so, when I look at my Smart Phone and see how fully interconnected I am to all people through the Web, how all information is immediately and instantly available, and that as I quiet my mind I can experience the Unity to all things through Consciousness, it does seem like we may be closing in on a truly transformative event that is bringing minds closer and closer together for the possible fusion of a totally new Being.)

Another group of visionaries who prophesized a culminating event occurring around the year 2012 were the Maya of Central America. Jose Arguelles has provided an extraordinary overview of Mayan cosmology as derived from their calendar, the tzolkin. [13] According to Arguelles, the Maya believed that time is harmonically structured as a series of nested hierarchical resonant cycles within cycles. The smaller cycles are influenced by harmonic resonances from the larger cycles, thus repeating certain patterns. Their calendar, according to Arguelles, is based on a twenty-eight day, thirteen lunation cycle that is synchronized to the natural cycles of the fractal Cosmos. Their calendar ends on December 21, 2012. Apparently, the Maya also saw great significance in the December 21, 2012 date, as it is the end date of a 5,125-year cycle, what they called the Great Cycle.

The end date of this Great Cycle happened to be in precise calibration to an alignment between the Earth, sun, and galactic center, which happens every twenty-six thousand years. As opposed to our irregular Gregorian calendar and linear time based on the mechanical clock, the Mayan calendar is cyclical and is based on seasonal, lunar, solar, zodiac, and galactic movements. They call the galactic center Hunab Ku, "the One Giver of movement and measure; the principle of intelligent energy that pervades the entire universe, animate or inanimate." [14] According to Arguelles, the Maya believed that the gravitational influences from the Galactic Center would initiate a transformation. "The end of this transformation is to raise the overall planetary field to a higher, more harmonic level of resonant frequency." [15]

The calculations upon which the Mayan calendar is based, we are told, are made from the ancient observations of what is currently called the Precession of the Equinoxes. [16] Ancient cultures with advanced astronomical systems, such as the Maya, Vedic Hindus of India, Tibetan, Egyptian, Hopi, and Aztec, to name a few, noticed that each zodiac constellation cycled in the heavens for a duration of 2,160 years. This 2,160-year cycle occurs due to the Precession of the Equinoxes, which is merely the product of what scientists' now know to be a wobble in the Earth's axis. A full wobble, or revolution, of the axis occurs every 25,920 years. As the wobble of the Earth's axis slowly turns a full circle, it points to and passes through all twelve heavenly zodiac constellations. The Earth points to and thus "enters" a new constellation every 2,160 years. During the last 2,100 years we have been in the Piscean constellation, and are currently transitioning into the constellation of Aquarius, ushering in the much-anticipated "Age of Aquarius."

The ancients gave great importance to what they called World Ages, and divided Earth's 25,625-year precession of the equinoxes through the twelve constellations of the zodiac into five (or four) world ages. According to the ancients, each of the five world ages lasts about 5,125 years and is marked by particular patterns, cultural styles, and mental expressions. Of course, the various cultures had variations, such that the Hindu Vedics outlined four yugas (world ages), the Hopi four worlds, and the Maya five Great Cycles. All Ages, however, adding up to one full precession of approximately twenty-six thousand years.

This twenty-six-thousand-year cycle also marks an interesting alignment between our wobbling axis and the center of our galaxy, which, according to the Mayan stargazers, was of great Cosmic importance. So not only does the Mayan calendar end on December 21, 2012, marking the end of one 5,125-year world age 'Great Cycle' (what we call recorded history) and the beginning of another (thus the so-called end of history), but it also signals the precise moment when our Earth's axis aligns with the rising winter solstice sun and the galactic center. Mayan scholar John Major Jenkins speculates:

> The end-date alignment can be thought of as an eclipse, and it shares with eclipses the basic alchemical meaning of "the transcendence of opposites." In Mayan metaphysics, this union has a more profound meaning that goes beyond the union of male and female and other pairs of opposites. Instead, it involves the nondual relationship between infinity and finitude, eternity and time -a union of lower and higher. Our higher and lower natures are reunited in eclipses, in the Quetzalcoatl myth of the sun joined with Venus, and in the 2012 eclipse of the galactic center by the solstice sun.... Time is restored to its relationship with timelessness when human consciousness reclaims the timeless, eternal perspective. The manifest world of appearances is restored to limitless possibilities when human consciousness reestablishes its connection to infinity. [17]

Some speculate that the gravitational pull from galactic center may be accelerating a process of change that has been building momentum since the beginning of time. The quickening that our planet is experiencing may be governed by this slow movement into alignment with our galaxy's center, affecting the physiosphere, life, and consciousness in ways that are becoming more and more apparent as we move through this transition. The current Earth changes, climatic changes, social/economic instability, accelerating technological advancement, ecological crisis, spread of global spirituality, scientific breakthrough, animal extinction, population explosion, financial meltdown, global revolutions, etc.—the list goes on—substantiate that something profound is happening on this beautiful planet. A deep, compassionate, and loving consciousness wants to break through, perhaps the second coming of Christ Consciousness, but the successful birth is not guaranteed.

Our Mother feels the birth pains of a new Consciousness, but miscarriage seems like a likely possibility as well. This process may very well have been initiated by the influence of vast gravitational fields emanating from the luminous core of our mysterious galactic center.

Interestingly enough, astrophysicists have recently discovered that at the center of our spiraling Milky Way galaxy lies a massive black hole, the center of which is a singularity. As we recall from our earlier chapters, a singularity is a point of such gravitational magnitude that it collapses upon itself infinitely, having infinite mass and curvature, thus literally tearing a hole through the space-time matrix. Physicists believe that our early universe sprang forth from a singularity, and it seems that the Omega point toward which we are heading is another one of these singularities. How can there be different points in space-time which separately move toward infinity? I believe the problem can be solved through Einstein's theory of relativity. If you were able to go into a singularity, the gravitational pull would be so strong that you would begin to accelerate exponentially (sound familiar?). As acceleration increased, you would eventually approximate the speed of light. According to Einstein's relativity formula, the faster you move relative to the rest of the universe, the more space-time dilates. This means that time slows down and space contracts relative to the rest of the evolving universe as you approach luminal speed. More happens, faster, from your frame of reference. So in your experienced one minute, you would witness billions of years of cosmic evolution, for example.

Since the singularity is of infinite mass and curvature, a person moving towards it would eventually reach the speed of light, piercing through and dissolving space-time in a blazing flash of pure light. Upon reaching the speed of light, time would completely end so that the entire expansion-contraction of the universe would be witnessed in a simultaneous flash. This means that the singularity stands beyond and outside of time-space(s) as an eternal infinite source of energy and information, which in essence is ever present, omniscient, and all pervasive, in-forming all universes with energy, life, and consciousness. If the universe sprang from this eternal point, then it seems logical that to that original primordial point of energy it shall return. The singularity *is,* prior to time, and thus exists everywhere and everywhen, since at the center one reaches the speed of light, obliterating space-time altogether in an always already simultaneity of nondual Being. An observer from this infinite point would watch, as time no longer exists there, the entire universal drama unfold spontaneously. All laws of physics break down in this center, as space contracts and dissolves, becoming a nonlocal a-causal connecting point to all other parts of the space-time continuum.

Let us recall that nonlocality is a principle that was developed by quantum physicists to describe the interaction between two particles without any observable physical influence. Old-fashioned Newtonian physics describes the world as a collection of isolated particles interacting by means of local force fields. A local field works according to the principle of mediated interaction. In order for a force, such as our Earth's gravity, to affect a body, such as the moon, this force must travel across the intervening space with a velocity no greater than the speed of light. Physicist John Bell was able to directly prove the quantum equations for nonlocality through an experiment measuring the spin of particles. Bell discovered that once any two atoms have interacted, they remain in complete entangled connection even after they are physically separated by space. He confirmed this nonlocal connection by measuring the spin of one proton and then measuring the spin of a proton that had been in contact with the first. He found that if the spin of the first proton was changed into a counter spin, the other proton reacted by shifting its spin in the opposite direction! This confirmed the notion that at the quantum level, time and space lose their ability to separate and divide, as communication between the two particles proved that faster-than-light-speed communication can occur due to the fact that at the quantum level there is no distance, past, or future.

As seen, it has been proposed that in the nucleus of every whirling particle is a "mini black-black," or singularity, which interconnects every pixel of our cosmic fabric, throughout space and time. [18] In other words, the "strong force" keeping the energy particle in a stable whirling pattern (i.e., holding the atomic nucleus together) is supra-gravitational. All this seems to imply that the infinite-eternal singularity prior to the big bang, the concrescent Omega point Attractor at the end of time, and the zero-point quantum essence at the core of material existence are all One Energy Source, existing outside yet projecting the moving stream of infinite space-time sequences. If these scientific findings have any validity, they imply that all of existence is literally nonlocally interconnected at the Center, where all points throughout space in all times intersect and become co-tangent. There is only One Singularity at the Center, out of which space, time, matter, life, and mind all emerge in a frantic struggle to find their way back to Source. If we follow our holographic analogy, were we to tap into this quantum singularity (the smallest conceivable part), the entire universal display would spontaneously unfold in a blinding instantaneous flash (the whole).

This is precisely what some explorers of Consciousness are saying happens in the deepest mystical experiences. Dr. Leary calls this level of Consciousness "Neuro-Atomic contelligence," where signals from the nucleus of the atom, the singularity, are received, Witnessed, and ultimately merged with as Being returns to the Source of all creation. "At this stage the basic energies which compose all structures in the universe are available for management. The metaphysiological contelligence constructs atoms, DNA chains, molecules, neurons; it sculpts, designs, architects all forms of matter by manipulating nuclear particles and gravitational force fields." [19] At this point in evolutionary awakening, all lower denser levels of manifestation have come to a complete rest, as Consciousness begins to tune in to the quantum signals within all of existence. McKenna explains this possibility:

> An explicit spatial dimension—of a co-dimension inclusive of our continuum—allows a hologram of other realized forms of organization, far distant, to become visible at certain levels of quantum resonance in the synaptic field. These levels have been damped by selection in favor of more directly relevant lines of information relating to animal survival. Thus, these quantum resonances carrying intimations of events at a distance only begin to acquire genetic reinforcement once a species has already achieved sufficient sophistication to be called conscious and mind-possessing. The use of hallucinogens can be seen as an attempt at medical engineering which amplifies, for inspection by consciousness, the quantum resonance of the other parts of the spatial continuum holographically at hand. [20]

At this level, that which Witnesses begins to tune into the subtlest frequencies of creation, the quantum foundation of being, eternally and nonlocally available in each moment. This quantum essence, or singularity, stands outside of space-time, projecting and receiving energy frequencies that manifest and dissolve in a basic pulsating, on/off, yin/yang rhythm of creative movement. At this stage the Witness goes into direct resonance with this Ground of Being and merges. Past and future fuse, and all that remains is an eternal Now, for the Witness taps into that Singularity that *is,* at all points simultaneously behind the moving image of space-time. A tunneling or spiraling effect is experienced, as in a near-death experience, [21] and one is sucked into this Central Oneness. Acceleration increases and the speed of light is reached as a realization that the Witness *is Pure Light*. Being made of pure Light, there is no time or space or form, and the dawning awakening that the Witness is present in all forms, throughout times, nonlocally, and simultaneously, but not bound by them, is revealed in an ecstatic mystical flash.

Modern researchers have been seeking a precise mechanism that can describe how the human mind may be able to directly interact with and access nonlocal quantum information. Anesthesiologist and consciousness researcher Dr. Stuart Hameroff has proposed that the answer may lie in microscopic structures that comprise neurons called microtubules. [22] Within every neuron there are thousands of tiny cylindrical polymers called microtubules, which form the cytoskeleton of the cell. Theses intricate cytoskeleton structures provide the structural support and scaffolding for all neurons, as well as a medium for information processing. Each microtubule is comprised of millions of protein subunits called tubulin, which are arranged in complex grid like molecular lattice formations. It has been observed that every nanosecond the tubulin proteins flex between an open or closed shape. This on/off, open/close, 1/0, yin/yang function acts as a microscopic computer driven by quantum-mechanical processes. Within a single neuron, the combined microtubule activity equals roughly one thousand trillion operations per second in computing power. According to Dr. Hameroff, our form of consciousness arises through theses countless quantum computations that magnify and amplify the latent field of conscious awareness embedded in the fabric of space-time geometry itself. In other words, the inherent, ever-present Awareness of the quantum vacuum is first articulated though the tubulin computations, which collectively amplify Awareness through the microtubules of the neuron. The neuron then houses this Awareness, projecting it throughout the neural networks of the brain, to be finally expressed as the fully articulated human mind. This fits the holographic model nicely, as every neuron, every microtubule, every tubulin, every quantum particle contains the Awareness that gets magnified and expressed throughout the levels to become the moment you, the reader, are having right now.

Another researcher, neuroscientist Dr. Ede Frecska, proposes that the cytoskeletal network, distributed throughout the brain in every neuron, could serve as the basis for the quantum computation that could be a medium for quantum holography. He speculates, "The cytoskeletal matrix may be immense enough to contain holographic information about the whole universe via nonlocal Interactions."[23] Dr. Frecska calls the cytoskeletal network of microtubules in every neuron the "quantum array antenna" of the brain, where the microtubules act like quantum hologram receptors. He continues: "based on the principle of nonlocality and with the quantum array antenna of cytoskeletal networks, the brain is in resonance with the whole universe." [24]

The basic image, then, is as follows: the fabric of every living cell is composed of intricate microfilaments that are in direct resonance with the frothing quantum foam behind matter. These microscopic networks act as highly sensitive antennas that are in constant communication with the rest of the cosmos via nonlocal interaction. As seen, the ZPF stores infinite information in the form of interference patterns due to its superconducting properties. All this cosmic information is selectively dampened and filtered, for it is seen as redundant by an organism trying to survive on a daily basis. At this advanced level (eight) of evolution, however, we may be ready to receive and download the cosmic information nonlocally and holographically available, as Consciousness begins to awaken to its original essence. So if our universe is holographic in nature, every quantum bit contains the information of the whole Cosmos as encoded interference wave patterns in the zero point field. As we activate this level of consciousness, we can begin to access said information via the quantum antenna arrays distributed throughout our body. This process would then hook the individual into the mainframe database of the cosmic brain, thereby truly activating what the mystical sages call Cosmic Consciousness, a "Cosmocentric" Awareness, as a direct line of communication would be made available between the individual and the Cosmos as a whole.

The universe as a giant brain is articulated by physicist Jack Sarfatti when he states, "Signals move through the constantly appearing and disappearing (virtual) wormhole connections, providing instant communication between all parts of space. These signals can be likened to pulses of nerve cells of a great cosmic brain that permeates all parts of space." [25] In level eight we access the "cosmic thoughts," so to speak, and become one with the cosmos through the activation of Cosmic Consciousness. From this perspective, the entire space-time matrix hologram is transceived at the subcellular quantum level as wave patterns, filtered, articulated, and translated through the levels so that it may be comprehended by the receiving human brain.

To review, the superconductive Unified Zero-Point Quantum Field may store all information from the entire Multiverse via standing interference wave patterns in what Ervin Laszlo calls the Akashic Field. [26] Waves encode and store vast amounts of information via interference patterns, and in a superconductive medium such as that of the ZPF, they have no resistance and thus fail to be subject to entropy and degradation. In essence they remain available eternally. This Field is nonlocal, accessible from every particle of creation, and contains the encoded blueprints of the cosmos. As such, all its information can be theoretically accessed within each quantum particle. There is mounting evidence that such is the case, as countless cases of "Akashic Experiences" have now been documented. Laszlo explains how this may occur within the brain:

> The process through which the brain can exchange information with holograms in the fields that surround the organism is "phase conjunction," more exactly, "phase conjunction quantum resonance." This means that the phase of the wavefronts of a hologram in the field is synchronized with the phase of the holographic receptors in the brain, bringing about resonance that enables the effective transmission of information from the hologram to the brain. The physiological structures that receive and process quantum information in the brain are the so-called cytoskeleton. [27]

Laszlo continues:

> If all things create waves in the unified field and interfering waves create quantum holograms in it, in principle our brain can receive information on some aspects or elements of all the things and events in the universe….In regard to information in the Akashic Field, the cytoskeletal fine structures of our individual brain provide the access code. When these structures are synchronized with a quantum hologram in the field, access is privileged: brain and hologram enter into phase-conjugate quantum resonance. [28]

The stored quantum interference wave-forms recorded from all Multiversal events in the ZPF may be theoretically accessible via these microfilament quantum antennas, as they are tuned to resonate in "phase conjugate resonance" with the standing-wave hologram. According to Laszlo, the zero point field may be the ultimate storage medium, our universal memory bank, and the brain is simply Consciousnesses retrieval and readout device. All memories may be stored in this timeless medium, and at this stage Awareness learns to retrieve the collective archives of the cosmos by transforming its imprinted wave interference patterns into holographic images accessible to the human transceiver, the brain.

In essence, at this level Consciousness begins to wake up to its creative foundation and Source, where all universal information is stored. The mystic at this level is no longer a person, but effectively a conduit for the transpersonal Awareness of the entire Cosmos. The universe begins to become aware of it-Self, as it awakens as the super organism that it is. The individual becomes a mere neuron in the Cosmic Brain, finally transceiving the information of the whole of Cosmic Consciousness. The Attractor at the end of time is our deepest Nature calling us back to full Awareness, as it pulls all forms toward its Unifying ends in the Omega Point.

Ontogenetic Expression

Who is this primordial essence behind all form? What is this eternal singularity projecting the manifest world? It is your Self! The original essence that always was, before the dance of evolution began. All world religions have their label for this most transcendent Source. God, Allah, Brahma, Yahweh, Great Spirit, Tao, Buddha Mind, Clear White Light, Creator, and Void are all words for that which is beyond words. Saints, mystics, and sages throughout the ages have been professing the true Reality, the ecstatic Source that comes into being in our myriad world of multiplicity. It is a dimensionless, timeless, spaceless Oneness that is the Unity of all things.

"The plentitude of this Consciousness can be attained by realizing the Identity of the individual self with the transcendent Self, the Supreme Reality." [29] As is expressed by the ageless sage Aurobindo, the Divine Essence beyond time and space can be directly accessed as our actual deepest *Identity*. Our higher Self, our Awareness, our Presence, our pure formless Consciousness that has been present along the entire developmental journey through time is God, Brahma, one-without-a second. In the deepest recesses of our soul we are one with our Creator: "Consciousness equals energy equals love equals awareness equals light equals wisdom equals beauty equals truth equals purity. It's all the same trip, it's all the same, any trip you want to take leads to the same place." [30]

What is required is a direct turning about in the deepest seat of Consciousness; a shift that turns Consciousness from its exteriorizing tendencies to a direct Witnessing of it-Self. As Consciousness turns to view it-Self, it dissolves and merges into it-Self, returning to the original, pure, unmanifest, formless Awareness that it always was. "It is omnipresent, silent and pure. And because it is omnipresent, there is no need to seek it. All seeking is brought on by ignorance." [31] As Zen master Kopp points out, the seeking of this higher Essence is ridiculous, for its presence stands eternally right behind the seeking. Can eyes see themselves? Can ears hear themselves? That Ultimate Reality is your Self, right behind the entire hierarchy of manifested forms. Only through a direct shift of focus from outward seeking to inward noticing can we discover the original Oneness that is our Self, the same Self in all animate and inanimate beings.

Up to this point we have been exploring the various incarnations of Consciousness. Now as we turn to examine Consciousness it-Self, various properties, by now familiar I hope, become apparent. Consciousness itself is nonlocal. It inhabits bodies localized in time and space, but in it-Self has no physical location. It is thus spaceless, interpenetrating all space. Consciousness expresses it-Self through time, but in it-Self is not bound by time. It is timeless. Being spaceless and timeless it is everywhere and everywhen, in all forms throughout time. This means that pure Consciousness-God is Here Now in every moment. To be truly Here is to be everywhere simultaneously. To be truly in the Now is to be always and forever. For if we reside in our pure formless Awareness, we contact all forms in which pure Awareness is. We tap into that placeless place within us that is infinite and eternal, pure Spirit.

The enlightened sages of all times and places agree that pure Consciousness is not temporal, not of time, but is rather eternally timeless. It knows no beginning, no birth, and no ending, no death. Ken Wilber illustrates the illusory nature of time:

> There is no past and future, for the past and future are simply the illusory products of a symbolic boundary superimposed upon the eternal now, a symbolic boundary which appears to split eternity into yesterday vs. tomorrow, before vs. after, time gone vs. time to come. Thus time, as a boundary upon eternity, is not a problem to get rid of, but an illusion which doesn't exist in the first place. [32]

This statement describes the fact that all you can ever experience is the present. All direct awareness is timeless, here and now, present awareness. This timeless present then acts as the foundation upon which the various levels of being, the boundaries, divisions, and habits, become superimposed, creating the multiplicity of the manifest world.

Spirit, it is said, can be "heard" in the complete stillness and silence of the moment. By quieting all lower structures of Being, from material desires to subtle energy currents, one is able to directly "hear" the essential, eternal vibration of Great Spirit. This vibration, the deepest essence that is your fundamental Self, has been called the holy Om in the Hindu Vedas. This ringing Om is the basic *nada,* or inner sound, that stands as the primordial energy Source for all creation. "In the beginning was the Word" of Genesis directly expresses the essential radiance of the formless, attributeless Source that brings form into being.

> Brahma is the absolute. Everything that exists is Brahma or the Sacred Word, which cannot be explained. It is without condition and without properties. It is the world-soul containing all single souls, as the ocean contains all drops of water of which it consists. Brahma is life. Brahma is joy. Brahma is void...Joy is truly the same as void. Void is truly the same as joy.[33]

If we are able to quiet our body-mind enough, we can directly listen to the primordial sound of the Big Bang, we can directly hear the quantum resonances humming within every atom of our being, we can directly resonate with Spirit who sings eternally the holy Om. Om is all sounds of the universe in One. The Clear White Light is all colors and lights of the universe in One. Om and the Clear White Light are One.

Buddhism has traditionally used the words Void and Emptiness to describe this unlimited and unconditioned transcendent Source of creation. This is because, as an experience, it is beyond being and nonbeing, existence and nonexistence; it is Empty and free of all attributes, formless and unmanifest. Called *Shunyata,* the Great Void, it stands as the naked Reality beyond all form and perception, silent and ever present.

"The Ground of Dzogchen is this fundamental, primordial state, our absolute nature, which is already perfect and always present." [34] In the *Tibetan Book of Living and Dying*, lama Rimpoche describes a series of bardos, or levels of reality which we have already explored, that arise as the person leaves the physical body in death. The lamas claim that initially the Clear Light, or Ground Luminosity, is revealed as the true Nature of Mind, but the unprepared fail to recognize it. A spiritually prepared person can recognize this primordial Light as their true nature and thus be liberated from *samsara,* the cycles of birth and death.

Raymond Moody has compiled a plethora of case studies with individuals who have had a near-death experience and have seen the "Clear White Light." He explains, "What is perhaps the most incredibly common element in the accounts I have studied, and is certainly the element which has the most profound effect upon the individual, is the encounter with a very bright light." [35] This experience has its version in all world religions, and is characterized as a warm, unconditional Love-Light that embraces and fully accepts the individual. Lama Rimpoche explains its appearance after death:

> In death all the components of our body and mind are stripped away and disintegrated. As the body dies, the senses and subtle elements dissolve, and this is followed by the death of the ordinary aspects of mind....Finally nothing remains to obscure our true nature, as everything that in life has clouded the enlightened mind has fallen away. And what is revealed is the primordial ground of our absolute nature, which is like a pure and cloudless sky. This is called the dawning of the Ground Luminosity, or "Clear Light," where consciousness itself dissolves into the all-encompassing space of truth. [36]

Light, or the Clear White Light, is of course *the* universal image for the Creator, from science to religion to poetry. Luminous and brilliant, radiating beams of light that coagulate into creation. Light is nondual, as it has neutral charge, and is everywhere at once, since it *is* the speed of light where distance and time have no meaning. From transcendent Source-Singularity, radiations of emanating brilliance illuminate the darkness of nonbeing, bringing light and birth into creation. The true meaning of enlightenment is the utter release of the individual into the luminous Awareness that shines upon the world—the final recognition that we are the Light, always have been, always will be.

Experience of Structure

Q: What do you see from this level?
A: Your true Self, Light, Emptiness, Essence, Spirit, God, pure Consciousness, Love.

The realization of this highest state of Being, the goal of evolutionary development, is truly Self becoming aware of it-Self. It is the universe waking up to its original formless essence in the singularity before it decided to bring forth the world of form. One can directly wake up to this mystical realization of the original Oneness, the Nature of Mind, through deep meditation. In level eight, Awareness completely untangles and dis-attaches itself from the defining parameters of the space-time-bound body-ego-mind. These earthly forces cease to have any hold over Spirit, as all duality is transcended through the direct merging of the individual soul (level seven) with unmanifest Spirit (level eight). This unmanifest Spirit is the original condition of everything before the mysterious impulse of creation initiated the evolutionary dance of time. Being the highest state of Consciousness (not really a state, but rather Consciousness in it-Self), it has been called the causal plane: the formless foundation of all being. Ken Wilber goes through the sequence of ascension:

> In the high subtle...the self was dissolved or reabsorbed in the Archetypal deity, as that deity; a deity which from the beginning has always been one's own Self and highest Archetype. Now at the low-causal, that deity-Archetype itself condenses and dissolves into final-God, which is simply the ground or essence of all the archetypal and lesser-god manifestations which were evoked, and identified with, in the subtle realms...In the high causal there is now perfect release into the radiance of formless consciousness. There is...no meditator, and no meditation...there is only radiance. [37]

As one awakens to the nature of one's own Being, there is a sense of release in which all that was formerly attributed to the separate self melts into the vastness of infinity.

The union or fusion of subject and object defines the next level of *samadhi* within Patanjili's Yoga Sutras, called *nirvikalpa samadhi.* In *nirvikalpa,* individual identity completely dissolves into a state of formless, unmanifest, pure Consciousness where all duality is annihilated. Here there is no content, only *satchitananda* (Absolute Existence-Knowledge-Bliss), and the yogi's mind is at its stillest. [38] In this state of *nirvikalpa samadhi,* the meditator and the meditation ceases as there is complete, unmanifest absorption into the ocean of pure Consciousness. There are no thoughts, no bodily perceptions, no subtle currents. There is only One. A total transcendence of time, space, and matter.

Within the Buddhist path of concentration, the deeper *samadhis* are mapped in the various *jhana* stages of increasing absorption into formlessness. The highest is the eighth *jhana*, where there is "neither perception nor nonperception, equanimity, and one-pointedness." [39] The meditator attains the formless states, the last four *jhanas,* by passing beyond all perception of form. To enter each successive formless *jhana*, the meditator substitutes progressively more subtle objects of concentration, refining one-pointedness and equanimity until nothing is left within the field of Awareness. When all content ceases, *nirvakalpa samadhi* is realized. Called "sphere of neither perception nor nonperception," there are no "mental states" present, approaching the ultimate limits of what we call perception. Goleman expresses one meditator's comment about the *eighth jhana*: it "is a state so extremely subtle that it cannot be said whether it is or is not." [40]

Within the Buddhist path of insight, the higher levels of the causal plane that arise from mindfulness meditation have been called nirvana, "where consciousness ceases to have an object," and ultimately nirodh, "total cessation of consciousness." [41] Goleman explains the practice: "On the path to nirodh, the meditator practices insight, using as a base each jhana in succession up to the eighth. With the cessation of this last state of ultrasubtle consciousness, he enters nirodh."[42] At these high levels of meditative consciousness, the paths of concentration and insight merge, as the formless Reality of Spirit becomes a deep realization that vanishes all technique, individuality, and manifestation. Nirodh is the naked purity of the Void, where all dualities disappear in the resonant silence of eternity. Absorbed in this totality, all notions of self, life, Earth, and existence disappear as the morning dreams disappear upon awakening. Life in a body on planet Earth becomes a faint memory ripple in an infinite ocean of Being, beyond being and nonbeing, that just *IS.* No meditator, no meditation, just stillness.

Another practice described by the ancient yogis is to pursue the inner sounds, *nada,* which become increasingly subtle as one tunes into them. Through direct resonance with internal vibrations, one merges with said sounds, to then hear a subtler one. The practice is to merge with each ascending frequency until complete formless Awareness is reached. All of these inner sounds are the subtler manifestations of the eternal Om. If one can become one with Om, one enters the causal Spirit, merging, fusing, and becoming the Supreme Identity. One wakes up to ones luminous Self, the original Witness that has been present throughout the entire evolutionary journey.

Lama Govinda describes this highest principle, the *Dharmakaya,* as "that in which all Enlightened Ones are the same: the experience of completeness, of universality, of the deepest super-individual reality of the *Dharma,* the primordial law and cause of all things, from which emanates all physical, moral, and metaphysical order." [43] He describes this higher Reality as the universal principle for all consciousness—the placeless place from which all individual sparks emanate and take on a life of their own, and the original H-omm-e to which they return. It is the Judeo-Christian God from whom all souls originate, and to whom they return: an eternal principle that is infinity itself, always present, within, and behind all things.

Vaughan summarizes this level in connection to the seventh chakra:

> At the seventh chakra, *sahasrara,* located at the crown of the head, the sense of Self disappears altogether. This is the realm of Absolute Spirit, the realm of non-duality, where all distinctions are transcended and one ceases to exist as a separate entity...all levels are seen to be manifestations of this one. This ultimate state of consciousness is not something apart from other states, but is intrinsically present in all states. [44]

The *sahasra* is the crowning lotus flower of the seventh chakra, spread out across the head as the branching fractal microfilaments in every neuron, transceiving, transducing, and manifesting the pure Consciousness that is the Unified Field of all creation into diversified form. The microfilaments picking up the original Light (level eight) of creation, focalizing it through the genetic code that imprints the pure Light with a subtle karmic pattern, the soul or subtle body of level seven, which then gets expressed and transduced throughout the programmed neural web of an individual's neurology (level six), which manifests as an individual body-mind (five), personality (four), thought patterns (three), emotional self (two), and physical body (one) on planet Earth. In level eight we transcend all other levels and access the basic interpenetrating Light behind all forms.

Other than the discussed deep meditative states, entheogenic intake, spontaneous mystical experience, near-death experience, or actual death, humans access this causal plane of formless Awareness regularly in the depths of deep, dreamless sleep every night. In deep, dreamless sleep, the brain enters the ultra subtle, super-still Delta brain wave frequency of only 0.5 to 3 (Hz) cycles per second. The body-mind enters its deepest healing state, as the parasympathetic nervous system of rest and repair is activated as little energy is used for mental activity. In deep, dreamless sleep, there is no thought, no dream, no content of any kind; just pure formless awareness. Of course most people forget this state as soon as they start dreaming (subtle Theta state), or as soon as they awaken (gross Beta states), leaving this supreme state of freedom in the "unconscious." The advanced practitioner of meditation, who can achieve the Delta frequency of *nirvikalpa Samadhi* upon demand, is also able to embrace and remember the deep, dreamless state due to the cultivation of constant Witnessing. With the well-established Witness in place, when the natural shutdown of the body-mind occurs at night, the Witness is able to remain aware, and thus merge with the silent totality of the Void-Light that unfolds when all grosser bodies are at rest. The naked substrate at the heart of creation is revealed every night, exposed in its splendor, unconditioned and free, as the *very* Witness of all other states. In other words, the Witnessing Awareness of all levels is revealed in its pure, raw form, and, if well developed, can maintain its Self-knowing through the deep darkness of the dreamless night. The formless spaciousness of the Witness becomes temporarily free of time, space, and form, and rests in its own radiance

Delata brain-wave frequencies measured in deep states of *nirvakalpa Samadhi* are not the only observations made by empirical neuroscience of the mystical state. Neuroscientists Newberg and D'Aquili have shown that the mystical experience can be mapped in the objective material brain. [45] Whereas spontaneous mystical experiences appear to involve circuitry that lies within the temporal lobe, as substantiated by their colleague Ramachandran, mystical experiences evoked by meditation appear to involve circuitry throughout the entire brain. The parietal lobe, which we recall establishes a three-dimensional sense of self by establishing a boundary between self and non-self, appears to have a dramatic *decrease* in activity. This decrease is experienced subjectively as a dampening in the sense of time and space and in the dissolution of the self/ non-self boundary. A shift in activity from left-brain analytical mind to right-brain holistic awareness can also be observed.

The frontal lobe, implicated in identity, attention, and focus, *increases* in activity in the area associated with attention, as it focuses one-pointedly on the object of meditation. This increase in activity may allow for the improved self-regulation of lower brain structures often associated with mindfulness. However, this same focus allows a filtering out of redundant thoughts, which is measured as a *decrease* in the

PFC areas surrounding the attention association centers, particularly in the mPFC and the PCC, effectively shutting down the Default Mode Networks (DMN) associated with ego-identity. So an increase in attention, and a decrease in overall PFC egoic-mental activity, are the hallmarks of meditation. Some researchers have measured brain-wave frequency in the temporal-lobe and the attention/ focus areas of the PFC at the Gamma brain-wave range, above 40 Hz, in advanced meditators. This implies that highly focused awareness may accelerate the energy in said brain structure, thereby moving consciousness toward deep levels of mystical experience. The visual areas of the temporal lobe also light up, with their connection to strong emotions and memory, infusing the visionary experience with deep feeling, significance, and meaning. And finally a *decrease* in activity in Broca's area and in the borders of the parietal and temporal lobes associated with verbal-conceptual expressions is also measured.

The fact that objective brain changes occur during these deep mystical experiences does not provide evidence against the validity of such experiences. The brain merely *reflects* the inner subjective experiences that lie in a dimension beyond our familiar space-time-matter continuum. Every time I listen to Mozart or look at a tree my brain lights up and changes its dynamic to reflect said experiences. The fact that my brain changes every time I have an experience does not refute the experience; it merely reflects in the material world an experience within the interior of Consciousness that cannot be touched by any current instrument. In the mystical state, the brain may change in the outside, as expected, but in the subjective within, Consciousness appears to discover its original nature. And in that discovery, realizes its connection to all that is *as a deeply felt gnosis, or knowing,* irrefutable by any other lines of reasoning. The all-knowing mystical flash of everything being the hallmark of this most transcendent experience, the implication is that it is deeper than circuitry and possibly connected to the quantum singularity-source of our space-time continuum.

Could this eternal Singularity found at the heart of Consciousness be the indestructible, all-knowledge-containing, all-powerful Philosopher's Stone? The concrescent monad that holographically contains the entire Cosmos? The all-seeing Crystal Ball, magically holding and reflecting the vast libraries of the Akashic Records? The access bindu point to unlimited zero-point energy? The final alchemical Union of opposites; pure nondual Tantric Ecstacy in the *Union Mystica*? The uncovering of the *materia prima,* the primary substance where subject merges with object in a radical flash? We embrace the entire material Cosmos with the Awareness that we experience in this moment, thereby discovering Eternal Life, pure Consciousness. All this is reflected, of course, in our shrinking technologies that are about to become indistinguishable from who and what we are. All eventually is discovered to be information made of Light, absolutely masterable with a little discipline and self-observation. Alchemists and mystics throughout time have stated, "the answer lies within." Our deepest "I Am" is ultimately omniscient, omnipotent, and omnipresent, they tell us, and once we awaken to that, the entire Cosmos awakens through us. We become identified to that which we already are: the totality of creation, pure and all-pervasive Spirit.

When I look to the past, I see the infinite oneness of the Singularity. When I face the future, I hear the eternally unifying Omega Point that beckons from the end of time. When we peer into matter, we see the undivided wholeness of the nonlocal zero-point quantum field. When I look into my Self, I see pure boundless Consciousness. When I listen to this moment, I hear none other than Spirit, eternally and perpetually smiling as its projections try to figure out what life is all about. If we push forward in all directions, we directly intersect infinity. And who do we find in this infinity? None other than our radiant Self, One-without-a-second.

Exercises:

1.) Tune into your breath. Slowly bring your entire being to a relaxed state. Next find the Witness within. Allow yourself to merge with that Witness. If phenomena arise, bring your awareness back to your breath, and find the Witness again. Continue this practice until you are able to rest as the contentless Witness, gradually diminishing the arising phenomena within Awareness. Turn your Witnessing upon itself, so that you are able to Witness the Witness. Who do you find? As moments of clear pure Awareness occur, merge with that space and attempt to prolong the experience. With time, moments of pure formless Awareness will increase, and you will find these experiences to be the source of your inner strength, joy, peace, and happiness.

2.) Connect yourself to your higher power. Lovingly merge with that power, regardless of the name you use to label that all-powerful Essence.

3.) Meditate on your seventh chakra, located at the crown of your head. Allow your Being to release itself through the top of your head. Feel the Light-Energy that moves in and out of your seventh chakra.

4.) Think about the singularity and the quantum ocean. Now meditate and attempt to *experience* these phenomena within yourself.

5.) Read about the effects of Ketamine and 5-MeO-DMT. How is it that these substances can reveal the nature of existence? Are the experiences reported mere hallucinations, or are they valid accounts of the structure of Being?

Further Transpersonal Explorations

My first exposure to meditation occurred in 1992 as I joined a Buddhist group of meditators who taught me basic mindfulness meditation. I dove deep into the practice as I noticed how the nature of my mind and life gradually began to change over time. I was able to let things go more easily and drift through the impermanent experiences that came and went without attachment. I began to discover that what I called self or ego was nothing more than a collection of thoughts, memories, and association with no inherent reality.

During my third year of college, and of mindfulness meditation practice, my roommate at the time, Matthew, invited me to attend a meditation class with him. With a slightly conceited and inflated attitude, I responded, "I don't need a class, I know how to meditate!" Nevertheless, I decided to join him just for fun. I was so high on myself at the time, thinking that I knew all there was to know about meditation, that I even refused to pay the meditation instructor and offered him three oranges instead. He accepted. As it turned out, the instructor was a Tantra Yoga master with much experience and who displayed a very deep understanding of the nature of Being. He had studied the ancient techniques of Tantra Yoga in India with a guru and had been teaching internationally for close to fifteen years. In his presence I quickly realized that I was only touching the tip of an iceberg of Consciousness so immense that I could barely conceive of its depth and magnitude. My inflation was quickly pierced, leaving me with a humble sense of awe at the mere possibilities.

One day I proceeded to excitedly tell him about my first mystical experience at the rave, feeling like this would impress him to no end. I shared how the past, present, and future merged into an eternal now, and that the now was pure Consciousness. I told him how my individual identity merged with an eternal-infinite totality that was the God-Singularity Source of all creation. Unmoved by my breathless story, he replied by stating, "That is an experience I have every time I meditate, and, furthermore, it is my ever-present state." Shocked, humbled, and inspired, I realized that "when the student is ready, the teacher appears." I was ready, so I felt, and he had appeared in my life at just the right time.

Eventually, the meditation master, Dr. Anatole Ruslanov (Acharya Abhidhyanananda Avadhuta), and I developed a relationship. He invited me to a small advanced meditation group which he led and taught privately. The four of us in the group meditated and talked about the issues and experiences we were having within a safe and sacred environment in the home of one of the members. After some time, Anatole offered me initiation into a particular meditation technique that had been passed down through the lineages of ancient India. The technique involved a mantra and a particular meditation on the chakras that I was told is to remain secret so that "it does not lose its power." I was formally introduced to an ancient meditation practice that is, in essence, the one-pointed concentration on the vibrations of this particular mantra. The night of my initiation, Anatole took me to a waterfall on a full moon and left me there alone to meditate with my newly acquired technique. The experience I had that night was close to identical to the one I had at the rave on LSD. I completely lost myself as I merged into what appeared as a Singular White Radiant Light. I had a glimpse into the Nature of Mind and tasted the true essence of my Being.

Needless to say, as I worked with this new Tantric concentration technique, it continued to take me to inner levels so deep that it made my previous mindful meditation practice seem like child's play in comparison. I began to have unitive experiences analogous to the sixth, seventh, and eighth formless *jhanas*. I became so involved with this particular practice and the mini-samadhis I was having that I became extremely attached to the formless Void behind all appearance. The bliss of focusing all of my conscious energy into a one-pointed center opened up a dimension of reality that made the external-consensus world seem like a pale and uninteresting shadow in comparison. I would remain in complete formless absorption in what is called *nivakalpa Samadhi* for hours at a time, exploring a level of reality that seemed fundamental and to lie outside the space-time continuum. To this day, this inner Source continues to fuel my inspiration, wisdom, compassion, and therefore in-form all aspects of my life. I have come to see this primordial Source within me as the purest expression of Love, and I have come to recognize it in every being I meet.

The above technique has ceased to be that important after twenty years of use, for it was merely a vehicle that helped me realize the underlying Field of ever-present Awareness, the Ground of all Being, which has always been there as the very Presence you and I feel right now. This sounds fancy, but in reality is only a rediscovery, breath by breath, of the underlying, ever-present Sentience of this moment that just is. The "I Am" at the core of all beings, radiating Life to all levels of creation, is who we are at the most fundamental level. When first revealed to me in the full-blown mystical experience, it was naked, beyond space-time-matter-ego, without sensory-mental disturbance, and formless. But now, as I meditate less, I try to connect to that spaciousness in each moment, as it is the silent background Om that interpenetrates all that is. I see that Source in the eyes of my kids, my family, my clients, the plants and animals around me, and in the radiance of the daily rising sun. When I start solidifying into unconscious behaviors and patterns, I step up my meditation time in order to remember and reconnect. At other times when life is busy, I meditate less and embrace the multiplicity of life's events. In the end it is all part of the One. Deep down within my deepest Self, the mantra continues to vibrate, however, like an ever-turning prayer wheel that keeps a good portion of my Awareness grounded and plugged in to that indestructible Core.

Nowhere is the naked Truth of who we really are as easily accessible as it is in the presence of death. I was honored to be in such Presence in 1998 as I volunteered for the Johns Hopkins Hospice program for a year while living in Baltimore, Maryland. As told earlier, this year was one dedicated to deep spiritual practice while working on my Transpersonal Psychology Master's degree. My role as a Hospice volunteer was to give caretakers a break while I sat with the dying client at his or her bedside. Normally we would sit in silence, as I found that the patients relaxed once their family members left the house. Fear, sadness, and recollection of past memories projected by the family members, I noticed, kept the dying person from being present with this most powerful event. A denial system, based on the family members' own fear of death, kept the person from facing the transformation under way. In their absence, I found that clients surrendered to their own inner process, as I had no agenda or relation to them, giving them the space to go through whatever they needed to go through. All I did was sit quietly, presently, centered on my breath and mantra, cultivating spaciousness and loving equanimity. I would witness my own emotions fluctuate in response to the fluctuating emotions of the client, but what was most remarkable was the subtle radiance that would emanate as the client and I would rest in quiet presence. A luminous quality would saturate the room, as a deeply hidden wisdom shone once the surface emotions of the struggling ego quieted down enough. The illusion of the ego became transparent as the body began to shut down, and pure Spirit was able to finally shine unobstructed in full, radiant glory. People became too weak to fight, as all defenses slowly collapsed to reveal a shimmering supernatural Light that seemed free and at peace. In one case a client left his body in my presence, and to my complete amazement, the only feeling I felt was utter peace. No more clinging or struggling; just release, as simple as an out breath. Control was no longer held by the active ego, but seemed to be taken over by a deep Intelligence that masterfully guided all aspects of what felt like not an ending, but a transformation. In the Presence of this Truth, I was blessed to touch Spirit in its rawest form, as I found my own awareness transformed by the merging I was being witness to. For this, I am eternally grateful to the beings who allowed me to be with them on their final days on this planet.

Today, as I write this last section, I notice that the date is April 12, 2012. As explained in the ontogenetic section of level eight, the year 2012 represents the mid-night of the twenty-six-thousand-year cycle of the Earth's wobble. When I wrote the first draft of this text twelve years ago (now seventeen), I naively assumed that due to the acceleration of change and novelty, 2012 would be the collective awakening of level eight in the Omega Point; the complete collective enlightenment of all beings on planet Earth. Now as I complete this work, I notice that this was extremely idealistic, despite the beauty and elegance of Terence McKenna's mathematical fractal model of time, and its correspondence to the end-date of the Mayan calendar. It now seems apparent that we are barely integrating level five, the Green meme, let alone level eight. Yet as I contemplate the events of the year 2011, I notice that there actually has been a collective movement toward unprecedented change. The Arab Spring uprisings, followed by the Occupy Wall Street movement and consequent protests worldwide, do point to the fact that transformation is in the air. Add to this process the fact that every protester has an Internet-connected smart phone, recording and transmitting every event worldwide simultaneously, and you can see that the Noosphere of level six may be truly awakening. In other words, every person is the eye of a collective Consciousness that is self-referencing, self-aware, and responsive to the whole. So it now feels to me like 2012 could possibly have bee the transition point into the Noosphere, level six, as the technologies are now in place to allow instantaneous knowledge transfer across all corners of the globe. Of course, now in 2017 we see a steep regression into lower levels of ego consciousness, epitomized by the Donald Trump phenomena, which I feel seems to represent the collapse of the old outdated and unsustainable structures necessary for the next wave of evolution to emerge. However, it is hard to really know anything for sure at this time in history, as the hallmark of these times is utter and complete uncertainty.

I am well aware that by the time any one reads this book, it will probably be well past 2012. I have left the December 21, 2012 date as the mark of a transformational event for its symmetric beauty. That date is the midnight of our twenty-six-thousand-year clock, and as we align with the Galactic center we create the opportunity for true evolutionary change. The work, of course, will continue, but due to the fact that my entire generation has grown up with this looming, archetypal meme of transformation, it seems appropriate to use it and create the transformation we've all been dreaming of. The Omega Point is, of course, an experience in Consciousness, and as more of us are initiated into the nature of mind via the *nirvakalpa Samadhi* experience, the more embodied the realization of Oneness will become.

I definitely do feel a current acceleration in the rate of change in life's events. I don't know toward what we are accelerating, but I do recognize that something is happening on this planet. A transformation seems to be under way, in myself, others, my community, and the entire planetary system. The environmental collapse brought about by extreme climate change, worldwide economic collapse, species extinction, peaking solar flares, peak oil, political absurdity, social unrest, and massive planetary protests seem to be symptoms of a metamorphosis in Consciousness. Into what we are transforming is hard to tell, but individual transpersonal experiences in levels six, seven, and eight seem to point the way. Personal inner experiences reveal the structure and nature of Consciousness, and, as we've been exploring, each level has a collective expression. Therefore, part of our work is to access these deeper dimensions of expanded identity individually so as to help transform the "external" collective manifestations. The deeper we are tapped, the more connected we are; therefore, the more united we live. By personally accessing the transpersonal domains inherent in our wholeness, the more able we are to help others enter that state of liberated unity. We must first free ourselves before we can help heal others, for healing is living in utter inner freedom. As free beings we can tap the creative engines of creation and help it continue its eternal art project of manifest existence.

A fascinating question still remains; how and why did the classical Maya end their calendar on December 21, 2012, with a whole mythology around death and rebirth surrounding this end date? One hypothetical reason could be that the astronomer-priest-shamans could literally see, through their shamanic visions, into the future. And in this visionary view of the temporal landscape, they could have seen an end point, a singularity, when humanity possibly discovered its Divine Spiritual Essence. They foresaw a time when the illusion of *maya* would be unveiled to reveal the naked Truth behind creation. The apocalypse, the "great revealing," when all falsehood dissolves and we stand at the threshold of a new spiral of possibility, may have been glimpsed by these visionaries. Some scholars believe, based on pictorial evidence, that these Mayan shamans may have used entheogens to connect with a higher dimensional plane in order to see McKenna's "temporal dwell point at the end of history." I interpret the "end of history" as the collapse and death of the current male-dominated, consumer-oriented, war-driven ego-culture (personified and epitomized in Donald Trump) that began five to six thousand years ago in the "dawn of civilization," with the eventual potential rebirth into a more compassionate, just, sustainable, regenerative, and loving culture. This last current "historical" Great Cycle has been dominated by ego, with great consequent achievements existing right next to its atrocities, but we are being once again signaled by the planet that it is time to evolve.

It seems more than likely that the Mayan shamans used the local flora and fauna to abstract the medicines that gave them access to the alternate higher dimensions. Psilocybin mushrooms abound in Southern Mexico and Central America, as do a variety of N, N-DMT containing plants and animals. One animal, the Sonora Desert toad, *Bufa Alvarius*, found throughout the tropics, produces high concentrations of 5-MeO-DMT (5-methoxy-DMT) in its glands, a product of serotonin synthesis also found in our bodies. While 5-MeO-DMT is a cousin of N, N-DMT, some argue it is many times more powerful. The experience is of similar short duration, five to twenty minutes, but is compared by psychonaut D. M. Turner as such: "5-Meo-DMT feels like sheer force, whereas N, N-DMT feels like sheer perfection." He continues; "on 5-MeO-DMT I can literally feel my mind exploding and expanding outward to encompass first the area near me, then the planet, and eventually the cosmos. This takes place over a span of fifteen seconds or so." [46]

The overwhelming majority of users, whose "tryp" reports can now be found logged on the educational website erowid.com, claim that on N, N-DMT one experiences visionary worlds with a variety of bejeweled beings in full multidimensional color, while on 5-MeO-DMT one's complete space-time-identity dissolves in a blinding flash of pure White Light. If N, N-DMT is the "Spirit Molecule," then 5-MeO-DMT has been called the "God Molecule." Explorer and writer James Oroc describes his research into this most-potent substance:

> After six years of fairly regular use of 5-MeO-DMT in both its natural and synthetic (lab-produced) forms, the following consistent patterns have emerged: I fully inhale the smoke, generally holding it in until my vision of my physical surroundings has began to break into fractals, and then I exhale. Virtually immediately upon exhalation, my vision experiences a field of light-fractals. My mind then dissolves into this white light, until the external vision of my eyes is no longer relevant

> (or at least no longer recognizes my physical environment). This white light—that blazes with the focused intensity of a laser and is both whiter-than-white, yet also sparkling with brilliant color—may be the crux of the experience. [47]

Another of Oroc's 5-MeO experiences reveals the level eight experience with great eloquence:

> As I let go I experience dissolution into an omniscient state of Oneness, a place where there is no difference with G/d, the physical universe, or me. We have ceased to exist as separate entities and now resonate as One. [48]

And finally, Oroc states his theory:

> My experiences with 5-MeO-DMT have led me to believe that when our consciousness is freed of the constraints of matter and mass, it spontaneously returns to the universal ground state of light, where it ultimately recognizes the true nature of reality as union with that light: union with G/d. [49]

In essence, Oroc is suggesting that this natural neuro-molecule has the capacity to release Awareness from the confines of the brain-bound, space-time locus, as "we are like a radio tuned in to the zero-point field, resonating with the vacuum energy." He continues with his hypothesis:

> Smoking 5-MeO-DMT (or DMT) briefly increases the coherence in the brain's Bose-Einstein condensate, causing all the neurons in the brain to fire simultaneously, which in turn "lifts the veil" from this reality by increasing the brain's resonant coherence with the Bose-Einstein condensate of the zero-point field. Then it is possible to experience the ground state of the zero-point field as a conscious entity of pure light. [50]

He speculates that the 5-MeO flash increases the brain wave coherence to such a level that it allows it to resonate with the underlying quantum vacuum of the zero-point field. The above experiential description of the encounter with the Light is, of course, a classic phenomenon in the near-death experience. The brief encounter with the Clear White Light, the same Light that Tibetan lamas introduce their disciples to in the transmission of the Ground Luminosity, seems to be the signature of the 5-MeO-DMT experience. The dawning of the Light in NDEs is really the revealing of the radiant Nature of Mind, the zero-point Ground state of all that arises.

Another substance that reportedly gives access to the quantum realm is ketamine, a general dissociative anesthetic used for children and elders in surgery due to the fact that it is a "gentle" anesthetic. It puts the body to sleep without depressing lung activity or interfering with the respiration process. It has also been known to have antidepressant effects. Its psychedelic properties were discovered when patients coming out of the anesthetic would report "reemergence" and out-of-body experiences. Further experiments showed that a dose much smaller than the anesthetic dose produces a dissociative experience of vast intensity. Subjects report that their senses turn off to the world, allowing consciousness to freely traverse beyond the confines of space and time.

This anesthetic dissociative reportedly puts the body to sleep by blocking and inhibiting NMDA/ glutamate receptors, while at the same time stimulating the awake mind via increased glutamate (remember, a major excitatory neurotransmitter) release. Normally, glutamate binds to the NMDA receptor sites and thus excites the ion channels. This process facilitates sensory perception and motor activity. Ketamine is an antagonist at the NMDA receptor, thus blocking the NMDA receptor site channel and inhibiting a signal. This process results in the attenuation of the sensory signals and a paralysis of the physical body. The excess glutamate excites other receptor sites, stimulating other brain functions such as cognitive, visual, and cerebellar functions. [51] Psychiatrist Dr. Karl Jansen believes the above mechanism to be responsible for all out-of-body experiences (OBE) and near-death experiences (NDE), naturally and with ketamine. He explains: "The link is tunnel blockade, a block that can happen naturally, for example, as a protective brain response if oxygen falls after heart attack, or that can be provided by ketamine. It is the block that can result in an NDE." [52] The NMDA receptor block shuts out the sensory-motor world while activating other, possibly unused pathways via the excess glutamate flood. Some speculate that the excess glutamate and its neural activation may increase neuroplasticity and the production of new neural pathways, thus its antidepressant effect, among others. Other than being an NMDA/glutamate receptor antagonist, Dr. Jansen reports, "ketamine also has direct and/or indirect effects on opioid, dopamine, serotonin, cannabinoid, nitric oxide, nor-adrenaline, sigma, GABA, and acytocholine systems, among others." [53]

In the context of our current discussion, Dr. Jansen speculates that, "ketamine may be one of the substances that 'retunes' the brain to allow awareness to enter 'the quantum sea'." [54] This appears evident to Jansen when he shares Trey Turner's ketamine experience:

> I had stumbled into the blast furnace at the heart of the cosmos, the engine that drives the process of creating manifest reality out of thoughts of the mind of God…I was seeing…that thoughts create manifest forms…It was kind of like a cosmic assembly line that was constantly churning out the alternate universes that some physicists theorize about which every conceivable possibility becomes an actual reality. [55]

Ketamine explorers often report (see erowid.com for "Special K" experiences) that consciousness is distilled to its purest essence, as all sensory awareness is transcended for the duration of one hour. As a point of consciousness, explorers report accessing alternate dimensions, parallel universes, and other probable realities accessible via "the quantum wormhole superhighways interconnecting the entire Metaverse." Explorers report that as one temporarily departs from the gravity-bound space-time identity structure, individual consciousness merges with an ocean of pure Consciousness, the Ground state of all creation. Again, this may occur as the five senses are quieted and stilled to a point that allows the indwelling Witnessing Awareness inherent in all form to access the information being received by the microtubules in every neuron. Without the noise of "external" sensory signals, the subtle reception of quantum Akashic information at the microfilament level may be accessible to the human as it is translated by the circuitry of the brain. D. M. Turner describes his ketamine experience;

> As the high is coming on there is a break in the continuity of consciousness. Soon after this point I find myself in a swirling psychedelic universe…. Frequently there is no recollection of ever having been myself, been born, had a personality or body,

> or even known planet earth. The experience is one of being in total orgasm with the universe. I feel like I'm in hyperspace, simultaneously connected to all things. Billions of images and perceptions are simultaneously flowing through my circuits. I am not bound into three dimensions. In the fourth dimension of time I am not locked into the current moment. I experience backwards and forwards in time as well, with the current moment being the center of intensity. [56]

As explored in earlier sections, there are a variety of technologies other than ketamine for achieving this departure process from the gravity-bound, 3-D, body-matter-space-time identity. The most familiar is falling asleep. Through certain physiological mechanisms, such as the channel blockade, the body becomes paralyzed as one falls asleep, allowing the active mind movement toward other dream-realities without the body responding in the material realm. The senses shut down, the body ceases to react to motor output, and Awareness journeys into the endless dreamscapes of deep Mind.

Sensory deprivation tanks are another excellent technology for attenuating physical stimuli so that Essence may travel within the inner invisible landscapes without distraction from the external world as mediated by sensory signals. *Pratyahara* from Raja Yoga is the precise step in Yoga which allows one to achieve this mastery on demand. As we recall, through the process of *pratyahara* we withdraw our conscious energy, *prana,* and Awareness from the senses and channel said energies toward higher centers and their respective dimensions of Being. I recommend the later, self-developed techniques for accessing these higher dimensions, for the mentioned substances can be very dangerous. Ketamine and 5-MeO-DMT are *not* recreational drugs for having some fun. They are serious chemicals that will fully dissolve any conception you have of your self and your reality. It is truly an ego death experience, often accompanied by intense fear and terror of total dissolution if surrender is not practiced. If you do not want to experience the complete annihilation of your individual personality and the space-time matrix you inhabit, I recommend you stay far away from these substances. You have been warned!

A possible speculative sequence could be as follows: the microtubules receive the Akashic quantum nonlocal information embedded in the Unified Field of Pure Consciousness (eight) and translate-transduce it to the DNA driven-templated neuron (seven). The neurons then translate, communicate, and network the translated signal across the human brain (six). The brain interprets the signal to make it accessible to the mind-body system (five). The body-mind system then runs it through the personality ego structure (four), which integrates the insight if relevant. The insight then manifests as a though pattern (three), eliciting an emotional reflex (two), with a corresponding physical reaction and sensation (one). Upon examination, it is seen that the body-sensation is made of matter, 99.9999 % of which physicists tell us is empty vacuum space. It all literally dissolves at the edge of perception, as matter is really an experience in Consciousness rather than something substantially solid and real.

The process works the other way. From the quantum Void a ripple creates a probability wave that collapses as a "material" pattern. A nervous system senses (collapses) that pattern as charge and runs it through the senses, the neuronal cord, and brain stem (one). After determining physio-survival relevance, it is channeled up to the limbic brain, eliciting an emotional response (two). After the emotional scan, it is further channeled up to the cortex to be analyzed by the rational mind (three). The rational mind then runs it by the PFC of the executive ego (four) for a decision to be made. The advanced personality opens up to the experience's multidimensional reality through a full mind-body resonant immersion (five). Upon examination from within, it is noticed and Witnessed that the multidimensional experience is a psychic pattern of holographic information with no inherent reality other than its neurological reconstruction (six). The information is assessed and recorded by the refined genetic intelligence in each neuron (seven), to then be reabsorbed back into the quantum ocean of probability waves as an eternal interference pattern. This ocean is, of course, pure Consciousness, the One who subjectively experiences the above sequence as it inhabits the interior of each level.

So, if the Void accessed in the deepest states of formless Samadhi is indeed identical to the Void that surrounds matter and interpenetrates it as the 99.9999 % empty space of the vacuum, then it should be possible to flip into its all-embracing vastness quite easily with a mere shift in focus. It would mean that formless Consciousness in a state of pure potential *is* the 99.9999 % (may even be the so-called mysterious dark matter and dark energy) empty vacuum that surround and interpenetrates matter; matter being the .00001 % that makes up our body and brain and material universe, the mere crystallizations and actualizations of that all-embracing Consciousness. In the deepest depths of our Being, Awareness exists in a state of unmanifest uncertainty, pure potentiality and probability, awaiting that secret signal for creation.

This unborn dimension is the ever-present Ground out of which everything is *still* arising. If our deepest Awareness is the Unified Field of Everything, the Ground of all realities, when we awaken to it we realize that we have always been that eternal Oneness before time began. From that placeless place, nothing ever was; only an Empty Absolute I AM out of which relative time, space, energy, matter, and mind vibrate into existence. Time travel, dimensional shifting, and access to the wormhole highways of the cosmos may literally be a possibility within our own deepest Being, *if* this Being is the substrate out of which all forms in the Multiverse creatively emerge, moment to moment. If it is all strung together by Consciousness, we may literally have access to unlimited energy, power, creativity, and information, for this pure deepest Consciousness is the Creator, One-without-a-second, within the deepest part of *You!* Zero Point Energy, fully accessible to the advanced Awareness, may be the jiggling energy that quietly hums behind all expressions of creation, awaiting its recognition as the very Power Source of your individual life and consciousness.

The Big Bang is not some event in the distant past. It is happening right here, right now, in the deepest level of your Being. As we zoom into our subatomic particles, or as we zoom out into the universe, we necessarily venture back in time to arrive at the Unified Field of the Singularity in the zero-point Ground state, outside and before time. This silent empty Void before the impulse of space-time was even a thought is your deepest Awareness, quietly resting outside all universes, actually found in the gap between your two thoughts. In the on/off of the frothing quantum foam, as in the movement of your thoughts, we witness the Big Bang over and over again as something emerges out of nothing, form appears from the formless, and vibrations resonate from the stillness of the empty Void. The ocean of Akashic Consciousness stores all holographic interference patterns in latent form, a.k.a. the Mind of God, awaiting a ray of willed light in order to manifest said vibratory patterns into fully articulated realities. If all info is encoded in the Akashic Field, and if this Field is pure Consciousness, then we theoretically have access to all of the encoded information within our very own Being!

Prior to and beneath all information and encoded patterns, the final release from time reveals the splendor of who we really are in that timeless essence that is our essential Self, the same Self that has Witnessed the entire journey across evolutionary space and time. As we look within, quiet the mind, and still the body, we begin to uncover the naked Radiant Light that hides beneath the hierarchy of manifestations, silently smiling as the Alpha-Omega state of total completion and perfection. And in that Light, where there is nothing to be or do, we find that it is all truly One. No birth, no death, just One. Always has been, always will be.

Conclusion

Nonduality: The All

"Love is the answer."

-John Lennon

Now that we have reached the Ultimate Source of all things, the highest possible state of Consciousness, are we done with our journey? According to various spiritual traditions, we have only just began. Buddhists say there is a danger of becoming too attached to the formless freedom and bliss of our deeper nature. According to them, this is the final duality, the last battle before reaching true enlightenment. Many renunciate traditions consider the causal plane, achieved in states of deep meditation, to be the final goal of spiritual evolution, as the Supreme Reality is discovered and the illusion of time-space is revealed. As monks, saddhus, sages, and priests have done throughout history, the turbulent tides of manifest existence are left behind for the personal Union with God. Cause and effect are transcended and one achieves personal liberation from the wheels of birth and death. This approach is practiced by various traditions, such as the Theravada "Hinayana" Buddhists, where liberation is sought individually. The mundane world is left behind for the peaceful pursuit of Nirvana through the 'Lesser Vehicle.' This approach is one of seeking individual salvation and liberation through devoted spiritual practice.

In contrast, Mahayana Buddhists seek the 'Great Vehicle.' This perspective approaches salvation not as an individual pursuit, but as collective process. "A critical difference between these two main Buddhist traditions is the Mahayana bodhisattva vow to gain enlightenment not just for oneself but for the sake of the salvation of all beings." [1] The bodhisattva is a being who has gone to the Void, merged with the formless, and seen the illusory nature of all phenomena. But out of the mystical realization that all is One, a deep compassion fills its Being. Out of this compassion the bodhisattva returns to the "marketplace" with helping hands. The deep insights from the subtle realms of creation move the bodhisattva to come back to the incarnation so as to help others wake up to their original Oneness. The bodhisattva realizes that in that Eternal Place, there is no time, so there is no hurry to Self-liberate. Instead the bodhisattva returns to the Earthly planes to help all beings attain enlightenment. They pursue this venture from an egoless stance as they reintegrate themselves into the manifest world as Divine agents of evolution. Their mission is to wake humanity up from its deep hypnotic dream so that it can rediscover the luminous potential latent within the core of every soul.

The bodhisattva vow is to liberate all beings, so that all can cross the great ocean of existence together in the Great Vehicle. "In the nondual traditions, you take a vow, a secret vow, which is the foundation of all of your training, and that vow is that *you will not disappear into cessation*—you will not hide in Nirvana, you will not evaporate in nirodh, you will not abandon the world by tucking yourself into nirvikalpa." [2] Through selfless service to humanity, these enlightened beings move quietly and unnoticed among the masses, exerting subtle influences that move and transform lives. Selfless services takes on many forms, from feeding homeless populations to doing dishes, and the transcendent becomes manifest in the simplicity of each moment.

Joseph Campbell noticed this pattern of transcendence and return in many of the world's myths and religions. [3] He called this eternal archetypal cycle the Hero's Journey, where an individual reaches the highest formless states after battling internal demons, to then return to the world and help the rest of humanity. There is a Buddhist analogy stating that when you initially begin to meditate, mountains are just mountains. As you advance into the deeper realms of meditation, mountains cease to be mountains. When you reach enlightenment, mountains are once again just mountains. Individual evolution takes you to the summit of Being, and once you have seen the Cosmic design you come back to your karmic incarnation and take your place in the worldly play. The only difference now is that you have seen the grand design, and thus come back with a mission to help illuminate and spread the Love that is the foundation of all being.

This enlightened state is known as nonduality, where "emptiness is form, form is emptiness." The formless radiance of Spirit (emptiness) is seen within every form, as every form is seen within the Empty embrace of Spirit. The Zen master is the perfect exemplar of this state. Her unshakable presence in the moment is a direct expression of the causal level of Consciousness living in the presence of multiplicity and manifestation. All is seen as different forms of Spirit, from the rock to the angel to the formless. The entire spectrum of manifest being is seen as different densities of pure Consciousness. The holographic model can help us visualize this perspective. The manifest world, or holomovement, is made out of vibratory interference patterns, strings, which through interaction create the various spectrums of being. Consciousness is like the *n*-dimensional laser-Light that produces the 4-D hologram when it shines through the interference patterns (habits) of the world. Like a shimmering hologram, we need both the subjective consciousness and the objective interference patterns to manifest our living world; both aspects, of course, being the two sides of the One Being.

In a rainbow spectrum, all the spectral colors are diffracted aspects of white light. Just as white light manifests as a spectrum of differentiated color frequencies as it passes through a prism, the manifest spectrum of Being is a diffraction of the original energy Source of the Clear White Light. All manifestations, like the various colors of the rainbow, are the spectral frequency densities originating from the Clear White Light Source. All things are simply differentiated configurations of a single Energy; an Energy that has an internal and an external dimension. This single Energy is Consciousness. All forms in existence are expressions of this One Consciousness, manifesting itself in ascending spectral degrees of density. All world religions agree on the fact that all is God, everything is Spirit. Thus the enlightened master sees God in a grain of sand, hears Spirit in the singing of the birds, feels Consciousness in the highest mountains, and senses the Divine in the stillness of each moment.

This Divine Energy, pure Consciousness, or White Light is nothing other than pure Love. Love is the energy that moves the Cosmos. Love, not as a mere human emotion (level two or five), but as the very Energy that bonds structures together, networks parts into wholes, and drives the Cosmos toward grander creations of ever-ascending beauty. Love as the Unified Force Field that unifies all four physical forces with the deepest sentience experienced in the heart of your Being. Love as the Union of inner and outer forces, the hidden impulse within every form that motivates the urge to re-Unite with the Beloved. The Alpha-Omega that attracts all toward its unconditional, all-embracing Oneness is the original Love that all beings long for. Christ was a bodhisattva who, after realizing in the desert that he and his father are One, came back to the marketplace to teach unconditional Love. He knew, as John Lennon did, that "Love *is* the answer," for Love is the very fabric of all that is. Through this powerful force of Love, the bodhisattva with Christ Consciousness comes to planet Earth to heal. Love-Light is healing energy in its purest form. Once a being has established a direct link to that Love-Light healing energy, miracles of all sorts are possible, for Love is a state of ever-present, healed wholeness. What is required is a complete surrendering of separate self, an ego death, and a full faith in Spirit and the unfolding process of evolution. A full acceptance of "destiny" and "fate" brings freedom, as in "not my will but Thy will," opening a clear channel for that Divine healing Light to enter and heal our suffering masses.

This pure unconditional Love can come through only in the Here and Now. In complete presence there is space, and in that space the silent Spirit works its miraculous magic. Pure Here and Now presence is complete nonduality, with no attachment, as the unmanifest and the manifest are seen as two sides of the One; "form is emptiness, emptiness is form." Love *is* nonduality, embracing both the highest and the lowest, the saint and the sinner, the good and the bad, in complete unconditional here and now loving-kindness. And in that here and now loving-kindness, there is healing, transformation, complete satori embrace of the All. This is the bodhisattva ideal, and through this presence all sentient beings move toward complete liberation.

In Patanjali's Yoga sutra terminology, the final level of realization is called *sahaj samadhi.* [4] One of the limits of the high causal state of *nivikalpa samadhi* is that it can be enjoyed only while the individual remains still, absorbed in deep meditation. The final step in Raja Yoga is extending the deep stillness of samadhi into all other realms of the individual's life (waking, dreaming, and deep sleep). If one is able to keep this Supreme level of Consciousness throughout life's everyday challenges, and remain conscious in every level of Being, then one is called *jivan-mukti,* a liberated man/woman. In this enlightened state of Being, the Supreme Void-formless state is integrated into the lower matrices as a constant Witnessing, and thus the *jivan-mukti* (bodhisattva) comes back to serve and advance the evolution of the collective body without attachment. In the nondual state, all levels are integrated as all aspects of being are fully delighted in and accepted as part of the One. It is a stage where you attempt to live consciously in all levels, as you realize that what gives the levels light, energy, life, and consciousness is the causal plane itself. This is true Wholeness. Enlightenment literally means "light emanating from within," and this Light is none other than your ever-present Awareness. In this sense we are all always enlightened and whole, always have been, but we needed to get to our current level of evolutionary complexity in order to realize this fact. The inherently enlightened Awareness had to necessarily get lost in its creations, but now has the possibility to awaken to its naked Self first (level eight), and then to the rest of its projections as aspects of it-Self in nonduality.

The Indian saint Ramana Maharashi proposed a simple operational definition for distinguishing between *nirvakalpa samadhi* and *sahaj samadhi* (jivan-mukti, or bodhisattva consciousness). "If there remains a difference between samadhi and the waking state, it is nirvakalpa samadhi at best; if no difference, the yogi has reached his goal of sahaj samadhi." [5] In sahaj samadhi, meditation is a self-sustained, spontaneous fact of the individual's existence. Life *becomes* the meditation. The individual expresses his/her stillness of mind and detachment from the separate body-ego-mind system though his/her presence and actions. The individual lives in an "eternal now" and does not distinguish himself/herself from others. He/she sees himself/herself in everything, as he/she sees everything within himself/herself. Every movement, gesture, and action is infused with transcendental Consciousness, and everything is seen as a full manifestation of the Absolute Brahma (God).

Ken Wilber beautifully illustrates the nondual state:

> The agitation of the separate-self sense profoundly relaxes, and the self uncoils in the vast expanse of all space. At that point, it becomes obvious that you are not "in here" looking at the world "out there," because that duality has simply collapsed into pure Presence and spontaneous luminosity. [6]

What is emphasized is that nonduality is not an actual state of consciousness, because all states have a beginning and an end, which by definition is not timeless, but is an ever-present fact awaiting recognition. Wilber declares, "The real aim is the stateless....Change of state is not the point; recognizing the Changeless is the point, recognizing primordial Emptiness is the point." [7] This primordial Emptiness is, of course, pure Awareness, the ever-present Witnessing Presence behind all form. Wilber continues:

> Resting in that Freedom and Emptiness—and impartially witnessing all that arises—you will notice that the *separate-self* (or ego) simply arises in consciousness *like everything else.* You can actually feel the self-contraction, just as you can feel your legs, or feel a table, or feel a rock, or feel your feet. [8]

This self-contraction, from the nondual stance, is not a problem because "the Witness loves everything that arises, just as it is." Wilber continues, "The Witness loves the ego, because the Witness is the impartial mirror-mind that equally reflects and perfectly embraces *everything* that arises." [9] As such, everything that arises is One with the Witness, as that Witness poses no resistance, just open space. Again, Wilber poetically points to this nondual reality:

> From that space of Freedom—and at some unbidden point—you may notice that the feeling of Freedom has no inside and no outside, no

> center and no surround. Thoughts are floating in this Freedom, the sky is floating in this Freedom, the world is arising in this Freedom, and you are That....This is the world of One Taste, with no inside and no outside, no subject and no object, no here versus there, without beginning and without end, without ways and without means, without path and without goal. And this, as Ramana said, is the final truth. [10]

In nonduality you *are* the world, you *are* the universe, you are the multiverses that arise and dissolve back into that Empty Ground of all Being, the deepest part of You, always and forever in the eternal now.

As all masters throughout the ages have pointed out, enlightenment is the simplest expression contained within each moment. It is the is-ness, the such-ness of things as they are, in each moment. "Nonduality of object and subject is the expression of immediate awareness." [11] Here there is no differentiation between past and future, you and I, me and it. All is contained within the totality of each breath. All that is arises within your Awareness, moment to moment, nothing else exists. The only Absolute Truth is the Now, all else is an abstraction. And in this all-embracing Now, sensations arise, perceptions arise, thoughts arise, self-contractions arise, images arise, yet all eventually return to the underlying stillness of the moment. Self and other merge, subject and object disappear, and all that remains is the rising sun on a clear blue sky.

Ultimately, the nondual realization eventually embraces the evolutionary process itself, seeing that Spirit *wants to manifest and experience* the diversities of its deepest creations. Consciousness wants to express itself in ascending levels of complexity and beauty, it wants to know itself in novel and creative ways, and it wants to play and dance throughout eternity. In nonduality, the understanding is that eternity is ever present, the backdrop against which all events take place, and therefore there is no hesitation to fully engage the world as the eternal Freedom is already inherently Here. We are already free, liberated, enlightened, and saved! This full realization, therefore, allows the full participation in the evolving drama, without fear, and the radical embodied engagement that moves evolution forward. Liberation is the self-evident reality of our immediate awareness that provides a feedback loop to the larger system, thereby helping it move toward collective evolution. Pure Awareness is already the perfected Omega state of eternity itself; therefore, there is no need to seek anything as it is radiantly here and now in every breath. Instead one enters the world with wonder, curiosity, creativity, and love as the boundaries of time and space gently dissolve. Life becomes a work of art, as we attempt to live as conscious a life as possible.

Andrew Cohen has called this nondual state of existence *Evolutionary Enlightenment*, stressing that *after* one realizes their essential nature as the formless One before time, the evolutionary process itself necessarily *needs* you in order to continue the evolutionary unfolding toward higher, undreamed of possibilities. Cohen has redefined the traditional concept of enlightenment by stating that you are not "only the eternal ground of Being but *also* the evolutionary impulse."[12] He continues by stating that the whole point of evolutionary enlightenment is "to be here—to participate fully, radically, *consciously* in the Universe Project. In this evolutionary context, the point of enlightenment is not merely to transcend the world so that you can be free of it but to *embrace* the world completely, to embrace the entire process as your self, knowing that you are the creative principle incarnate, and *you* have a lot of work to do." [13] In other words, once one has awakened to one's original nature outside of space and time, the imperative is to return *as the evolutionary impulse itself* in order to continue the journey of creation toward higher spirals of creativity and potential. And if the Ground is one with the quantum ocean of zero-point energy, the evolutionary and creative potential of the awakened soul is truly of godlike proportions. We may truly be becoming godlike in our creative and manifesting powers, harnessing the momentum that has driven the unfolding process for the past fourteen billion years to manifest a whole new spiral of creation. Tapped into our One God-Self, we manifest as individual godlike entities that reflect, through our unique gifts and talents, the Power of the One out of which we all emanate.

This final chapter is by no means the "conclusion," but the beginning of a higher octave, a higher harmonic of unfolding possibility and probability. The Source, of course, is and will always be the unmoved, unchanged, ever-present eternal Light, but the projections continue to evolve on the "shoulders" of the recorded patterns of the past. As harmonic emanations, an enlightened culture will (if it ever gets there) unfold the deepest realms of the imagination in ways that reflect the very Big Bang itself, as creativity spins into accelerated rates that break all known so-called laws of physics. Currently, as far as we know, we humans represent the leading edge of complexity. Therefore, universal evolution seems to be focusing its intent on us by pushing-pulling us toward a higher spiral of development.

Whether this higher spiral of evolution happens with a material reflection in the material realm, or whether it transcends the physical boundaries all together and ascends into octaves within the subtle plane, is impossible to know. Many spiritual traditions claim that there is an entire evolutionary process occurring in higher, non-material planes of existence. They insist that there are subtle worlds of ethereal energy with highly evolved entities that live as subtle light bodies, without any connection to our material universe. We *can* access these realms, as explored in level seven, but grounded in our material bodies and brain. Potentially at death we enter the subtle realms without our bodies, and, if we do not reincarnate, can continue to evolve as ascended masters of inconceivable light and power. Until then, whether through the evolutionary process or at the time of death, the call now is to embrace this life, this planet, this universe in all its manifestations. The nondual stance then embraces the whole spectrum, from the material foundations, to the ethereal subtle realms beyond matter, to the formless Ground of all creations.

One of the traditions that works from this radically nondual stance is Advaita Tantra, the tradition into which I was initiated twenty-two years ago. Besides giving me precise techniques for accessing the causal formless Ground, Tantra has also provided me with the philosophical, experiential, and practical tools that have allowed me to practice nonduality. Tantra means *that which liberates,* or *liberation through expansion.* Tantra can also mean continuum, which denotes the continuity between Spirit and matter. It is a system that rejects the renunciate model that proclaims Spirit/transcendence as good, and matter/nature/sensuality/body as bad. The Tantric system claims that All is an expression of the Divine, from worldly to sublime, profane to sacred. As such, the Tantric practitioner uses *all* experiences for spiritual development and ultimate emancipation from suffering. Yes, even sex!

Tantra teaches that before time or space there is simply One-Without-a-Second, Brahma, Source of all creation. Out of this Eternal Field there is a mysterious impulse that gives rise to the first separation from the One. Now there are two, and from the two the dance of time, energy, and life embarks on the epic journey that we are the inheritors of. So from the neutral Void, the universe divides itself into on/off, positive/negative, light/dark, yin/yang that spirals creation into existence like the opening of a flower. The Tantric yogis and yoginis personified these two basic Cosmic forces, as humans often do, in anthropomorphic forms: Shiva, the God of pure Consciousness (*Purusha*—the inner, subjective aspect), and Shakti, Goddess of creative Energy (*Prakriti*—the outer, objective aspect). Ultimately, Shiva and Shakti are One, but separated each other in order to facilitate creation. Without two, in relationship, there is no creation. It takes two to dance. According to Tantra, the whole process of evolution is driven by the urge for return to that initial state of wholeness, Oneness, the final re-Union in Love. And from that return to original Love, the "Big Crunch," some would say, "Big Bang" new creative universes into existence in endless cycles of creation and destruction. You could say Shiva and Shakti like to Bang!

"As above, so below" is an internalized practice for the Tantric adept. Yoga teaches that the human body has two major subtle energy currents that run through our main *nadis,* the subtle channels that spiral like the helical DNA up and down our spine and its central *nadis,* the *Shusumna.* The left current (right brain) runs through the *Ida nadis* and is the lunar current of Shakti. The right current (left brain) runs through the *Pingala nadis* and is the solar current of Shiva. This yogic understanding parallels Carl Jung's assertion that all humans, regardless of gender or sex, have a masculine aspect, animus (yang), and a feminine aspect, anima (yin). A truly whole and integrated individual has a balance of energies both in body and in psyche. A series of yogic practices are precisely employed to facilitate this harmonization of energies to achieve wholeness and integration, and ultimately an experience of the essential nondual Oneness of all existence.

One conception of the forces describes Goddess kundalini-Shakti as the serpentine creative power-energy that resides coiled up deep in the core of the Earth (remember Her?), connecting us to Earth via our root chakra at the base of the spine. This is the force of creativity, Nature, birth/death, becoming, and manifestation, and is represented by the cyclical motions of Earth and sister Moon. Shiva, according to this yogic metaphor, represents the Solar God of radiant transcendent formless Consciousness, residing at the top of the head in the crown chakra. Through various Tantric and yogic practices the adept raises the Shakti and brings down the Shiva principle, allowing the two forces to meet and intermingle at the seven centers as yin/yang vortices or wheels that spin as the two forces are balanced. All chakras contain both yin/yang elements, as both are needed to spin the wheels.

As can be seen, the Tantric tradition is radically nondualistic, worshiping the Divine Mother Goddess of creation, the light of Father God, and the transcendent Unity beyond both aspects. As such, equal value is given to transcendent states of pure unmanifest Consciousness, *and* immersion in the world of immanent activity, cycles, evolution, manifestation, and becoming. Christ said, "in the world but not of this world," and Buddha proclaimed, "form is emptiness, emptiness is form," meaning that the transcendent Emptiness and spiritual bliss beyond form is of the same Divine energy as the everyday manifestations of everyday life. Yet to be stuck on either side of the coin, according to Tantra, is to not be ultimately free. Purely living in the world with all its desires, worries, attachments, and complexities is like being in prison, while living in a cave in total absorption in the Light is also an alienated place that separates and denies the evolutionary art project that is life and existence. One merged in individual Samadhi becomes irrelevant to the unfolding destiny of the Cosmos, unless he/she returns as the nondual sage that catalyzes evolution toward its higher potentials.

Tantra offers a refreshing approach that promotes spiritual development and growth, while simultaneously encouraging the full embodiment, participation, and enjoyment of all of life's, Earth's, and Nature's gifts. The complete union of body and mind, spirit and matter, heaven and earth, transcendence and immanence, subject and object, being and becoming, male and female, *within one's own Being.* One can achieve this full union, wholeness, or integration individually, as we all have, or rather *are*, these two aspects of reality: both spiritual and worldly realities seen as moment-to-moment expressions of the Sacred, the Divine marriage of your present Awareness and all that arises.

Cohen would argue that being engaged in the evolutionary process *as* the embodied expression of that Divine drive *is* to grow spiritually, ultimately leading to spiritual awakening. [14] Of course, the full awakening cannot occur unless one temporarily leaves the noise of the lower matrices behind so as to find the Source in the deepest stillness. Once accessed, however, one can then return to the lower realms of creation to creatively engage the evolutionary process and thus attempt to help others and the collective body evolve toward higher potentials. In nonduality we see that we are all part of the One Being. Therefore, the imperative becomes one of helping all sentient beings move toward the enlightened recognition of their essential Oneness, thereby reducing the inherent suffering of a separate existence.

Here and Now

My life at this moment in time, currently 2017 real time, actually, has become a dedication to this mysterious process of healing, growth, development, and evolution. Practicing to be fully grounded in the Here and Now, I attempt to connect with the entire evolutionary process we have just explored as the essence of what and who I am. I attempt to live what Ken Wilber calls an "integrally informed" life, [15] acknowledging and working with all dimensions of Being with every breath, every interaction, every decision I make. He encourages all to take up an "integral life practice," practices that work to strengthen all levels, in all their manifestations. Everyone can create his or her own "integral life practice," adopting techniques and practices that reflect his or her own predispositions and temperament. I've described some of mine in the preceding *further personal and transpersonal explorations*. I will outline them here to illustrate how I attempt to work with each level, each dimension, so as to move from and toward wholeness in this lifetime. I am by no means impeccable, the shadow side always quietly living in each dimension, but this is what I strive to maintain in moments of balance. All in all, it is actually the inevitable balancing influences of the shadow side that keep the practices turning toward Health. Therefore i've included the shadow.

Level1—Material Plane—Exercise my physical body through running and physical work. Eat whole natural organic local food. Keep my home and physical environment clean and aesthetically pleasing. Seek right livelihood as a psychotherapist. Keep my family safe.

Shadow side (SD) - Ill, sick, in physical pain, stressed, fearful, lazy, unconscious.

Level 2—Bio-Emotional Plane—Nurture my emotional body by cultivating positive relationships. Love my kids and partner, and cherish family time. Enjoy friends, and find time to just hang out. Attempt to keep home environment positive, happy, and centered around loving kindness. Make love.

SD – Depressed, anxious, angry, moody, resentful, fighting, jealous, dramatic.

Level 3—Conceptual Plane—Read, research, learn, discuss, and write this book. Share ideas, educate self and others, and explore diverse cultures. Read and play music.

SD – Dogmatic, know-it-all, wrong, confused, irrational, illogical, misinformed, habituated thought, ruminating thoughts.

Level 4—Social Personality Plane—Use my social role and identity as psychotherapist not only to make a living, but to help others and my community. Serve as an agent of social change. Be a soccer coach for my kid's soccer team. Vote for the least destructive politicians.

SD - Inflated ego, sense of separateness, prideful, conceited, rigid boundaries, selfish, egotistical.

Level 5—Holistic Plane—Practice Yoga daily. Work on our farm, our community garden, and our local school gardens. Take care of fruit trees and participate in raising grass-fed organic cows. Connect with larger community to strive toward self-sustainability, self-reliance, ecological awareness, and environmental protection. Install solar panels, wind turbines, and establish grey water systems. Build soil, practice permaculture, and engage in bioremidatiobn.

SD – Drive an air-polluting car, use and throw away plastic, eat junk food, waste water, shop at Wal-Mart, pollute my body.

Level 6—Psychic Plane—Practice daily meditation, mindfulness in daily life, and engage the collective Noosphere via Internet participation. Practice psychotherapy from deep place of Witnessing, as the meta-programmer of all realities.

SD – Mindless, unconscious, restless, full of random thoughts, low clarity, unfocused, repressed childhood issues.

Level 7—Subtle Plane—Engage in ritual, participate in ceremony, honor the seasons, and take occasional shamanic journeys into the spirit world to connect with ancestors, guides, spirit helpers. Work with plants and Nature to access the Gaian evolutionary mind so as to find guidance and strength. Honor the Goddess of creation in all Her manifestations. Help heal the planet through small acts, activism, and engagement. Reduce carbon footprint.

SD – Negative energies, dark entities, the entire shadow side itself, violent tendencies, still repressed trauma, historical human trauma, planetary ecocide.

Level 8—Causal Plane—Meditate, access Ground with every breath, see Spirit in all forms. Teach meditation to others to help all wake up to their luminous Essence. Know that we are all truly One. Experience the freedom of knowing my true timeless nature. Rest in ever-present Awareness. Bliss out on the Void. Be One with God.

SD – Ignorant, disconnected, unloving, cruel, lost, in despair, unwise, death.

Nonduality—Love every person, experience, event, and help humanity heal as I continue to seek personal healing. Engage the evolutionary process without fear.

Embrace and witness the shadow side and fill it with Light. Serve, from a selfless bodhisattva ideal, so as to help all sentient beings find peace, freedom, and joy in this very lifetime. Live Here and Now. Swami Sivananda sums it up best: "*serve, love, meditate,* and *realize.*"

Exercise: Design your own integral life practice!

Ken Wilber advices us, "Practice them diligently, and coordinate your integral efforts to unfold the various potentials of the bodymind—until the bodymind itself unfolds in Emptiness, and the entire journey is a misty memory from a trip that never even occurred." [16]

Other than attempting to live now-here (nowhere), fully grounded in my body while accessing the deepest freedom of inherent Awareness, I attempt to manifest the integral vision through the aforementioned Integral Life Practices. In the last eight years I have been able to ground this vision professionally as I have joined a group of healers to create a community healing center for body, mind, and spirit. Our center, called Global Healing Arts, comprises two massage therapists (deep tissue, shin jyutsu, trigger point, therapeutic massage, etc.), two acupuncturists and a traditional Chinese medicine practitioner, Yoga and Tai Chi teacher, and nutritionist. I provide "integrally informed" traditional and transpersonal psychotherapy and host weekly meditation groups and classes. Our mission statement reads: *Our vision is to provide a healing environment that integrates leading-edge modalities with ancient practices aimed at facilitating health and wellness for the whole person. In this endeavor, we bring together techniques and wisdom from East and West, North and South, to create total wellness in body, mind, and spirit with individuals, couples, families, and groups. Only by engaging the entire person can we initiate a healing that extends into the community, and ultimately our planet, creating true Global Healing.* Only by engaging the entire spectrum of Being can we initiate true healing, in the individual and in the collective.

Another focus of my personal Integral Life Practice has become the creation and cultivation of community gardens. For the last twenty years my partner and I have been working with the soil to cultivate organic fruits and vegetables no matter where we've lived. In the last nine years we have engaged our local extended community to create a community garden that feeds our community members with fresh seasonal produce. Excess food is donated to the food bank, as we experience the abundance that our planet has for every living being. Community gardens not only feed our physical bodies, but they nurture the soul by providing a space to meet, connect, and commune with our neighbors. Gardens also feed the soul by providing beauty and a naturally biodiverse habitat for animals and insects, creating a central place of communion for all sentient beings. As we create and expand green spaces, we aid the struggling atmosphere by growing plants that absorb carbon dioxide to produce fresh oxygen. By adopting biodynamic, permaculture, and bioremediation practices we can initiate the regeneration and healing of our suffering biosphere.

In the last few years we have collaborated with my brother and sister-in-law, who happen to be our neighbors and closest community allies, to create community school gardens in our local elementary school and middle school, and a full farm at the local high school. Both are teachers in said schools and have worked hard to bring all local county agencies together to support and finance these visionary projects. The aim is to not only create community, cultivate healthy food, and teach kids and family members about growing food, but to heal our nutritional deficit that has our society living in such un-health and dis-ease. Our goal is to bring the healthy veggies grown by the kids into the cafeteria, therefore educating the community on right nutrition and healthy eating. In this effort we strive to raise healthy kids, a radiant community, and reinforce the budding ecological and environmental awareness of the Green meme slowly tacking hold at this time. Community school gardens serve as living classrooms to educate and teach experientially, while producing the very nutrition that our kids so badly lack. My brother and sister-in-law already have the vegetables sampled in the classroom once they are grown, and the kids love them. We hope to install cooking and nutrition classes and create a central meeting place for all county agencies to network their efforts toward community health and healing.

In working with community members to create community gardens I have come to the conclusion that one of the answers to our current global crisis *is* community gardens. Imagine if every school, every community, every home, every urban rooftop had organic vegetable gardens. Nutritious food would abound, no one would go hungry, and the increased vegetation would help rebalance the ecological devastation that humanity has inflicted on our planet in the last couple of centuries. Healthy soil-water-air-temperature = healthy environment. Healthy environment = healthy food. Healthy food= healthy kids and families. Healthy families = healthy communities. And healthy communities = healthy planet. The root of health and healing is wholeness, and in that wholeness we ultimately realize that we are all part of the One.

Many claim that the above vision is not realistic for the suburban and city dwellers, as there is more cement and cars then there is open space in most of the world's cities. The answer to this hesitation I encountered in my brother's neighbor's backyard, reminding me of John Lennon's statement, "there are no problems, only solutions." My brother lives in San Ramon, California, which is a typical suburban sprawl that reflects the majority of people's living space. His neighbor, an aging hippie from the sixties actually, has created a permaculture paradise in her backyard, which is no bigger than the average American's backyard. There in her edible landscape she grows all the fruits, berries, nuts, vegetables, eggs, honey, and herbs that she could ever need. She cans and stores the surplus, and shares with her friends and family. She has no energy bill as she has solar panels on her roof that produce all the energy she could ever need. She claims she is 80 % self-sustained, and the other 20 % she tries to barter with others in her local community. And this is happening in the backyard of a mainstream, typical American neighborhood.

The revelation here is that every backyard can ultimately become a mini farm, and every home a producer rather than a consumer. Every rooftop could have solar panels so that people's energy is locally harnessed from the light of the daily rising sun. We could decentralize the energy grid by creating a distributed and diversified network of solar energy, wind turbines, geothermal, and hydroelectric power guaranteeing energy independence and security for all bioregional communities. Energy, as well as information, can be a Peer-to-Peer, Open-Source network of symbiotic cooperation. In big cities there are now green building designs that are not only carbon neutral, but actual producers of energy. Imagine, every city rooftop green with vegetables and flowers, catching water, the rays of the sun, and the movement of the wind to power the building and its inhabitants. Imagine, every city street lined with fruit and nut trees, community vegetable gardens in every neighborhood, and renewable energy sources distributed throughout the cities. We have the knowledge, the technologies, and the techniques needed to repurpose our systems so that all sentient beings can enjoy the abundance that our planet freely offers to all Her inhabitants. What are we waiting for? What is the resistance? No ego-based power structure is strong enough to hold back the evolutionary impulse that lives in the heart of all beings.

System theorist Buckminster Fuller (1895–1983) said that our planet has more than enough resources to feed our planetary populations many times over, but we need to model our systems after nature if this is to occur. With a no-waste philosophy, Fuller believed that through a complete system redesign, we can not only reverse our environmental impact, but create a sustainable and regenerative world of abundance for all of its inhabitants. His design revolution, which includes homes (he invented the geodesic dome), communities, cities, transportation, and energy, among other systems, is modeled after the structures and functions of nature. Energy, power, food, water, and resources decentralized, communally shared, and freely available to all living beings.

Fuller's design revolution seems like an obvious step if we are to "break through" rather than "break down," as Laszlo would say. We already posses the technologies that can allow for a swift transition from the centralized power-energy-resources controlled by the dominator culture to a decentralized partnership society to occur. Using the vast informational networks of social media and the internet, we could initiate a massive re-education campaign that can help in the reshaping of behavioral habits; from the destructive ego-based consuming mentality to one of cooperation and altruistic production. Energy is everywhere, and is a birthright for every being born to this planet. Why should the 1 % hoard all the resources while the rest struggle to make ends meet? This new green design modeled after nature requires no pathological hierarchies of power and control. Energy can and should be locally and bioregionally produced via renewable solar, wind, water, and soil technologies, as energy is everywhere. With the new emerging technologies for so called "free energy" we will even be able to tap the infinite energy available in the zero-point field. As we evolve, we will eventually learn to harness the creative zero-point energies that power the expanding cosmos and all its fractal subsystems. With access to this unlimited energy, anything is possible.

Governments should also be decentralized, in my view, creating a true democratic society entangled and wired through the Internet, with power equally distributed amongst all educated adults. "One iPhone, one vote" will be all that is required for the collective to take democratic action as a whole. Bickering between the two-party dinosaurs is no longer effective or efficient. We are currently grid-locked in outdated ideologies based on ethnocentric views, while the obvious fact of an overpopulated planet with limited resources stares us in the face. Resources should be locally and bioregionally produced and consumed, creating the living cycle of a locally thriving yet globally oriented community. Currencies should become local, taking the interest and debt-based system off the menu to create wealth for the many, not the few. Beyond local currencies, we should consider a gift economy fueled by altruism and worldcentric love, where giving gives the giver more than the receiver in terms of inner fulfillment. All products should be locally produced by local community members, therefore decreasing the multibillion-dollar power structures of the wealthy corporations now running the planet. Food should be completely decentralized, using bioregional climates and biodynamic resources to sustain communities and their nutritional health. Leaders and politicians should take a vow of poverty, as Gandhi suggested, so that governance is pure and not corrupted by the pursuit of power, wealth, and control.

Polluters should be stopped, as they take away not only our life-sustaining rights to a clean environment, but that of the next "seven generations."

Of course, the current paradigm of military control, corporate rule, energy hoarding, consumption madness, centralized energy-power-food-wealth, and disregard for Nature are all expressions of a deeply separated ego living in its media controlled and produced illusion. Evolution is inviting us to grow up and partake of the dream that beckons from "beyond history." As I write these words, a revolution is under way. The Occupy movement initiated in 2011 is only the beginning, as humans are finally waking up and learning that they have a right to "Occupy the Planet." It is time to reclaim the creative powers we all share, so that we can initiate the Golden Age that our ancestor seers prophesied. First we must clean up the polluted mess, heal the suffering ego, and redesign our systems so that all may be healthily sustained and thrive. Then we can re-channel our creative efforts to manifest higher aesthetic potentials, artistic possibilities, and imaginative creations that can take us all into the next world age of peace, love, enlightenment, and abundance.

With a healthy planet and a healthy people as foundation, humanity can then follow its most visionary aspirations where technology miniaturizes to the point of disappearing from physical space. Nanotechnology, virtual realities, genetic engineering, AI, a telepathic global village, space migration, teleportation, and zero-point energy are all possible, *if* consciousness shifts toward its inherent unity within. If it does not, the separate, paranoid ego will have powers that could wipe out all life on this planet in one fell swoop. Perhaps to leave this used-up planet and head for the stars is part of the process, but somehow this scenario does not seem to represent a more "evolved state." Evolving consciousness beyond separate body-ego-minds while dancing in the fertile lands of Gaia, possibly guided by cyber techno-shamans initiating the masses into an ocean of inner beauty through advanced nano and sound technologies, for example, seems like a higher more evolved scenario to me.

Tim Leary's SMI^{2}LE captures a likely future if we don't destroy our selves first: Space Migration, Intelligence Increase, and Life Extension. [17] With these things in place, our planetary culture could be one driven by art and the pursuit of harmony and beauty, as nature has always done, making us true co-creative engines for a Transpersonal Meta-Cosmic Intelligence that silently guides all structures and forms. We would all be aligned and inspired by inner spiritual guidance, rather than by centralized, self-interested power elites, becoming living embodiments of the evolutionary impulse itself. True Cosmic Beings awakening to the conscious creative power of evolution, while simultaneously tapped into the One: the Core out of which everything is derived.

Within the context and fervor of our current historical predicament, the beginning of a post- 2012 world age cycle, we are called by our suffering planet to the act of self-less service. Our planetary crisis has reached such disproportionate levels that only a collective movement toward planetary healing will save it from death. Any ego-driven motivation will perpetuate the vast problems of today, for indeed these problems are direct expressions of the ego and its imposed boundaries. We do not have to reach enlightenment to realize this fact. "All we are saying is give peace a chance," John Lennon and his generation loudly sang. Planetary healing will only occur if we come together to celebrate our divinity, our oneness, and the original Love that was lost in the turmoil of history. We must reclaim our planet, our freedom, and by letting go of our self-created boundaries our human family will once again become One. This is our dream. This is our Vision.

Exercise 1:

0.) Find a comfortable position with an aligned back, neck, and head and tune into your breath. Allow the breath to slow, deepen, and become more rhythmic. Use the out breath to release and let go of whatever arises. As all biorhythms slow, begin to feel the underlying Radiance of that which is Aware within you. Notice how this Awareness has no boundaries in its quiet state. Begin to notice the space between your thoughts and prolong it by lengthening the exhale. Notice how behind the thoughts, Awareness exists as that Field of infinite probability: the Akashic Field, existing in a state of form-less potential, pregnant with all information.

1.) Within this Field of Awareness, of infinite possibility, notice the densest and grossest of the available signals. You may come to see that it is the physical sensations, eliciting the world of materiality and solidity. Notice your sensations throughout your body by conducting a brief body scan, or "sweeping." Notice your painful and pleasurable sensations as programmed and transmitted by your very cells. Watch the fluctuating sensory patterns with total Witnessing Presence, not pushing or pulling at sensations, but calmly abiding in the equanimity and spaciousness of pure Being. Watch the sensations of the 'physical' world arise and dissolve back into the Field of Consciousness. Now gather all that sensual energy and ground it in your first chakra, Earth, and let it ground you via the felt gravitational pull of the Earth below you.

2.) Now, clear the mind by inhaling and exhaling deeply in order to explore the next dimension of your Being. As the field of your Awareness begins to return to Zero, the Ground State, notice the next grossest signal arising within that Field of

Witnessing. Notice that subtler to your felt sensation is an emotional undercurrent. Take a moment and notice, as you continue to breathe, your current emotional state, your "pain body," and the feelings running through your pranic channels. Notice their slightly faster vibratory rate, yet that they are still highly intertwined with the physical body. On the next inhale gather all of your emotional energy and ground it in your second chakra, feeling its fluid Water-element nature and its life giving power.

3.) On your next exhale, again clear the mind and allow the breath to bring you back to the ever-present Witness, the One who views all that arises. As the Field returns to zero vibration, formless awareness, notice the subtler mental commentary behind the emotions and sensations. Notice the endless thoughts that fill the Field with endless holographic expressions. Notice the belief structures, the biases, the conditioning, and the ongoing mind loops. Returning to breath, inhale all mental expressions and exhale them out, grounding the mental power in the third chakra, the solar plexus, and feeling the Fire in the power of thought.

4.) Clear the Field of your Awareness once again, returning to pure Consciousness, state of pure potential, via breath. Now notice your subtle identity structure. Notice your self-concept, and witness how it is merely a collection of associations, memories, beliefs, and identifications. Notice the vibratory, cyclical, and fluctuating nature of what you call your personality. See its non-reality, its fleeting nature, and the images that reinforce it from a state of equanimity and spaciousness. Feel this ego as grounded still in the third, Fire-Power Hara chakra.

5.) Once again return to the still zero-point, releasing all content within Awareness as you breathe out. On your next deep inhale, feel all the air and prana enter your entire body and brain. Feel the air-prana enter every channel of your body-mind system. Experience your entire body-mind, the Whole of your experience, in this moment. Notice how what we call the body (one and two) and mind (three and four) are really an integrated unit of experience. Feel the entire gestalt with each breath, breathing in clean, clear, fresh, healing prana and releasing tensions, stress, contractions, knots, blocks, emotions, and thoughts. As the body-mind calms and clears, take a deep inhale and ground this body-mind connection in the Heart of the system, the fourth chakra. Feel the entire lower body meet the higher body in the center of the chest, feeling the all-embracing Air element of compassion, inspiration, and altruistic love. Breathe from the center of your heart chakra.

6.) As your body-mind begins to fully relax and let go, I invite you now to turn toward that which lies behind the signals by contacting the Witness. As you find some identity with that which is Aware, notice mindfully the various signals come and go within that Field that is your Awareness. Notice perceptions and sensations as they arise, or an emotional undercurrent, a fleeting thought, or contractions of the ego. Notice how all those signals create the gestalt that is your current body-mind state. On the next breath, notice how all of these signals are ultimately vibratory in nature, bits of information, coming and going with no inherent reality, bleeps of mind-stuff, ultimately psychic in nature. We notice mind to be a co-creative force in nature. On your next breath, ground that creative vibratory psychic power in your fifth throat chakra. Activate your voice, your truth, your authentic creative expression as you tap into the Ether element of space that interconnects all things.

7.) At this point, your body-mind should be so quiet, calm, and at rest that all the signals from the personal domain begin to recede into the vast expanses within the ocean of pure Consciousness. Watch what you call your life, personality, and material existence fade into the shimmering luminous ocean out of which it all came. Notice how all the above signals are ultimately made of Light. Different configurations of Light, mere data, pure information, all undulating into endless forms. Notice how behind your personal existence is a realm of light and information that provides the blueprints and molds for your life. Begin now to draw up the energy from the base of the spine all the way past all chakras, up to the third eye, sixth chakra. Collect the various frequencies of sensation, emotion, thought, and spirit, and begin to focalize them all into the third eye. As you breathe in, feel all signals, energy, and prana merge into one-point, and dissolve into pure Light on the out breath. Awareness being extremely sensitive and subtle at this point, notice the imagery in the fields of light. Notice the fractal patterns, the web of light-information that is the subtle Genetic-Gaian backdrop of our organic Planet. Feel the deep Intelligence(s) interpenetrating us, possibly maintained by the DNA antennas arrays distributed throughout your body and the environment in which it lives. Sense the spirits and sentient energy movements as you open your intuitive third eye.

8.) Finally, allow the entire subtle light show to slow down and fade back into the silent, empty Void of your pure Awareness. Return Home, once again, to that state of total fulfillment inherent in the quiet Mind. Let all vibrations stop, and rest in the empty expanse of your True Nature. Let every sense of yourself dissolve into the ocean of quantum potential that surrounds and is behind every bit of your existence. On the next inhale from the sixth chakra allow all the energy-prana to shoot up the seventh chakra, top of the head, dissolving into the Radiant White Light of pure Spirit. Feel yourself connect with everything, and know in a flash that YOU ARE THAT! Rest in that eternal freedom.

9.) After enjoying the Bliss of your Essential formless Nature, let the Light emanating from the top of your head, which connects you to the entire Cosmos, cascade down and surround your entire Being. Visualize the torus, interconnecting all the chakra energies of your Being as they spiral around your central Empty axis, the *shusumna*. Feel all your chakras spinning and vibrating in complete harmony and health. Watch as every level, every signal, every emanation occurs within the empty embrace of Consciousness, all as One moment. In this moment, allow all the levels and dimensions of your Being to coexist in harmony. And in that harmony, see it all become One. Not two, but One timeless Being.

Exercise 2:

Find a comfortable position and tune into your breath. As your body-mind begins to relax, visualize a golden point of Light in your heart chakra. With each exhale, feel that golden warm healing light expand, first enveloping your entire being; your body, emotions, thoughts, personality, and soul. Feel the healing of every cell within your body as the warm light penetrates and infuses your being with healing energy. After you feel this Light, this Presence, throughout your body, allow it to expand with each breath, first enveloping your loved ones, family, and friends. Next, allow the expanding golden circle of Love-Light to envelop your community, your continent, and finally the entire planet. Feel the warm Love-Light heal each sentient being, each cell of the planetary body. Experience the dissolution of boundaries, divisions, and fragmentations. Next, in rhythm with your breath, feel the Love-Light moving out into space, embracing our solar system, our galaxy, our galactic cluster, and finally the entire Cosmos. Feel the entire universe as it is cradled by this nurturing Light, radiating warm Love-Light energy to each and every particle of manifestation. Picture this radiance embracing everything that is and ever was. Feel how the All is within this Love-Light. Now recognize how this Love-Light is your Awareness. Recognize how that boundless Love is really your true Self.

Epilogue

What does life look like if we truly live *as if* our deepest Awareness is one with the physicists' Unified Field of Everything? If the Unified Field contains all recorded information, and if our deepest Consciousness is *identical* to this all-pervasive Akashic Field, what can we expect for the evolution of the Cosmos as it becomes conscious of its underlying Essence? These are some of the questions explored in my second book, *Dimensions of Being*[2]: *An Explorer's Guide to* Higher *Consciousness.* The basic notion, and experience, that the Cosmos is really an expression of Consciousness unlocks a series of possibilities that allow humans to become conscious of evolution and the creative creation process itself. It awakens us, the cells, into a larger Field of Intelligence that we as individuals are mere fragments of. Only by accessing this deeper interconnected Wisdom can we even hope to reengineer our systems so that they may equitably sustain all of its inhabitants.

In *Dimensions of Being*[2] I explore the latent power and potential within us all. By asserting the basic assumption, based on subjective experience derived from various mystic techniques and practices, that the Unified Field is pure Consciousness, we immediately enter a new level of conscious evolution where we become true co-creators of reality. The future is not predetermined; it awaits our conscious participation so that it may manifest the next dream. As we discover our individual connection to the Source within, we initiate the shift in identity so that we remember who we truly are. In that recognition we awaken to our multi-dimensional nature and heal. This is the promise of the ancient prophecies. Post 2012 existence will be about information, Consciousness, multidimensionality, and the concrescence of all minds into a Unified Intent. There is no other way. We either join in an altruistic alliance with each other and the rest of biology, or we destroy ourselves in one atomic flash. The current global pressures are catalyzing the next spiral of evolution, where through information and Awareness evolution is becoming aware of itself. And as it discovers its driving inner impulse and its connection to all that is, it necessarily accelerates to realms impossible to currently imagine. Infinite energy, infinite information, infinite power, and enlightened Awareness underlie all of existence. Therefore, as we awaken to this Reality, we activate inherent potentials that will completely transform our world. And in that transformation, we will be reborn as a new, *higher* Being. Being^2.

May your journey through and into Consciousness be filled with awe, wonder, and Love. May you find the inherent freedom and peace that *is* your essential nature. Namaste!

Notes

Preface

1. Davies, P., *God and the New Physics* (New York: Simon and Schuster, 1983).

My Journey Through Consciousness: Brief Autobiography

1. Orwell, G., *1984* (New York: Signet Classic, 1949).
2. Huxley, A., *Brave New World* (New York: Harper Row, 1932).
3. Davies, P., *God and the New Physics* (New York: Simon and Schuster, 1983).

Introduction: Considerations for Exploring Consciousness

1. Lilly, J., *The Center of the Cyclone* (New York: Bantam Books, 1972).
2. James, W., *The Varieties of Religious Experience* (New York: Harper Row, 1902).
3. Mitchell, S., *Tao Te Ching* (New York: HarperSanFrancisco, 1988), p. 1.
4. Suzuki, S., *Zen Mind, Beginner's Mind* (New York: Weatherhill, 1970), p. 128.
5. James, op. cit.
6. Godwin, R. W., *One Cosmos Under God: The Unification of Matter, Life, Mind, and Spirit* (St. Paul, MN: Paragon House, 2004), p. 21.
7. Wilber, K., *Sex, Ecology, Spirituality: The Spirit of Evolution* (Boston: Shambala 1995).
   ------, *A Brief History of Everything* (Boston: Shambala, 1996).
8. Suzuki, op. cit., p. 41.
9. Huxley, A., *The Doors of Perception* (New York: Harper Row, 1954).
10. Leary, T., *The Game of Life* (Phoenix: New Falcon Publications, 1979), p. 2.
11. Ibid.
    ------, *Info-Psychology* (Phoenix: New Falcon Publications, 1987).
12. Wilber, K., "An Approach to Integral Psychology." *Journal of Transpersonal Psychology*, 31 (2), 109–136, (1999).
13. Huxley, A., *The Perennial Philosophy* (New York: Harper Row, 1970).

14. Goswami, A., *The Self-Aware Universe: How Consciousness Creates the Material World* (New York: Penguin Putnam, 1993), p. 48.
15. Bohm, D., *Wholeness and the Implicate Order* (London: Routledge and Kegan Paul, 1980).
16. Govinda, A., *Foundations of Tibetan Mysticism* (New York: Samuel Weiser, 1974), pp. 66-67.
17. Wilber, K., *Quantum Question* (Boston: Shambala, 1985).

Part 0:

The Void

1. Mitchell, S., *Tao Te Ching* (New York: HarperSanFrancisco, 1988).
2. Dass, R., *Be Here Now* (New York: Crown Publishing, 1971).
3. Gribbin, J., *Genesis: The Origins of Man and the Universe* (New York: Delacorte Press, 1981), p. 5.
4. Laszlo, E., *Science and the Akashic Field: An Integral Theory of Everything* (Rochester, VT: Inner Traditions, 2004).
5. Ibid., p. 108.
6. Turner, M. S., "The Origins of the Universe." *Scientific American*, Vol. 301 no. 3. (2009).
7. Hawking, S., *A Brief History of Time* (New York: Bantam Books, 1988).
8. Hagelin, J., *Manual for a Perfect Government* (Fairfield, IA: Maharishi University of Management Press, 1998), p. 47.
9. Ibid., p. 48.
10. Greene, B., *The Elegant Universe: Superstrings, Hidden Dimensions, and the Quest for the Ultimate Theory* (New York: Vintage Books, 2003).
11. Hagelin, J., *Manual for a Perfect Government* (Fairfield, IA: Maharishi University of Management Press, 1998), p. 48.
12. Ibid., pp. 48-49.
13. Lazlo, op. cit., p. 47.
14. Haisch, B., *The God Theory: Universes, Zero-Point Fields, and What's Behind It All* (York Beach, ME: Red Wheel/Weiser, 2009), p. 70.
15. Wolf, F. A., and B. Toben, *Space-Time and Beyond: Toward an Explanation of the Unexplainable* (New York: Bantam Books, 1982).
16. Haisch, op. cit.

17. Wilber, K., *Sex, Ecology, Spirituality: The Spirit of Evolution* (Boston: Shambala, 1995), p. 117.
18. Amoraea, D. S., *Divine Human Blueprint Course Manual* (Self-publish: Divine- Blueprint.com, 2010).
19. Haramein, N., M. Hyson, and E. A. Rauscher, "Scale Unification—A Universal Scaling Law for Organized Matter,"(www.theresonanceproject.org/pdf/scallinglaw _paper.pdf), p.1.
20. Hagelin, op. cit., p. 52.
21. Evans-Wentz, W. Y., *The Tibetan Book of the Great Liberation* (London: Oxford University Press, 1969), p. 1.
22. Ibid., p. 2.
23. Mishra, R., *The Textbook of Yoga Psychology* (New York: Julian Press, 1987).
24. Ibid., p. 26.
25. Wilber, K., *The Holographic Paradigm and Other Paradoxes* (Boston: Shambala, 1985), p. 274.
26. Penrose, R., *Shadows of the Mind: A Search for the Missing Science of Consciousness* (London: Vintage Books, 1994).

Part 1: Birth of a World

Level 1
Physio-Survival: Material Plane

1. Neruda, P., *Late and Posthumous Poems 1968–1974* (New York: Grove Press, 1988), p. 85.
2. Leary, T., *Psychedelic Prayers and Other Meditations* (Berkeley: Ronin Publishing, 1966), p. 77.
3. Loomis, W. F., *Four Billion Years: An Essay on the Evolution of Genes and Organisms* (Sunderland, MA: Sinauer Associates, 1988).
4. Knight, A. V., *The Meaning of Teilhard de Chardin* (Old Greenwich, CT: Devin-Adair, 1974), p. 35.
5. Gribbin, J., *Genesis: The Origins of Man and the Universe* (New York: Delacorte Press, 1981), p. 187.
6. Reader, J., *The Rise of Life: The First 3.5 Billion Years* (New York: Alfred A. Knopf, 1986), p. 25.
7. Wilber, K., *A Brief History of Everything* (Boston: Shambala, 1996), p. 31.

8. Daintith, J., *Dictionary of Physics* (New York: Harper and Row Publishers, 1981).
9. Wilber, op. cit., p. 145.
10. Ibid.
11. Loomis, op. cit.
12. Grof, S., *The Holotropic Mind: The Three Levels of Human Consciousness and How They Shape Our Lives* (San Francisco: HarperSanFrancisco, 1993), p. 38.
13. Frager, R., and J. Fadiman., *Personality and Personal Growth* (New York: Longman, 1998), p. 27.
14. Ibid., p. 28.
15. Maslow, A., *Toward a Psychology of Being* (New York: Van Nostrand, 1968).
16. Erikson, E., *Childhood and Society* (New York: Norton, 1963).
17. Wilber, op. cit.
18. Leary, T., *Neuropolitique* (Tempe, AZ: New Falcon Press, 1988), p. 54.
19. Vaughan, F., *The Inward Arc: Healing in Psychotherapy and Spirituality* (Grass Valley, CA: Blue Dolphin Press, 1995), p. 101.
20. Ibid., p. 102.
21. Capra, F., *The Tao of Physics* (Boston: Shambala, 1991), p. 225.
22. Kent, J. L., *Psychedelic Information Theory: Shamanism in the Age of Reason* (Seattle, WA: PIT Press/Supermassive, 2010), p. 60.
23. Julien, R. M., *A Primer of Drug Action* (New York: Worth Publishers, 2001), p. 226.

Level 2
Emotional- Territorial: Bio-emotional Plane

1. Reader, J., *The Rise of Life: The First 3.5 Billion Years* (New York: Alfred A. Knopf, 1986), p. 70.
2. Ibid.
3. Leary, T., *Info-Psychology* (Phoenix: New Falcon Publications, 1987), p. 84.
4. Ibid., p. 84.
5. Hooper, J., and D. Teresi., *The 3-Pound Universe: The Brain* (New York: Dell Publishing, 1986), p. 36.
6. Wilber, K., *A Brief History of Everything* (Boston: Shambala, 1996), p. 165.
7. Ibid., p. 163.

8. Sullivan, H. S., *The Interpersonal Theory of Psychiatry* (New York: W. W. Norton, 1953).
9. Frager, R., and J. Fadiman., *Personality and Personal Growth* (New York: Longman, 1998), p. 28.
10. Ibid., p. 199.
11. Lorenz, K., *On Aggression* (London: University Paperbacks, 1967).
12. Leary, op. cit.
13. Vaughan, F., *The Inward Arc: Healing in Psychotherapy and Spirituality* (Grass Valley, CA: Blue Dolphin Press, 1995), p. 103.
14. Dharma, S. K., and C. Stauth, *Meditation as Medicine* (New York: Pocket Books, 2001), p. 115.
15. Vaughan, op. cit.
16. Frager, op. cit., p. 25.
17. Reich, W., *Character Analysis* (New York: Pocket Books, 1976), p. 393.
18. Julien, R. M., *A Primer of Drug Action* (New York: Worth Publishers, 2001), p. 98.
19. Ibid., p. 98.
20. Ibid., p. 99.

Level 3
Mental-Symbolic: Conceptual Plane

1. Nelson, H., and R. Jurmain, *Introduction to Physical Anthropology* (New York: West Publishing, 1991), pp. 441-442 and 458.
2. Ibid.
3. McKenna, T., *Food of the Gods* (New York: Bantam Books, 1992), p. 24.
4. Ibid.
5. Hooper, J., and D. Teresi., *The 3-Pound Universe: The Brain* (New York: Dell Publishing, 1986), p. 43.
6. Gebser, J., *The Ever-Present Origin* (Athens: Ohio University Press, 1985).
7. Leary, T., *Info-Psychology* (Phoenix: New Falcon Publications, 1987), p. 88.
8. Gebser, op. cit.
9. Ibid.
10. Wilber, K., *Sex, Ecology, Spirituality: The Spirit of Evolution* (Boston: Shambala, 1995).

------, *A Brief History of Everything* (Boston: Shambala, 1996).

11. Piaget, J., *The Theory of Stages in Cognitive Development* (New York: McGraw Hill, 1969).
12. Kohlberg, L., *Moral Development* (New York: Macmillan, 1968).
13. Frager, R., and J. Fadiman, *Personality and Personal Growth* (New York: Longman, 1998), p. 200.
14. Leary, T., *The Game of Life* (Phoenix: New Falcon Publications, 1979).
    ------, *Info-Psychology* (Phoenix: New Falcon Publications, 1987).
15. Piaget, op. cit.
16. Kohlberg, op. cit.
17. Erikson, E., *Childhood and Society* (New York: Norton, 1963), p. 124.
18. Frager, op. cit., pp. 30-31.
19. Vaughan, F., *The Inward Arc: Healing in Psychotherapy and Spirituality* (Grass Valley, CA: Blue Dolphin Press, 1995), pp. 104-106.
20. Skinner, B. F., *The Behavior of Organisms* (New York: Appleton-Century-Crofts, 1938).
21. Ramachandran, V. S., and S. Blakeslee, *Phantoms in the Brain* (New York: William Morrow, 1998).
22. Davies, P., *God and the New Physics* (New York: Simon and Schuster, 1983).
23. Reader, J., *The Rise of Life: The First 3.5 Billion Years* (New York: Alfred A. Knopf, 1986).
24. Julien, R. M., *A Primer of Drug Action* (New York: Worth Publishers, 2001), p. 185.
25. Ibid., p. 199.
26. Ibid., p. 203.

Level 4

Social Role- Identity: Personality Plane

1. Leary, T., *Info-Psychology* (Phoenix: New Falcon Publications, 1987), p. 94.
2. Wilber, K., *Sex, Ecology, Spirituality: The Spirit of Evolution* (Boston: Shambala, 1995).
   ------, *A Brief History of Everything* (Boston: Shambala, 1996).
3. Gebser, J., *The Ever-Present Origin* (Athens: Ohio University Press, 1985).
4. Russell, B., *A History of Western Philosophy* (New York: Simon and Schuster, 1945).

5. Ibid.
6. Wilber, op. cit., p. 267.
7. Ibid., p. 261.
8. Vaughan, F., *The Inward Arc: Healing in Psychotherapy and Spirituality* (Grass Valley, CA: Blue Dolphin Press, 1995), p. 29.
9. Stevenson, L., and D. Haberman, *Ten Theories of Human Nature* (New York: Oxford University Press, 1998).
10. Neitzcche cited in Stevenson, L., and D. Haberman, *Ten Theories of Human Nature* (New York: Oxford University Press, 1998), p. 170.
11. Leary, T., *Chaos and the New Cyber Culture* (Berkeley: Ronin Publishing, 1994), pp. 47-48.
12. Goswami, A., *The Self-Aware Universe: How Consciousness Creates the Material World* (New York: Penguin Putnam, 1993).
13. Gribbin, J., *In Search of Schrodinger's Cat: Quantum Physics and Reality* (New York: Bantam Books, 1984).
14. Herbert, N., *Elemental Mind: Human Consciousness and the New Physics* (New York: Plume Books, 1993).
15. Piaget, J., *The Theory of Stages in Cognitive Development* (New York: McGraw Hill, 1969).
16. Kohlberg, L., *Moral Development* (New York: Macmillan, 1968).
17. Miller, D., *Adolescence: Psychology, Psychopathology, and Psychotherapy* (New York: Jason Aronson, 1974).
18. Ibid.
19. Erikson, E., *Childhood and Society* (New York: Norton, 1963).
20. Ibid., pp. 261-262.
21. Maslow, A., *Toward a Psychology of Being* (New York: Van Nostrand, 1968).
22. Ibid.
23. Leary, op. cit., p. 96.
24. Erikson, op. cit.
25. Conze, E., *Buddhist Scriptures* (London: Penguin Books, 1959).
26. Vaughan, F., *The Inward Arc: Healing in Psychotherapy and Spirituality* (Grass Valley, CA: Blue Dolphin Press, 1995), p. 30.
27. Wilber (1996), op. cit.
28. Frager, R., and J. Fadiman, *Personality and Personal Growth* (New York: Longman, 1998), p. 26.

29. Wilber, op. cit.
30. Julien, R. M., *A Primer of Drug Action* (New York: Worth Publishers, 2001), p. 234.
31. Ibid., p. 226.
32. Ibid., p. 226.

Part 2: Back Toward the Light

Level 5
Mind-Body Centaur: Holistic Plane

1. Aurobindo, A., *The Future Evolution of Man: The Divine Life upon Earth* (Wheaton: The Theosophical Publishing House, 1974), p. 68.
2. Knight, A. V., *The Meaning of Teilhard de Chardin* (Old Greenwich, CT: Devin-Adair, 1974), p. 136.
3. Aurobindo, op. cit., p. 39.
4. Leary, T., *The Politics of Ecstasy* (Berkeley: Ronin Publishing, 1968), p. 5.
5. Lattin, D., *The Harvard Psychedelic Club* (New York: HarperOne, 2010), p. 1.
6. Wilber, K., *One Taste: The Journals of Ken Wilber* (Boston: Shambala, 1999).
7. Wilber, K., *A Brief History of Everything* (Boston: Shambala, 1996).
8. Leary, op. cit.
9. Wilber, K., *Sex, Ecology, Spirituality: The Spirit of Evolution* (Boston: Shambala, 1995).
10. Perls, F., "Psychiatry in a New Key." *Gestalt Journal*, 1 (1), 32–53, (1978).
11. Frager, R., and J. Fadiman, *Personality and Personal Growth* (New York: Longman, 1998), p. 141.
12. Reich in Ibid., p. 230.
13. Wilber, K., *The Essential Ken Wilber* (Boston: Shambala, 1998), pp. 73-74.
14. Leary, T., *Info-Psychology* (Phoenix: New Falcon Publications, 1987), pp. 106-108.
15. Tart, C., *States of Consciousness* (El Cerrito, CA: Psychological Processes, 1983), p. 110.
16. Leary, op. cit.
17. Hastings cited in Tart, C., *Altered States of Consciousness* (New York: HarperSanFrancisco, 1990), p. 412.

18. Ramsdale, D., and E. Ramsdale, *Sexual Energy Ecstasy: A Practical Guide to Lovemaking Secrets of the East and West* (New York: Bantam Books, 1993), p. 14.
19. Wilber, op. cit.
20. Vaughan, F., *The Inward Arc: Healing in Psychotherapy and Spirituality* (Grass Valley, CA: Blue Dolphin Press, 1995), pp. 106-108.
21. Lidell, L., and G. Rabinovitch, *The Sivananda Companion to Yoga* (New York: Simon and Schuster, 1983).
    Mishra, R., *The Textbook of Yoga Psychology* (New York: Julian Press, 1987).
    Eliade, M., *Patanjali and Yoga* (New York: Schocken Books, 1975).
22. Ibid.
23. Ibid.
24. Dharma, S. K., and C. Stauth, *Meditation as Medicine* (New York: Pocket Books, 2001), p. 118.
25. Ibid.
26. Lidell, op. cit. and, Mishra, op. cit.
27. Dharma, op. cit. p. 125.
28. Weil, A., *Spontaneous Healing* (New York: Fawcett Columbine, 1995).
29. Chopra, D., *Quantum Healing: Exploring the Frontiers of Mind/Body Medicine* (New York: Bantam Books, 1990).
30. Ibid.
31. Elias, J., and K. Ketchman, *In the House of the Moon* (New York: Warner Books, 1995), p. 86
32. Martinez, M., *The New Prescription: Marijuana as Medicine* (Oland, CA: Quick American Archives, 2000).
33. .Julien, R. M., *A Primer of Drug Action* (New York: Worth Publishers, 2001), p. 303.
34. Ibid., pp. 303-304.
35. Ibid., p. 334.

Level 6

Awareness of Mind: Psychic Plane.

1. Crowley, A., *Eight Lectures on Yoga* (Dallas: Sangreal Foundation, 1972).
2. Leary, T., *Chaos and the New Cyber Culture* (Berkeley: Ronin Publishing, 1994), p. 3.

3. McLuhan, M., *Understanding Media: The Extension of Man* (New York: McGraw-Hill, 1964).
4. McKenna, T., The Jeweled Net of Indra. *Psychedelic Illumination.* 1 (8), (1996), p.51.
5. Ibid. p. 52.
6. Rudhyar, D., *The Planetarization of Consciousness: From the Individual to the Whole* (New York: Harper Colophon Books, 1970).
7. De Chardin, T., *The Phenomena of Man* (New York: Harper and Row, 1959).
8. Knight, A. V., *The Meaning of Teilhard de Chardin* (Old Greenwich, CT: Devin-Adair, 1974).
9. Arguelles, J., *Manifesto for the Noosphere* (Berkeley: Evolver Edition, 2011), p. 9.
10. Leary, op. cit., p. 35.
11. Leary, T., *Info-Psychology* (Phoenix: New Falcon Publication, 1987).
12. Lilly, J., *The Center of the Cyclone* (New York: Bantam Books, 1972).
13. Leary, op. cit., p. 45.
14. Ibid., p. 59.
15. Ibid., p. 64.
16. Schawartz, J., "Mindful Awareness and Self-Directed Neuroplasticity: Integrating Psychospiritual and Biological Approaches to Mental Health with a Focus on OCD." (www.ocdcentre.com, 2002.), p. 7.
17. Ibid., p. 1.
18. Ibid., p. 3.
19. Holmes, D. A., *Psyche's Palace: How the Brain Generates the Light of the Soul* (The Library of Consciousness, 2008), p. 29.
20. Ibid., p. 30.
21. Ibid., p. 42.
22. Ibid., p. 30.
23. Pribram, K., *Language and the Brain* (Monterey, CA: Brooks/Cole Publishing, 1971).
24. Pribram, K., "The Neurophysiology of Remembering." *Scientific American* (22), 1969), p. 77.
25. Leary, op. cit., p. 116.
26. Yeshe, L., *Becoming Your Own Therapist* (Boston: Lama Yeshe Wisdom Archive, 1999).

27. Engler in Walsh, R., and F. Vaughan, *Path Beyond Ego: The Transpersonal Vision* (New York: G. P. Putnam's Sons, 1993).
28. Blofeld, J., *The Tantric Mysticism of Tibet: A Practical Guide* (New York: E. P. Dutton, 1970), p. 54.
29. Ibid., p. 53.
30. Yeshe, op. cit.
31. Mishra, R., *The Textbook of Yoga Psychology* (New York: Julian Press, 1987), p. 247.
32. Crowley, op. cit.
33. Vaughan, F., *The Inward Arc: Healing in Psychotherapy and Spirituality* (Grass Valley, CA: Blue Dolphin Press, 1995), pp. 109-110.
34. Mishra, op. cit., p. 414.
35. Goleman, D., *The Meditative Mind: The Varieties of Meditative Experience* (New York: G. P. Putnam Book, 1988), p. 15.
36. Ibid., p. 15.
37. Govinda, A., *Foundations of Tibetan Mysticism* (New York: Samuel Weiser, 1974), p. 150.
38. Ibid., 151.
39. Goleman, op. cit., p. 24.
40. Ibid. p. 24.
41. Dass, R., *Be Here Now* (New York: Crown Publishing, 1971), p. 33.
42. Grof, S., *LSD Psychotherapy* (Sarasota, FL: MAPS, 2001).
43. Julien, R. M., *A Primer of Drug Action* (New York: Worth Publishers, 2001), p. 334.
44. Kent, J. L., *Psychedelic Information Theory: Shamanism in the Age of Reason* (Seattle, WA: PIT Press/Supermassive, 2010), p. 61.
45. Ibid., p. 45.

Level 7
Soul: Subtle Plane

1. McLuhan, M., *Understanding Media: The Extension of Man* (New York: McGraw-Hill, 1964).
2. McKenna, T., *The Archaic Revival* (New York: HarperSanFrancisco, 1991), p. 230.

3. McKenna, T., The Jeweled Net of Indra. *Psychedelic Illumination*, 1 (8), (1996), p. 54.
4. Leary, T., *The Game of Life* (Phoenix: New Falcon Publications, 1979), p. 219.
5. Bohm, D., *Wholeness and the Implicate Order* (London: Routledge and Kegan Paul, 1980).
6. Sheldrake, R., *A New Science of Life* (Los Angeles: Jeremy P. Tarcher, 1982).
7. McKenna, T., and D. McKenna, *The Invisible Landscape: Mind, Hallucinogens, and the I-Ching* (New York: HarperSanFrancisco, 1993), p. 52.
8. Leary, T., *Info-Psychology* (Phoenix: New Falcon Publication, 1987), p. 123.
9. McKenna, op. cit.
10. Narby, J., *The Cosmic Serpent: DNA and the Origins of Knowledge* (New York: Tarcher/Putnam, 1999).
11. Leary, op. cit., p. 121.
12. McKenna, op. cit.
13. McKenn, T., *Food of the Gods* (New York: Bantam Books, 1992).
14. Schultes, R., and A. Hofmann, *Plants of the Gods: Their Sacred, Healing, and Hallucinogenic Powers* (Rochester: Healing Arts Press, 1992).
15. McKenna (1991), op. cit., p. 218.
16. Ibid., pp. 219-220.
17. McKenna (1993), op. cit., pp. 203-204.
18. Ibid., pp. 80-81.
19. Ibid,. pp. 91-92.
20. Narby, op. cit.
21. Popp, F. A., "On the Coherence of Ultraweak Photon Emission from Living Tissue." In *Disequilibrium and Self-Organization*, edited by C. W. Kilmister, (Dordrecht: Reidel,1986), pp. 207–230.
22. Narby, op. cit., p. 127.
23. Ibid., pp. 130-131.
24. Ibid., p. 160.
25. Amoraea, D. S., *Divine Human Blueprint Course Manual*. (Self-publish: Divine- Blueprint.com, 2010), pp. 19-20.
26. Ibid., p. 20.
27. Eliade, M., *Shamanism* (Princeton: University Press, 1972), p. 5.

28. Drury, N., *The Shaman and the Magician: Journeys Between the Worlds* (London: Routledge and Kegan Paul, 1982), p. 1.
29. McKenna, T., *The Shaman.* (CD recording, 1992).
30. Castenada, C., *The Teachings of Don Juan* (Berkeley: Simon and Schuster, 1973).
31. Frager, R., and J. Fadiman, *Personality and Personal Growth* (New York: Longman, 1998), p. 67.
32. McKenna (1991), op. cit., p. 94.
33. Russell, B., *A History of Western Philosophy* (New York: Simon and Schuster, 1945), pp. 121-122.
34. Ibid., p. 122.
35. Wilber, K., *A Brief History of Everything* (Boston: Shambala, 1996), pp. 217-218.
36. Ibid., p. 211.
37. Narby, op. cit., p. 129.
38. Strassman, R., S. Wojtowicz, L. E. Luna, and E. Frecska, *Inner Paths to Outer Space* (Rochester, VT: Park Street Press, 2008).
39. Hooper, J., and D. Teresi, *The 3-Pound Universe: The Brain* (New York: Dell Publishing, 1986), p. 354.
40. Govinda, A., *Human Dimensions: The Tibetan Book of the Dead* (Buffalo: Human Dimensions Institute, 1972), p. 56.
41. Mishra, R., *The Textbook of Yoga Psychology* (New York: Julian Press, 1987).
42. Goleman, D., *The Meditative Mind: The Varieties of Meditative Experience* (New York: G. P. Putnam Book, 1988), p. 24.
43. Ibid., p. 15.
44. Conze, E., *Buddhist Scriptures* (London: Penguin Books, 1959), p. 221.
45. Rimpoche, S., *The Tibetan Book of Living and Dying* (New York: HarperSanFrancisco, 1992).
46. Ibid., p. 103.
47. Ibid., 276.
48. Ibid., p. 278.
49. Govinda, A., *Foundations of Tibetan Mysticism* (New York: Samuel Weiser, 1974), p. 213.
50. Ibid., p. 215.
51. Vaughan, F., *The Inward Arc: Healing in Psychotherapy and Spirituality* (Grass Valley, CA: Blue Dolphin Press, 1995), p. 111.

52. Strassman, R., *DMT: The Spirit Molecule* (Rochester, VT: Park Street Press, 2001), p. 69.
53. Ibid., pp. 68-69.
54. McKenna (1993), op. cit., p. 86.
55. Strassman (2008), op. cit., p. 39.
56. Ibid., p. 65.
57. Ibid., pp. 65-66.
58. Turner, D. M., *The Essential Psychedelic Guide* (San Francisco, CA: Panther Press, 1994), pp. 55-56.

Level 8
Pure Spirit: Causal Plane

1. McKenna, T., *The Shaman* (CD recording, 1992).
2. Russell, P., *The White Hole in Time* (New York: HarperSanFrancisco, 1992), p. 200.
3. Anderla and Vallee quoted in Wilson, R. A. *Prometheus Rising* (Phoenix, AZ: New Falcon Publications, 1983).
4. McKenna, T., *The Archaic Revival* (New York: HarperSanFrancisco, 1991). McKenna, T., and D. McKenna, *The Invisible Landscape: Mind, Hallucinogens, and the I-Ching* (New York: HarperSanFrancisco, 1993).
5. McKenna (1991), op. cit., p. 100.
6. Ibid., pp. 101-102.
7. De Chardin, T., *The Phenomena of Man* (New York: Harper and Row, 1959).
8. Knight, A. V., *The Meaning of Teilhard de Chardin* (Old Greenwich, CT: Devin-Adair, 1974), p. 133.
9. Kurzweil, R., *The Singularity is Near: When Humans Transcend Biology* (New York: Penguin Books, 2005).
10. Brown, D. J., *Conversations on the Edge of the Apocalypse* (New York: Palgrave Macmillian, 2005), p. 111.
11. Ibid., p. 111.
12. Ibid., p. 115.
13. Arguelles, J., *The Mayan Factor: Path Beyond Technology* (Santa Fe: Bear, 1987).
14. Ibid., p. 197.
15. Ibid., p. 118.

16. Jenkins, J. M., "The Origins of the 2012 Revelation." In *The Mystery of 2012* (Boulder, Co: Sounds True, 2007).
17. Ibid., p. 46.
18. Wolf, F. A., and B. Toben, *Space-Time and Beyond: Toward an Explanation of the Unexplainable* (New York: Bantam Books, 1982).
    Sarfatti, J., and B. Toben, *Space-Time and Beyond* (New York: E. P. Dutton, 1975).
19. Leary, T., *Info-Psychology* (Phoenix: New Falcon Publications, 1987), p. 129.
20. McKenna (1991), op. cit., p. 251.
21. Moody, R., *Life After Life* (New York: Bantam Books, 1975).
22. Hameroff, S. R., *Ultimate Computing: Biomolecular Consciousness and Nanotechnology* (Amsterdam: North Holland, 1996).
23. Strassman, R., S. Wojtowicz, L. E. Luna, and E. Frecska, *Inner Paths to Outer Space* (Rochester, VT: Park Street Press, 2008), p. 191.
24. Ibid., p. 192.
25. Sarfatti, op. cit.
26. Laszlo, E., *Science and the Akashic Field: An Integral Theory of Everything* (Rochester, VT: Inner Traditions, 2004).
27. Laszlo, E., *The Akashic Experience: Science and the Cosmic Memory Field* (Rochester, VT: Inner Traditions, 2009), pp. 249-250.
28. Ibid., p. 251.
29. Aurobindo, A., *The Future Evolution of Man: The Divine Life upon Earth* (Wheaton: The Theosophical Publishing House, 1974), p. 132.
30. Dass, R., *Be Here Now* (New York: Crown Publishing, 1971), p. 5.
31. Kopp, W., *Zen: Beyond All Words* (Boston: Charles E. Tuttle, 1993), p. 38.
32. Wilber, K., *No Boundary: Eastern and Western Approaches to Personal Growth* (Boston: Shambala, 1979), p. 65.
33. Berendt, J., *The World is Sound: Nada Brahma* (Rochester: Destiny Books, 1983), p. 17.
34. Rimpoche, S., *The Tibetan Book of Living and Dying* (New York: HarperSanFrancisco, 1992), p. 151.
35. Moody, op. cit., p. 58.
36. Rimpoche, op. cit., p 259.
37. Wilber, K., *One Taste: The Journals of Ken Wilber* (Boston: Shambala, 1999), p. 317.
38. Mishra, R., *The Textbook of Yoga Psychology* (New York: Julian Press, 1987).

39. Goleman, D., *The Meditative Mind: The Varieties of Meditative Experience* (New York: G. P. Putnam Book, 1988), p. 15.
40. Ibid., p. 19.
41. Ibid., p. 24.
42. Ibid., p. 36.
43. Govinda, A., *Foundations of Tibetan Mysticism* (New York: Samuel Weiser, 1974), p. 213.
44. Vaughan, F., *The Inward Arc: Healing in Psychotherapy and Spirituality* (Grass Valley, CA: Blue Dolphin Press, 1995), p. 112.
45. D'Aquili, E., and A. B. Newberg, *The Mystical Mind: probing the biology of religious experience* (Augsburg Fortress Publishers, 1999).
46. Turner, D. M., *The Essential Psychedelic Guide* (San Francisco, CA: Panther Press, 1994), pp. 53-54.
47. Oroc, J., *Tryptamine Palace: 5-MeO-DMT and the Sonora Desert Toad* (Rochester, VT: Park Street Press, 2009), pp. 6-7.
48. Ibid., p. 9.
49. Ibid., p. 168.
50. Ibid., p. 175.
51. Julien, R. M., *A Primer of Drug Action* (New York: Worth Publishers, 2001).
52. Jansen, K., *Ketamine: Dreams and Realities* (Sarasota, FL: MAPS, 2001), p. 116.
53. Ibid., p. 115.
54. Ibid., p. 146.
55. Ibid., p. 139.
56. Turner, op. cit., pp. 64-65.

Conclusion
Nonduality: The All

1. Goleman, D., *The Meditative Mind: The Varieties of Meditative Experience* (New York: G. P. Putnam Book, 1988), p. 82.
2. Wilber, K., *A Brief History of Everything* (Boston: Shambala, 1996), p. 239.
3. Campbell, J., *The Hero with a Thousand Faces* (New Jersey: Princeton University Press, 1968).
   ------, *Myths, Dreams, and Religion* (New York: Dutton, 1970).
4. Mishra, R., *The Textbook of Yoga Psychology* (New York: Julian Press, 1987).

5. Goleman, op. cit., p. 76.
6. Wilber, K., *The Essential Ken Wilber* (Boston: Shambala, 1998), p. 13.
7. Ibid., p. 15.
8. Ibid., p. 135.
9. Ibid., p. 136.
10. Ibid., pp. 137-138.
11. Wilber (1996), op. cit., p. 232.
12. Cohen, A., *Evolutionary Enlightenment* (New York: SelectBooks, 2011), p. 66.
13. Ibid., p. 53.
14. Ibid.
15. Wilber, K., *Integral Spirituality* (Boston: Integral Books, 2007).
16. Wilber (1998), op. cit., p. 107.
17. Leary, T., *Chaos and the New Cyber Culture* (Berkeley: Ronin Publishing, 1994).

Bibliography

Amoraea, D. 2010. *Divine Human Blueprint Course Manual.* Self-publish: Divine-Blueprint.com.

Arguelles, J. 1987. *The Mayan Factor: Path Beyond Technology*. Santa Fe: Bear.

------. 2011. *Manifesto for the Noosphere*. Berkeley: Evolver Edition.

Aurobindo, A. 1974. *The Future Evolution of Man: The Divine Life upon Earth.* Wheaton: The Theosophical Publishing House.

Berendt, J. 1983. *The World is Sound: Nada Brahma*. Rochester: Destiny Books.

Blofeld, J. 1970. *The Tantric Mysticism of Tibet: A Practical Guide*. New York: E. P. Dutton.

Bohm, D. 1980. *Wholeness and the Implicate Order*. London: Routledge and Kegan Paul.

Brown, D. J. 2005. *Conversations on the Edge of the Apocalypse*. New York: Palgrave Macmillian.

Campbell, J. 1968. *The Hero with a Thousand Faces*. New Jersey: Princeton University Press.

------. 1970. *Myths, Dreams, and Religion*. New York: Dutton.

Capra, F. 1991. *The Tao of Physics*. Boston: Shambala.

Castenada, C. 1973. *The Teachings of Don Juan*. Berkeley: Simon and Schuster.

Chopra, D. 1990. *Quantum Healing: Exploring the Frontiers of Mind/Body Medicine.* New York: Bantam Books.

Cohen, A. 2011. *Evolutionary Enlightenment*. New York: SelectBooks.

Conze, E. 1959. *Buddhist Scriptures*. London: Penguin Books.

Crowley, A. 1972. *Eight Lectures on Yoga*. Dallas: Sangreal Foundation.

Daintith, J. 1981. *Dictionary of Physics*. New York: Harper and Row Publishers.

D' Aquili, E., and A. B. Newberg. 1999. *The Mystical Mind: Probing the Biology of Religious Experience.* Augsburg Fortress Publishers.

Dass, R. 1971. *Be Here Now*. New York: Crown Publishing.

------. 1973. *The Only Dance There Is*. New York: Anchor Books Doubleday.

David-Neel, A., and L. Yongden. 1967. *The Secret Oral Teachings in Tibetan Buddhist Sects*. San Francisco: City Lights Books.

Davies, P. 1983. *God and the New Physics*. New York: Simon and Schuster.

De Chardin, T. 1959. *The Phenomena of Man*. New York: Harper and Row.

Dharma, S. K., and C. Stauth. 2001. *Meditation as Medicine*. New York: Pocket Books.

Drury, N. 1982. *The Shaman and the Magician: Journeys Between the Worlds*. London: Routledge and Kegan Paul.

Eliade, M. 1972. *Shamanism*. Princeton: University Press.

------. 1975. *Patanjali and Yoga*. New York: Schocken Books.

Elias, J., and K. Ketchman. 1995. *In the House of the Moon*. New York: Warner Books.

Erikson, E. 1963. *Childhood and Society*. New York: Norton.

Evans-Wentz, W. Y. 1969. *The Tibetan Book of the Great Liberation*. London: Oxford University Press.

Frager, R., and J. Fadiman. 1998. *Personality and Personal Growth*. New York: Longman.

Gebser, J. 1985. *The Ever-Present Origin*. Athens: Ohio University Press.

Godwin, R. W. 2004. *One Cosmos Under God: The Unification of Matter, Life, Mind, and Spirit*. St. Paul, MN: Paragon House.

Goleman, D. 1988. *The Meditative Mind: The Varieties of Meditative Experience*. New York: G. P. Putnam Book.

Goswami, A. 1993. *The Self-Aware Universe: How Consciousness Creates the Material World*. New York: Penguin Putnam.

Govinda, A. 1972. *Human Dimensions: The Tibetan Book of the Dead*. Buffalo: Human Dimensions Institute.

------. 1974. *Foundations of Tibetan Mysticism*. New York: Samuel Weiser.

Greene, B. 2003. *The Elegant Universe: Superstrings, Hidden Dimensions, and the Quest for the Ultimate Theory*. New York: Vintage Books.

Gribbin, J. 1981. *Genesis: The Origins of Man and the Universe*. New York: Delacorte Press.

------. 1984. *In Search of Schrodinger's Cat: Quantum Physics and Reality*. New York: Bantam Books.

Grof, S. 1993. *The Holotropic Mind: The Three Levels of Human Consciousness and How They Shape Our Lives*. San Francisco: HarperSanFrancisco.

------. 2001. *LSD Psychotherapy*. Sarasota, FL: MAPS.

Hagelin, J. 1998. *Manual for a Perfect Government*. Fairfield, IA: Maharishi University of Management Press.

Haisch, B. 2009. *The God Theory: Universes, Zero-Point Fields, and What's Behind It All*. York Beach, ME: Red Wheel/Weiser.

Hameroff, S. R. 1996. *Ultimate Computing: Biomolecular Consciousness and Nanotechnology*. Amsterdam: North Holland.

Haramein, N., M. Hyson, and E. A. Rauscher. "Scale Unification—A Universal Scaling Law for Organized Matter." www.theresonanceproject.org/pdf/scall-inglaw _paper.pdf.

Hawking, S. 1988. *A Brief History of Time*. New York: Bantam Books.

Herbert, N. 1993. *Elemental Mind: Human Consciousness and the New Physics*. New York: Plume Books.

Holmes, D. A. 2008. *Psyche's Palace: How the Brain Generates the Light of the Soul*. The Library of Consciousness.

Hooper, J., and D. Teresi. 1986. *The 3-Pound Universe: The Brain*. New York: Dell Publishing.

Huxley, A. 1932. *Brave New World*. New York: Harper Row.

------. 1954. *The Doors of Perception*. New York: Harper Row.

-----. 1970. *The Perennial Philosophy*. New York: Harper Row.

James, W. 1902. *The Varieties of Religious Experience*. New York: Harper Row.

Jansen, K. 2001. *Ketamine: Dreams and Realities*. Sarasota, FL: MAPS.

Jenkins, J. M. 2007. "The Origins of the 2012 Revelation." In *The Mystery of 2012*. Boulder, Co: Sounds True.

Julien, R. M. 2001. *A Primer of Drug Action*. New York: Worth Publishers.

Kent, J. L. 2010. *Psychedelic Information Theory: Shamanism in the Age of Reason*. Seattle, WA: PIT Press/Supermassive.

Knight, A. V. 1974. *The Meaning of Teilhard de Chardin*. Old Greenwich, CT: Devin-Adair.

Kohlberg, L. 1968. *Moral Development*. New York: Macmillan.

Kopp, W. 1993. *Zen: Beyond All Words*. Boston: Charles E. Tuttle.

Kurzweil, R. 2005. *The Singularity is Near: When Humans Transcend Biology*. New York: Penguin Books.

Laszlo, E. 2004. *Science and the Akashic Field: An Integral Theory of Everything*. Rochester, VT: Inner Traditions.

------. 2009. *The Akashic Experience: Science and the Cosmic Memory Field*. Rochester, VT: Inner Traditions.

Lattin, D. 2010. *The Harvard Psychedelic Club*. New York: HarperOne.

Leary, T. 1966. *Psychedelic Prayers and Other Meditations*. Berkeley: Ronin Publishing.

------. 1968. *The Politics of Ecstasy*. Berkeley: Ronin Publishing.

------. 1979. *The Game of Life*. Phoenix: New Falcon Publications.

------. 1987. *Info-Psychology*. Phoenix: New Falcon Publications.

------. 1988. *Neuropolitique*. Tempe, AZ: New Falcon Press.

------. 1994. *Chaos and the New Cyber Culture*. Berkeley: Ronin Publishing.

Lidell, L., and G. Rabinovitch. 1983. *The Sivananda Companion to Yoga*. New York: Simon and Schuster.

Lilly, J. 1972. *The Center of the Cyclone*. New York: Bantam Books.

Loomis, W. F. 1988. *Four Billion Years: An Essay on the Evolution of Genes and Organisms*. Sunderland, MA: Sinauer Associates.

Lorenz, K. 1967. *On Aggression*. London: University Paperbacks.

Martinez, M. 2000. *The New Prescription: Marijuana as Medicine*. Oakland, CA: Quick American Archives.

Maslow, A. 1968. *Toward a Psychology of Being*. New York: Van Nostrand.

McKenna, T. 1991. *The Archaic Revival*. New York: HarperSanFrancisco.

------. 1992. *Food of the Gods*. New York: Bantam Books.

------. 1996. The Jeweled Net of Indra. *Psychedelic Illumination*. 1 (8), 51–54.

McKenna, T., and D. McKenna. 1993. *The Invisible Landscape: Mind, Hallucinogens, and the I-Ching*. New York: HarperSanFrancisco.

McLuhan, M. 1964. *Understanding Media: The Extension of Man*. New York: McGraw-Hill.

Moody, R. 1975. *Life After Life*. New York: Bantam Books.

Miller, D. 1974. *Adolescence: Psychology, Psychopathology, and Psychotherapy*. New York: Jason Aronson.

Mishra, R. 1987. *The Textbook of Yoga Psychology*. New York: Julian Press.

Mitchell, S. 1988. *Tao Te Ching*. New York: HarperSanFrancisco.

Narby, J. 1999. *The Cosmic Serpent: DNA and the Origins of Knowledge*. New York: Tarcher/Putnam.

Nelson, H., and R. Jurmain. 1991. *Introduction to Physical Anthropology*. New York: West Publishing.

Neruda, P. 1988. *Late and Posthumous Poems 1968–1974*. New York: Grove Press.

Oroc, J. 2009. *Tryptamine Palace: 5-MeO-DMT and the Sonora Desert Toad*. Rochester, VT: Park Street Press.

Orwell, G. 1949. *1984*. New York: Signet Classic.

Penrose, R. 1994. *Shadows of the Mind: A Search for the Missing Science of Consciousness*. London: Vintage Books.

Perls, F. 1978. "Psychiatry in a New Key." *Gestalt Journal*, 1 (1), 32–53.

Piaget, J. 1969. *The Theory of Stages in Cognitive Development*. New York: McGraw Hill.

Popp, F. A. 1986. "On the Coherence of Ultraweak Photon Emission from Living Tissue." In *Disequilibrium and Self-Organization*, edited by C. W. Kilmister, pp. 207–230. Dordrecht: Reidel.

Pribram, K. 1969. "The Neurophysiology of Remembering." *Scientific American* 22.

------. 1971. *Language and the Brain*. Monterey, CA: Brooks/Cole Publishing.

Ramachandran, V. S., and S. Blakeslee. 1998. *Phantoms in the Brain*. New York: William Morrow.

Ramsdale, D., and E. Ramsdale. 1993. *Sexual Energy Ecstasy: A Practical Guide to Lovemaking Secrets of the East and West*. New York: Bantam Books.

Reader, J. 1986. *The Rise of Life: The First 3.5 Billion Years*. New York: Alfred A. Knopf.

Reich, W. 1976. *Character Analysis*. New York: Pocket Books.

Rimpoche, S. 1992. *The Tibetan Book of Living and Dying*. New York: HarperSanFrancisco.

Rudhyar, D. 1970. *The Planetarization of Consciousness: From the Individual to the Whole*. New York: Harper Colophon Books.

Russell, B. 1945. *A History of Western Philosophy*. New York: Simon and Schuster.

------. 1985. *The ABC of Relativity*. New York: Mentor Books.

Russell, P. 1992. *The White Hole in Time*. New York: HarperSanFrancisco.

Sarfatti, J., and B. Toben. 1975. *Space-Time and Beyond*. New York: E. P. Dutton.

Schawartz, J. 2002. "Mindful Awareness and Self-Directed Neuroplasticity: Integrating Psychospiritual and Biological Approaches to Mental Health with a Focus on OCD." www.ocdcentre.com.

Schultes, R., and A. Hofmann. 1992. *Plants of the Gods: Their Sacred, Healing, and Hallucinogenic Powers*. Rochester: Healing Arts Press.

Sheldrake, R. 1982. *A New Science of Life*. Los Angeles: Jeremy P. Tarcher.

Skinner, B. F. 1938. *The Behavior of Organisms*. New York: Appleton-Century-Crofts.

Stevenson, L., and D. Haberman. 1998. *Ten Theories of Human Nature*. New York: Oxford University Press.

Strassman, R. 2001. *DMT: The Spirit Molecule*. Rochester, VT: Park Street Press.

Strassman, R., S. Wojtowicz, L. E. Luna, and E. Frecska. 2008. *Inner Paths to Outer Space*. Rochester, VT: Park Street Press.

Sullivan, H. S. 1953. *The Interpersonal Theory of Psychiatry*. New York: W. W. Norton.

Suzuki, S. 1970. *Zen Mind, Beginner's Mind*. New York: Weatherhill.

Tart, C. 1983. *States of Consciousness*. El Cerrito, CA: Psychological Processes.

------. 1990. *Altered States of Consciousness*. New York: HarperSanFrancisco.

Turner, D. M. 1994. *The Essential Psychedelic Guide*. San Francisco, CA: Panther Press.

Turner, M. S. 2009. "The Origins of the Universe." *Scientific American*, Vol. 301 no. 3.

Vaughan, F. 1995. *The Inward Arc: Healing in Psychotherapy and Spirituality*. Grass Valley, CA: Blue Dolphin Press.

Walsh, R., and F. Vaughan. 1993. *Path Beyond Ego: The Transpersonal Vision*. New York: G. P. Putnam's Sons.

Weil, A. 1995. *Spontaneous Healing*. New York: Fawcett Columbine.

Whaley, L., and D. Wong. 1999. *Nursing Care of Infants and Children*. Baltimore: Mosby.

Wilber, K. 1979. *No Boundary: Eastern and Western Approaches to Personal Growth*. Boston: Shambala.

------. 1985. *The Holographic Paradigm and Other Paradoxes*. Boston: Shambala.

------. 1985. *Quantum Question*. Boston: Shambala.

------. 1995. *Sex, Ecology, Spirituality: The Spirit of Evolution*. Boston: Shambala.

------. 1996. *A Brief History of Everything*. Boston: Shambala.

------. 1998. *The Essential Ken Wilber*. Boston: Shambala.

------. 1999. "An Approach to Integral Psychology." *Journal of Transpersonal Psychology*, 31 (2), 109–136.

------. 1999. *One Taste: The Journals of Ken Wilber*. Boston: Shambala.

------. 2007. *Integral Spirituality*. Boston: Integral Books.

Wilson, R. A. 1983. *Prometheus Rising*. Phoenix, AZ: New Falcon Publications.

------. 1993. *Quantum Psychology*. Phoenix, AZ: New Falcon Publications.

Wolf, F. A., and B. Toben. 1982. *Space-Time and Beyond: Toward an Explanation of the Unexplainable*. New York: Bantam Books.

Yeshe, L. 1999. *Becoming Your Own Therapist*. Boston: Lama Yeshe Wisdom Archive.

71551285R00189

Made in the USA
Columbia, SC
31 May 2017